Learn Java

with examples in BlueJ

(A beginner's hands-on approach to learning Java)

G. Suden

ISBN: 9781096927792

Printed by Kindle Direct Publishing, An Amazon.com Company

Available from Amazon.com, Amazon Europe, other online stores and retail outlets.

Contents

Chapter 1

Introduction to Object Oriented Programming Concepts

Introduction to Object Oriented Programming Concepts

W ELCOME to the exciting world of Computer Applications. You must have heard people talking about using an App, Application, or a Program. But what does it precisely mean?

In simple words, an Application allows you to perform a set of specific tasks to solve a particular problem. These days, Computer Applications are used in almost every field: education, banking, engineering, designing, healthcare services, and so forth.

Computer Applications are written using the block of codes known as *Programs*. Creating a computer program can be like making a recipe for any dish. As in both the cases you provide a set of instructions on what to do, how to do and when to do, you get the desired output. For example, Figure 1.1 demonstrates a recipe to make Tomato Pasta, where the stepwise instructions and ingredients give you a solution to this.

Figure 1.1: Making Tomato Pasta

Computer - A problem-solving machine
You have been hearing all along that computer is a problem-solving machine. But how exactly does it solve a problem? Well, it solves the problem just like the recipe, with the same two things – a set of instructions and the ingredients. A computer uses the set of instructions and data (ingredients) to solve a problem. When both the aspects are put together, it is called a *computer program*.

Just like the instructions of a good recipe are written clear enough so that anyone can follow them, the programs too are written with step-by-step instructions so that a computer can follow them to get the desired output. The computer simply executes these instructions in the sequence in which they occur in the program, one after the other. In the program, the data is processed as per the instructions.

These instructions may look like:

- Print your name on the screen

- Calculate the area of a circle

- Compute simple interest

- Show your account balance on an ATM machine

The data required for the above instructions may look like:

- Your name

- The radius of the circle

- Amount, rate, and time

- The balance amount in my account

A **Programmer** is a person who writes a computer program. **Programming** is the process of writing a computer program. A **Programming Language** is a set of commands and syntax used to create a computer program.

1.1 Evolution of Programming Languages

As we use any common language to communicate with each other, similarly, we use programming languages to communicate with the computer. Since the invention of the computer, many programming languages have been developed to communicate with it. Let us have a look at various generations of programming languages that have evolved over a period of time.

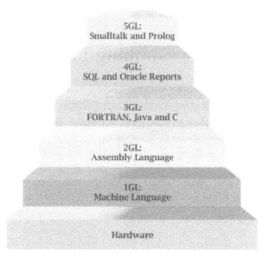

Figure 1.2: Programming Languages

1.1.1 First Generation Programming Language

A first-generation language (1GL) is the first programming language used by the programmers and is regarded as *machine language*. Machine language instructions are expressed as binary numbers called *machine code*. A binary number is made up of just two digits – zero (0) and one (1). Thus, a machine language instruction is just a sequence of zeros and ones. Machine language is a *low-level language*.

1.1.2 Second Generation Programming Language

Assembly language is regarded as a second-generation language (2GL). Assembly language uses symbolic operations called mnemonics instead of binary digits. These mnemonics can have up to maximum five letter combinations, for example:

```
ADD – used to add two data items
SUB – used to subtract two data items
MOV – used to move a data item from one location to another
```

Assembly language is also a *low-level language*.

1.1.3 Third Generation Programming Language

A third-generation language (3GL) is close to English in vocabulary. Writing programs in these languages is much easier than using their predecessors. These languages are easier to read and require less time to write programs. A sample code snippet is shown below:

```
if age >= 18 then
    Print "Candidate can vote"
else
    Print "Candidate cannot vote"
```

Third-generation programming languages are *high-level programming languages*, such as FORTRAN, Java, C, and C++.

1.1.4 Fourth Generation Programming Language

A fourth-generation language (4GL) is closer to a natural language (for example, English) than a third-generation language. The fourth-generation languages are *non-procedural*. This means, the programmer specifies what is required as opposed to how it is to be done. In other words, the desired results are outlined by the programmer and the computer is expected to provide them. A sample code snippet is shown below:

```
Select Name, Age, Marks
From StudentsDatabase
Where Marks > 90
```

In this example, the required series of instructions to get the `Name`, `Age`, and `Marks` from the `StudentsDatabase` is decided by the computer. The user only specifies what is required. Database languages such as Structured Query Language (`SQL`), report generators such as `Oracle Reports`, and `Python` are examples of fourth-generation languages.

1.1.5 Fifth Generation Programming Language

A fifth-generation language (5GL) is designed to solve a given problem using constraints given to the program, rather than using an algorithm written by a programmer. The fifth-generation languages are mainly used in Artificial Intelligence.

`Smalltalk`, `Prolog`, and `Mercury` are good examples of the fifth-generation languages. It is expected that using 5GLs the computer will directly understand human beings! Understanding the speech would be common to computers, and people would be able to talk to computers.

Now, let us learn different ways of writing computer programs.

1.2 Programming Paradigms

A programming paradigm is an approach or style of programming that is used to classify programming languages. Each programming language uses one or more programming paradigms (see Figure 1.3). Each programming paradigm supports a set of concepts that makes it the best for a certain kind of problem. For example, **Procedure Oriented Programming (POP)** paradigm is best suited for problems with step-by-step instructions whereas the **Object Oriented Programming (OOP)** paradigm is best suited for problems with a large number of related data.

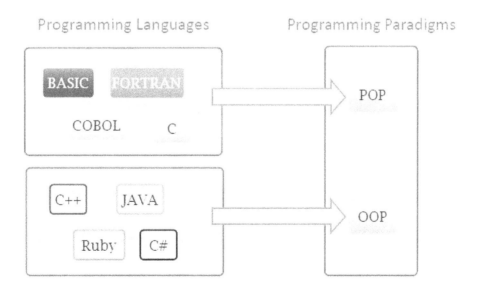

Figure 1.3: Programming Paradigms

Let us now discuss the Procedure Oriented Programming and the Object Oriented Programming paradigms in detail.

1.2.1 Procedure Oriented Programming (POP)

Procedure Oriented Programming is a programming paradigm based on the concept of using procedures. A *procedure* is a sequence of instructions to be executed. The best-known early language which uses this type of paradigm is FORTRAN (FORmula TRANslation), which was developed in the 1950s. During later developments in the 1970s-80s, a structured programming approach was making its mark. This programming approach used the following guidelines:

- Break down a large program into several tasks or parts.

- Find the solution for each part separately, by treating it as a new problem which itself can further be broken down into several parts.

- Repeat this process as it will eventually lead you up to parts which can be solved directly and do not require any further break down.

- Combine all the previous solutions into the final solution.

The solution to each part is usually termed as a function or procedure. A function[1] is effectively a set of instructions to be carried out. It has a defined purpose and usually "takes in" data (called input), processes it, and "returns" a result (called output). Therefore, with this approach, a large program can be split into more manageable functions or procedures. This approach allows functions to be independently developed and tested.

Figure 1.4: Functions

Figure 1.5 shows the main program calling a number of functions. A function can also call any other function.

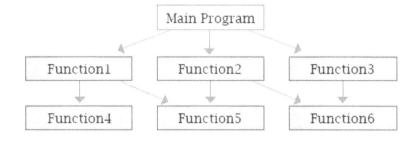

Figure 1.5: Procedure Oriented Programming Approach

---

[1]Functions are also referred as modules, methods, procedures or sub-routines but they all mean the same thing.

Procedural programming is the way we first approached programming a computer because it corresponds most closely to the way the computer works:

A computer takes one instruction at a time and executes it.
A procedural program is a step-by-step list of instructions to solve a problem.

This perfectly matched with what a computer can do. Therefore, if you want a computer to do something, you should provide step-by-step instructions on how to do it. For example, using the recipe analogy, the first step is to boil the water and the next is to add pasta and so forth. It is, therefore, no surprise that most of the early programming languages were all procedural. FORTRAN, BASIC, COBOL, and C are good examples of the procedural languages.

Having gone through the details, let us formally define the term, Procedure Oriented Programming.

> **Definition**
>
> A programming paradigm where a complex programming problem is solved by dividing it into smaller problems using functions (or procedures) is known as Procedure Oriented Programming.

Since we started at the top and then worked our way downwards towards finding the solution of each part, this style of programming is termed as a *top-down approach*.

Therefore, using the top-down approach, you can solve a large programming problem by dividing it into a number of subtasks (functions). When using these functions in the main program, you can ignore lower-level details of how computations are dealt with. You can reuse these functions whenever they are required. This results in a neat, precise and smaller code.

As experts progressed in software engineering, it was realised that this approach to solving problems was incomplete. Remember, it was previously stated that there are two aspects to a program – instructions and data. The above problem-solving approach is mainly dealing with the instructions aspect only. The data aspect is not given as much thought and consideration as is given to the instructions. Let us understand what it means:

1. Functions share global data in a program (see Figure 1.6). The global data is declared in a way that makes it available to every other part of the program. Therefore, its value can be changed by the main program or any function. There is no protection of data from the unauthorised access and misuse.

   > **Note**
   >
   > The local data is declared in a way that makes it only available within a specific function. Therefore, its value can be changed in that function only.

2. It is difficult to keep track of where in the program the global data has been changed or why it was changed.

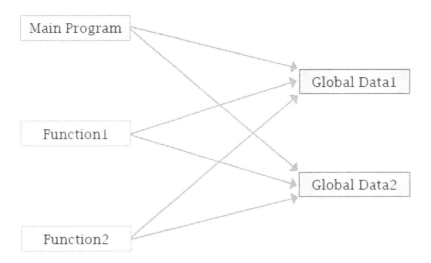

Figure 1.6: Data Sharing POP

The issue in sharing global data may sound trivial in small programs. However, in large and complex programs, it is difficult to maintain the legitimacy of such global data if a number of functions are operating on it.

1.2.1.1 Characteristics of Procedural Programming

(i) Procedural programming follows a top-down approach.

(ii) The program is divided into blocks of codes called functions, where each function performs a specific task.

(iii) Procedural programs model real-world processes as 'procedures' operating on 'data'.

(iv) The data and functions are detached from each other.

(v) The data moves freely in a program.

(vi) It is easy to follow the logic of a program.

(vii) A function can access other function's data by calling that function.

1.2.1.2 Limitations of Procedural Programming

(i) Procedural programming mainly focuses on procedures or functions. Less attention is given to the data.

(ii) The data and functions are separate from each other.

(iii) Global data is freely moving and is shared among various functions. Thus, it becomes difficult for programmers to identify and fix issues in a program that originate due to incorrect data handling.

(iv) Changes in data types need to be carried out manually all over the program and in the functions using the same data type.

(v) Limited and difficult code reusability.

(vi) It does not model real-world entities (e.g., car, table, bank account, loan) very well where we, as a human being, perceive everything as an object.

(vii) The procedural programming approach does not work well for large and complex systems.

The above limitations gave rise to a totally different programming paradigm called Object Oriented Programming (OOP). Let us learn about it in the next section.

1.2.2 Object Oriented Programming (OOP)

Before we proceed further with Object Oriented Programming, let us understand what an Object is.

Everything is an Object
In the broadest term, everything we see around us is an object. This can be a tangible[2] thing, such as a car, pen, book, mobile, chair, and an ATM. Or it can be an intangible[3] thing, such as a bank account, fee account, an email, and an mp3 file.

Figure 1.7: Examples of Real-world Objects

An *object* is an identifiable entity with some attributes and behaviour. For example, we can say that a car is an object. It has *attributes*, such as its colour, make, model, and engine size. Its *behaviour* includes driving forward, backward, accelerating, halting, etc.

Let us take another example of the mobile phone object. It has *attributes*, such as its model, colour, weight, size, and camera resolution. Its *behaviour* includes dialling the number, starting the call, ending the call, taking a picture, etc.

---

[2]Tangible refers to things that can be seen and touched.
[3]Intangible refers to things that may or may not be seen, but they cannot be touched.

Now, let us take an example of an intangible object – `bank account`. It has *attributes*, such as account number, account holder's name, and balance amount. Its *behaviour* includes depositing money, withdrawing money, showing balance, etc.

In Object Oriented Programming, as the name suggests, the problem-solving aspect focuses on objects. In order to solve a problem in OOP, you start by identifying the *objects* involved in the problem. Then you identify the *attributes* and *behaviour* of these objects. The attributes of an object are represented by the data, and the behaviour is represented by the functions or operations the object can perform. The whole object-oriented program is divided into objects.

In this problem-solving approach, we start at the bottom by identifying the objects and then work upwards towards the solution of the problem. This style of programming is termed as *bottom-up approach*.

> **Definition**
>
> Object Oriented Programming (OOP) is a programming paradigm in which data and functions are wrapped into a single unit.

What is a Class?

The term *class* is used to describe a group of objects that have some common attributes and behaviour. For example, consider lions, giraffes, and cows. They all share common attributes such as all have eyes, hair, ears, and four legs. They all share common behaviour, such as: all of them eat, sleep, walk, and run. Therefore, they can be grouped into a class called `Animal`.

Similarly, mangoes, apples, and oranges all share some common attributes and behaviour belonging to the `Fruit` class.

Figure 1.8: Animal Class

Figure 1.9: Fruit Class

A class can be thought of as a template or blueprint for multiple objects with similar features. An object belonging to a particular class is called an *instance* of that class. Therefore, we can say that mango is an instance of the `Fruit` class.

Figure 1.10 shows data sharing in procedure-oriented programming. As can be seen, the global data is freely available to the main program as well as to all the functions.

Figure 1.11 shows data sharing in object-oriented programming. As can be seen, the data is accessed through defined functions only. The data is not freely available, due to the fact that the only way of accessing the data is by calling the relevant function.

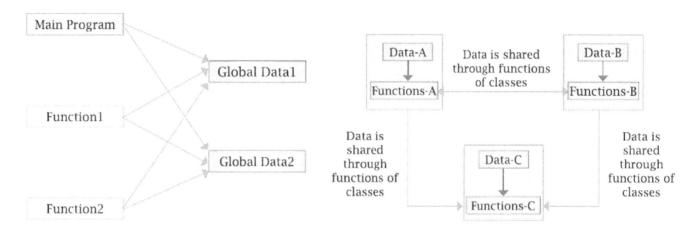

Figure 1.10: Data Sharing POP   Figure 1.11: Data Sharing OOP

1.2.2.1 Characteristics of Object Oriented Programming

(i) OOP follows a bottom-up approach.

(ii) The program resulting from object-oriented programming is a collection of objects. Each object has its own data and a set of operations.

(iii) OOP restricts the free movement of data and the functions that operate on it. It uses a data/information hiding technique that allows better control over data. We will learn about it in the subsequent sections.

(iv) A properly defined class can be reused, giving way to code reusability.

(v) The concept of object-oriented programming models real-world entities very well.

(vi) Due to its object-oriented approach, it is extremely useful in solving complex problems.

1.2.2.2 Limitations of Object Oriented Programming

(i) The size of the programs created using this approach may become larger than the programs written using procedure-oriented programming approach.

(ii) Software developed using this approach requires a substantial amount of pre-work and planning.

(iii) OOP code is difficult to understand if you do not have the corresponding class documentation.

(iv) In certain scenarios, these programs can consume a large amount of memory.

1.3 Principles of Object Oriented Programming

For a programming language to claim to be object-oriented, it should have the ability to work with classes and objects. In addition, it must use and implement the following four fundamental object-oriented principles:

- Data Abstraction

- Encapsulation

- Inheritance

- Polymorphism

A programming language that does not adhere to these four principles cannot claim to be object-oriented. Let us now understand these principles in detail.

1.3.1 Data Abstraction

In order to use something, you do not need to know how it works. A coffee-making machine, for example, is complex. But you do not need to know how it actually works. You just need to know which coffee you want. Just press the relevant button, it will make some quirky noises and you will get a nice cup of coffee. That is abstraction.

Figure 1.12: Coffee Maker

Abstraction refers to the act of representing essential features without including the background details. Here, the abstraction presents only the essential features i.e. dispensing buttons of the coffee machine. The dispensing buttons hide all the complexity of making coffee behind them.

In real life, we use abstraction all the times. Abstraction helps to hide internal implementation details that are not relevant to the user. Moreover, abstraction is relative to the perspective of the viewer. It means that there can be different abstractions of an entity depending on the viewpoint of the user.

Let us understand different abstractions of an entity with the help of some examples.

While using an ATM machine to withdraw money, you insert your Debit card in the provided slot and follow the on-screen instructions. After providing the correct PIN number and entering the desired amount, you collect the money from the machine. Here, the user interacts only with the essential features of an ATM machine - card reading slot, touch screen for input and the money dispensing slot. The user does not need to know or understand the background processes the machine performs, such as:

- Reading the card details

- Verifying the PIN

- Checking the account balance

- Counting the cash

However, an ATM's technician does need to understand these background processes so that he can identify and fix issues with the ATM machines. For him, the essential feature of the money dispensing slot is not the same as it is for a normal ATM user. The essential features for him will be the mechanism of counting and dispensing cash behind the scenes. Therefore, there can be two abstractions of an ATM machine – one for the ATM user and the other for the ATM technician. Figure 1.13 shows these two perspectives in the pictorial form.

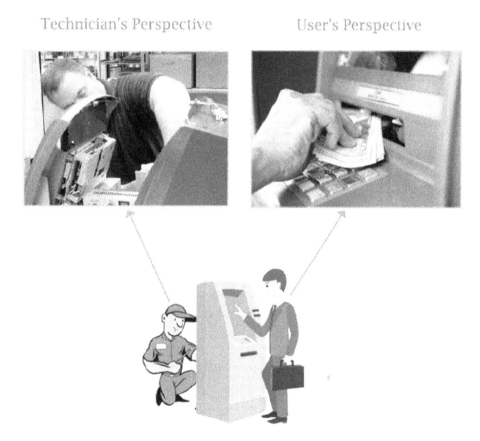

Figure 1.13: Two Abstractions of an ATM

Data/Information Hiding

Using abstraction, the objects expose only the essential features to the outside world and hide the rest of the details. The outside world only sees a simplified version of the actual object. This is called data/information hiding. The details of how features are implemented inside the object are not important to the outside world, as long as they perform their assigned role correctly.

Note: Applying the concept of abstraction to data is termed as data abstraction.

1.3.2 Encapsulation

You are all familiar with the volume control knob, as shown in Figure 1.14, which you use to control the volume of music playing on stereos. It encloses a lot of information about its implementation, such as the value of the resistance transistors, current voltage, and the position of the knob. But when you want to change the level of volume, you have only one method of affecting this complex encapsulation, which is by moving the knob clockwise or anti-clockwise.

Figure 1.14: Volume Control Knob

You cannot change the level of volume by using any other control on the music player. For example, pressing the play, pause, forward or reverse button would not change the volume. In this scenario, the volume control knob is said to be well encapsulated from other controls (objects) or the outside world.

Encapsulation is a mechanism that binds the data and code (functions) together into a single unit. It keeps them both safe from the outside world, preventing any unauthorised access or misuse. Access to the data and code inside a class is strictly controlled. Only the functions that are inside the class can access data. In this way, the data and functions are said to be encapsulated into a single entity, as if enclosing them both into a capsule (See Figure 14.1).

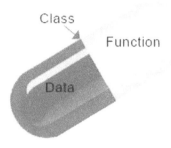

Figure 1.15: Encapsulation

> **Note**
>
> Remember that the attributes of an object are represented by the data and the behaviour is represented by the functions the object can perform.

Let us take another real-life example of a washing machine as shown in Figure 1.16. The start button on the washing machine encapsulates lots of complexity behind it. Here, the abstraction shows only the essential feature i.e., the Start button. The encapsulation helps to hide all the internal details of washing, i.e.,

- filling up the water

- starting the drum

- spinning

- rinsing, etc.

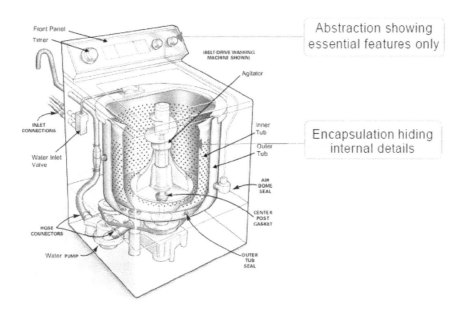

Figure 1.16: Washing Machine (Encapsulation & Abstraction example)

1.3.3 Inheritance

You might have studied the term heredity in biology, which means children inheriting characteristics of their parents. For example, hair colour, nose shape, and eye colour. Similarly, Java being an object-oriented programming language, allows one class to inherit from the other. Thus, the classes developed in Java are much closer to the real world. Let us understand it with the help of an example.

There are objects that are related to each other in a hierarchical way such as Birds, Walking Birds and Ostrich. All kinds of birds have attributes, such as their name, size, colour, and average lifespan. They also have certain behaviour, such as eating, sleeping and breathing. These can be considered as the generic attributes and behaviour of a Birds class definition. These attributes and behaviours will be shared amongst all birds unless they have specific differences that separate them from the rest.

From the `Birds` class, specific types of birds can be inherited, for example, `Flying Birds`. The `Flying Birds` class needs to define only its own unique attributes, such as flying distance, timings of flying and places where they fly. The rest of the generic attributes and behaviour are inherited from the `Birds` class.

In this illustration, the Flying Birds class is said to be a derived class of the Birds class, thereby inheriting all of its characteristics and behaviour. Meanwhile, the Birds class is said to be the parent class of the Flying Birds class (see Figure 14.2).

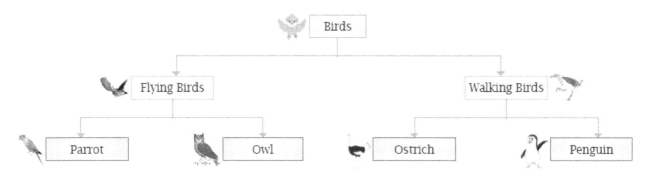

Figure 1.17: Inheritance Example

With this understanding, let us now define inheritance in terms of OOP:

Definition

Inheritance is a powerful mechanism by which one class acquires the properties of another class. For inheritance, first of all, you define the common class that contains the generic features of an entity. Then you define another class as an extension of the common class, inheriting everything from the common class.

The common class that gets inherited is called the *parent class* or the *base class* or the *super class*. The class that inherits from the common class is called the *child class* or the *derived class* or the *sub class*. As can be seen in Figure 14.2, inheritance is not just limited to one level. You can have sub classes of `Flying Birds` as `Parrot` and `Owl`. Thus, a derived class can be a base class of other classes forming an inheritance hierarchy.

Figure 1.18: Base and Derived Class

The inheritance mechanism makes it possible for an object to be a specific instance of a more generic object. If you do not apply inheritance, each object would need to define all of its characteristics explicitly. It will be time-consuming first to create a class and then be compelled to create another brand new one that has similar functionality. However, using inheritance, an object needs to define only those qualities that make it unique within its class. The rest of the general qualities are inherited from the parent class.

Inheritance is Transitive

Inheritance is transitive. It means that all the attributes and behaviour are passed down from a parent class to the child class and then from the child class to their children and further. Using Figure 14.2 as an example, an instance of class `Parrot` also inherits all the attributes and behaviour of the `Flying Birds` class and the `Birds` class.

Figure 1.19: Transitivity

But, how does inheritance help in Object Oriented Programming?

The inheritance mechanism is a very powerful tool in the object-oriented design which enables you to reuse existing code easily and flexibly. Using inheritance, you can progressively build up classes with extensive capabilities, with minimal effort. The capabilities at each stage are added in a clear and simple manner, making the code easy to manage and maintain.

1.3.4 Polymorphism

The word Polymorphism means "many forms". It comes from the Greek word *poly* (meaning many) and *morphos* (meaning form). *Polymorphism* is the ability of a function or an object to acquire multiple forms.

Let us understand the concept of Polymorphism with the help of classic "Shape" example. Here, the parent class is `Shape`. Each object in the `Shape` class has attributes, such as size, number of sides, colour and corners. The behaviour of each shape includes being drawn, erased, coloured, etc. Therefore, each object in this class will have the corresponding functions, such as `Draw()`, `Erase()` and `Colour()` respectively. From this base class, specific types of shapes are inherited – `Circle`, `Rectangle`, and `Triangle`.

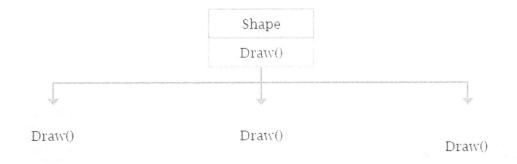

Figure 1.20: Polymorphism – Draw Command

As shown in Figure 1.20, the same `Draw()` function can be used to handle different shapes irrespective of whether it is a `Circle`, `Rectangle` or `Triangle`. However, calling the `Draw()` function for the `Circle` object causes different code to be executed than that of the `Rectangle` or

`Triangle`. With this understanding, let us now define Polymorphism in terms of OOP:

> **Definition**
>
> Polymorphism is a mechanism by which you can send the same message to different objects, and each object can respond in a different way based on its class.

Just like a `Draw()` message can draw a circle, rectangle or a triangle, an `Accelerate()` command can accelerate a train, a car or an aeroplane.

Figure 1.21: Polymorphism – Accelerate Command

But, how does Polymorphism help in Object Oriented Programming?
Polymorphism helps in reducing the complexity by allowing one interface to specify a general type of action. Code designed and written with the polymorphic capabilities is unaffected by the addition of new types. For example, in our previous illustration, a new `Boat` class can be added that can use the same `Accelerate()` command. Adding new types is the most common way of extending object-oriented programs, thereby reducing the software development and maintenance cost.

1.4 All Principles Working Together

In the real-life, a mobile phone is an excellent example of an object-oriented design. Let us understand how it uses all the four OOP principles.

Making a call hides a tremendous amount of complexity behind a very simple interface. As an end user of the mobile, do you ever need to know how this call will be connected to the other person? No, you just use the interface provided. Here, the abstraction helps to show only the essential features to make a call, i.e., the dial button. The encapsulation helps to hide all the complexity of making a call, i.e., connecting to the other device via circuitry and the mobile network (see Figure 1.22).

You, as end users of the mobile, rely on inheritance to operate different types of mobile phones. Remember, when you say different types in everyday language, it means subclasses in OOP! Whether the mobile phone is an iPhone, Samsung or Xiaomi, they all more or less operate in the same way to make a phone call because they are all subclasses of the same superclass Mobile (see Figure 1.23). Just key-in the number and press the dial button. However, a few smart phones may have different Graphic User Interfaces. But, it takes only a short time to adjust to a different interface because you understand the key features of the superclass `Mobile`.

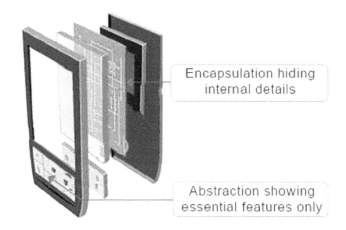

Figure 1.22: Mobile - Abstraction and Encapsulation

Finally, let us see how polymorphism comes into the picture. Mobile manufacturers offer a wide range of phones but the way of operating the phone is essentially the same. For example, iPhone X has the models iPhone XS, iPhone XS Max, and iPhone XR (see Figure 1.23). With any of these forms of the iPhone X, you still press the dial button to make a call and press the end button to end the call. The same interface is used to control a number of different implementations.

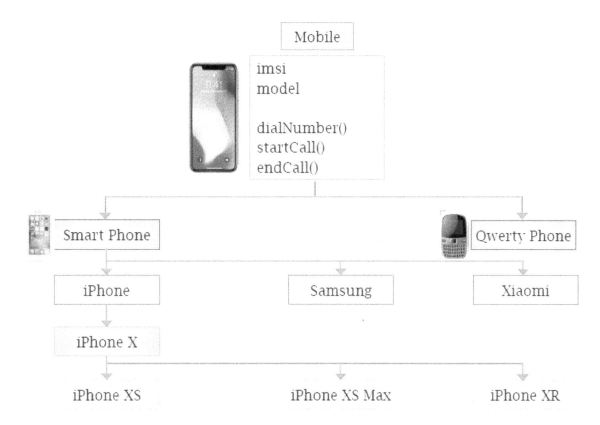

Figure 1.23: Mobile Class Hierarchy

You have understood now that with the help of the four pillars of OOP (Abstraction, Encapsulation,

Inheritance, and Polymorphism), the individual components are transformed into a real-world Phone object, which is a complete entity in itself. Since the human mind is more used to seeing things as whole objects, you can apply the same principles to the computer programs. In a computer program, you can apply:

- Abstraction to identify data objects.

- Inheritance to allow classes to acquire the properties of another class.

- Encapsulation to hide complexity from the outside world so that no unauthorised access or action takes place. It also ensures that a user is not overwhelmed with additional details.

- Polymorphism to design a generic interface to specify a general type of action.

1.5 Difference between POP and OOP

Having studied the POP and OOP, let us summarise the key differences between the two programming paradigms as shown in Table below.

Difference between POP and OOP		
Basis	*POP*	*OOP*
Approach	Follows a top-down approach	Follows a bottom-up approach
Orientation	Algorithmic in nature, i.e., instruction oriented.	Data oriented in nature.
Abstraction	The abstraction is at procedure (function) level.	The abstraction is at object (class) level.
Division	The sequence of events in a large program is divided into functions.	Entire program is divided into objects.
Interaction	Interaction with the program is via direct function calls.	Interaction with the program is via functions defined in the class only.
Real World	Real world is represented by 'procedures' operating on 'data'.	Real world is represented by objects and the operations which can be performed on these objects.
Data	Data and functions are separate.	Data and functions are encapsulated into a single entity.
Data Security	Data security is less as it contains lesser features to protect the data.	It is more secure as one of its primary features includes data hiding.
Data Sharing	A function can access any other function's data by calling that function.	Only the data whose access has been granted can be accessed by another function.
Code Reusability	Limited and difficult code reusability.	Versatile and easy code reusability.

Basis	POP	OOP
Code Maintenance	Code is difficult to modify, extend and maintain.	Code is easy to modify, extend and maintain.
Example Languages	C, COBOL, and Pascal	Java, C++, and C#

(table heading: Difference between POP and OOP contd...)

Multiple Choice Questions

1. Procedure Oriented Programming gives importance to ....

    A. Instructions only   C. Data only

    B. Instructions and data   D. None of the above

2. Procedure Oriented Programming mainly uses ....

    A. Top-down approach   C. Bottom-up approach

    B. Top-down and bottom-up approach   D. None of the above

3. Object Oriented Programming mainly uses ....

    A. Top-down approach   C. Bottom-up approach

    B. Top-down and bottom-up approach   D. None of the above

4. An object belonging to a particular class is known as a/an .... of that class.

    A. Interface   C. Alias

    B. Instance   D. Member

5. Objects that share the same attributes and behaviour are grouped together into a/an ....

    A. Interface   C. Alias

    B. Instance   D. Class

6. .... is the technique of binding both data and functions together to keep them safe from unauthorised access and misuse.

    A. Abstraction   C. Encapsulation

    B. Inheritance   D. Polymorphism

7. .... refers to the act of representing essential features without including the background details.

    A. Abstraction   C. Encapsulation

    B. Inheritance   D. Polymorphism

8. .... is the feature by means of which one class acquires the properties of another class.

    A. Abstraction   C. Encapsulation

    B. Inheritance   D. Polymorphism

9. The ability of a function or object to take on multiple forms is called ....

    A. Abstraction   C. Encapsulation

    B. Inheritance   D. Polymorphism

10. The term OOP stands for ....

    A. Object Oriented Procedure   C. Object Oriented Programming

    B. Object Oriented Packet   D. Object Orientation Procedure

---

State whether the given statements are True or False:

☐ Low-level languages are closer to computer hardware.

☐ In a procedural language, code and data are held separately.

☐ In object-oriented programming, code and data are held separately.

☐ Wrapping up data and related functions in a single unit represents encapsulation.

☐ The object is also known as an instance.

☐ The class that is derived from another class is called a superclass.

☐ Classes can be derived from other classes.

☐ Inheritance allows a class to acquire the properties of another class.

☐ A class is a blueprint for the attributes and behaviours of a group of objects.

☐ Objects from the same class do not share the same definition of attributes and behaviours.

Assignment Questions

1. What are programming languages? Describe the various generations of programming languages.

2. What are programming paradigms? Briefly explain two popular programming paradigms.

3. What are the characteristics of procedural programming?

4. What are the limitations of procedural programming?

5. Write a short note on Object Oriented Programming.

6. Explain the phrase, "Everything is an object".

7. What are the characteristics of object-oriented programming?

8. What are the limitations of object-oriented programming?

9. What do you mean by Abstraction? Give suitable examples.

10. Differentiate between the Owner's and the Vet's perspective in Figure 1.24.

Figure 1.24: Abstraction using the Dog Model

11. Differentiate between the Car Mechanic's and Car Driver's perspective in Figure 1.25.

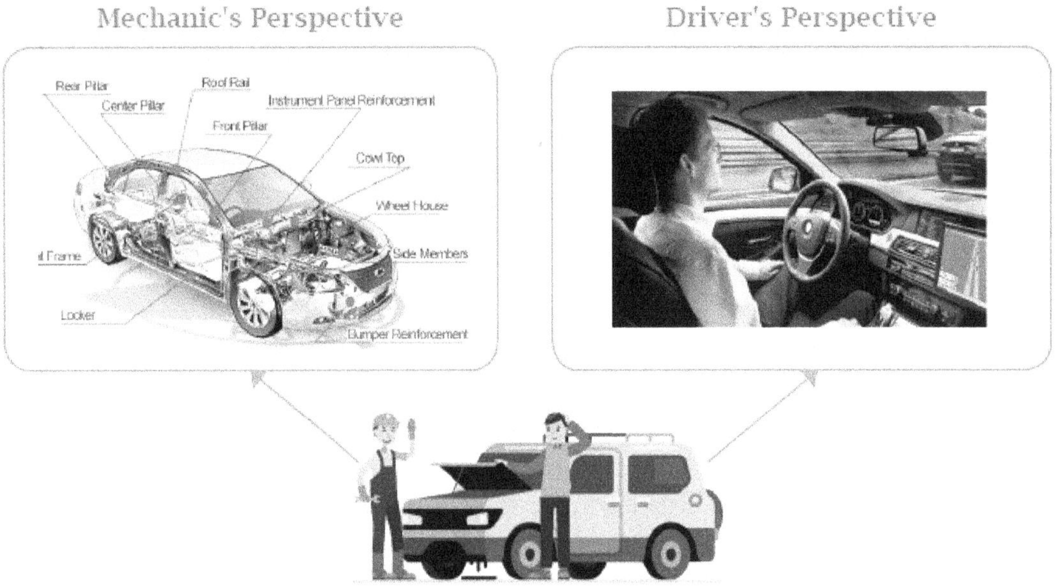

Figure 1.25: Abstraction using the Car Model

12. Explain the term, Encapsulation using appropriate examples.

13. Provide real-life examples to explain the term Inheritance.

14. Polymorphism means different forms. Explain Polymorphism in Java and provide examples to support your answer.

15. Write a short note on the principles of Object Oriented Programming.

16. Explain the difference between Inheritance and Encapsulation with suitable examples.

17. What are the differences between Procedural Programming and Object Oriented Programming?

Answers To Objective Questions

Multiple Choice Questions

1. A	3. C	5. D	7. A	9. D
2. A	4. B	6. C	8. B	10. C

True or False

1. True	3. False	5. True	7. True	9. True
2. True	4. True	6. False	8. True	10. False

Chapter 2

Introduction to Java

Introduction to Object Oriented Programming Concepts

Java is a full-featured, general purpose object-oriented programming language that can be used to develop robust mission-critical applications. It was used to develop the code to communicate with the robotic rover on Mars. Developed by James Gosling at Sun Microsystems, Java was initially designed for consumer electronic devices such as televisions, washing machines, microwaves, and other similar electronic devices. Since these devices used different platforms, there was a need for a platform independent language, such as Java.

Java applications are platform independent, which means that Java applications can run on any platform. The term platform refers to a specific combination of hardware and system software (operating system). For example, an application running on a computer with *Intel Core i7* processor (hardware) and Windows 7 may not run on a computer with Macintosh (Operating System). Java has become enormously popular. Its rapid rise and wide acceptance can be traced to its design characteristics, particularly its promise that you can write a program once and run it anywhere.

> **Note**
>
> The capability of a computer program to run on multiple platforms is referred to as platform independence.

2.1 Types of Java Programs

There are two types of Java programs: stand-alone applications and internet applets.

2.1.1 Stand-alone Java Application

A stand-alone Java application refers to a Java program that can run independently on a computer. Acrobat PDF Reader is an excellent example of this type of application. Java stand-alone applications can either be console-based or with a Graphical User Interface (GUI). A Console-based Java application uses a text-only interface. A GUI-based Java application uses a graphical interface, such as command buttons, text fields, and a mouse.

2.1.2 Java Applets or Java Internet Applets

While browsing the internet, often the graphical user interface and animation that you see have been developed using Java. The Java programs that run in a web browser are called Java applets. The applet is capable of performing many tasks on a web page, such as displaying graphics, playing sounds, and accepting user input (see Figure 2.1). Applets are also used to create animation and interactive games. They can be transported over the internet from one computer to another through a Java-enabled browser or an applet viewer.

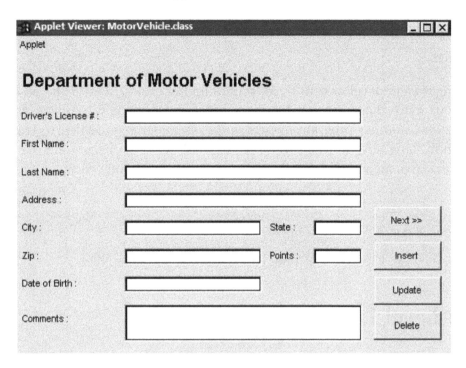

Figure 2.1: Java Applets – User Input Example

2.2 Machine Language

Computers were developed to carry out instructions that were written in its native language called machine language. Machine language instructions are expressed as binary numbers called machine code. A binary number is made up of just two digits – zero (0) and one (1). Each digit, zero or one, is called a *bit*. Thus, the machine language instruction is just a sequence of zeros and ones.

A machine language instruction may look like:

```
000000 00001 00010 00110 00000 100000
```

Although most computers perform the same kind of operations, they use different sets of binary codes for each instruction. Due to this, the machine code of one type of computer is not the same as that of another type of computer. For example, machine code of UNIX computer is different from that of Windows computer. Note that a computer can directly execute a program only if it is written in its own machine language.

2.3 Assembly Language

Programming in machine language was a tedious process and was prone to errors. In addition to this, these programs were very difficult to read and modify. To overcome these issues, assembly languages were developed which allowed programs to be written using symbolic operations called mnemonic codes. For example, instead of using `100101`, you can use mnemonic `ADD`. Assembly language instructions may look like:

```
ADD AX, BX
MOV AL, 61h
```

Assembly languages were developed to make programming easier. Although these programs were relatively easier to write than machine language programs, but they were not recognised by the computer. Therefore, another program known as an assembler was needed to translate programs written in assembly language into machine language as shown in Figure 2.2. An *assembler* is a program that translates an assembly language program into machine code.

Figure 2.2: Code Translation by an Assembler

2.4 High-Level Languages

In the 1950s, a new generation of programming languages known as high-level languages emerged. A high-level language is quite similar to the English language and is easy to learn and use. There are many high-level programming languages, and each was designed for a specific purpose. Basic, C, Java, etc. are good examples of some high-level languages. A high-level language statement may look like:

```
VolumeOfCuboid = Length * Width * Height;
```

A program written in a high-level programming language is called a *source program* or source code. Since the program written in the high-level language is not recognised by the computer, a translator program is needed to translate it into the machine language equivalent. The translation can be done using either an interpreter or a compiler.

2.4.1 Interpreter

An *interpreter* is a program that translates the source code instructions into machine code line-by-line. The interpreter runs in a loop, reading the next statement from the source code and translating it into the necessary machine code. Note that the execution of an interpreted program is slow.

Figure 2.3: Code Translation by an Interpreter

2.4.2 Compiler

A *compiler* is a program that translates code written in a high-level language into machine code all at once before the program is executed. A machine language version of the source code is called the *object code*. During program execution, the object code is loaded into the computer memory. The computer then directly executes the object code. Note that the execution of a compiled program is fast.

Figure 2.4: Code Translation by a Compiler

2.5 Traditional Compilation Process

The object code generated by the compilation process is specific to the platform you are compiling on, as shown in Figure 2.5. For example, if you compiled your source code on UNIX platform, the resulting program would run only on the UNIX platform. To run the same program on any other platform, for example, Macintosh, you need to compile the original source code with a compiler suitable for Macintosh. The compiler for one high-level language is different from the other. For example, a C++ language compiler can be used to convert a C++ source code file only and cannot be used for converting a Java source code file.

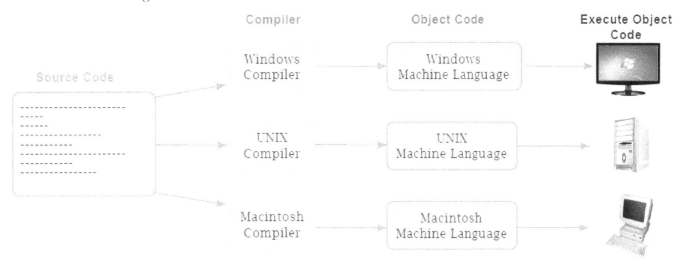

Figure 2.5: Traditional Compilation Process

2.6 Java Compilation Process

You have already learnt that in the traditional compilation process, an equivalent machine code is generated for a particular platform. So, the source code written in Java language is also compiled into a machine code. However, Java compilation process is different. Here, the machine code is for a virtual machine known as *Java Virtual Machine* or *JVM*. The machine code for the Java Virtual Machine is called *Bytecode*. This Bytecode needs a Java Interpreter to convert it into the machine code of the computer on which it is to be executed. This interpreter is a part of the Java Virtual Machine or JVM (see the zoomed-out part of Figure 2.6). The Java source code file has a ".java" extension, and the Bytecode file has a ".class" extension.

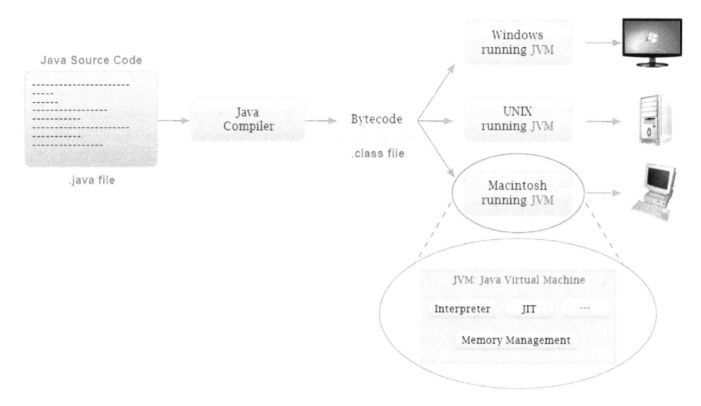

Figure 2.6: Java Compilation Process

A different Java Bytecode Interpreter is needed for each type of computer (i.e., Windows, UNIX, and Macintosh). However, once the computer has the required Java Bytecode Interpreter, it can run any Java Bytecode program.

The JVM also includes a *Just-In-Time (JIT)* compiler that compiles selected portions of Bytecode into executable code[1] (see Figure 2.7). The remaining code is simply interpreted. JRE is an acronym for Java Runtime Environment. The JVM, along with many other class libraries, constitutes the JRE.

Figure 2.7: JRE and JVM

---

[1] In computing, executable code or an executable file causes a computer "to perform a series of instructions when it is opened".

2.7 Features of Java

Java has many features that make it one of the most popular programming languages in the world. Let us understand some of its important features:

2.7.1 Object Oriented

Java is an object-oriented programming language because it treats everything as an object. The entire program code and data reside within objects and classes. This enables us to easily use and extend the object model.

2.7.2 Robust

Java is a robust and reliable programming language. It has strict compile time and runtime checking for data types. Memory allocation and de-allocation is automatic in Java, so there is less for the programmer to worry about.

2.7.3 Platform Independent

The concept of "Write once, run anywhere", is one of the most important features of Java, which makes it a very powerful language. Java applications can run on any platform that has the corresponding JVM installed on it.

2.7.4 Simple

Java is a simple and easy to learn programming language. The removal of many unreliable features of C and C++ (its predecessors) has simplified its understanding and implementation.

2.7.5 Secure

Security becomes an important issue for a language that is used for programming on the internet. Java allows applets to confine to the Java runtime environment only. Applets cannot access any other part of the computer when downloaded on the web browser. This helps to eliminate any damage due to malicious software and viruses.

2.7.6 Multithreaded

Java is also a multithreaded programming language. This means that you do not need to wait for an application to finish one task before starting another. Multithreading works in a similar way as multiple processes run on one computer. For example, listening to audio while scrolling a web page and downloading an applet.

> **Note**
>
> Java uses a combination of compilation and interpretation.

2.8 Working with BlueJ

BlueJ is an Integrated Development Environment (IDE) specifically designed for teaching Java at an introductory level. The BlueJ environment was developed as part of a university research project to teach object-oriented programming to beginners. It was developed and maintained by a joint research group at Deakin University in Melbourne, Australia, and the University of Kent in Canterbury, UK. The BlueJ Development Environment provides a single Graphical User Interface (GUI) that contains:

- Code Editor – to write the program code

- Java Compiler – to compile your code

- Virtual Machine – to execute the Java program

- Terminal – to view the output

- Debugger – to find problems in the code

2.8.1 Starting BlueJ

In order to start BlueJ, click on Start > All Programs > BlueJ > BlueJ as shown in Figure 2.8.

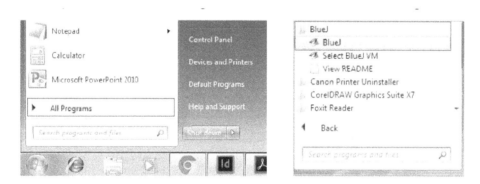

Figure 2.8: Starting BlueJ

Or, you can also start BlueJ by double-clicking on the BlueJ icon on your desktop.

2.8.2 Creating a BlueJ Project

To write programs in the BlueJ IDE, you need to create a project. This is because all Java programs are created as part of a BlueJ project. The steps to create a new project are as follows:

- Click on the Project menu and choose the `New Project` option:

- You will now see `New Project` dialog box. Provide the *Name* as BlueJWork and the Location as `C:\`. Click on the `OK` button.

A new project will be created. The `Project Window` containing a README file appears.

2.8.3 Creating a Class

As you have already learnt that a class is a template for creating objects and holds its attributes (member variables) and behaviours (member methods), let us now create a class containing only a member method, which will display a welcome message on the screen.

Steps to create a class in BlueJ are as follows:

- There are two ways to add a class to your project.

    1. In the BlueJ window, click on the **New Class** button. Or,

    2. Click on the Edit menu in the toolbar and select the **New Class** option (see Figure 2.9).

- A dialog box **Create New Class** appears as shown in Figure 2.10. Enter the *Class Name* as **Welcome** and select the *Class Type* as **Class**. Click on the **OK** button.

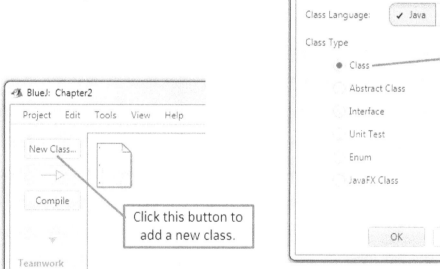

Figure 2.9: Adding a New Class   Figure 2.10: Defining the Class Name and Class Type

> **Note**
>
> If you change the name of the class, the class icon in the Project window will also reflect the change.

In the Project window, you will find an icon representing the newly created class `Welcome` as shown in Figure 2.11. The *stripes* on the icon indicate that the class has not been compiled yet.

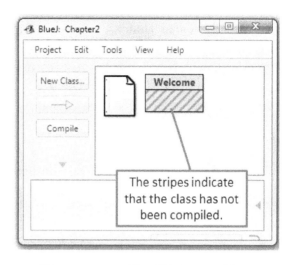

Figure 2.11: The Welcome Class

2.8.4 Editing the Class Code

In order to edit the class code, you need to open the class in the Editor. To do so, either double-click on the class icon or right click on the class icon and select the `Open Editor` option as shown in Figure 2.12.

The class will have some pre-written code already in it. Just press `Ctrl+A` together (to select everything in the Editor window) and press the `Delete` key to remove the entire selection.

Figure 2.12: Opening Editor

Type the code as shown in Figure 2.13. It is a very basic program demonstrating the use of a member method to print a message.

After writing the code in the Editor window, save the changes by clicking on the `Save` option in the `Class` menu. It is a good programming practice to keep saving your work at regular intervals.

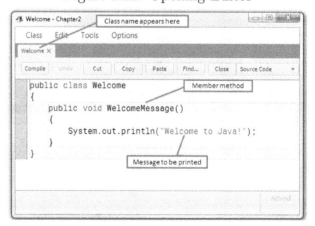

Figure 2.13: Writing the Class Code

Now, as you have successfully written your first Java program, let us quickly go through the code and understand what each line of the code does.

> **Note**
>
> The line numbers on the left-hand side are not part of the code. The numbers are displayed so that these lines can be referred to in the code explanation that follows.

Listing 2.1: Welcome.java

```java
1  public class Welcome
2  {
3      public void WelcomeMessage()
4      {
5          System.out.println ("Welcome to Java!");
6      }
7  }
```

Code Walkthrough:

◈ Line 1:

- The keyword `public` is an access specifier that defines the scope of a class.

- The keyword `class` denotes that this is a `class` with the name `Welcome`.

◈ Line 2:

- The first opening curly bracket marks the beginning of the class code.

◈ Line 3:

- This statement creates a new member method called `WelcomeMessage`.

- The keyword `public` is an access specifier that defines the scope of the member method.

- `void` is a Java keyword which signifies that this method will not return a value.

- The name of the member method is `WelcomeMessage()`. The method name is programmer specified, which cannot be a Java keyword.

◈ Line 4:

- The opening curly bracket indicates the beginning of the method code.

◈ Line 5:

- `System.out.println()` statement prints the text in double quotes ("") as an output. You will learn about it in the following chapters.

- The semicolon (;) indicates the end of a statement. In Java programming, you have to terminate every statement with a semicolon. The absence of this leads to a compile-time error.

◈ Line 6:

- The closing curly bracket indicates the end of the method code.

◈ Line 7:

- The last closing curly bracket marks the end of the class code.

Note the indentation of the code. It helps in improving the readability and makes a block of code easy to spot in a long, complicated program.

2.8.5   Compiling Java Code

The file you have just saved with the .java extension is known as the *source file*. As mentioned earlier that a computer understands only machine language, let us transform our source code to a machine-readable format. To convert the source code (.java file) into the machine language (bytecode file with .class extension), click on the Compile button as shown in Figure 2.14.

If the compiler finds any error, the cursor will move to the location of the error, and it will be marked with a red underline. The error message will be displayed in the text floating nearby. For example, if you use capital P in the println keyword, the compiler will highlight the incorrect code as shown in Figure 2.14.

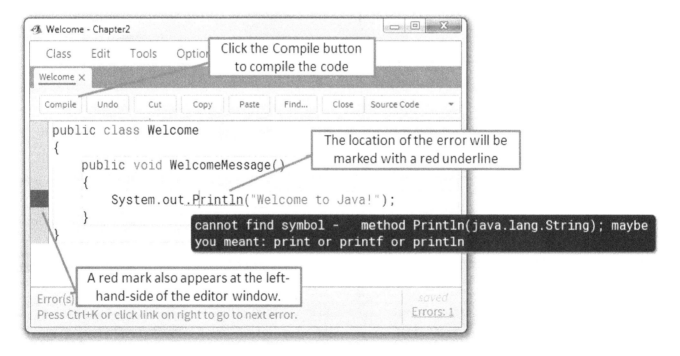

Figure 2.14: Compiling Code with Errors

> **Note**
>
> If there are multiple errors, they are displayed as separate red underlines and red marks. If an error underline is visible, you can hover the mouse over it to display the corresponding error message.

If there are no errors, the compiler displays the message: *Class compiled - no syntax errors*, as shown in Figure 2.15. Note that when you press the **Compile** button, your changes are automatically saved.

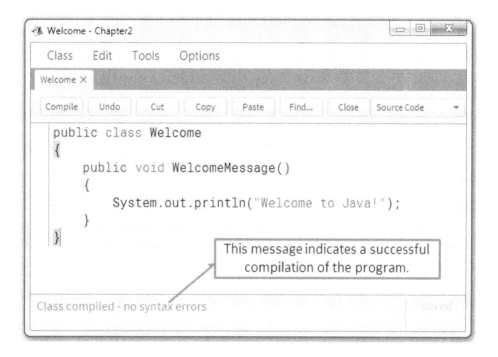

Figure 2.15: Successful Code Compilation

2.8.6 Creating an Object

After successful compilation of the code, the blueprint or template required to create objects is ready. Let us now create an object named as `welcome1` of class type `Welcome`.

To create an object of the `Welcome` class, right click on the class icon and select the option `new Welcome()`. The `new` keyword is used to create an object of the class type. The keyword allocates memory for the new object. You will learn about it in detail in the following chapters.

The `Create Object` dialog box appears. Provide the *Name of Instance*, i.e., name of the object as `welcome1` and click on the `OK` button. BlueJ creates an instance named `welcome1` and shows a red-coloured icon in the Object Bench within the Project window as shown in Figure 2.16.

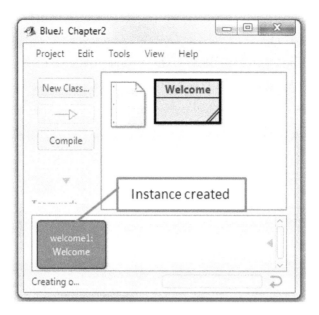

Figure 2.16: Object Bench

2.8.7 Executing the Member Methods

BlueJ has excellent features to execute a program after it has been compiled successfully. Let us learn how you can execute the method `WelcomeMessage()` using the instance `welcome1`. In other words, how you can send a message to instance `welcome1` to perform its action `WelcomeMessage()`. In the Object Bench, right click on the `welcome1` icon and select method `void WelcomeMessage()`. The execution starts, and the message `Welcome to Java!` is displayed in a separate Terminal Window as shown in Figure 2.17.

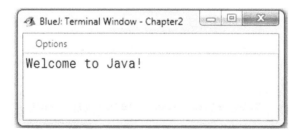

Figure 2.17: The Terminal Window

Since the Terminal Window is not automatically cleared when you re-run the program, you can clear it by selecting the `Clear` option from the `Options` menu. You can also instruct BlueJ to automatically clear the Terminal Window before the execution of a method by selecting `Clear screen at method call` option from the `Options` menu.

2.8.8 The main() Method

So far, you have learnt that you can execute a member method using the following steps:

- Create an object (instance) of the class.

- Right-click on the instance and select the method to execute.

The above technique is used to execute class methods within the BlueJ IDE, for example, executing `WelcomeMessage()` in the `Welcome` class. However, if you want to execute your Java program outside the BlueJ IDE then your program may compile but would not execute unless you add a `main()` method. The `main()` method is the first method which executes when the Java Virtual Machine (JVM) loads the class for execution. The rest of the program is executed following the instructions from this method.

Let us see how to create a Java program with a `main()` method.

- Add a new class `WelcomeAgain`.

- Double-click on the `WelcomeAgain` class icon to open the Editor window.

- Replace the pre-written code with the code as shown in Figure 2.18 .

- Compile the code and close the Editor window.

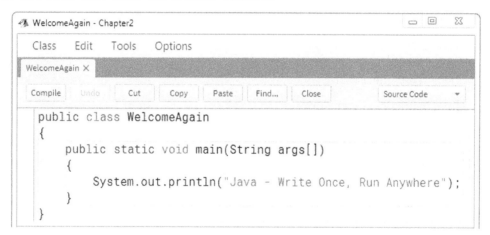

Figure 2.18: Program with main() Method

After successful compilation, right-click on the class icon in the Project window. You will see a shortcut menu with various options. Select the `void main(String[] args)` option from the list. A Method Call dialog box appears. Click on the `OK` button. The program execution starts. The Terminal Window will show the output of this program as shown in Figure 2.19.

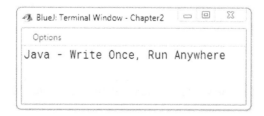

Figure 2.19: Executing Program with main() Method

You have successfully executed the class as an application (or program) with the `main()` method.

Multiple Choice Questions

1. Which language does the CPU understand?

   A. Machine language   C. High-level language

   B. Assembly language   D. English language

2. Stand-alone Java applications .... for execution.

   A. need Java-compatible web browser   C. do not need Java-compatible web browser

   B. need an assembler   D. need a linker

3. What is the full form of JVM?

   A. Java Visual Monitor   C. Java Virtual Monitor

   B. Java Video Monitor   D. Java Virtual Machine

4. The full form of JRE is ....

   A. Java Runtime Editor   C. Java Runtime Expression

   B. Java Runtime Environment   D. Java Runtime Enabler

5. Java uses .... for execution.

   A. compilation and interpretation   C. compilation only

   B. interpretation only   D. None of the above

6. A program that translates code written in a high-level language into machine code is called ....

   A. Assembler   C. Compiler

   B. Linker   D. None of the above

7. A program that translates an assembly language program into machine code is called ....

   A. Assembler   C. Compiler

   B. Linker   D. None of the above

8. Feature(s) of Java include ....

A. Robust   C. Secure

B. Object-Oriented   D. All of the above

9. Java can be used to write ....

     A. stand-alone applications only

     B. both stand-alone and internet applications

     C. internet applications only

     D. None of the above

10. Java applications can run on ....

     A. Windows platform   C. UNIX platform

     B. Macintosh platform   D. All of the above

11. Java applications ....

     A. are platform dependent   C. are platform independent

     B. do not need a platform to run   D. cannot run on Windows

12. A Java program can run as a stand-alone application only if it has ....

     A. a void method   C. an overloaded method

     B. an overloaded method   D. no methods

13. What is the extension of a Java source code file?

     A. .java   B. .txt   C. .class   D. .BlueJ

14. What is the extension of a Java class file?

     A. .obj   B. .java   C. .class   D. .BlueJ

15. Choose the correct statement.

     A. Applets can be executed in a web browser only.

     B. Applets can be executed in an applet viewer only.

     C. Applets can be executed in both web browser and applet viewer.

     D. Applet cannot be executed.

Assignment Questions

1. Write a short note on types of Java programs.

2. How is Java platform independent?

3. Which language does the CPU understand?

4. Describe the traditional compilation process with a suitable diagram.

5. Describe the Java compilation process with a suitable diagram.

6. What is the difference between an interpreted language and a compiled language?

7. How is traditional compilation process different from Java compilation process?

8. What are JVM and JIT?

9. Distinguish between the following:

    (i) Source code and Object code
    (ii) Compiler and Interpreter
    (iii) ".java" file and ".class" file

10. What is Java Bytecode?

11. Describe the slogan, "Write once, run anywhere" in relation to Java.

12. Describe four features of Java.

13. What is the difference between machine code and Bytecode?

14. What role does the Java Virtual Machine play in the compilation and interpretation process?

15. Can Java run on any machine? What is required to run Java on a computer?

16. How is Java more secured than other languages?

Multiple Choice Questions

1. A	4. B	7. A	10. D	13. A
2. C	5. A	8. D	11. C	14. C
3. D	6. C	9. B	12. C	15. C

Chapter 3

Elementary Concepts of Objects and Classes

Elementary Concepts of Objects and Classes

T HE two most important concepts in Object-Oriented Programming are the objects and classes. We live in a world that is comprised of real-life objects, like cars, pens, chairs, tables, computers, etc. A class is a blueprint for multiple objects with similar features. Although the objects and classes have been discussed in Chapter 1, let us learn about these concepts further in this chapter.

3.1 Modelling Entities - Abstraction Revisited

All objects in the real world are entities. An entity is something that exists as itself, either in concrete or in conceptual form. Everything that happens in the world is a result of the interactions that occur between these objects. In object-oriented software, objects are entities that are used to model a system. However, an entity can have different perspectives depending on who is looking at it!

Let us revisit the car example. The car, as an entity, can have two different abstraction[1] views (see Figures 3.1 and 3.2):

1. **Driver's view**: For the driver, a car is one single object, which can be operated using gears, indicators, accelerator, brake, etc. The driver doesn't need to know or understand the internal mechanisms of how these components actually work.

2. **Mechanic's view**: Car mechanics need to know and understand how the internal mechanisms like gears, indicators, accelerator, brake, etc. actually work so that they can identify and fix issues with the cars. For a mechanic, each car part is a single object.

> **Note**
>
> In this example, certain attributes would be common for both. For example, model, engine size, petrol/diesel, etc.

---

[1] Abstraction refers to the act of representing essential features without including the background details.

Figure 3.1: Abstraction Driver

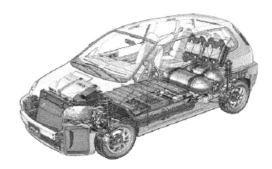

Figure 3.2: Abstraction Mechanic

Abstraction for Car Driver

- Model

- Engine size

- Petrol

- Number of seats

- Seat type

- Comfort level

- Insurance group

- Transmission type (Automatic/Manual)

Abstraction for Car Mechanic

- Model

- Engine size

- Petrol

- Transmission type (Automatic/Manual)

- Axle

- Bearing

- Brake pad

- Exhaust

So which abstraction model would you adopt?

The answer is: one that suits your requirement.

In other words, you choose the abstraction model based on your project: if you are writing the object-oriented software from a car driver's perspective, you design your objects based on the car driver's abstraction (Figure 3.1).

On the other hand, if you are writing the object-oriented software from a car mechanic's perspective, you design your objects based on the car mechanic's abstraction (Figure 3.2).

> **Note**
>
> You model the entities and their behaviour based on what is relevant to the problem that you are trying to solve and choose the appropriate abstraction model.

Let us understand this with the help of another entity called `Customer`. In a banking application, a customer can have attributes such as `Name` and `Address`. However, in a hair salon one of the attributes a customer has is `Hair colour`, and in a restaurant, the attribute may be `Favourite` `drink`. Thus, there can be three different abstractions to represent the Customer entity as shown in Figures 3.3, 3.4 and 3.5.

Figure 3.3: Bank   Figure 3.4: Salon   Figure 3.5: Restaurant

Abstraction for Bank

- Name

- Address

Abstraction for Salon

- Name

- Address

- Hair Colour

Abstraction for Salon

- Name

- Address

- Favourite drink

Having understood how to look at an entity in different perspectives, let us delve into the composition of an object in the next section.

3.2   What is an Object?

When you look around, you will see objects everywhere. The chair you are sitting on, the table, pen, book, fan, door, etc. These objects can be divided into one of the following categories:

1. **Tangible objects**: These are the objects which you can see and touch. For example, chair, and computer. In fact, you are also an object.

2. **Conceptual objects**: These are intangible objects and exist as a conceptual entity. You cannot see and touch them. For example, an email or a bank account.

3. **Roles**: Roles played by people like a student, a teacher or a clerk.

4. **Events**: An event is something occurring in a system. For example, a sale or purchase in a departmental store.

Objects are the basic units of an object-oriented system. An *object* is an identifiable entity that has its own set of attributes, behaviour and state. Note that a third component has now been added – state.

- *Attributes* are individual characteristics that differentiate one object from the other.

- *Behaviour* is defined by the set of functions or operations an object can perform.

- *State* is defined by the set of values held by its attributes.

Let us understand the attributes, behaviour, and state of an object using the `Mobile` object.

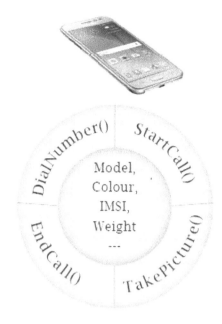

Mobile Object		
Attributes	*Behaviour*	*State*
Model	Dial the number	Model: Samsung A6
IMSI	Start call	IMSI: xyz223344
Colour	End call	Colour: White
Weight	Take a picture	Weight: 152gm
Camera resolution		Camera resolution: 16mp
Status (On/Off)		Status: On

Figure 3.6: Mobile Object

Let us take another example of a `Motor-Bike` object.

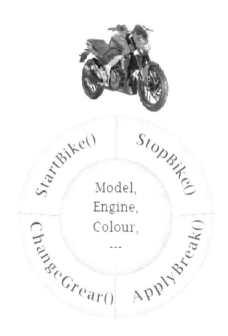

Motor-Bike		
Attributes	*Behaviour*	*State*
Model	Dial the number	Model: Harley Davidson Street 500
Registration number	Start call	Registration number: GB133453
Colour	End call	Colour: Red
Engine	Take a picture	Air-cooled
Status		Status: broken-down

Figure 3.7: Motor-Bike Object

In the real world, you are also an object - a `Person` object.

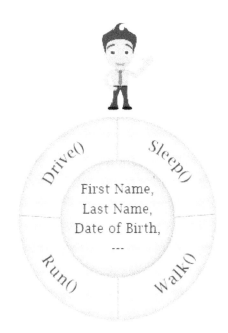

Person Object		
Attributes	*Behaviour*	*State*
First name	Sleep	First name: John
Last name	Walk	Last name: Dee
Date of birth	Run	Date of birth: 15-Oct-2001
Colour of eyes	Drive	Colour of eyes: Blue
Address		Address: 45, Reading Street, UK

Figure 3.8: Person Object

Just like human beings interact with each other, objects also interact with each other. Thus, you can say that the `Person` (object) can `Drive` (behaviour) the `Car` (object). Observe that an object interacts with another object via its behaviour.

Figure 3.9: The Person object driving the Car object

3.3 Class - The Object Factory

In the real world, you will often find many individual objects that are all of the same kind. For example, there may be thousands of other mobiles that have the same make and model as yours. Each mobile has been built from the same set of blueprints and therefore contains the same attributes and behaviour. In object oriented programming terms, it is said that your mobile is an instance of the `Mobile` class.

Objects that share the same attributes and behaviour are grouped together into a class. A class is a template or blueprint for multiple objects with similar features and may be regarded as a specification for creating similar objects. Due to this reason, class is also called an *object factory* that produces multiple objects of the same type.

Once a class has been defined, you can create many objects belonging to that class. An object belonging to a particular class is known as an *instance* of that class. Therefore, you can say that a `mango` is an instance of the `Fruit` class. The terms *object* and *instance* are often interchangeable.

The `Mobile` class in Figure 5.6 specifies the attributes and behaviour of a mobile in the abstract form. Two concrete instances of the `Mobile` object have been created with the same attributes and behaviour. Each object has its own state i.e., each attribute in the instance has a specified value. For example, attribute `Model` of `Object1` has a value *Samsung A6* whereas the same attribute of `Object2` has a value *iPhone X*.

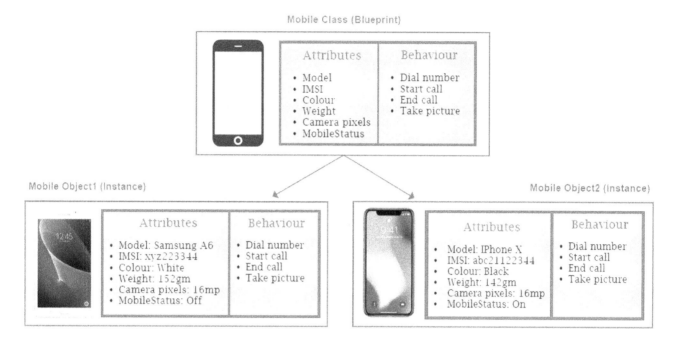

Figure 3.10: The Mobile Class with two Instances

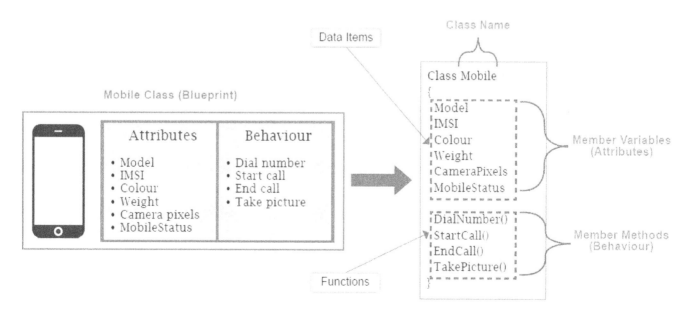

Figure 3.11: Schematic representation of the Mobile class

Figure fig:MobileClassSchematic shows a schematic (pseudo form) representation of the Mobile class. In object-oriented programming terms, these attributes are represented through data items in a class known as member variables or instance variables. The behaviour is represented through functions or methods known as member methods or simply methods.

> **Note**
>
> Note that a class is a logical construct whereas an object has a physical reality. A class is a specification of a set of objects and not the actual object.

Let us take another example of the **Account** class. The **Account** class serves as a blueprint to create different bank accounts, for example, **myAccount** and **yourAccount**.

The object – **myAccount** - is an instance of the **Account** class. Similarly, the object – **yourAccount** - is another instance of the same **Account** class (see Figure 3.12).

Both, **myAccount** and **yourAccount**, share the same attributes and behaviour i.e. both will have attributes like account number, balance, etc., and behaviours like deposit, withdrawal, etc. However, both the instances have their own state, i.e. each attribute in the instance has a specified value.

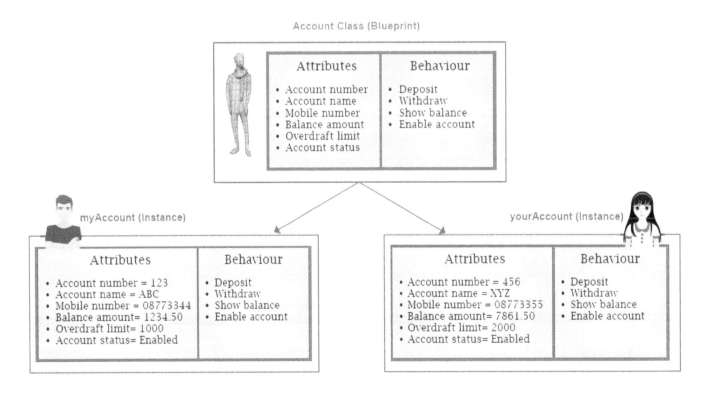

Figure 3.12: The Account Class

Figure 3.13 shows a schematic representation of the **Account** class:

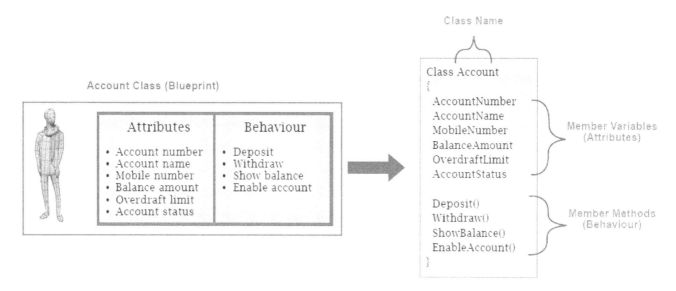

Figure 3.13: Schematic representation of the Account class

How a Class is different from an Object?

One major difference between a class and an object is the way attributes and methods are treated in a class and an object. A class is just a specification[2] of the object. The attributes and methods in a class are thus declarations that do not contain any values. However, an object is a concrete instance of a class with properly defined values of each attribute and behaves as per the methods of the class.

How objects encapsulate state and behaviour?

An object stores its state in member variables and exposes its behaviour through the member methods. The member methods operate on member variables (object's state) and serve as the primary mechanism to interact with the object. Only the member methods which are defined inside the class can access the data and change its state. Hence, the state and behaviour are said to be encapsulated by the object, hiding internal state and requiring all interaction to be performed through the methods of an object.

3.4   Class as a User Defined Data Type

In programming terms, the following statement defines a variable of the integer data type:

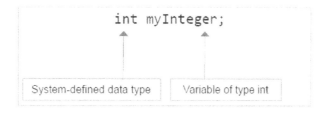

Figure 3.14: Integer Data Type

---

[2]A specification is a detailed description about something.

Here int is said to be a system-defined data type as it is provided by the programming language. Using the concept of a class, you can make the data and the methods of an object a user-defined data type. The class may now be considered as a data type and an object as a variable of that data type. For example, once the Account class has been defined, the following statement will create a myAccount object belonging to the Account class.

Figure 3.15: Account Data Type

Similarly, once the Mobile class has been defined, the following statement will create an iPhoneX object belonging to the Mobile class.

    Mobile iPhoneX;

Hence, a class is a user-defined data type, which has its own functionality and behaves like built-in data types for example, int, and float.

3.5 Message Passing between Objects

Let us recap what you have learnt so far:

- What is an object?

- How to identify the abstract attributes (member variables) and behaviour (member methods) of the object and use them to define the class.

- Each class specifies a set of methods, which are the actions (behaviours) that its objects support.

But how do you interact (or communicate) with an object or how do multiple objects interact with each other in a program? Let us learn about it in the following sub-sections.

3.5.1 Message to an Object

In real life, we communicate with each other by passing messages. For example, asking a bank clerk to deposit money in your account, or asking the gardener to water the plants.

Similarly, communicating with an object means sending a message to it. A *message* is a request to an object to perform an action (behaviour).

Let us first understand what a message to an object means in programming terms. To do so, let us refer to the `iPhoneX` object belonging to the `Mobile` class as follows:

```
Mobile iPhoneX;
```

Now if you want the `iPhoneX` object to dial a number, you simply send a message to the object like:

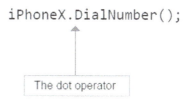

Figure 3.16: Send Message

This statement is a request to the `iPhoneX` object to call its member method `DialNumber()` using the dot (.) operator[3]. You may also specify a mobile number as an argument[4] to the `DialNumber()` method. Therefore, the method call may look like:

```
iPhoneX.DialNumber("08130100123");
```

Let us take another example of the `Account` object that you defined earlier:

```
Account myAccount;
```

Here, if you want to deposit money into this account, you will simply send a message to the `myAccount` object like:

```
myAccount.Deposit(1050);
```

This will add £1050 to the Balance amount member variable!

3.5.2 Message between Objects

Objects communicate with each other by sending messages. The message sending object requests the message receiving object to perform an action. A message sending object is called the *sender* while the message receiving object is called the *receiver*.

Let us take the example of depositing money in a bank account. There are two objects involved here. The first one is the person (the `Person` object), the holder of the bank account and the second one is the account itself (the `Account` object).

```
Person Simon;
Account myAccount;
```

---

[3]You will learn about the dot operator in the following chapters.

[4]You will learn about the arguments in the following chapters.

The message passing between these two objects may look like as shown in Figure3.17:

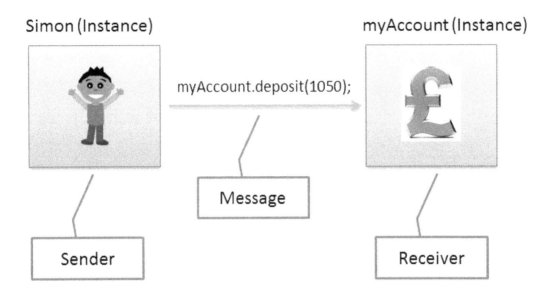

Figure 3.17: Message Passing between Objects

Multiple Choice Questions

1. An object has ....

    A. Attributes   C. Behaviour

    B. State   D. All of the above

2. A class is ....

    A. An object factory   C. A specification for objects

    B. A blueprint to create objects   D. All of the above

3. .... represents an entity in the real-world with its identity and behaviour.

    A. A class   C. A procedure

    B. An object   D. A function

4. .... is a template to create similar objects that share common characteristics and behaviour.

    A. A function   C. An attribute

    B. A procedure   D. A class

5. The values of an object's .... represent the state of the object.

    A. Methods   C. Attributes

    B. Procedures   D. Classes

6. The terms object and .... are often interchangeable.

    A. Instance   C. Attribute

    B. Behaviour   D. State

State whether the given statements are True or False:

□ A class is a specification about the object.

□ Only one instance can be created from a single class.

□ A class is a user-defined data type.

□ Real world objects encapsulate state and behaviour.

□ There can be multiple abstractions of the same entity.

□ Objects interact with each other through messages.

Assignment Questions

1. What are objects? Give five examples.

2. Explain the anatomy of an object.

3. Explain the following statement – "Class is a specification for objects".

4. Explain the following statement – "Abstraction is relative to the perspective of the viewer".

5. Identify five possible attributes and three possible behaviours of the following entities:

    (i) School

    (ii) Student

    (iii) Teacher

    (iv) Computer

    (v) Television

    (vi) Washing Machine

    (vii) Chair

    (viii) Person

6. Explain in detail how a class is different from an object.

7. Give the reason why a class is known as:

    (i) An object factory

    (ii) A composite data type

    (iii) A user-defined data type

8. How are classes and objects inter-related? Support your answer with an example.

9. What do you understand by the term objects encapsulate state and behaviour?

10. Explain how objects communicate with each other.

Answers To Objective Questions

Multiple Choice Questions

1. D	2. D	3. B	4. D	5. C	6. A

True or False

1. True	2. False	3. True	4. True	5. True	6. True

Chapter 4

Values and Data Types

Values and Data Types

B FORE writing programs in any language, you need to understand the basic concepts required for programming. Every programming language has its own syntax rules, data types, and range of values. This chapter introduces Java fundamentals to you so that you can start writing your own programs.

4.1 Character Set

A character set is a defined list of characters recognised by a language. It is comprised of:

(i) Alphabets: letters, `A-Z` (uppercase) and `a-z` (lowercase)

(ii) Numerals: digits, `0-9`

(iii) Special Characters: `?`, `%`, `}`, `>`, , etc.

Collectively, the alphabets and numerals are known as the *alphanumeric character set*. Two standard character sets are ASCII and Unicode.

4.2 ASCII Character Set

ASCII stands for American Standard Code for Information Interchange. It is a 7-bit set of codes that defines 128 different characters ($2^7 = 128$). For example, letter 'A' can be represented using the 7-bit code `100 0001`. The ASCII character set is enough to represent every uppercase letter, lowercase letter, digit, and special character used in the English language keyboard.

> **Note**
>
> The Extended ASCII code is an 8-bit character set that defines 256 different characters ($2^8 = 256$), including the standard 7-bit ASCII characters.

4.3 Unicode Character Set

Unicode is an international character set designed to represent all the characters found in languages around the world, such as English, Hindi, Japanese, Chinese, French, and German. It can use 8 to 32 bits to represent a character. The first 128 characters in the Unicode character set are the same as those of the ASCII character set, and the next set of 128 characters is the same as the Extended ASCII character set. The rest are used to represent characters from all over the world making it the largest set of characters. Java uses the Unicode character encoding. It enables you to handle text in any language.

The following table shows some letters represented using the Unicode character set. The specific Unicode character is expressed using the escape sequence '\u' followed by its four digits hexadecimal code. You will learn about escape sequences in a later section.

Unicode Characters		
Character	*Unicode*	*Remarks*
£	'\u00A3'	Pound sign
$	'\u0024'	Dollar sign
€	'\u20AC'	Euro sign

Listing 4.1: UnicodeChars.java

```
1  public class UnicodeChars
2  {
3      public static void main(String args[])
4      {
5          System.out.println("\u00A3");
6          System.out.println("\u0024");
7          System.out.println("\u20AC ");
8      }
9  }
```

Output
£
$
€

4.4 Tokens

All characters in a Java program are grouped into symbols called `Tokens`. These are the smallest individual units in a program. There are five categories of tokens in Java as shown in Figure 4.1. Various language features are built from these five tokens.

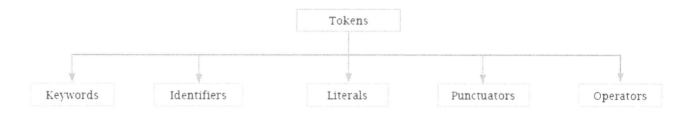

Figure 4.1: Tokens

4.4.1 Keywords

`Keywords`, also known as `Reserved Words`, are the words that have a special meaning to the Java compiler. Java compiler reserves these keywords for its own use, and hence they are not available as names for variables or methods. Some of the Java keywords are listed below:

Java Keywords			
abstract	continue	goto	protected
boolean	default	if	public
break	do	import	return
byte	double	int	short
case	else	long	static
char	final	new	switch
class	float	package	void
const	for	private	while

> **Note**
>
> Keywords `goto` and `const` are not currently used in Java. The literal values `true`, `false`, and `null` are not keywords, just like the literal value 1729. However, you cannot use them as variable names, just as you cannot use 1729 as a variable name.

4.4.2 Identifiers

Identifiers are fundamental building blocks of a program and are used to name different components of a program, such as variables, methods, and objects.

Java Identifiers Naming Conventions

It is recommended to follow these naming conventions:

(i) An identifier can consist of any combination of letters, digits, the underscore character (_), and the dollar sign ($).

(ii) It cannot begin with a digit.

(iii) It may be of any length.

(iv) Both uppercase and lowercase letters can be used in naming an identifier.

(v) Java is case sensitive, which means that two identifier names that differ only in uppercase and lowercase characters are considered to be different identifiers. Therefore, `total`, `Total`, `ToTaL`, and `TOTAL` are all different identifiers.

(vi) An identifier cannot be a `keyword` or a `boolean` literal or a `null` literal.

Examples of some valid identifiers are:

- `customerName`
- `$M1Math`
- `student3`
- `_Grade`
- `INTEREST`
- `CheckPrime`
- `$10_to_20`
- `very_long_identifier_-name_for_testing`

Examples of some invalid identifiers are:

- `continue` – It is a Java keyword.

- `Income tax` – Space is not allowed in the identifier name.

- `2M_Value` – Identifier name cannot begin with a digit.

- `Discount-amount` – Special characters other than (_) and ($) are not allowed.

- `Birth.Date` – Special characters other than (_) and ($) are not allowed.

4.4.3 Literals

Literals are a sequence of characters that represent values in a program and are stored in variables. Literals are made of digits, letters and other characters. Java supports the following types of literals:

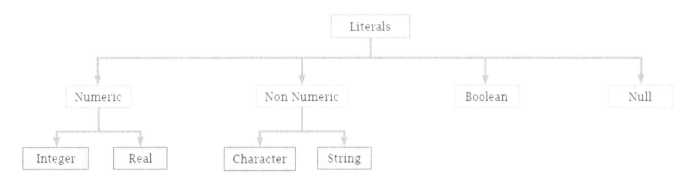

Figure 4.2: Literals in Java

4.4.3.1 Numeric Literals

Numeric literals are values that may consist of digits (0 to 9), a decimal point (.), a positive (+) or negative (-) sign. They are of two types:

4.4.3.1.1 Integer Literals Integer literals are values, which represent whole numbers only. They can be positive or negative values. The integer value that contains no sign represents the positive value by default. Examples of some valid integer literals are:

- 1455
- +345
- -101

Some invalid integer literals are:

- 67 678 – Space not allowed

- 876,453 – Comma not allowed

4.4.3.1.2 Real Literals Real literals are also called *floating point literals* as they represent values with a decimal point. These can be written either in fractional or exponential form.

A real literal in the *fractional form* consists of signed or unsigned digits, including a decimal point between the digits. Examples of some valid real literals in the fractional form are:

- 42.33
- +2334.05
- 0.001729
- -23.90
- 7348.009

Some invalid real literals in the fractional form are:

- 233 – It must have a decimal point.
- 2355. – It must have at least one digit after the decimal point.
- .25 – It must have at least one digit before the decimal point.
- 42.16.77 – Two decimal points are not allowed.
- 34,543.50 – Comma is not allowed.

A real literal in the *exponential form* consists of two components: mantissa and exponent. For example: 7.04 x 1034 can be written in the exponential form as 7.04E34, where

- 7.04 is the mantissa (component before E).
- 34 is the exponent (component after E).

Examples of some valid real literals in the exponential form are as follows:

- 67.E7
- -350E4
- 5.600E32
- 234E+8

Some invalid real literals in the exponential form are as follows:

- 55.5E – No digit specified after the exponent, i.e., after E.
- 52.3E9.6 – The exponent must be an integer value.
- .23E7 – It must have at least one digit before the decimal point.
- 45,22E25 – Comma is not allowed.

4.4.3.2 Non-numeric Literals

Java offers two types of non-numeric literals. These are:

4.4.3.2.1 Character Literals Literals of this type represent exactly one character enclosed in single quotes. Some examples are:

- 'G'
- ' '
- '#'
- '3'

4.4.3.2.2 String Literals One or more characters enclosed in double quotes are string literals. For example:

- "abc"
- "Maya\'s "
- "z+5"

- "Chicago"
- "D"
- "7+7"

4.4.3.3 Boolean Literal

The logical values `true` and `false` are the boolean literals. During a logical evaluation, the true/false literals represent on/off, yes/no, and presence/absence of something.

4.4.3.4 The Null Literal

This is a special kind of literal which is represented by the keyword null or escape sequence '\0'.

4.4.4 Punctuators

Punctuators (also called *separators*) are symbols used for grouping and separating the code. Folliing Table lists the various punctuators and their purpose.

Punctuators		
Punctuator	**Name**	**Purpose**
;	Semicolon	The most commonly used separator in Java is the semicolon. It is used to separate statements.
,	Comma	It is used to separate consecutive identifiers in a variable declaration.
	Curly Brackets	Curly brackets are used to define a block of code in a Java program. They are also used to initialise the values of arrays.
()	Parenthesis	Parenthesis or round brackets are used to define methods. They are also used to define the precedence of operators in an expression and conditions in control structures.
[]	Square Brackets	Square brackets are used to declare arrays and refer to values at a particular index.
.	Period	The period operator in Java is used to access member variables and methods. It is also used to differentiate the package names from sub - packages and class names.

4.4.5 Operators

Operators are symbols which are used to perform arithmetic or logical operations in a given expression. The main categories of operators in Java are shown in the following Table. Each of these operators consists of 1 or 2 special characters.

Java Operators						
Unary Operators	+(unary)	-(unary)				
Assignment Operator	=					
Arithmetic Operators	+	-	*	/	%	
Relational Operators	>	<	>=	<=	==	!=
Increment/Decrement Operators	++	--				
Logical Operators	&&	||	!			
Bitwise Operators	&	|	^	~	«	»
Conditional/ Ternary Operator	?:					

4.5 Escape Sequences

An Escape Sequence is a set of characters that has a special meaning to the Java compiler. In the escape sequence, a character is preceded by a backslash (\\). An escape sequence causes the character following it to escape its normal interpretation. For example, when you print the character 'n', the same character is displayed on the screen, but when it is prefixed with '\\', it is read as an escape sequence. Following Table shows some common Java escape sequences.

Escape Sequences	
Escape Sequence	**Short Description**
\n	Inserts a newline in the text at this point (shifts control to the next line)
\t	Inserts a tab in the text at this point
\\	Inserts a backslash character in the text at this point
\"	Inserts a double quote character in the text at this point
\'	Inserts a single quote character in the text at this point
\r	Inserts a carriage return in the text at this point (same as pressing the Enter key)
\?	Inserts a question mark in the text at this point
\a	Produces an audible bell (beep sound)
\0	Represents a null character

For example, if you want to put quotation marks within the other quotation marks, you must use the escape sequence \" as displayed in the following statement:

```
System.out.println("Programming in Java is \"fun!\"");
```

Listing 4.2: EscapeSequence.java

```java
public class EscapeSequence
{
    public static void main(String args[])
    {
        System.out.println("Programming in Java is \"fun!\"");
    }
}
```

Output

Programming in Java is "fun!"

4.6 Data Types

Java has a variety of data types that allows programmers to choose the data type suitable to the needs of the application. These data types can broadly be divided into the following two categories:

Primitive Data Types: The fundamental data types that are an integral part of the Java programming language are called *primitive data types*. They are also called *intrinsic* or *built-in data types* because these are part of the programming language. There are eight primitive data types in Java. These are `byte`, `short`, `int`, `long`, `char`, `float`, `double`, and `boolean`.

Non-Primitive Data Types: The data types that are derived from the primitive types are called *non-primitive data types*. They are also called *reference types*, *derived types* or *composite data types*. There are three non-primitive types in Java: classes, arrays, and interfaces. The storage mechanism of non-primitive types is different from that of the primitive types. You will learn about this in later chapters.

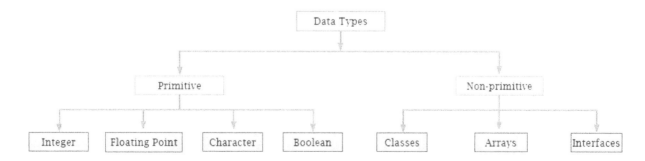

Figure 4.3: Data Types in Java

4.6.1 Primitive Types

The primitive data types can be grouped into the following four categories.

4.6.1.1 Integer Data Types

Integer data types are used to store whole numbers, for example, 767, 5050, and -745. There are further four types of integers in Java as shown in Figure 4.4. These are byte, short, int, and long. The values that can be stored in these depend on which data type is being used in the program.

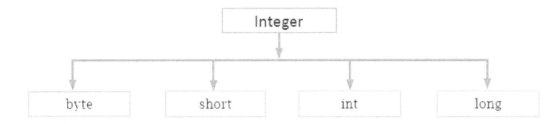

Figure 4.4: Integer Data Types

Integer Data Types			
Type	Size	Short Description	Range
byte	8 bits (1 byte[1])	Byte-length integer	-128 to 127 (-2^7 to $2^7 - 1$)
short	16 bits (2 bytes)	Short integer	-32,768 to 32,767 (-2^{15} to $2^{15} - 1$)
int	32 bits (4 bytes)	Integer	-2 billion to +2 billion (approx.) (-2^{31} to $2^{31} - 1$)
long	64 bits (8 bytes)	Long integer	-9E18 to +9E18 (approx.) (-2^{63} to $2^{63} - 1$)

4.6.1.2 Floating Point Data Types

Since integer data types can store only whole numbers, they cannot be used to store decimal values. Thus, the floating point data types are used to store numbers with decimal values (fractional numbers). Floating point data types can further be divided into float and double data type.

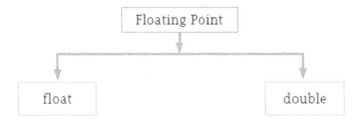

Figure 4.5: Floating Data Types

---

[1]1 byte = 8 bits

Floating Point Data Types				
Type	*Size*	*Description*	*Precision*	*Range*
float	32 bits (4 bytes)	Single-precision floating point	Up to 7 significant decimal digits	1.4e-045 to 3.4e+038
double	64 bits (8 bytes)	Double-precision floating point	Up to 15 significant decimal digits	4.9e-324 to 1.8e+308

The float data type can be used to store values with low precision digits, such as temperature, salary and percentage. The double data type is usually required to store high precision values, such as scientific readings, the location of celestial bodies and their distances. If a numeric literal contains a decimal point, then it is **double** by default. To designate a literal constant of the type **float**, you must append the letter f or F, for example, 6.7f or 5.2F.

4.6.1.3 Character Data Type

Characters in Java are stored using **char** data type. This data type supports the Unicode character set and occupies 2 bytes (16 bits) in the memory. The following table lists the size and range.

Character Data Type			
Type	*Size*	*Short Description*	*Range*
char	16 bits (2 bytes)	Single character	0 – 6553

A character data type is always enclosed within single quotes, for example, 'K', 'A', and 'q'.

Strings are widely used in Java programming and are a sequence of characters. It must be noted that a string is always enclosed within double quotes, e.g., "Java", "X", and "Save Water".

4.6.1.4 Boolean Data Type

Logical values are stored using **boolean** data type. There are only two values the boolean data type can have - **true** or **false**.

The following table lists the size and range of the boolean data type.

Boolean Data Type			
Type	*Size*	*Short Description*	*Range*
boolean	8 bits (1 byte) but uses only 1 bit	Binary or boolean values	true or false

Although the boolean data type needs only one bit of storage, the Java compiler reserves 8 bits (= 1 byte) for it.

The complete set of data types supported by Java is shown in Figure 4.6.

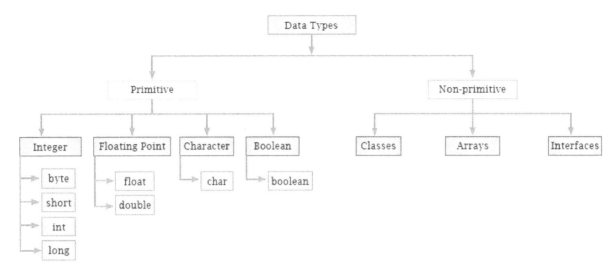

Figure 4.6: Data Types - Summary

Now, let us learn how to store the values of these data types in the computer memory using variables.

4.7 Variables

A variable is an identifier that denotes a location in computer memory to store a data value. The variable may take different values at different times during the execution of a program. It is the computer's job to keep track of the location where the data is stored. You, as a programmer, only need to remember the name of this variable.

Variable names are chosen by the programmer. It is suggested to use meaningful names so that anyone reading your code can easily comprehend what they represent, for example, instead of using the name `tM` to represent total marks, use `totalMarks`.

4.7.1 Variable Declaration

Variable declaration plays a key role in a Java program. The variable can be used in the Java program only if it has been declared. During program execution, when the computer encounters a variable declaration, it performs the following two tasks:

- Sets aside memory for the variable.

- Associates the variable name with that memory location.

A simple variable declaration has the following syntax:

```
data-type variable-name;
```

where, the data-type can be any primitive data type, and the variable-name is the name of the variable. Since the variable is an identifier, all the identifier naming conventions also apply (see section 4.4.2). The following statement will declare an integer type variable `feeAmount`.

```
int feeAmount;
```

Figure 4.7: Schematic Representation of Variable Declaration

A declaration statement must end with a semicolon. Similarly, the following statements will also declare a `float` type variable `simpleInterest` and a `char` type variable `choice`:

```
float simpleInterest;
char choice;
```

If you need to declare more than one variable of the same type, you can declare them all in one line. For example:

```
short day, month, year;
float grossPay, netPay;
```

4.7.2 Variable Initialisation

Storing data in a variable means assigning a value to it. Let us understand some ways to initialise variables:

(i) You can assign a value to the variable at the time of its declaration. For example, the following statement would declare an integer type variable `feeAmount` and assign an initial value of 750 to it.

```
int feeAmount = 750;
```

Figure 4.8: Schematic Representation of Variable Initialisation

Here, the variable `feeAmount` is said to be initialised with an initial value of 750.

(ii) You can declare a variable and initialise it separately as shown below:

```
int accountNumber;
accountNumber = 1000020456;
```

(iii) You can assign values to multiple variables in one statement or choose to declare some and initialise the others. For example:

```
short day = 10, month = 12, year = 2020;
int p, q = 7, r;
```

(iv) The initial value does not have to be a literal only. It can be any expression also. For example:

```
int x = 2, y = x+5;
```

4.7.3 Default Value of Variables

Variables that are declared but not initialised are given a default value by the compiler. Table on the right lists the default values for the data types supported by Java. However, not depending on such default values is generally considered to be a good programming practice.

Data Type	Default Value
byte	0
short	0
int	0
long	0L
float	0.0f
double	0.0d
char	'\u0000'
boolean	false
Non-primitive or reference data type	null

Let's write a program in Java to demonstrate various data types.

Listing 4.3: JavaDataTypes.java

```
1  public class JavaDataTypes
2  {
3      public static void main(String args [])
4      {
5          byte byteVar = 125;
6          short shortVar = 1729;
7          int intVar = 123456;
8          long longVar = 1234567890;
9          float floatVar = 656.55F;
10         double doubleVar = 3422.36D;
11         char charVar = 'D';
12         String stringVar = "Save Water";
```

```
13        boolean booleanVar = false;
14
15        System.out.println("byteVar: " + byteVar);
16        System.out.println("shortVar: " + shortVar);
17        System.out.println("intVar: " + intVar);
18        System.out.println("longVar: " + longVar);
19        System.out.println("floatVar: " + floatVar);
20        System.out.println("doubleVar: " + doubleVar);
21        System.out.println("charVar: " + charVar);
22        System.out.println("stringVar: " + stringVar);
23        System.out.println("booleanVar: " + booleanVar);
24    }
25 }
```

```
Output
byteVar: 125
shortVar: 1729
intVar: 123456
longVar: 1234567890
floatVar: 656.55
doubleVar: 3422.36
charVar: D
stringVar: Save Water
booleanVar: false
```

4.8 Constants (Named or Symbolic Constants)

Sometimes, you may not want to change the value of a variable once it has been initialised. For example, in a program that calculates simple interest, you may want to keep the interest rate 0.08 (i.e., 8%) throughout the entire program. In Java, the modifier final can be used in the variable declaration to ensure that the value stored in the variable cannot be changed after the variable has been initialised. The keyword **final** makes the variable a constant, i.e., whose value cannot be changed. Consider the following statement:

```
final double INTEREST\_RATE = 0.08;
```

In the above example, the value of **INTEREST_RATE** cannot be changed anywhere else in the program. The **final** modifier instructs the Java compiler that this value will not change. Any assignment statement that tries to assign a value to **INTEREST_RATE** will be flagged as a syntax error by the compiler as shown in Figure 4.9.

Note that in the variable name, only underscores have been used to separate the English words in uppercase letters. Java does not require this particular style for constants, but it helps in improving the readability of the code. There are a number of advantages of using constants like this as given below:

(i) It improves the readability of the program and makes it easier for someone to understand the code.

(ii) Any unintentional changes to such variables are flagged by the compiler.

(iii) Later, if there is a change in the value of such variable (e.g., interest rate change), you just need to modify its value at one place and all the other occurrences will be taken care of automatically.

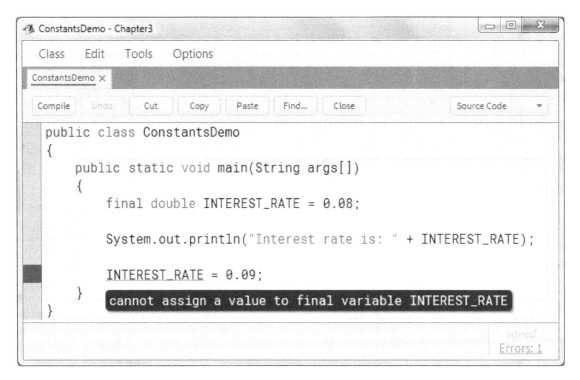

Figure 4.9: Changing a Variable with final Modifier

Write a program to compute the surface area of a sphere.
Hint: Surface area of sphere = $4\pi r^2$

Listing 4.4: Sphere.java

```
1  public class Sphere
2  {
3      public static void main(String args[])
4      {
5          final double PI = 3.14159;
6          double radius = 17.8;
7          double surfaceArea;
8
9          surfaceArea = 4 * PI * radius * radius;
10
11         System.out.println("Surface area of sphere with radius " + radius ↵
              ↪ + " is " + surfaceArea);
12     }
13 }
```

Output
Surface area of sphere with radius 17.8 is 3981.5255024000003

4.9 Comments in Java

Writing fully commented code is a good programming style. Comments are usually added in a program to give an overview of the code and provide additional information that is not readily available in it. The primary purpose of comments is to document the code so that even a layperson can understand the purpose of the written code. Comments are ignored by the Java compiler and do not affect the execution of the program. Comments can appear anywhere in your code except in the middle of an identifier, a reserved word, or a literal constant. Java programs can have three styles of comments: single line, multiline, and documentation comments.

4.9.1 Single Line Comment

It is the simplest comment in Java that appears in a single line. This type of comment begins with a double slash (//) and continues to the end of the line. During the compilation process, once the compiler encounters a double slash, it ignores any text following it.

4.9.2 Multiline Comment

Sometimes, multiple lines are required to explain the logic of a program. In such cases, the programmer can use a multiline comment. This style of comment starts with the initiating slash-asterisk (/*) and ends with the terminating asterisk-slash (*/). Therefore, the comment can extend over multiple lines. Note that there must be no space between the slash and the asterisk.

4.9.3 Documentation Comment

Documentation comment is a special comment (called javadoc) that looks like a multiline comment, but it is generally used to generate external documentation about the source code. This type of comment begins with a forward slash followed by two asterisks (/**) and ends with an asterisk followed by a forward slash (*/). The compiler ignores this kind of comments, just like other comments.

Listing 4.5: CommentsDemo.java

```java
1  /* CommentsDemo.java
2   * This is a comment in Java          ◄--------------- Multiline comment
3   * that spans multiple lines.
4   */
5  public class CommentsDemo
6  {
7      //The main() method declaration ◄--------------- Single line comment
8      public static void main(String args[])
9      {
10         String fruit = "Mango";    //Declare and initialise variable
11         /* Program logic */ ◄---------------
12     }
                                    Multiline comment style in single line
13 }
```

Key points to remember while using comments:

(i) You should keep your comments clear and concise.

(ii) Always arrange them in the code such that they are easy to see and it is clear what they document.

(iii) If comments are too long or are all over the statements, they may make the code more difficult to read.

Multiple Choice Questions

1. Java uses .... character set.

    A. ASCII only   C. Unicode

    B. Extended ASCII only   D. None of the above

2. ASCII stands for ....

    A. American Standard Code for Information Interchange

    B. American Simulated Code for Information Interchange

    C. American Standard Code for Interchange of Information

    D. American Standard Code for Interaction of Information

3. ASCII is ....

    A. 6-bit set of codes   C. 7-bit set of codes

    B. 8-bit set of codes   D. 16-bit set of codes

4. Extended ASCII is ....

    A. 6-bit set of codes   C. 7-bit set of codes

    B. 8-bit set of codes   D. 16-bit set of codes

5. The smallest individual component in a program is called ....

    A. Token   B. Identifier   C. Keyword   D. Method

6. Which of the following is not a token?

    A. Keyword   B. Identifier   C. Operator   D. Procedure

7. Which of the following is a keyword?

    A. character   B. break   C. object   D. attribute

8. Which of the following is not a legal identifier?

A. _room
          C. 10thClass

B. $PayAmount
          D. nullValue

9. Which of the following is a default value of float data type?

    A. 0   B. 0float   C. 0f   D. 0.0f

10. Which of the following is a default value of boolean data type?

    A. `true`   B. `false`   C. `null`   D. `void`

11. Which of the following is an invalid integer?

    A. 2222   B. 22222   C. 222 22   D. 222

12. Which of the following is not a character literal?

    A. '\n'
          C. 'n'

    B. "n"
          D. All of the above

13. Which of the following punctuator is the statement terminator in Java?

    A. ;
          C. ,

    B. .
          D. All of the above

14. Which of the following is not a primitive data type in Java?

    A. boolean   B. short   C. float   D. class

15. What is the size of a long data type in Java?

    A. 32 bits   C. 48 bits   type is not   in Java.

    B. 64 bits   D. long   data   supported

16. What is the size of a boolean data type in Java?

    A. 1 bit
          C. 8 bits

          D. boolean data type does not take
    B. 16 bits   any space in memory.

17. Single line comments can be added using ....

    A. //
          C. \\

    B. /* */
          D. both A and B

18. Which of the following changes a variable declaration into a constant?

A. const   B. constant   C. static   D. final

19. The ASCII codes of A-Z are represented by decimal range ....
    A. 65-90   B. 66-91   C. 97-122   D. 98-123

20. Which of the following is a primitive data type?
    A. array   B. interface   C. class   D. boolean

State whether the given statements are True or False:

☐ Java supports the use of the ASCII character set only.

☐ The ASCII code for character 'Z' is 90.

☐ The smallest unit in a Java program is known as `token`.

☐ The Unicode character set uses 8 to 32 bits per character.

☐ In an escape sequence, a character is preceded by a backward slash (\).

☐ In Java, an identifier can begin with a $ sign.

☐ The `boolean` data type is used for storing logical values.

☐ Java offers five types of `tokens`.

☐ Identifiers in Java may be of any length.

☐ The `char` data type reserves 8 bits in memory.

☐ Default value of reference data type is `null`.

☐ To designate a literal constant of the type `float`, you must append the letter L to it.

☐ Default value of `char` data type is '\u0000'.

☐ If a literal constant contains a decimal point, then it is of the type `double` by default.

☐ A variable can be used in a Java program even if it has not been declared.

Assignment Questions

1. Why does Java use the Unicode character set?

2. What are escape sequences in Java? Give three examples.

3. What is the result of evaluating the following expression?

    `(3 + 6 * 7) / 3 + 2`

---

4. What is a `token` in Java? Name the tokens available in Java.

5. Why can a `keyword` not be used as a variable name?

6. Which of the following are Java `keywords`?

    `area, input, class, public, int, x, y, radius, long, Hello.java`

7. What are identifiers in Java? List three identifier formation rules.

8. Explain the following statement – "In Java, `total`, `Total`, `ToTaL`, and `TOTAL` are all different identifiers".

9. Which of the following are invalid identifiers?

    (i) ten   (iv) Coffee   (vii) _var

    (ii) "Hello"   (v) $dollar

    (iii) 5678   (vi) 4Variables

10. How would you print characters like \, ' and " in Java?

11. Distinguish between the following:

    (i) Token and Identifier   (iii) Character and String Constant

    (ii) Keyword and Identifier   (iv) Integer and float Constant

12. Distinguish between `"A"` and `'A'`.

13. What is wrong with the following statement?

    `float flt = 7895.0345;`

14. Describe primitive data types in Java.

15. List the size of primitive data types in Java.

16. Which integer and floating point data types take up the same number of bits in computer memory?

17. What is variable initialisation in Java? What are the default values of the following type of variables?

    `short, int, long, float, double, char.`

18. Provide the declaration for two variables called `xCoordinate` and `yCoordinate`. Both variables are of type `int` and both are to be initialised to zero in the declaration.

19. Write a Java assignment statement that will set the value of the variable `interestAmount` to the value of the variable `balanceAmount` multiplied by the value of the variable `rate`. The variables are of type `double`.

20. Explain the statement, "a well-documented code is as important as the correctly working code".

21. How can you write single line comments in Java?

22. Write a Java constant declaration that gives the name **TAX_RATE** to the value **15%**.

23. If you want to change the precedence of operations in an expression, which symbols do you use?

24. What are symbolic constants? How are they useful in writing programs?

25. What is the output produced by the following lines of program code?

```
char x, y;
x = 'y';
System.out.println(x);
y = 'z';
System.out.println(y);
x = y;
System.out.println(x);
```

Answers To Objective Questions

Multiple Choice Questions

1. C	5. A	9. D	13. A	17. D
2. A	6. D	10. B	14. D	18. D
3. C	7. B	11. C	15. B	19. A
4. B	8. C	12. B	16. C	20. D

True or False

1. False	4. True	7. True	10. False	13. True
2. True	5. True	8. True	11. True	14. True
3. True	6. True	9. True	12. False	15. False

Chapter 5

Operators in Java

Values and Data Types

AFTER getting familiar with various values and data types supported by Java, let us learn how to use them in expressions. An expression is built using variables, literals or values. Operators are symbols which are used in expressions to perform arithmetic or logical operations. The variable or literal on which the operator is applied is known as an *operand*. The operator needs one or more operands to perform any operation as shown in Figure 5.1.

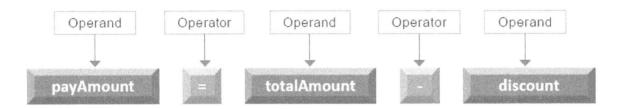

Figure 5.1: Operand and Operator

5.1 Form of Operators

There are three forms of operators in Java as described in the following subsections.

5.1.1 Unary Operator

An operator that has just one operand is known as a *unary operator*. Examples of unary operators are +, -, ++, -, !, etc.

5.1.2 Binary Operator

An operator that has two operands is known as a *binary operator*. Examples of binary operators are +, %, >, &&, etc.

5.1.3 Ternary Operator

An operator that has three operands is known as a *ternary operator*. An example of ternary operator is ?:.

5.2 Types of Operators

5.2.1 Arithmetic Operators

As in most other languages, Java allows you to form expressions using variables, constants, and the arithmetic operators: + (addition), - (subtraction), * (multiplication), / (division), and % (modulus, remainder). Table below lists the arithmetic operators available in Java.

Operator	Symbol	Expression (x = 13, y = 2)	Result
Addition	+	x + y	15
Subtraction	-	x - y	11
Multiplication	*	x * y	26
Division	/	x / y	6
Remainder (Modulus)	%	x % y	1

Let us go through these operators in more detail.

5.2.1.1 Addition Operator (+)

The addition operator adds the two operands, thereby giving the sum of two values. For example,

    25 + 7 evaluates to 32
    z + 12 evaluates to 22 (when z = 10)
    x + y evaluates to 20 (when x = 12 and y = 8)

The operands may be of the integer data type (`byte`, `short`, `int`, `long`) or the floating point data type (`float`, `double`).

5.2.1.2 Subtraction Operator (-)

The subtraction operator subtracts the second operand from the first, thereby giving the difference between the two values. For example:

    19 - 8 evaluates to 11
    z - 12 evaluates to -7 (when z = 5)
    x - y evaluates to 3 (when x = 7 and y = 4)

The operands may be of the integer data type (`byte`, `short`, `int`, `long`) or the floating point data type (`float`, double), as for the addition operator.

5.2.1.3 Division Operator (/)

The division operator divides the first operand by the second operand, thereby giving the quotient.

If both the operands are integers then the result of the division will also be an integer, i.e., the decimal part will be truncated (removed). However, when either of the operands or both are float or double, the result of the division is a real number. For example,

38/5 results in 7 (integer division)

38/5.0 results in 7.6 (real division)

38.0/5 results in 7.6 (real division)

38.0/5.0 results in 7.6 (real division)

5.2.1.4 Remainder or Modulus Operator (%)

The modulus operator (%) gives the remainder of a division operation. For example, when 20 is divided by 3, you get the remainder 2, i.e., 20 % 3 results in 2.

Similarly, x % 5 results in 3, when x = 23.

Listing 5.1: ArithmeticOperators.java

```
1  public class ArithmeticOperators
2  {
3      public static void main(String args[])
4      {
5          int x=13, y=2;
6
7          System.out.println("x+y evaluates to " + (x+y));
8          System.out.println("x-y evaluates to " + (x-y));
9          System.out.println("x*y evaluates to " + (x*y));
10         System.out.println("x/y evaluates to " + (x/y));
11         System.out.println("x%y evaluates to " + (x%y));
12     }
13 }
```

Output

x+y evaluates to 15

x-y evaluates to 11

x*y evaluates to 26

x/y evaluates to 6

x%y evaluates to 1

In addition to the binary form, the plus and minus operators also have a unary form where they can operate on just one operand, as detailed below.

Unary + Operator

The unary plus operator (+) is written before the operand. This operator results in the same value as the operand. For example:

If x = 15, then +x results in 15.

If x = -7, then +x results in -7.

If x = 0, then +x results in 0.

Unary - Operator

The unary minus operator (-) also precedes an operand. This operator negates the value of an operand, i.e., if an operand is a positive value, it converts the value of that operand to its negative value and vice-versa.

If x = 15, then -x results in -15.

If x = -7, then -x results in 7.

If x = 0, then -x results in 0.

String Operator (+)

You have already seen how the + sign can be used to concatenate1 strings. Some other examples of concatenation are as follows:

"6" + "5" will result in "65"

"Room " + "39" will result in "Room 39"

"15 " + "August" will result in "15 August"

5.2.1.5 Relational Operators

Relational operators determine the relationship between the two operands by comparing them. The outcome of these operations is a boolean value which is either true or false. Java provides six types of relational operators as shown in Table below. Relational operators are binary operators as they operate on two operands.

Operator	Symbol	Expression (x = 23, y = 14)	Result
Greater than	>	x > y	true
Less than	<	x < y	false
Equal to	==	x == y	false
Greater than or equal to	>=	x >= y	true
Less than or equal to	<=	x <= y	false
Not equal to	!=	x != y	true

Listing 5.2: RelationalOperators.java

```
1  public class RelationalOperators
2  {
3      public static void main(String args[])
4      {
5          int x = 23, y = 17;
6          System.out.println("x > y is: " + (x > y));
7          System.out.println("x < y is: " + (x < y));
8          System.out.println("x == y is: " + (x == y));
9          System.out.println("x >= y is: " + (x >= y));
10         System.out.println("x <= y is: " + (x <= y));
11         System.out.println("x != y is: " + (x != y));
12     }
13 }
```

Output
x > y is: true
x < y is: false
x == y is: false
x >= y is: true
x <= y is: false
x != y is: true

Note that relational operators have lower priority than the arithmetic operators.

5.2.1.6 Logical Operators

Logical operators operate only on boolean operands and are used to construct complex decision-making expressions. The table on the right lists some of the logical operators.

Logical Operators	
Operator	*Symbol*
Logical AND	&&
Logical OR	||
Logical NOT	!

5.2.1.6.1 Logical AND Operator (&&) .

The logical AND operator (&&) is a binary operator and is used to combine two conditions or expressions. The resultant value is a boolean value. The result is true if both the values are true, and the result is false if either of the values is false. Table on the right shows the Truth Table for the AND operator. It has the following syntax:

Logical AND Operator (&&)		
operand1	*operand1*	*Result*
true	true	true
true	false	false
false	true	false
false	false	false

```
operand1 && operand2
```

Let us take an example as follows:

```
(25 > 33) && (25 < 27)
```

This will evaluate as:

```
false && true ==> false
```

The result is false because the first expression evaluates to false.
Note that the logical AND operator has lower priority than the relational operators.

5.2.1.6.2 Logical OR Operator (\|\|) .

The logical OR operator (\|\|) is a binary operator and is used to combine two conditions or expressions. The resultant value is also a boolean value. The result is true if either of its operands is true, or if both are true. Table on the right shows the Truth Table for the OR operator. It has the following syntax:

Logical OR Operator (||)		
operand1	*operand1*	*Result*
true	true	true
true	false	true
false	true	true
false	false	false

```
operand1 || operand2
```

For example, consider the expression:

```
(38 > 33) || (33 < 33)
```

This evaluates to:

```
true || false ==> true
```

Note that the logical OR operator has lower priority than the relational operators.

5.2.1.6.3 Logical NOT Operator (!) .

The logical NOT operator (!) is a unary operator and is written before a single operand. The logical NOT operator negates the result of the expression following it, i.e., if the expression returns a **true** value then the logical NOT operator will return **false**, and vice versa. Table on the right shows the Truth Table for the NOT operator. It has the following syntax:

Logical NOT Operator (!)	
operand	*Result*
true	false
false	true

```
!operand
```

For example, consider the expression:

```
!(23 > 43)
```

This evaluates to:

```
!false ==> true
```

Note that the logical NOT operator has higher precedence than the relational and arithmetic operators.

Let us now learn the implementation of the logical operators with the help of the following program.

Listing 5.3: LogicalOperators.java

```
1  public class LogicalOperators
2  {
3      public static void main(String args[])
4      {
5          System.out.println("(25 > 33) && (25 < 27) is " + ((25 > 33) && ↵
                (25 < 27)));
6          System.out.println("(38 > 33) || (33 < 33)) is " + ((38 > 33) || ↵
                (33 < 33)));
7          System.out.println("!(23 > 43) is " + (!(23 > 43)));
8      }
9  }
```

Output
(25 > 33) && (25 < 27) is false
(38 > 33) || (33 < 33)) is true
!(23 > 43) is true

5.2.1.7 Assignment Operators

Assignment operator is used to assign the value of an expression to a variable. It has the following syntax:

```
variable = expression;
```

For example, consider the following assignment:

```
totalMarks = 780;
```

The value of `totalMarks` after assignment will be 780. Any previous value stored in the `totalMarks` is destroyed and replaced by the new value.

Let us see another example:

```
counter = counter + 1;
```

Assuming that the original value of the `counter` was 10, the new value of the `counter` after assignment will be 11. The computer would deal with the assignment statement `counter = counter + 1` by taking the old value of the `counter`, and adding 1 to it. Finally, it will store the answer as the new value of the `counter`.

The assignment operator is a binary operator.

Difference between = and ==

The = operator is an assignment operator. It sets a variable equal to some value. For example, `age = 15` sets the variable named `age` equal to 15.

The == operator is a comparison operator. You use it to check if something equals something else. For example, `age == 17` checks if the value that `age` holds is equal to 17.

5.2.1.7.1 Shorthand Assignment Operators

Java offers several variations of the assignment operator that are referred to as shorthand assignment operators. For example, consider the following statement:

```
x = x + 2;
```

You can rewrite the above assignment statement as:

```
x += 2;
```

This version of the statement uses += shorthand assignment operator. Both perform the same action, i.e., increment the value of variable `x` by 2. Assuming that the initial value of `x` was 7, the new value of `x` will be 9 (7+2) after the execution of the above statement.

Java offers shorthand assignment operators for all the arithmetic binary operators. Therefore, any statement which includes the following syntax:

```
variable = variable operation expression;
```

can be rewritten, using the shorthand operator, as:

```
variable operation= expression;
```

For example, x = x + 3; can be rewritten as, x += 3;

There are two advantages of using shorthand assignment operators as given below:

(i) They save a little bit of typing time.

(ii) The use of shorthand operators results in an efficient code as they are implemented most efficiently by the Java run-time environment as compared to their long forms.

The following table shows the main shorthand operators.

Operator	Simple	Shorthand	Result X = 10 and Y = 3
+=	x = x + 1	x += 1	11
-=	x = x - 1	x -= 1	9
*=	x = x * y	x *= y	30
/=	x = x / y	x /= y	3
%=	x = x % y	x %= y	1

Listing 5.4: ShorthandOperators.java

```java
public class ShorthandOperators
{
    public static void main(String args[])
    {
        int x, y;
        x = 10; y = 3;
        System.out.println("x += 1 is " + (x += 1));
        x = 10; y = 3;
        System.out.println("x -= 1 is " + (x -= 1));
        x = 10; y = 3;
        System.out.println("x *= y is " + (x *= y));
        x = 10; y = 3;
        System.out.println("x /= y is " + (x /= y));
        x = 10; y = 3;
        System.out.println("x %= y is " + (x %= y));
    }
}
```

Output
```
x += 1 is 11
x -= 1 is 9
x *= y is 30
x /= y is 3
x %= y is 1
```

5.2.1.8 Increment and Decrement Operators

You often encounter situations in programming where you need to increment or decrement a variable by 1. For example, have a look at the following statements:

```
counter = counter + 1;
i = i + 1;
j = j - 1;
```

These statements can also be rewritten as:

```
counter++;
i++;
j--;
```

The operators ++ and - are called increment and decrement operators, respectively. These are unary operators, having the following two versions each:

Prefix increment: when the increment operator (++) is put before its operand like, ++x
Postfix increment: when the increment operator (++) is put after its operand like, x++
Prefix decrement: when the decrement operator (--) is put before its operand like, --x
Postfix decrement: when the decrement operator (--) is put after its operand like, x--

Note: Remember, the Pre stands for before and the post stands for after.

Usually, the operators ++ or -- are used in statements like x++; or ++x;. These statements change the value of x. The two versions of the operators have the same effect on the operand (i.e., the final values of ++x and x++ are the same). However, you can use x++, ++x, x--, or --x as expressions or as part of the larger expressions. When used as expressions or part of larger expressions, their impact is different (see Table below).

Operator	Name	Example (x=1)	Result	Rule
x++	Post increment	int z = x++;	z is 1, x is 2	First use, then increment
++x	Pre increment	int z = ++x;	z is 2, x is 2	First increment, then use
x--	Post decrement	int z = x--;	z is 1, x is 0	First use, then decrement
--x	Pre decrement	int z = --x;	z is 0, x is 0	First decrease, then use

Let us now understand the postfix and prefix operators in greater detail. Consider the following statement.

```
z = y++;
```

According to the statement, you need to increment the value of y by 1 and also assign the value of y to z. Assuming the value of y is 15, the statement z = y++ will first use the value of y, i.e., assign it to z, yielding z = 15. It will then increment the value of y, yielding y = 16.

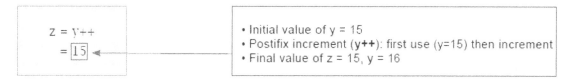

Figure 5.2: Postfix Expression Evaluation

> **Note**
>
> Remember the rule in the Postfix increment: first use, then increment.

Figure 5.3 shows the memory status during the evaluation process.

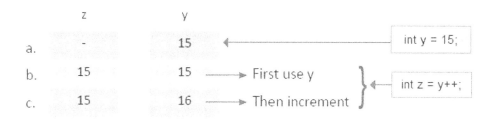

Figure 5.3: Postfix Increment

Let us understand this process step by step.

a. Initially, the value of variable y is 15, and the value of variable z is not defined.

b. As it is a Postfix operation, you first use y, which is 15, hence z is assigned the value 15.

c. Now, you increment the value of y by 1. Thus, the final value of y = 16.

The following program is the implementation of Figure 5.3.

Listing 5.5: PostfixIncrement.java

```java
public class PostfixIncrement
{
    public static void main(String args[])
    {
        int y = 15;
        int z = y++;
        System.out.println("y: " + y);
        System.out.println("z: " + z);
    }
}
```

Output
y: 16
z: 15

Now, consider the following statement

```
z = ++y;
```

Here, **++y** is defined to be the new value of y after 1 has been added. So, if y is 15 then both y and z will have the value 16, i.e., it first increments the value of y and then uses its value as shown in Figure 5.4.

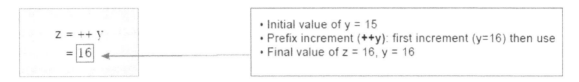

Figure 5.4: Prefix Expression Evaluation

> **Note**
>
> Remember the rule in the Prefix increment: first increment, then use.

Figure 5.5 shows the memory status during the evaluation process.

Figure 5.5: Prefix Increment

Here is the stepwise explanation of what happens:

a. Initially, the value of variable y is 15, and the value of variable z is undefined as it has not been declared yet.

b. When you use the prefix operation, the value is first incremented, thus the value of y becomes 16. The variable z remains undefined since the value of y has not been used yet.

c. After incrementing, the value of y is used, i.e., assigned to z. Thus, z becomes 16.

The following program is the implementation of Figure 5.5.

Listing 5.6: PrefixIncrement.java

```
1  public class PrefixIncrement
```

```
 2  {
 3      public static void main(String args[])
 4      {
 5          int y = 15;
 6          int z = ++y;
 7          System.out.println("y: " + y);
 8          System.out.println("z: " + z);
 9      }
10  }
```

Output

```
y: 16
z: 16
```

In short, we can say:

- The postfix operator first assigns the value to the variable on the left and then increments the value of the operand.

- The prefix operator first increments the value of the operand and then assigns it to the variable on the left.

5.2.2 Conditional Operator (?:)

The conditional operator is also called a ternary operator because it has three operands. Its syntax is:

```
boolean-expression ? expression1 : expression2
```

The operator works as follows: the `boolean-expression` is evaluated first. If it evaluates to `true`, then the value of the entire expression is `expression1`; otherwise, the value of the entire expression is `expression2`. Note that only one of the expressions (either `expression1` or `expression2`) is evaluated.

A classic example of the conditional operator is to find the smallest of two numbers `a` and `b` as shown in the following program.

Listing 5.7: FindMin.java

```
1  public class FindMin
2  {
3      public static void main(String args[])
4      {
5          int a = 127, b = 113;
6          System.out.println("Minimum number is: " + ((a > b) ? a : b));
7      }
8  }
```

Output

```
Minimum number is: 113
```

5.3 Precedence and Associativity of Operators

An expression may contain a wide variety of operators in Java. When two or more operators are used in an expression, the Java runtime environment decides which operator should be evaluated first. This decision is made on the basis of the precedence and associativity of the operators, as explained below:

Precedence: Each operator has a precedence associated with it. *Precedence* is the priority of an operator according to which it is evaluated. This precedence is used to determine the order of evaluation of an expression involving more than one operator. There are different levels of precedence from high to low. An operator belonging to a higher level is evaluated first.

Associativity: If two operators have the same precedence (priority), then they are either evaluated from "Left to Right" or from "Right to Left". This is termed as *associativity*, which tells the direction of execution of operators ("Left to Right" or "Right to Left") when operators in an expression have the same precedence.

Table below shows the Java operators from the highest to the lowest precedence, along with their associativity.

1	[]	Array index	Left to Right
	()	Method call	
	.	Member access	
2	++	Pre or postfix increment	Right to Left
	--	Pre or postfix decrement	
	+, -	Unary plus, minus	
	~	Bitwise complement	
	!	Logical NOT	
3	(type cast)	Type cast	Right to Left
	new	Object creation	
4	*	Multiplication	Left to Right
	/	Division	
	%	Modulus (remainder)	
5	+, -	Addition, subtraction	Left to Right
	+	String concatenation	

6	<	Less than	Left to Right
	<=	Less than or equal to	
	>	Greater than	
	>=	Greater than or equal to	
7	==	Equal to	Left to Right
	!=	Not equal to	
8	&&	Logical AND	Left to Right
9	||	Logical OR	Left to Right
10	? :	Conditional (ternary) operator	Right to Left
11	=	Assignment and shorthand assignment operators	Right to Left
	+=		
	-=		
	*=		
	/=		
	%=		

Let us take an example of the following expression:

```
x - y + z
```

If you check the above table, both the + and - operators have the same precedence (5). That means the computer will apply associativity rule for the direction of execution which is "Left to Right" in this case (see precedence row 5 in the Table). This means that the expression:

```
x - y + z
```

will be evaluated as:

```
(x - y) + z
```

and not as:

```
x - (y + z)
```

What if you want the computer to evaluate y + z first? Well, you might have already guessed it, use brackets. You can always change the order in which an expression will be evaluated by using brackets.

Let us take another example of operators having the same precedence:

```
System.out.println("Eight " + 4 + 4);
```

The output of the statement will be:

    Eight 44

Instead of:

    Eight 8

This is due to the + operator in the string concatenation having the same precedence as the + operator for addition (see precedence row 5 in the Table). As the associativity is from "Left to Right" for this level, the concatenation of "Eight " with the string equivalent of 4 takes place first. The resultant string is again concatenated with the string equivalent of 4 giving us the output "Eight 44".

Let us see what happens when you use the following statement:

    System.out.println(4 + 4 + " Eight");

This time, the output of the statement will be:

    8 Eight

The + operator in the string concatenation has the same precedence as the + operator for addition (see precedence row 5 in the Table) but the associativity is from "Left to Right" for this level. Thus, the addition of 4 with 4 takes place first. The string equivalent of the resultant is then concatenated with the string that follows it, giving you the output "8 Eight". To give preference to the integer addition, you must use brackets like:

    System.out.println("Eight " + (4 + 4));

The correct output of the statement will now be:

    Eight 8

This is illustrated in Program 4.8.

Listing 5.8: Associativity.java

```
1  public class Associativity
2  {
3      public static void main(String args[])
4      {
5          System.out.println("Eight " + 4 + 4);
6          System.out.println(4 + 4 + " Eight");
7          System.out.println("Eight " + (4 + 4));
8      }
9  }
```

Output

Eight 44
8 Eight
Eight 8

5.4 The new Operator

Earlier you learnt that using the concept of a class, you can make the entire data and methods a user-defined data type. The class may be considered as a data type, and an object as a variable of that data type. Creating the object of the class type involves two steps:

(i) Declaring a variable of the class type.

(ii) Allocating memory for the object where details of the object can be stored.

The **new** operator is used to allocate memory for the object. The above two steps take the following syntax:

```
Classname objectname;
objectname = new Classname();
```

Here, `Classname` is the name of the class that is being instantiated (i.e., the class whose instance is being created). The `objectname` is a variable of the type `Classname` that is being created.

Let us consider the `Mobile` class as shown in Figure 5.6.

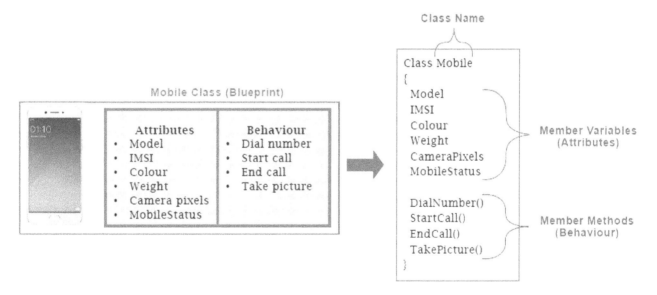

Figure 5.6: Schematic Representation of the Mobile Class

When you create an object of this class type, the statements will have the following syntax:

```
Mobile myMobile;
myMobile = new Mobile();
```

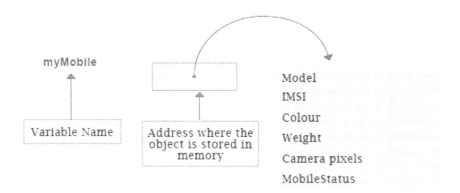

Figure 5.7: Creating an Object of the Mobile Class

Note the difference between defining a primitive data type (for example, an integer) and an object:

For an integer, the variable contains the value itself whereas for an object, the variable contains the address where the object is stored. An arrow has been used in the above figure to indicate that the content is an address and not the value itself.

You can also use the following combined syntax to declare and allocate memory in one statement:

```
Classname objectname = new Classname();
```

Let us now create various objects using the new operator.

```
Mobile myiPhoneX = new Mobile();
Mobile mySamsung = new Mobile();
Mobile myBlackberry = new Mobile();
```

The **new** operator in each of the above statements will allocate memory for each object at the run-time as shown in the Figure 5.8.

myiPhoneX	mySamsung	myBlackberry
Model	Model	Model
IMSI	IMSI	IMSI
Colour	Colour	Colour
Weight	Weight	Weight
- - -	- - -	- - -

Figure 5.8: Instance Memory Allocation

Let us summarise some key points about the class:

- A class is a template or blueprint specifying the attributes and behaviour of objects.

- It acts as a data type to create objects.

- Class is a logical construct whereas object is a concrete reality occupying space in memory.

5.5 The dot (.) Operator

Once the objects have been declared and the memory has been allocated, member variables and member methods can be accessed using the dot (.) operator. Syntax of the dot operator is:

```
Objname.memberVariable;
Objname.memberMethod();
```

Let us see how to use the dot operator to assign values to the member variables of the `Mobile` objects.

```
Mobile myiPhoneX = new Mobile();
Mobile mySamsung = new Mobile();
Mobile myBlackberry = new Mobile();
myiPhoneX.Colour = "Gold";
mySamsung.Model = "A7";
myBlackberry.Weight = 145;
```

These statements will update the memory as shown in Figure 5.9. The data for one object is separate from the data for another.

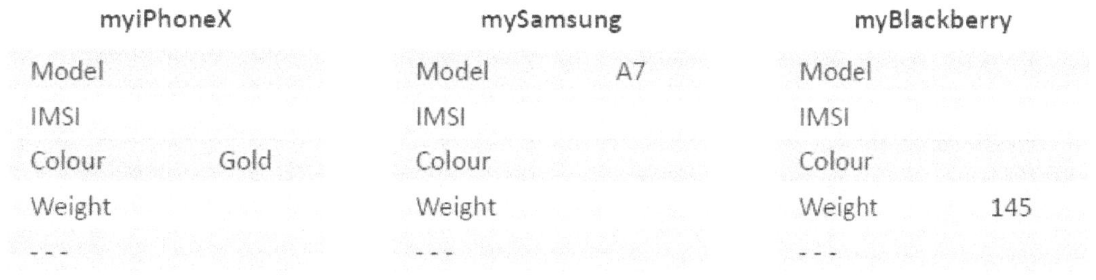

myiPhoneX		mySamsung		myBlackberry	
Model		Model	A7	Model	
IMSI		IMSI		IMSI	
Colour	Gold	Colour		Colour	
Weight		Weight		Weight	145
- - -		- - -		- - -	

Figure 5.9: Instances with Data

Similarly, you can access the member methods as shown below:

```
myiPhoneX.DialNumber();
mySamsung.StartCall();
myBlackberry.EndCall();
```

5.6 Expressions

An expression is a combination of constants, variables, operators and method calls. It is constructed according to the syntax of the language. The expression when evaluated returns a single value. Literals, variables, and method calls are simple expressions. The value of one expression can be combined with other expressions to form a complex expression. When several operators appear in an expression, you use precedence and associativity to determine the order of evaluation of the operators.

Java expressions can be categorised into various types:

5.6.1 Arithmetic Expression

An arithmetic expression represents a numeric value. It can be further categorised into three subtypes, namely integer, real, and mixed expressions.

5.6.1.1 Integer Expression

An expression containing integer constants and variables joined by arithmetic operators is known as an *integer expression*. The integer expression evaluates to an integer value. Consider the following declarations:

```
int a, x, y, z, radius;
```

Some examples of the integer expressions using the above declarations are:

- 55
- x * x + y

- a + 15
- a * (x + y + z)

- 2 * radius
- -z + (5 * x)

5.6.1.2 Real Expression

An expression containing real constants and variables joined by arithmetic operators is known as a *real expression*. The real expression evaluates to a real value. Consider the following declarations:

```
float a, x, y, z, radius;
```

Some examples of the real expressions using the above declarations are:

- 55.0
- 6.5 * x * x + y

- a + 15.0
- x * (y + z)

- 22/7 * radius
- -x + (3.0 *y)

5.6.1.3 Mixed Expression

An expression which contains a combination of integer and real expressions is known as a *mixed expression*. Consider the following declarations:

```
int a, x, radius;
\textbf{float y, z;}
```

Some examples of the mixed expressions using the above declarations are:

- a + 45.0
- 2 * x * x + y

- a - 15.0
- x * (y + z)

- 3.14 * radius
- -x + (3.0 *y)

5.6.2 String Expression

A string expression represents a string value. You cannot add and subtract strings, like numbers, but Java does provide a + operator for concatenation of strings. Some examples of string expressions are as follows:

- "Java " + "Programming" will result in "Java Programming"

- "123" + "789" will result in "123789"

- "The square of 25 is " + square
  Assuming that the square variable has a value of 625, the above-mentioned string expression will result in:
  "The square of 25 is 625"

5.6.3 Boolean (or Logical) Expression

A boolean expression represents a boolean value – true or false. In addition to the arithmetic and relational operators, a boolean expression can contain boolean operators. Some examples of boolean expressions are:

- i <= 5

- salary > 25000 || salary <= 50000

- option == 'A' || opton == 'B'

- a != b && a != c

- i < j

- (x - y) <= (z - 3)

- inputValue == 3

- (i + j) < 10

5.7 Type Conversions

While programming, it is sometimes necessary to convert a data item of one type to another type. When an arithmetic expression consists of constants and variables of the same data type, the result of the expression is also of the same data type. For example, if the data type of length and breadth is int, then the result of the expression length * breadth will also be an int.

A type conversion takes place when an arithmetic expression consists of constants and variables of different data types (mixed expressions). A type conversion is a process that converts a value of one data type to another data type. There are two forms of type conversions in Java: Implicit and Explicit conversions.

5.7.1 Implicit Type Conversions

The type conversions which are automatically performed by the Java compiler are known as *implicit type conversions*. There are a lot of other names given to implicit type conversions. These are automatic type conversion, type promotion, widening conversion or coercion.

Here are the conversion steps followed by the Java compiler while evaluating an expression that has different types of variables and constants:

Step 1: If either operand is of the type `double`, then the other operand is converted to `double`.

Step 2: Otherwise, if either operand is of the type `float`, then the other operand is converted to `float`.

Step 3: Otherwise, if either operand is of the type `long`, then the other operand is converted to `long`.

Step 4: Otherwise, both operands are converted to `int`.

Let us take a simple example and see how the Java compiler applies these rules.
Example 1:

```
long longNumber, myResult;
int intNumber;
```

Let us evaluate the following expression which has mixed data types.

```
myResult = longNumber + intNumber;
```

Here is a graphical representation of the evaluation process:

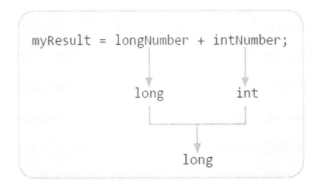

Figure 5.10: Expression Type Evaluation

The step by step explanation of the evaluation process is as follows:

(i) Compiler reads the expression. Since neither operand is of the type `double`, the compiler moves to the next step.

(ii) It re-evaluates and deduces that neither operand is a `float`, so it moves to the next step.

(iii) Here, the compiler identifies that one operand is `long`, so the other operand is converted to `long` and their result is of `long` type.

Let us now evaluate the following expression which has mixed data types.
Example 2:

```
double myDouble, myResult;
float myFloat;
int myInt;
char myChar;
myResult = myInt + myChar + myFloat / myDouble;
```

Here is a graphical representation of the evaluation process:

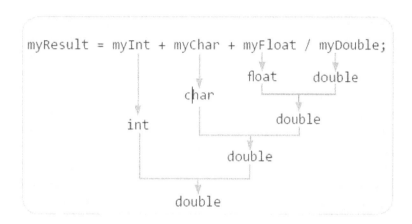

Figure 5.11: Expression Type Evaluation

The step by step explanation of the evaluation process is as follows:

(i) The division operation is solved first because it has a higher precedence. Since operand `myDouble` is `double`, the other operand `myFloat` is converted to a `double`, and their result is of `double` type.

(ii) Now, the addition between character (`myChar`) and `double` datatype is performed. Variable `myChar` is converted to a `double`, and their result is of `double` type.

(iii) Finally, when the result of the previous step is evaluated with an integer (`myInt`), `myInt` is converted to a `double`, and their result is of `double` type.

5.7.2   Explicit Type Conversions

Consider a scenario, where you need to assign an `int` value to a `byte` variable. This time, the conversion will not be performed automatically because the `byte` data type is smaller in size than `int`. Recall that the `byte` data type can only hold up to 8 bits whereas the `int` data type can hold up to 32 bits. In such cases, a programmer has to force the conversion and is referred to as *explicit type conversion* or type casting.

To create a conversion between two incompatible types, a cast must be used. A cast is simply an explicit type conversion. Its syntax is:

    (data-type) expression

Here, the data-type is any primitive data type. The expression may be a constant, variable or any expression.

Scenario 1 - Let us consider the scenario where a **double** value is typecast into an integer as per the following statement:

    int a = (int) 19.73;

The above statement will cast the **double** value 19.73 into an **int**. The value of variable a will be 19.

Listing 5.9: DoubleToInt.java

```
1  public class DoubleToInt
2  {
3      public static void main(String args[])
4      {
5          int a = (int) 19.73;
6          System.out.println("a = " + a);
7      }
8  }
```

```
Output
a = 19
```

When you perform a cast, it can lead to a loss of precision. Therefore, when a **double** value is assigned to an **int** type, the fractional component is lost. In this example, the value 19.73 was truncated to 19.

Scenario 2 - Let us consider the scenario where a **float** value is typecast into an integer as per the following statement:

    float a = 76.89F;
    int b;
    b = (int) a;

In the above example, the **float** value 76.89 will typecast into an integer. The value of **b** will be 76. Note that explicit casting does not affect the original value. In this example, the cast operator **(int)** does not affect the value of variable **a**. The data type of variable a remains **float** with the value of 76.89 in the other parts of the program as shown in Program 5.10.

Listing 5.10: FloatToInt.java

```java
1  public class FloatToInt
2  {
3     public static void main (String args [])
4     {
5        float a = 76.89F;
6        int b;
7
8        b = (int)a;
9
10       System.out.println("b = " + b);
11       System.out.println("a = " + a);
12    }
13 }
```

```
Output
b = 76
a = 76.89
```

Scenario 3 – Let us now consider a scenario where XYZ Company charges Rs.50,000 per mile to survey roads on a highway. Suppose, you know the number of **feet** surveyed. A programmer wrote a simple program to compute the total price as given below:

```
totalPrice = 5000 * (feet / 5280);
```

(1 Mile = 5280 Feet)

Here is the program and its output.

Listing 5.11: ComputeCost.java

```java
1  public class ComputeCost
2  {
3     public static void main (String args [])
4     {
5        int feet = 2700;
6        float totalPrice;
7        totalPrice =  5000 * (feet / 5280);
8
9        System.out.println("Total Price = " + totalPrice);
10    }
11 }
```

```
Output
Total Price = 0.0
```

Clearly, the output is wrong as integer division is taking place when dividing integer value of **feet** by 5280, resulting in zero output.

You can correct this problem by casting one of the operands into **float** data type as shown in Program 5.12. Now, a real-division takes place and correct value of the total price is displayed.

Listing 5.12: ComputeCostWithCast.java

```
1  public class ComputeCostWithCast
2  {
3     public static void main (String args[])
4     {
5        int feet = 2700;
6        float totalPrice;
7        totalPrice =  5000 * ((float)feet / 5280);
8
9        System.out.println("Total Price = " + totalPrice);
10    }
11 }
```

Output

Total Price = 2556.818

Multiple Choice Questions

1. If a = 8 and b = 4, the value of a %= b is ....

    A. 2   B. 0   C. 4   D. 8

2. An operator taking only single operand for its operation is called ....

    A. A unary operator   C. A ternary operator

    B. A binary operator   D. None of the above

3. Which one of the following is not a binary operator?

    A. AND   B. %   C. ==   D. !

4. Which one of the following is not a valid operator in Java?

    A. <=   B. !==   C. !=   D. ==

5. The statement i = i +1 is equivalent to ....

    A. i++   C. ++i

    B. i += 1   D. All of the above

6. For x = 5, the statement sum = ++x + 8 evaluates to ....

    A. sum = 12   B. sum = 13   C. sum = 14   D. sum = 15

7. Assuming x=1 with the following code snippet:

    ```
    int y = --x;
    ```

    Which one of the following is true?

    A. x=1, y=1   B. x=0, y=0   C. x=1, y=0   D. x=0, y=1

8. The statement (1>0) && (1<0) evaluates to ....

    A. 0   B. 1   C. false   D. true

9. The statement (1>0) || (1<0) evaluates to ....

| A. 0 | B. 1 | C. false | D. true |

10. The statement (1==1)? 1: 0 evaluates to ....
| A. 0 | B. 1 | C. false | D. true |

11. The expression 17 % 4 gives the output ....
| A. 4 | B. 3 | C. 2 | D. 1 |

12. Consider the following code snippet:
```
float x = 8.25F;
int y;
y = (int) x;
```

What are the values of x and y?
| A. x = 8.25, y = 8 | C. x = 8, y = 8.25 |
| B. x = 8.0, y = 8.0 | D. x = 8, y = 8 |

13. The expression 13 / 3 gives the output ....
| A. 4 | B. 3 | C. 0 | D. 1 |

14. The statement System.out.println("six " + 3 + 3); gives the output ....
| A. six 33 | B. six 6 | C. 33 six | D. 6 six |

15. The expression 4 + 8 % 2 gives the output ....
| A. 6 | C. 4 |
| B. 8 | D. None of the above |

16. Implicit type conversion is also known as ....
| A. Automatic type conversion | C. Widening conversion |
| B. Type promotion | D. All of the above |

State whether the given statements are True or False:

☐ There is only one ternary operator in Java.

☐ Arithmetic operators + and - also have a unary form.

☐ Operators = and == perform the same operation in Java.

☐ The expression 14 % 2 evaluates to 0.

☐ The expression 7 / 13 evaluates to 0.

☐ The output of `System.out.println (!true);` is false.

☐ The expressions 6 + 7 and "6" + "7" evaluate to the same value.

☐ The expression `m = m + 2` is same as `m =+ 2`.

☐ The new operator allocates memory during runtime.

☐ The statements `n = 25` and `n == 25` are same.

☐ The expression `p =- 9` is same as `p = p-9`.

☐ The assignment operator (=) is a binary operator.

☐ The output of `System.out.println(1==1);` is true.

☐ Explicit type conversion is also known as coercion.

Assignment Questions

1. We have two variables x and y. Write Java statements to calculate the result of division of y by x and calculate the remainder of the division.

2. Assign the value of pi (i.e., 3.142) to a variable with requisite data type.

3. What are logical operators? Give an example of each.

4. What is an assignment operator? Give an example.

5. Explain the shorthand assignment operator with an example.

6. What is the purpose of the new operator?

7. What is the use and syntax of a ternary operator?

8. State the difference between = and ==.

9. If a = 5, b = 9, calculate the value of:
   ```
   a += a++ - ++b + a
   ```

10. Distinguish between the following:
    (i) Prefix and Postfix Increment
    (ii) Prefix and Postfix Decrement
    (iii) Unary and Binary Operators
    (iv) Increment and Decrement Operator
    (v) / and % operator

11. If `m=5, n=2`; what will be the output of m and n after execution?
    (i) `m -= n`
    (ii) `n = m + m/n`

12. If `x = 3, y = 7`, calculate the value of:
    ```
    x -= x++ - ++y
    ```

13. What will be the output of the following if `x=5`?
    ```
    5 * ++x
    5 * x++
    ```

14. What is type conversion? How is an implicit type conversion different from explicit type conversion?

15. What do you understand by type conversion?

16. Explain the term 'typecasting'.

17. What are precedence and associativity?

18. Evaluate the following expressions, if the values of the variables are:
    a = 2, b = 3 and c = 3
    (i) a - (b++) * (--c)
    (ii) a * (++b) %c

19. Write the Java expressions for the following:
    (i) $(a + b)^2 + b$
    (ii) $a^2 + b^2$
    (iii) $z = x^3 + y^3 + \dfrac{xy}{3}$
    (iv) $f = \dfrac{a^2 + b^2}{a^2 - b^2}$
    (v) $z = \dfrac{ab + bc + ca}{3abc}$
    (vi) $0 <= x <= 50$
    (vii) $z = \dfrac{(0.05 - 2y^3)}{x - y}$
    (viii) $z = \dfrac{(a + b)^n}{\sqrt{3} + b}$
    (ix) $z = \dfrac{a^x b^y}{\sqrt[3]{x} + ^3\sqrt{y}}$

20. Rewrite the following statements without using shorthand operators.
    (i) p /= q
    (ii) p -= 1
    (iii) p *= q + r
    (iv) p -= q - r

21. Determine the output of the following program.
```
public class Test
{
    public static void main(String[] args)
    {
        int a = 1, b = 2;
        System.out.println("Output1: " + a + b);
        System.out.println("Output2: " + (a + b));
    }
}
```

22. What is the difference between the following two statements in terms of execution? Explain the results.
```
x -= 5;
x =- 5;
```

23. What is concatenation? On what data type is concatenation performed?

24. Determine the output of the following program.

```
public class PredictOutput1
{
    public static void main(String args[])
    {
        int a = 4, b = 2, c = 3;
        System.out.println("Output 1: " + (a = b * c));
        System.out.println("Output 2: " + (a = (b * c)));
    }
}
```

25. Determine the output of the following program.

```
public class PredictOutput2
{
    public static void main(String args[])
    {
        int a = 6, b = 2, c = 3;
        System.out.println("Output 1: " + (a == b * c));
        System.out.println("Output 2: " + (a == (b * c)));
    }
}
```

26. Determine the output of the following program.

```
public class PredictOutput3
{
    public static void main(String args[])
    {
        int a = 2, b = 2, c = 2;
        System.out.println("Output 1: " + (a + 2 < b * c));
        System.out.println("Output 2: " + (a + 2 < (b * c)));
    }
}
```

Answers To Objective Questions

Multiple Choice Questions

1. B	3. D	5. D	7. B	9. D	11. D	13. A	15. C
2. A	4. B	6. C	8. C	10. B	12. A	14. A	16. D

True or False

1. True	3. False	5. True	7. False	9. True	11. False	13. True
2. True	4. True	6. True	8. False	10. False	12. True	14. False

---

Chapter 6

User-defined Methods

User-defined Methods

A program is a set of instructions given to the computer to solve a particular problem. These instructions are specified in the form of methods in Java. In other programming languages, the *methods* are known as *functions*, *procedures*, *modules*, *subroutines* or *sub-programs*. These methods exist inside a class, and each method performs a specific task. There are two types of methods:

(i) **System-defined methods** – The methods defined by the developers of Java are called *system-defined methods*. They are also known as *library methods* or *built-in methods*. For example, `Math.sqrt()` and `Math.round()`.

(ii) **User-defined methods** – The methods defined by the user are called *user-defined methods*. These methods are defined as per the need of the user to create customised and reusable blocks of code.

This chapter deals with the discussion of user-defined methods. You will learn how to create your own custom methods and use them in your programs.

6.1 Need/Advantages of Methods

A class with only data items and without methods that operate on this data is of a little or no use. The objects created by such a class cannot perform any operation. Therefore, you must add methods that are necessary for processing the data contained in the class. There are a number of reasons to use methods. Some of them are listed below:

(i) Methods can be reused in a program without the need to rewrite the same code. Thus, methods provide the means to avoid duplication of the code and help in code reusability.

(ii) They help divide complex programs into manageable code blocks.

(iii) They help us in understanding the flow of a program.

(iv) They help in improving the readability of code.

(v) They make debugging of the code easier.

6.2 Method Definition

The methods are defined inside the class immediately after the member variables. The syntax of a method definition is:

```
[access-modifier] type method-name ([parameter-list])
{
    method-body;
}
```

The first line of the method definition is called *method prototype* or *method header*. See Figure 6.1 depicting a simple method that just displays a message on the screen. The `method-body` within curly brackets contains a block of statements that is executed to perform a task. The statements within the method body are executed when the method is called.

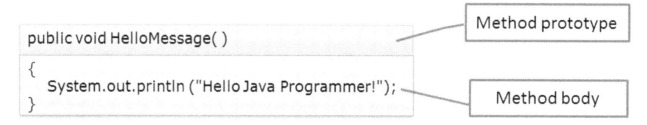

Figure 6.1: Method Definition

The method definition can be divided into five main parts:

(i) The method prototype may begin with an `access-modifier`, which can be `public`, `private` or `protected`. These modifiers determine the type of access to the method. They are called *access modifiers* or *access specifiers* because they specify if elements outside the class can use this method. The square brackets (see syntax) indicate that this part of the *method definition* is optional.

(ii) The type of data returned by the method can be any valid Java data type. If the method does not return a value, then it must return a `void` type.

(iii) The `method-name` can be any valid Java identifier. You should always give meaningful names to the methods so that their purpose is clear by reading their names, for example, `ComputeSimpleInterest` rather than `CmpSI`.

(iv) The `parameter-list` is a sequence of data type and identifier pair(s) separated by commas. The `parameter-list` is also called *parameters* or *arguments*. If a method has no parameters, then its parameter list will be empty, but you must use empty round brackets, (). Notice in the syntax that the parameters are optional.

(v) The statements within the `method-body` describe the tasks to be performed.

Method Signature

The method name along with the list of parameters used in the method prototype is known as *method signature*. It is a part of the method prototype.

Let us understand the various parts of a method with some examples.

Example 1:
Figure 6.2 shows various parts of the `HelloMessage()` method.

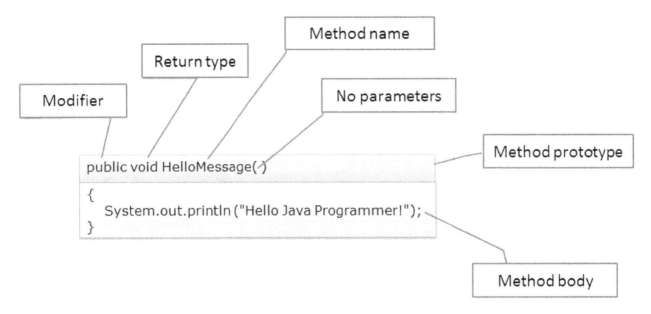

Figure 6.2: Method Prototype and Body

In this example:

- The method prototype is:
  `public void HelloMessage()`

- The method signature is: `HelloMessage()`

- The access modifier `public` signifies that the method can be accessed by other classes.

- The return type is `void` which signifies that the method does not return a value.

- The parameter list is empty (i.e., no parameters); therefore, no values can be passed to this method.

Example 2

Figure 6.3 shows various parts of the `FindCube()` method. The method calculates the cube of a number passed as an argument and returns the calculated value.

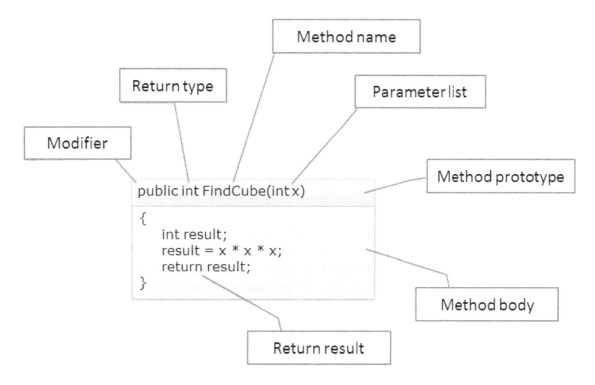

Figure 6.3: Method with a Return Value

In this example:

- The method prototype is:
  `public int FindCube(int x)`

- The method signature is:
  `FindCube (int x)`

- The access modifier `public` signifies that the method can be accessed by other classes.

- The return type is `int`, which signifies that the value returned by the method will be of int data type.

- The method has only one parameter. The data type of the parameter is `int`, and the name of the identifier is `x`.

Example 3

Figure 6.4 illustrates a method that finds out the maximum of two numbers passed as arguments and returns the maximum value.

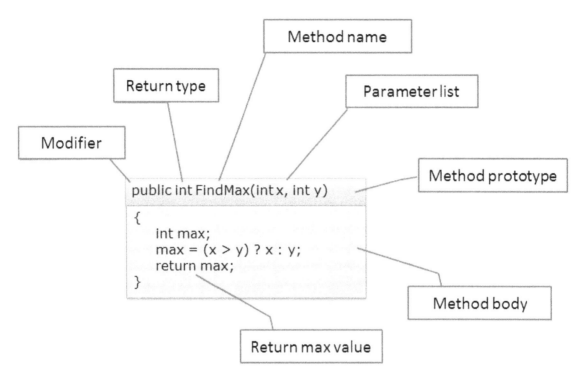

Figure 6.4: Method with Two Arguments

In this example:

- The method prototype is:
  `public int FindMax(int x, int y)`

- The method signature is:
  `FindMax(int x, int y)`

- The modifier `public` signifies that the method can be accessed by other classes.

- The return type is `int`, which signifies that the method returns a value of int data type.

- The method has two parameters. The data type of both the parameters is `int`, and the names of the identifiers are `x` and `y`.

6.3 Method Parameters

Parameters are given in round brackets after the method name in the heading of a method definition. A parameter provides a mechanism for passing information to the method. The schematic representation of the `FindCube()` method may look like as shown in Figure 6.5.

Figure 6.5: Schematic Representation of the FindCube() Method

As we have discussed earlier, the parameter list of **FindCube()** method, (**int x**), specifies that the method has one parameter. The data type of the parameter is **int**. Within the body of the method, the parameter can be used in the same way as a variable.

Notice that there is nothing in the method definition that gives a value to the parameter. The parameter gets its initial value from outside of the method. When the **FindCube()** method is invoked, a value must be provided for the parameter in the method call statement. The corresponding argument in the method definition is then initialised with the parameter value. The parameter in the method invocation can be a literal, such as **7** or **'G'**, a variable, or any expression that yields a value of the appropriate type.

6.4 Invoking Methods

By defining a method in a class, all you are doing is telling the computer that the method exists with some functionality. The method does not actually get executed until it is invoked. The method can be *invoked* (or *called* or *executed*) by specifying its name, followed by parameters being sent enclosed in the round brackets. For example, the **FindCube()** method defined earlier could be invoked using the following call statement:

```
FindCube(num);
```

where, **num** needs to be of the **int** data type. This method invoke statement could occur anywhere in the class. Let us understand how you can invoke this method in a program:

```
1   public class ComputeCubeDemo
2   {
3       public int FindCube (int x)
4       {
5           int result;
6           result = x * x * x;
7           return result;
8       }
9
10      public void ComputeCube ()
11      {
12          int num = 5;
13          int myResult;
14          myResult = FindCube (num);
15          System.out.println ("Cube of " + num + " is " + myResult);
16      }
17  }
```

❷ Control transfers to the method definition

❶ The method calling statement

❸ Control transfers back to the calling statement

In this program, a method `FindCube()` has been defined which computes the cube of a number. The number whose cube is to be computed is passed as an argument. When such a method is invoked:

- The invoke statement must provide all the parameter values.

- The type and number of parameters in the invoke statement must match with those of the method prototype.

  For example, the method prototype at Line 3 has only one parameter and is of `int` data type. Therefore, the invoking statement at Line 14 provides only one parameter whose data type is `int`.

- The order of parameters in the invoke statement must match with that of the method prototype.

  For example, if the method prototype is:

  ```
  public int GradingMethod(int a, float b, char c)
  ```

  The invoke statement should be:

  ```
  GradingMethod(77, 55.5, 'Z');
  ```

> **Note**
>
> When the method call statement is encountered, the program control is transferred to the method definition, i.e., the statements in the method body are executed, and then the control transfers back to the calling statement.

6.4.1   Actual and Formal Parameters

In the discussion so far, the term parameter has been used in two different, but related, concepts. There are parameters used in the method invocation, such as num at Line 14 in the statement `FindCube(num)`. On the other hand, there are parameters used in the method definition, such as x at Line 3 in the statement `FindCube (int x)`.

The parameters that appear in the method invocation are called *actual parameters*. The parameters that appear in the method definition are called *formal parameters* (see Figure 6.6).

> **Note**
>
> Formal parameters are also known as *dummy parameters*.

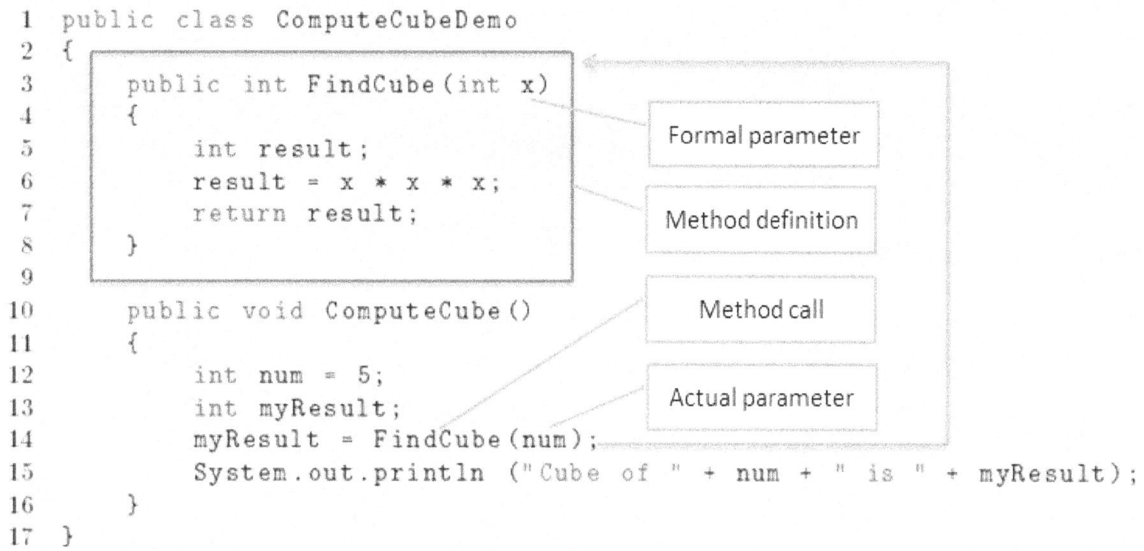

```
1   public class ComputeCubeDemo
2   {
3       public int FindCube(int x)
4       {
5           int result;
6           result = x * x * x;
7           return result;
8       }
9
10      public void ComputeCube()
11      {
12          int num = 5;
13          int myResult;
14          myResult = FindCube(num);
15          System.out.println ("Cube of " + num + " is " + myResult);
16      }
17  }
```

Formal parameter

Method definition

Method call

Actual parameter

Figure 6.6: Actual and Formal Parameters

In the above-mentioned example, x is the formal parameter whereas num is the actual parameter.

Sometimes, the method call statement may contain an expression as an argument. In such cases, the actual parameters in the method call statement are first used to evaluate the expression, and the values are then assigned to the formal parameters in the method definition. Using these values, the body of the method is executed. For example, you can have a call statement, such as:

```
myResult = FindCube(3 * num);
```

In this case, the expression 3 * num will be evaluated first using the actual parameter. Its value will then be assigned to the formal parameter x, and the body of the FindCube() method will be executed. For example, if the value of num is 4, the formal parameter x would be assigned the computed value, 12 (i.e., 3*4).

6.5   Returning from Methods

Just as invoking a method is important, returning from a method is equally important. You know that by invoking a method, the program control transfers to the invoked method. Once the method execution finishes, the control transfers back to the invoking statement. There are two ways in which the control can transfer back to the invoking statement.

(i) The return statement is encountered in the invoked method.

(ii) The last statement in the invoked method is executed.

6.5.1 The Return Statement

Generally, the methods you create process some data and give a calculated value. For example, the `FindCube()` method calculates the cube of an integer. The calculated value remains within the method unless it is returned back to the invoking method. Such methods specify the return value via the `return` statement. The syntax of the `return` statement is:

```
return expression;
```

The `return` statement can only be used inside the method body. The data type of the return value must match the type specified in the method header.

The `return` statement fulfils two purposes:

(i) It returns a value to the calling statement.

(ii) It causes an exit from the method and transfers the control back to the calling method.

The `return` statement always ends a method invocation. Once the `return` statement is executed, the method ends, and any remaining statements in the method definition are not executed. The definition of a method that returns a value must have one or more return statements.

As you have seen in the `HelloMessage()` example, there is no return statement. In such cases, the control transfers back to the calling statement once the method execution finishes. The return type of such methods must always be `void`.

There is no need to have return statement in a `void` method, but you can place the return statement in the `void` method if there are situations that require the method to end before the entire code is executed. In this case, you can use the `return` statement without any expression as given below:

```
return;
```

6.5.2 Returning Values

All methods must return a value except the methods defined as `void`. This returned value must be of the same data type as defined in the method prototype. If `return` statement is missing in such methods, an error message is displayed in the Code Editor as shown in Figure 6.7.

> **Note**
>
> A method can return only a single value although there can be multiple return statements in the method.

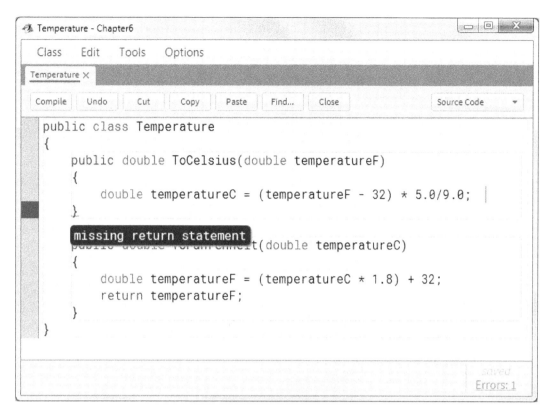

Figure 6.7: Missing return Statement

Let us see an example how to execute a method with parameters using BlueJ.

Listing 6.1: Temperature.java

```java
public class Temperature
{
    public double ToCelsius(double temperatureF)
    {
        double temperatureC = (temperatureF - 32) * 5.0/9.0;
        return temperatureC;
    }

    public double ToFahrenheit(double temperatureC)
    {
        double temperatureF = (temperatureC * 1.8) + 32;
        return temperatureF;
    }
}
```

The program has two methods:

(i) `ToCelsius()` - to convert temperature from Fahrenheit to Celsius

(ii) `ToFahrenheit()` - to convert temperature from Celsius to Fahrenheit

When you execute the `ToFahrenheit()` method in BlueJ, a Method Call dialog box appears as shown in Figure 6.8. Enter value of temperature in Celsius, say 37.4, and click the OK button.

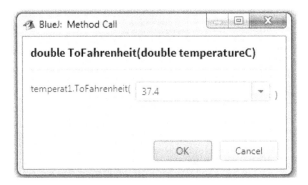

Figure 6.8: Method Call with Parameter

A Method Result window appears displaying the temperature in Fahrenheit.

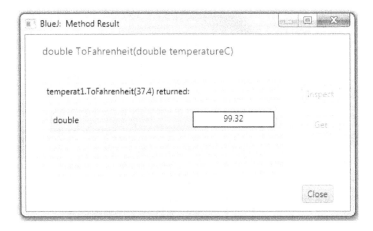

Figure 6.9: Method Result

6.6 Passing Values to Methods

By now, you have understood that a method is a part of the program. It receives the arguments passed from the calling method performs the necessary operations and returns the control back to the calling method. You can pass two types of arguments to the Java method:

- any primitive data types, i.e., `char`, `byte`, `short`, `int`, `long`, `float`, `double`, and `boolean`

- reference data types, i.e., objects or arrays

You can pass values to a method in Java in two ways: pass by value and pass by reference, which are also referred to as call by value and call by reference, respectively.

6.6.1   Pass by Value (Call by Value)

When you pass parameters to a method by value, the values of actual parameters are copied to the formal parameters. Hence, the called method creates its own copy of the argument values and uses them. By doing so, any change in the formal parameter values does not reflect in the actual parameters. Thus, the actual parameter values remain the same. Let us understand the concept using the following example.

```java
1   /* PassByValueDemo.java */
2   class PassByValueDemo
3   {
4       int num;
5
6       public void Compute(int n)       // Formal parameter
7       {
8           n = n * 2;
9           System.out.println("Value in the method call: " + n);
10      }                                // Value of num is copied to n.
11
12      public void TestCompute()
13      {
14          num = 5;   //assign a value
15          System.out.println("Original value: " + num);
16          Compute(num);                // Actual parameter
17          System.out.println("Value after method call: " + num);
18      }
19  }
```

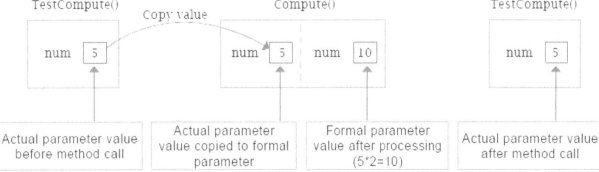

Figure 6.10: Pass by Value Operation

As shown in Figure 6.10, the value of the actual parameter num before the method call is 5. This value gets copied to the formal parameter **n** when the **Compute()** method is invoked. When the instructions inside the `Compute()` method are processed, the value of the formal parameter **n** changes to 10. However, the value of the actual parameter num remains the same, i.e. 5, even after the method call. When you execute the `TestCompute()` method in BlueJ, you will see the following output.

Output
Original value: 5
Value in the method call: 10
Value after method call: 5

The best thing about passing parameters by value is that the value of the variables used in the method call cannot be changed as the method works on a copy of the variables. All primitive data types in Java are passed by value.

6.6.2 Pass by Reference (Call by Reference)

In the pass by reference technique, the reference of the actual parameter is passed to the formal parameter. Remember that the reference denotes the memory location of a variable. As a result, both the actual parameter and the formal parameter represent the same memory location. Hence, the called method works with the original data rather than its own copy. Thus, any changes made to the value of the formal parameter also get reflected in the actual parameter. Let us understand the concept using the following example.

```
1   /* PassByRefDemo.java */
2   class PassByRefDemo
3   {
4       int num;                                    Formal parameter
5
6       public void Compute(PassByRefDemo obj)
7       {
8           obj.num = obj.num * 2;
9           System.out.println("Value in the method call: " + obj.num);
10      }                                           Object reference is passed.
11
12      public void TestCompute()
13      {
14          PassByRefDemo testObject = new PassByRefDemo();
15          testObject.num = 5; //assgin a value
16          System.out.println("Original value: " + testObject.num);
17          Compute(testObject);
18          System.out.println("Value after method call: " + testObject.num);
19      }                       Actual parameter
20  }
```

As shown in the Program, when the `compute()` method is invoked, the address of the actual parameter `testObject` gets passed to the formal parameter `obj`. This method now works with the original data, and the change in the value of the formal parameter gets reflected in the value of actual parameter (see Figure 6.11).

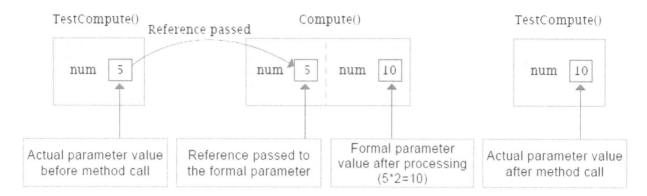

Figure 6.11: Pass by Reference Operation

When you execute the `TestCompute()` method in BlueJ, you will see the following output this time.

```
Output
Original value: 5
Value in the method call: 10
Value after method call: 10
```

Clearly, changes made to the value of the formal parameter are reflected in the actual parameter. In Java, arrays and objects are passed to methods by reference automatically.

> **Note**
>
> The `String` objects are immutable in Java, which means they cannot be changed once they are created. Even if the strings are passed by reference, they cannot be changed.

6.7   Pure and Impure Methods

Methods in Java classes are used to perform specific tasks based on the logic of the program. Java methods in the course of their execution may or may not change the state of an object. On this basis, the methods can be classified into pure and impure methods.

6.7.1   Pure Methods

A method is considered pure if:

- It does not change the original state of an object.

- It always returns the same value when the same arguments are given.

Pure method generally returns a value to its calling method. The return value is either a primitive data type or an object. Invoking a pure method has no side effects, such as changing the state of an object, modifying the argument or printing[1]. Consider the following example that demonstrates a pure method.

Listing 6.2: PureMethodDemo.java

```java
class PureMethodDemo
{
    public int PureMethod(int num)
    {
        num = 5 * num + 5;
        return num;
    }

    public static void main(String args[])
    {
        int param = 2;
        int result;

        PureMethodDemo myObject = new PureMethodDemo();

        System.out.println("Value of argument before calling the ←
            ↪ PureMethod(): " + param);

        result = myObject.PureMethod(param);
        System.out.println("Return value from the PureMethod(): " + ←
            ↪ result);

        System.out.println("Value of argument after calling the ←
            ↪ PureMethod(): " + param);
    }
}
```

Output

Value of argument before calling the PureMethod(): 2
Return value from the PureMethod(): 15
Value of argument after calling the PureMethod(): 2

---

[1]Printing is impure because it involves Input/Output (I/O). I/O, by definition, is impure because of the presence of external state of the I/O device.

In this example:

- The value of the actual argument param remains the same, before and after invoking the method. The value of param (i.e., 2) is passed to the method `PureMethod()` where it is processed. During the course of action, the value of actual argument param does not change even if there is a change in the value of formal parameter `num`.

- Irrespective of the number of times the `PureMethod()` is called, it returns the same value when the same arguments are given.

6.7.2 Impure Methods

A method is considered impure if:

- It does change the original state of an object.

- Every time it is called, it does not return the same value when the same arguments are given.

Invoking an impure method causes side effects. Impure methods may or may not return a value. Consider the following example that demonstrates an impure method.

Listing 6.3: ImpureMethodDemo.java

```
1  class ImpureMethodDemo
2  {
3      int accountNumber;
4      double accountBalance;
5
6      public double Deposit(double amount)
7      {
8          accountBalance = accountBalance + amount;
9          return accountBalance;
10     }
11
12     public static void main(String args[])
13     {
14         double result;
15
16         ImpureMethodDemo myAccount = new ImpureMethodDemo();
17
18         System.out.println("Value of accountBalance before calling the ↵
                ↪ Deposit() method: " + myAccount.accountBalance);
19
20         result = myAccount.Deposit(12000);
21         System.out.println("Return value from the Deposit() method: " + ↵
                ↪ result);
22
23         System.out.println("Value of accountBalance after calling the ↵
                ↪ Deposit() method first time: " + myAccount.accountBalance);
```

```
24
25      result = myAccount.Deposit(12000);
26      System.out.println("Return value from the Deposit() method: " +
            result);
27
28      System.out.println("Value of accountBalance after calling the
            Deposit() method second time: " + myAccount.accountBalance);
29    }
30 }
```

Output
Value of accountBalance before calling the Deposit() method: 0.0
Return value from the Deposit() method: 12000.0
Value of accountBalance after calling the Deposit() method first time: 12000.0
Return value from the Deposit() method: 24000.0
Value of accountBalance after calling the Deposit() method second time: 24000.0

In this example, each time the `Deposit()` method is invoked:

- The state of the object changes, i.e., the member variable `accountBalance` is updated.

- It will return a different value even when the same argument is given.

6.8 Static and Non-Static Methods

Depending on how they can be accessed, Java methods are of two types:

- Static methods

- Non-static methods

The static methods are created with the **static** keyword in their method prototype as shown below:

```
public static return-type method-name(parameter-list)
{
      Method-body
}
```

The non-static methods are created without the **static** keyword in their method prototype as shown below:

```
public return-type method-name(parameter-list)
{
      Method-body
}
```

You have learnt that once a method has been defined in a class, you can use an instance to access it. For example, you were required to create an instance of the ComputeCubeDemo class to use its method ComputeCube().

The methods which are accessed via an instance of the class are known as *non-static methods*. On the other hand, the methods which can be accessed without an instance of the class are known as *static methods*. For a method to be static, the keyword **static** must precede its declaration.

Let us understand the difference between static and non-static methods with the help of a program. This program defines two methods: one static (**FindCubeStatic**) and the other non-static (**FindCube**).

Listing 6.4: DemoClass.java

```java
1  public class DemoClass
2  {
3      public static int FindCubeStatic(int y)
4      {
5          int result;
6          result = y * y * y;
7          return result;
8      }
9
10     public int FindCube(int x)
11     {
12         int result;
13         result = x * x * x;
14         return result;
15     }
16
17     public static void main(String args[])
18     {
19         int a, b;
20         DemoClass classObject = new DemoClass();
21         a = classObject.FindCube(4);
22         System.out.println("Non-static method result " + a);
23
24         b = DemoClass.FindCubeStatic(4);
25         System.out.println("Static method result " + b);
26     }
27 }
```

Output
Non-static method result 64
Static method result 64

Code Walkthrough:

◈ Lines 3 - 8: Define the static method **FindCubeStatic()**. Notice the keyword **static** in the method prototype.

◈ Lines 10 - 15: Define the non-static method **FindCube()**.

◈ Line 20: Creates an instance of the class.

◈ Line 21: The instance named `classObject` is used to invoke the non-static member method `FindCube()`.

◈ Line 24: The class name `DemoClass` is used to invoke the `static` member method `FindCubeStatic()`. Notice that there is no need of using the instance to invoke the static method.

Let us summarise the key points you have just learnt:

- An instance is required to invoke a non-static method (also known as an *instance method*). In order to create an instance of the class, you use the following generic syntax:

    ```
    ClassName objectName = new ClassName();
    ```

    And to invoke the non-static method, you use the following generic syntax:

    ```
    objectName.Non-staticMethodName();
    ```

- An instance is not required to invoke a `static` method. It can be invoked using the class name. When you declare a method with the `static` modifier, it belongs to the class rather than to the objects of that class. Hence, it is also known as a *class method*. To call the static method, you use the following generic syntax:

    ```
    ClassName.StaticMethodName();
    ```

6.9 Method Overloading (Polymorphism)

So far, you have been defining methods with unique names within a class. However, it is possible in Java to define two or more methods within the same class that have the same name, as long as their parameter declarations are different. When this is the case, the methods are said to be overloaded, and the process is referred to as *method overloading*. Method overloading is one of the ways by which Java implements polymorphism.

Consider the following two method declarations:

```
max(int num1, int num2)
max(double num1, double num2)
```

The above-mentioned two methods have the same name but different parameter declarations. If you call `max()` with `int` parameters, the `max()` method that expects `int` parameters will be invoked. If you call `max()` with `double` parameters, the `max()` method that expects `double` parameters will be invoked. This is referred to as method overloading, and the method `max()` is said to be overloaded.

> **Definition**
>
> The process of defining two or more methods with the same name but different signatures in a class is called method overloading.

6.9.1 Need for Method Overloading

You have already learnt that objects have attributes and behaviour. The behaviour of an object is implemented through methods in a class. Sometimes, an object is intended to perform similar operations with slight change in the parameters. For example, finding the maximum of two numbers. The arguments can be `int` or `double`, depending on user's choice, as described above.

You must be wondering why you cannot define two methods with two different names for such cases. Of course, you can. You can define the above-mentioned two methods as:

```
maxInt(int num1, int num2)
maxFloat(double num1, double num2)
```

However, in your program you need to write code to decide which method needs to be executed. For example,

```
if (choice == 'i')
    maxInt(intNum1, intNum2)
else if (choice == 'd')
    maxFloat(doubleNum1, doubleNum2)
else
    System.out.println("Invalid choice");
```

Wouldn't it be better if the computer decided which method gets executed? In larger projects, it would reduce the number of lines of code and increase the efficiency of the application because such unnecessary comparisons are excluded.

When an overloaded method like `max()` is invoked, Java uses the type and/or number of parameters as its guide to determine which version of the overloaded method to call. Java simply executes that version of the method whose parameters match the arguments used in the call.

6.9.2 Defining Overloaded Methods

The signature of a method plays a vital role in method overloading. A method name along with the list of parameters used in the method prototype is known as *method signature*. For example, consider the following method heading:

```
public int compute(int num, double dbl, String name)
```

Its signature is:

```
compute(int num, double dbl, String name)
```

Note that the return type of the method is not a part of the method signature.

If two methods have the same type and number of arguments in the same order, they have the same signatures. For example, consider the following two method signatures:

```
max(int x, int y)
max(int n, int m)
```

These methods are said to have the same signatures even though they are using different parameter variable names. In Java, you can overload a method, provided the methods with the same name have different signatures. The signatures can differ in the type of parameters or in the number of parameters or both.

When a method has been declared more than once in a class, Java uses the following steps as its guide to determine the overloading:

(i) If the signature of a method matches with that of the previous method, then that method is treated as a redeclaration of the first method.

(ii) If the signatures of the two methods match but differ in their return types, the second declaration is flagged as a syntax error, as shown in Figure 6.12.

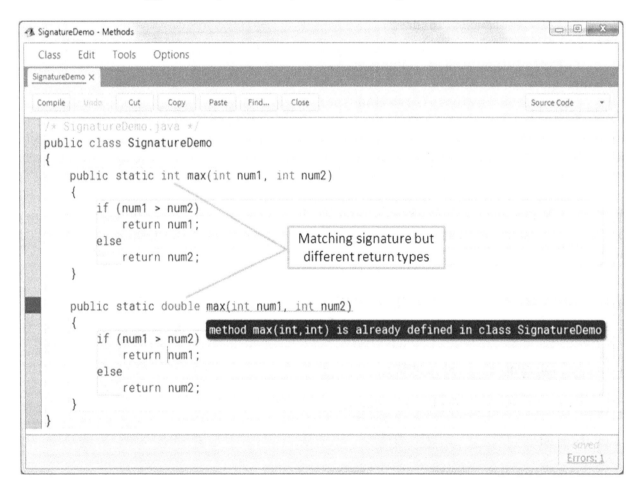

Figure 6.12: Erroneous Declaration of an Overloaded Method

(iii) If the signatures of the two methods differ in the type of parameters or in the number of parameters or both, the two methods are considered as overloaded.

6.9.3 Invoking Overloaded Methods

You can invoke overloaded methods just like any other method. Java uses the type and/or number of parameters as its guide to determine which version of the overloaded method to call. Consider the following two method declarations:

```
max(int num1, int num2)
max(double num1, double num2)
```

If you call `max()` with `int` parameters, the `max()` method that expects `int` parameters will be invoked. If you call `max()` with `double` parameters, the `max()` method that expects `double` parameters will be invoked.

To understand the concept of overloading, let us now consider a program that creates three methods as follows:

(i) The first method finds the maximum of two **integer** numbers.

(ii) The second method finds the maximum of two **double** numbers.

(iii) The third method finds the maximum of three **double** numbers.

All three methods are named `max()` and hence, are overloaded.

Listing 6.5: OverloadingMethods.java

```
1  public class OverloadingMethods
2  {
3
4      //find the maximum of two int values
5      public static int max(int num1, int num2)
6      {
7          if (num1 > num2)
8              return num1;
9          else
10             return num2;
11     }
12
13     //find the maximum of two double values
14     public static double max(double num1, double num2)
15     {
16         if (num1 > num2)
17             return num1;
18         else
19             return num2;
20     }
21
22
```

```
23    //find the maximum of three double values
24    public static double max(double num1, double num2, double num3)
25    {
26        return max(num1, max(num2, num3));
27    }
28
29    public static void main(String[] args)
30    {
31        System.out.println("Invoking the max() method with int values 11 ←
              ↪ and 13");
32        System.out.println("Maximum value is: " + max(11, 13));
33
34
35        System.out.println("Invoking the max() method with double values ←
              ↪ 21.3 and 20.9");
36        System.out.println("Maximum value is: " + max(21.3, 20.9));
37
38
39        System.out.println("Invoking the max() method with three double ←
              ↪ values 33.3, 33.7 and 33.0");
40        System.out.println("Maximum value is: " + max(33.3, 33.7, 33.0));
41    }
42 }
```

Output
Invoking the max() method with int values 11 and 13
Maximum value is: 13
Invoking the max() method with double values 21.3 and 20.9
Maximum value is: 21.3
Invoking the max() method with three double values 33.3, 33.7 and 33.0
Maximum value is: 33.7

6.9.3.1 Ambiguous Invocation

Sometimes, there are two or more possible matches in the invocation of an overloaded method. In such cases, the compiler cannot determine the most specific match. This is referred to as an *ambiguous invocation*. The ambiguous invocation causes a compile-time error as shown in Figure 6.13, where a reference to the overloaded max() method is made.

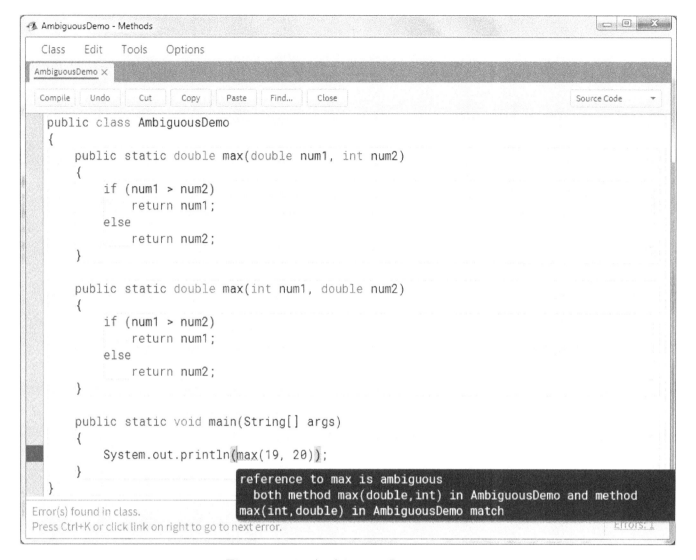

Figure 6.13: Ambiguous Invocation

To avoid such ambiguity, you can use constant suffixes, such as F, L and D, to differentiate between such values. This will indicate compiler to decide which overloaded method to call. For example, in the above program, the ambiguity can be resolved using the following invocations:

```java
System.out.println(max(19D, 20));
```

Or

```java
System.out.println(max(19, 20D));
```

Here, the suffix D or d makes the value a double. Similarly, the suffix L or l makes the value a long.

Design a class to overload a method `volume()` as follows:

(i) `double volume(double r)` – with radius 'r' as an argument, returns the volume of sphere using the formula:
$$v = \frac{4}{3}\pi^3$$

(ii) `double volume(double h, double r)` – with height 'h' and radius 'r' as the arguments, returns the volume of a cylinder using the formula:
$$v = \pi r^2 h$$

(iii) `double volume(double 1, double b, double h)` – with length 'l', breadth 'b' and height 'h' as the arguments, returns the volume of a cuboid using the formula: $v = l*b*h$

Listing 6.6: VolumeOverload.java

```java
public class VolumeOverload
{
    double volume(double r)
    {
        double vol = 4.0 / 3 * 22 / 7 * Math.pow(r, 3);
        return vol;
    }
    double volume(double h, double r)
    {
        double v = 22.0 / 7 * Math.pow(r, 2) * h;
        return v;
    }
    double volume(double 1, double b, double h)
    {
        double v = 1 * b * h;
        return v;
    }
}
```

Design a class to overload a function `SumSeries()` as follows:

(i) `void SumSeries(int n, double x)` – with one integer argument and one double argument to find and display the sum of the series given below:

$$s = \frac{x}{1} - \frac{x}{2} + \frac{x}{3} - \frac{x}{4} + \frac{x}{5} + \ldots\ldots \text{ to n terms}$$

(ii) `void SumSeries()` – To find and display the sum of the following series:

$$s = 1 + (1 \times 2) + (1 \times 2 \times 3) + \ldots + (1 \times 2 \times 3 \times 4 \ldots \times 20)$$

Listing 6.7: SeriesOverload.java

```java
public class SeriesOverload
{
    public void SumSeries(int n, double x)
    {
        double sum = 0;
        for (int i = 1; i <= n; i++)
        {
            if (i % 2 == 1)
                sum = sum + (x / i);
            else
                sum = sum - (x / i);
        }
        System.out.println("Sum of series = " + sum);
    }
    public void SumSeries()
    {
        long sum = 0;
        for (int i = 1; i <= 20; i++)
        {
            long product = 1;
            for (int j = 1; j <= i; j++)
            {
                product = product * j;
            }
            sum = sum + product;
        }
        System.out.println("Sum of series = " + sum);
    }
}
```

Design a class to overload a function `area()` as follows:

(i) `double area(double a, double b, double c)` with three double arguments, returns the area of a scalene triangle using the formula:

$$area = \sqrt{s(s-a)(s-b)(s-c)} \qquad \text{where } s = \frac{a+b+c}{2}$$

(ii) `double area(int a, int b, int height)` with three integer arguments, returns the area of a trapezium using the formula:

$$area = \frac{1}{2} height(a+b)$$

(iii) `double area(double diagonal1, double diagonal2)` with two double arguments, returns the area of a rhombus using the formula:

$$area = \frac{1}{2}(diagonal1 * diagonal2)$$

Listing 6.8: AreaOverload.java

```java
public class AreaOverload
{
   public double area(double a, double b, double c)
   {
      double s = (a + b + c) / 2;
      double area = Math.sqrt(s * (s - a) * (s - b) * (s - c));
      return area;
   }
   public double area(int a, int b, int height)
   {
      double area = 0.5 * height * (a + b);
      return area;
   }
   public double area(double diagonal1, double diagonal2)
   {
      double area = 0.5 * (diagonal1 * diagonal2);
      return area;
   }
}
```

Design a class to overload a function `polygon()` as follows:

(i) `void polygon(int n, char ch)`: with one integer argument and one character type argument that draws a filled square of side `n` using the character stored in `ch`.

(ii) `void polygon(int x, int y)`: with two integer arguments that draws a filled rectangle of length `x` and breadth `y`, using the symbol '@'

(iii) `void polygon()`: with no argument that draws a filled triangle shown below.

Example:

(i) Input value of n=2, ch='O'
Output:
O O
O O

(ii) Input value of x=2, y=5
Output:
@ @ @ @ @
@ @ @ @ @

(iii) Output:
```
*
* *
* * *
```

Listing 6.9: PolygonOverload.java

```java
1  public class PolygonOverload
2  {
3     public void polygon(int n, char ch)
4     {
5        for (int i = 1; i <= n; i++)
6        {
7           for (int j = 1; j <= n; j++)
8           {
9              System.out.print(ch);
10          }
11          System.out.println();
12       }
13    }
14    public void polygon(int x, int y)
15    {
16       for (int i = 1; i <= x; i++)
17       {
18          for (int j = 1; j <= y; j++)
19          {
20             System.out.print("@");
21          }
22          System.out.println();
23       }
24    }
25    public void polygon() {
26       for (int i = 1; i <= 3; i++)
27       {
28          for (int j = 1; j <= i; j++)
29          {
30             System.out.print("*");
31          }
32          System.out.println();
33       }
34    }
35 }
```

Multiple Choice Questions

1. A method that does not return a value has a .... return type.

    A. double   B. class   C. float   D. void

2. A method can return ....

A. any number of values   C. only 1 value

B. 2 values   D. 3 values

3. If a method returns a value, then it must be ....

    A. of the same data type as defined in its prototype

    B. `void` type

    C. `double` type

    D. `boolean` type

4. Parameters in the method definition are called ....

    A. actual parameters   C. informal parameters

    B. formal parameters   D. void parameters

5. The parameters that are passed to the method when it is invoked are called ....

    A. formal parameters   C. informal parameters

    B. actual parameters   D. void parameters

6. The method that changes the state of an object is known as ....

    A. pure method   C. perfect method

    B. impure method   D. imperfect method

7. The scope of a local variable is limited to the ....

    A. Windows   C. Class

    B. Multiple programs   D. Method or block it is declared in

8. The technique in which the change in the formal parameter gets reflected in the actual parameter is known as ....

    A. call by reference   C. call by argument

    B. call by value   D. call by method

9. In which technique are the values of actual parameters copied to the formal parameters?

    A. Windows   C. Class

    B. Multiple programs   D. Method or block it is declared in

10. A method with many definitions is known as ....

A. many method

B. multiple method

C. void method

D. overloaded method

| State whether the given statements are True or False: |

☐ A method may contain any number of **return** statements.

☐ The non-static methods need an instance to be called.

☐ A method can return more than one value.

☐ Methods defined as **void** must return a value.

☐ The **static** methods need an instance to be called.

☐ In Java, all primitive types are passed by value and all reference types are passed by reference.

☐ You can place the **return** statement in a **void** method without any expression.

☐ If a method returns a value, then it must be of the same data type as defined in the method prototype.

☐ Parameters in the method definition are called dummy parameters.

☐ Methods reside in a class in Java.

☐ Method overloading is one of the ways by which Java implements polymorphism.

☐ The scope of a local variable is limited to the method or the block it is declared in.

☐ The keyword **static** makes a method a class method.

☐ An impure method always returns the same value when the same arguments are given.

| Assignment Questions |

1. What is a method? Explain the various parts of a method.

2. What is a method signature?

3. How do you define and invoke a method?

4. What does the **return** statement do in a method?

5. What does **void** signify in the method prototype?

6. Explain the difference between actual and formal parameters.

7. Explain **static** and non-static methods.

8. What happens when an argument is passed by reference?

9. When a method has been declared more than once in a class, how does Java determine the overloading?

10. What is an ambiguous invocation? Give an example.

11. Given below are the two method definitions:

(i) `public static double Check(double x, double y)`

(ii) `public static double Check(int x, double y)`

Which of the two methods is invoked for the following?

(i) `double z = Check (6, 5);`

(ii) `double z = Check (5.5, 7.4);`

12. . What is the signature of the following method heading?

`public void CoolMethod(int xx, char yy, int zz)`

13. Which OOP principle implements function (method) overloading?

14. A palindromic prime is a prime number and also palindromic. For example, 131, 313, and 757 are prime numbers and also palindromic prime numbers. Write a program that displays the first 100 palindromic prime numbers.

15. Differentiate between the following:

(i) Call by value and Call by reference

(ii) Pure and Impure methods

(iii) Simple Method and Overloaded method

Answers To Objective Questions

Multiple Choice Questions

1. D	3. A	5. B	7. D	9. B
2. C	4. B	6. B	8. A	10. D

True or False

1. True	3. False	5. False	7. True	9. True	11. True	13. True
2. True	4. False	6. True	8. True	10. True	12. True	14. False

Chapter 7

Input in Java

Input in Java

MOST useful applications or programs have some flexibility built into them, and they can produce different results when provided with a different set of data. Generally, the user of the program provides this data, and thus has some control over the program execution. A common term, known as data entry, is used to represent the activity of the program that accepts data from the user. So far you have been using literals or have assigned values to variables to use data in your program. However, in addition to these, there are a number of other ways to input data to a program or an application. For example, the keyboard, mouse, disk files and network. In this chapter, we will discuss the following three types of data input techniques in Java:

(i) Input using Initialisation or literals

(ii) Input using Parameters (BlueJ)

(iii) Input using Scanner Class

Before we delve into these techniques, first let us learn about an important concept, packages in Java.

7.1   Introduction to Packages

A *package* is a named collection of Java classes that are grouped on the basis of their functionality.

A package can be understood like a toolbox. The toolbox contains various tools, each providing a special functionality. Similarly, the package contains multiple classes each providing a special functionality, that can be used as and when required.

Classes within a package can access each other's non-private members, which can save you programming effort and make it more efficient to access their data. Moreover, while programming large projects comprising thousands of lines of code, the programmers face a challenge of providing each class with a unique class name. For example, if the programmer defines a class named `"Math"`, then this class would conflict with the `Math` class in the Java library.

Java packages help us resolve this sort of unique challenges. You can define multiple classes that have the same name, provided these classes belong to different packages.

Packages can be compiled separately and imported into your code. Together with the access modifiers, packages provide the means for implementing encapsulation because they allow you to distribute your classes as *Bytecode* files.

7.1.1 Common Packages in Java

Java provides a number of built-in methods and features that are all stored in a named package. These pre-written classes (packages) can easily be used in your programs. Figure 7.1 shows some commonly used packages.

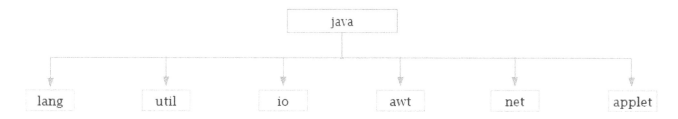

Figure 7.1: Java Packages

A package that is contained in another package is called a *sub-package*. As can be observed in the diagram, a number of standard sub-packages are included in the java package. One of the commonly used sub-packages in `java` is the `util` package. Since `util` is contained within the `java` package, it is written as `java.util`. Table 7.1 shows a brief description of the classes contained within the `java` package.

Package	Short Description
java.lang	Provides classes that are fundamental to the design of the Java programming language such as primitive data types, String, and Math functions.
java.util	Provides classes for printing, scanning, etc.
java.io	Provides classes for input and output of data.
java.awt	Provides classes to implement Graphical User Interfaces.
java.net	Provides classes for networking.
java.applet	Provides classes for implementing applets.

Table 7.1: Classes in the Java Package

These packages are organised in a hierarchical structure. Figure 7.2 shows a graphical representation of the nesting levels in the Java packages. Here nesting refers to a package containing a sub-package, the sub-package containing another package and so on. For example, the java package contains the util package, which in turn contains various classes required to implement the scanning and printing.

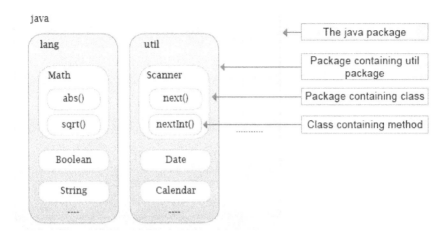

Figure 7.2: Nesting in Java Packages

The class that implements the scanning features is known as the **Scanner** class. Since this class is contained in the `java.util` package, its complete name is `java.util.Scanner`.

7.1.2   Using Packages

Let us now understand how to incorporate built-in Java packages in the programs. In doing so, you will learn to use the Calendar class of the java.util package. The Calendar class is an abstract class[1] that provides methods for converting between a specific instant in time and a set of calendar fields such as YEAR, MONTH, DAY_OF_MONTH, HOUR, and so on. Consider the following program that displays the current date using the Calendar class of the java.util package.

Listing 7.1: CalendarClassDemo.java

```
1  public class CalendarClassDemo
2  {
3      public static void main(String args[])
4      {                                                       Fully qualified name
5          java.util.Calendar   cal = java.util.Calendar.getInstance();
6
7          String strDate="Today is: " + cal.get(java.util.Calendar.DATE) +
8                  "/" + (cal.get(java.util.Calendar.MONTH) + 1) +
9                  "/" + cal.get( java.util.Calendar.YEAR );
10
11         System.out.println(strDate);          Fully qualified name
12     }
13 }
```

Output

Today is: 20/4/2019

---

[1]An abstract class is a class that is declared with the abstract keyword. Abstract classes cannot be instantiated, but they can be subclassed.

Code Walkthrough:

◈ Line 5: Creates a `Calendar` object named `cal` and gets a calendar using the default time zone and locale.

◈ Line 7: Uses the `get` method to get the value of the calendar field `Date`. This field stores the day of the month. The first day of the month has value 1.

◈ Line 8: Uses the `get` method to get the value of the calendar field `Month`. This field stores the month of the year. The first month of the year in the Gregorian and Julian calendars is JANUARY, which has a value 0. Hence, 1 has been added to the month value.

◈ Line 9: Uses the `get` method to get the value of the calendar field `Year`. This field stores the year and is calendar-specific.

In the above example, the `Calendar` class within the `java.util` package is said to be used with a fully qualified name. The fully qualified name of a class includes its package name. Thus, the fully qualified name of the `Calendar` class is `java.util.Calendar`. Its non-qualified name is just `Calendar`. However, if you try to use a non-qualified name (i.e., without `java.util`), BlueJ will throw an error as shown in Figure 7.3.

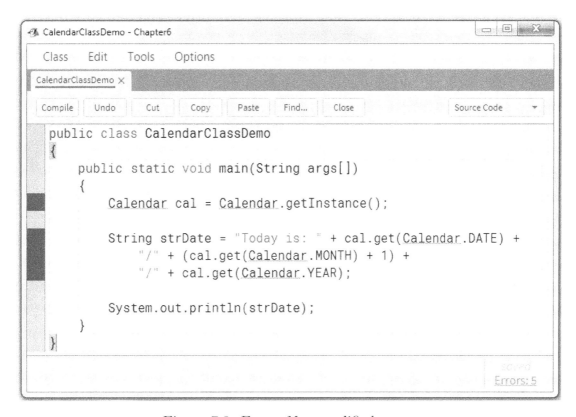

Figure 7.3: Error: Non-qualified name

As evident from the program, it can be a tedious task to type long, dot-separated names every time you use the class. For this reason, Java provides a feature called `import` statement to bring certain classes or an entire package into the current program. Once imported, a class can be referred directly, using only its name.

7.1.3 Importing Packages

The import statement allows a program to refer to classes defined in other packages without using the fully qualified class names. Its syntax is:

```
import package1[.package2] [.package3].classname;
```

Here package1 is the name of the top-level package, package2 is the name of the package that is inside package1, and so on (even beyond package3, if needed). You can have any number of packages in a package hierarchy. Finally, specify the explicit classname.

The syntax error that occurred in the previous example (see Figure 7.3) can be resolved using an import statement. For example, the statement

```
import java.util.Calendar;
```

imports the Calendar class, and therefore the class name can now directly be used in the program. There is no need to use the package name to qualify the class. The import statement must appear at the top of the class file, before any declarations. Only blank lines, comments, and package statements may precede the list of import statements. Program 7.2 shows the updated code with an import statement.

Listing 7.2: CalendarClassDemo2.java

```
1  import java.util.Calendar;      ◄----------------- import statement
2
3  public class CalendarClassDemo2
4  {
5      public static void main(String args[])
6      {                                              ----- Non-qualified name
7          Calendar  cal = Calendar.getInstance();
8
9          String strDate = "Today is: " + cal.get(Calendar.DATE) +
10             "/" + (cal.get(Calendar.MONTH) + 1) +
11             "/" + cal.get( Calendar.YEAR );
12                                         ---------------- Non-qualified name
13         System.out.println(strDate);
14     }
15 }
```

Code Walkthrough:
◈ Line 1: The import statement makes the Calendar class available for use in your program.
◈ Line 7, 9, 10, and 11. The Calendar class in the package java.util can now be used directly, i.e., without typing the package name.

Instead of the classname, you can also use an asterisk (*), known as a wildcard character, which indicates that the Java compiler should import the entire package. For example:

```
import java.util.*;
```

The above statement will import all the classes in the `java.util` package.

7.1.4 Advantages of using Packages

A package is Java's way of forming a library of classes. There are a number of advantages of using packages, such as:

(i) Packages group related classes so that they can be managed effectively.

(ii) The classes contained in other packages can easily be reused.

(iii) You can declare multiple classes with the same name in different packages.

(iv) Encapsulation can be implemented by using packages.

7.2 Input using Initialisation or Literals

You can provide inputs to a program by initialising variables with the desired values or providing literal values. In this form of input, the required data is decided before the program execution starts. This form of input is also referred to as "hard-coded values". Let us understand this concept using the following example which calculates the volume of a sphere.

Listing 7.3: Sphere.java

```java
1  public class Sphere
2  {
3     public static void main(String args [])
4     {
5        double radius ;
6        //Initialse radius with the desired value
7        radius = 5;
8        double volume = SphereVolume(radius );
9        System.out.println("Volume of sphere with radius " + radius + " ↵
              ↳ is " +  volume );
10
11       //Use literal value 7.8 to calculate volume
12       volume = SphereVolume(7.8) ;
13       System.out.println("Volume of sphere with radius 7.8 is " + ↵
              ↳ volume );
14    }
15
16    public static double SphereVolume(double rad)
17    {
18       double vol = 4.0/3.0 * Math .PI * Math . pow (rad , 3);
```

		Output
19	`return vol ;`	Volume of sphere with radius 5.0 is 523.5987755982989
20	`}`	Volume of sphere with radius 7.8 is 1987.798769261791
21	`}`	

The main drawback of this type of data input technique is that whenever a programmer needs to get an output using a different set of input values, the program has to be modified and recompiled. This can be a cumbersome task! Thus, to avoid the modification and recompilation, the technique of Input using Parameters can be used.

7.3 Input using Parameters (BlueJ)

In this form of input, the required data is decided at the time of program execution. The variables whose values are to be input must be used as parameters to the method. Let us understand this form of input with the following example.

Write a program that uses parameters as the form of input to compute simple interest.

Listing 7.4: ComputeSimpleInterest.java

```
1  public class ComputeSimpleInterest
2  {
3      public double SimpleInterest(double principal, double rate, double ↵
          ↪ time)
4      {
5          double interest = (principal * rate * time)/100.0;
6          return interest ;
7      }
8  }
```

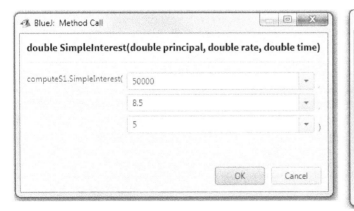

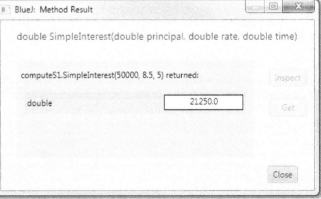

7.4 Input using the Scanner Class

The Scanner class is the latest development in Java and was introduced in JDK 5. The Scanner class reads the input data from a stream and converts it into values of various data types, thus making it easier for the programmer to read all types of numeric values, strings, and other types of data. The Scanner class is in the java.util package. The following line, which should be placed near the start of your program file, tells Java where to find the definition of the Scanner class:

```
import java.util.Scanner;
```

Before we proceed further, the term 'stream' needs some explanation, so let us understand it first.

What is a Stream?

Java programs perform Input/Output (I/O) operations using streams. A stream is a path along which the data flows. It transfers data from a source to a destination.

A stream can be understood like a hose pipe along with which the water flows, as shown in Figure. In this illustration, the water container is the source, shrubs are the destination, and the pipe serves as the stream which carries water (data).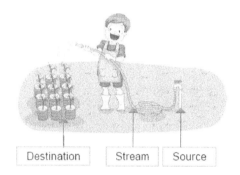

As an analogy, you input data to a program via the keyboard (source). The data is then stored in the computer memory (destination) for further processing. The keyboard uses a special stream called System.in to transfer the entered data to its destination. The output of this stream is in bytes as shown in Figure 7.4.

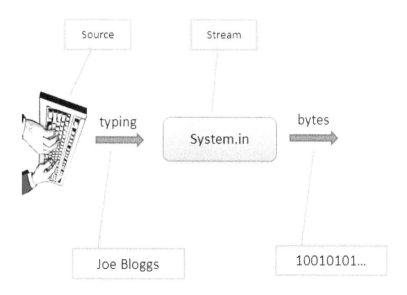

Figure 7.4: Data Input using System.in

`System.in` stream is known as the *Standard Input*. Therefore, whenever in a program you need input from the keyboard, you can use the `System.in` stream.

`System.out` is another stream that is used as the *Standard Output* (display monitor). You have been using the `println()` method of the `System.out` stream to print your program output on the screen. BlueJ considers this standard output as the Terminal Window.

7.4.1 The Scanner Class

Figure 7.5 shows the schematic representation of a user entering data using the keyboard and the `Scanner` class. Note that the `Scanner` class can be used to read input from the keyboard, a file, a string, or any other source.

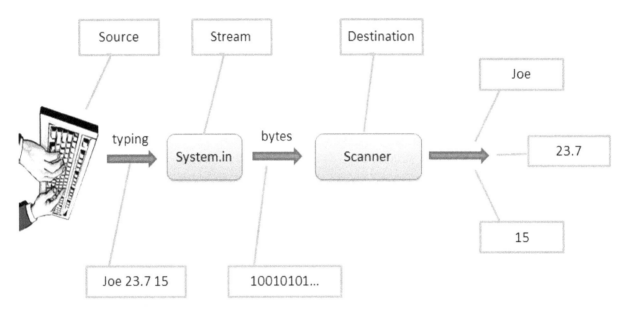

Figure 7.5: Data Input using Scanner Class

How does the Scanner work?

The input received by the Scanner class is broken into tokens using a delimiter pattern. A delimiter is a sequence of one or more characters that separates two tokens. The default delimiter is a whitespace (the space bar). Whitespace is any string of characters, such as blank spaces, tabs, and line breaks. Figure 7.6 shows the entered data using the default delimiter. Figure 7.7 shows the entered data using the comma delimiter.

> **Note**
>
> To use the Scanner Class, you would need JDK 5 or a later version, along with the BlueJ 2.5 or a later version.

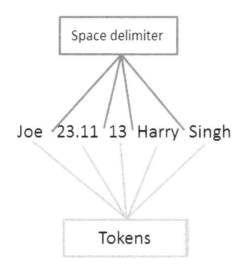

Figure 7.6: Tokens with Space Delimiter

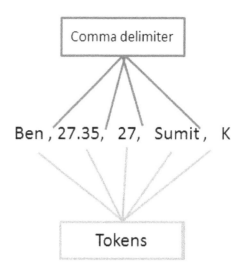

Figure 7.7: Tokens with Comma Delimiter

You can use methods of the Scanner class to read tokens (data) that the user types on the keyboard. Sometimes, you may need to convert these tokens into different formats. Java provides various **next** methods to convert the entered tokens into the required data type values. For example, to read the next input token as a `float`, you can invoke the `nextFloat()` method of the `Scanner` class. The following table lists various next methods along with their usage.

Method	Short Description
next()	This method is used to read the next complete token (until the delimiter is encountered) from the Scanner object. It returns the token as a string value.
nextLine()	This method is used to read a complete line of text. It returns the token as a `String` value.
nextShort()	This method is used to read a short. It returns the token as a `short` value.
nextInt()	This method is used to read an integer. It returns the token as an integer value.
nextLong()	This method is used to read a long. It returns the token as a long integer value.
nextFloat()	This method is used to read a float. It returns the token as a `float` value.
nextDouble()	This method is used to read a double. It returns the token as a double value.
next().charAt(0)	This method is used to read the complete token, and then the first character is returned using the `charAt(0)` method.

While reading the input, if a token cannot be converted to the desired type (for example, if you try to read "xyz" as an integer via the `nextInt()` method), a runtime error will occur. You can avoid this runtime error by making sure that the specified type of input is available via the `hasNext()` method. For example, you can use the `hasNextInt()` method before using the `nextInt()` method to ensure that an integer data type token is available to read before attempting to convert it, thereby preventing a possible runtime error. Following Table lists various `hasNext` methods and their usage.

Method	Short Description
hasNext()	Returns true if this scanner has another token in its input.
hasNextLine()	Returns true if this scanner has another line in its input.
hasNextShort()	Returns true if the next token in this scanner's input can be interpreted as a short value.
hasNextInt()	Returns true if the next token in this scanner's input can be interpreted as an int value.
hasNextLong()	Returns true if the next token in this scanner's input can be interpreted as a long value.
hasNextFloat()	Returns true if the next token in this scanner's input can be interpreted as a float value.
hasNextDouble()	Returns true if the next token in this scanner's input can be interpreted as a double value.

7.4.2 Creating the Scanner Object

To read data from the keyboard, you need to create an object of the `Scanner` type which accepts the `System.in` stream as an input source. The `new` operator is used to create an instance of the `Scanner` class. Figure 7.8 shows the syntax of creating a scanner object named `keyboard`.

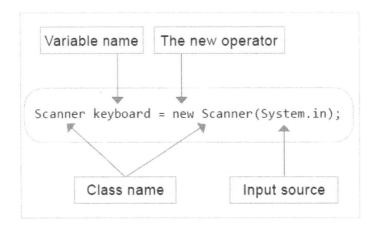

Figure 7.8: Creating the Scanner Object

Let us put all this knowledge into practice and write some programs using the **Scanner** class.

Listing 7.5: NextMethods.java

```
1  import java.util.Scanner;
2
3  public class NextMethods
4  {
5      public static void main(String args[])
6      {
7          Scanner keyboard = new Scanner(System.in);
8
9          System.out.print("Enter a sentence: ");
10         String strValue = keyboard.nextLine();
11
12         System.out.print("Enter an integer value: ");
13         int intValue = keyboard.nextInt();
14
15         System.out.print("Enter a long value: ");
16         long longValue = keyboard.nextLong();
17
18         System.out.print("Enter a double value: ");
19         double dblValue = keyboard.nextDouble();
20
21         System.out.print("Enter a character value: ");
22         char charValue = keyboard.next().charAt(0);
23
24         System.out.println("You entered the following data:");
25         System.out.println("line: " + strValue);
26         System.out.println("int: " + intValue);
27         System.out.println("long: " + longValue);
28         System.out.println("double: " + dblValue);
29         System.out.println("char: " + charValue);
30
31         keyboard.close();
32     }
33 }
```

Output

```
Enter a sentence: Better late than never
Enter an integer value: -45
Enter a long value: 1234567890
Enter a double value: 1729.45
Enter a character value: z
You entered the following data:
line: Better late than never
int: -45
long: 1234567890
double: 1729.45
char: z
```

Code Walkthrough:

◈ Line 1: The import statement makes the `Scanner` class available for use in your code.

◈ Line 7: Uses the **new** operator to create an instance **keyboard** of the `Scanner` class which takes `System.in` as an input source.

◈ Line 31: Closes the Scanner, and no further inputs are accepted by the computer.

Write a program by using class `Employee` to accept Basic Pay of an employee. Calculate the allowance/deductions as given below. Finally, find and print the Gross and Net Pay.

Allowance/Deduction	Rate
Dearness Allowance (DA)	30% of Basic Pay
House Rent Allowance (HRA)	15% of Basic Pay
Provident Fund (PF)	12.5% of Basic Pay

```
Gross Pay = Basic Pay + Dearness Allowance + House Rent Allowance
Net Pay = Gross Pay - Provident Fund
```

Listing 7.6: Employee.java

```java
1  import java.util.Scanner;
2  public class Employee
3  {
4      public static void main(String args[])
5      {
6          Scanner scanner = new Scanner(System.in);
7
8          System.out.print("Enter Basic Pay: ");
9          double basicPay = scanner.nextDouble();
10
11         double dearnessAllowance = basicPay * 0.3; //30% of Basic Pay
12         double houseAllowance = basicPay * 0.15;    //15% of Basic Pay
13         double providentFund = basicPay * 0.125;    //12.5% of Basic Pay
14         double grossPay = basicPay + dearnessAllowance + houseAllowance;
15         double netPay = grossPay - providentFund;
16
17         System.out.println("Gross Pay: " + grossPay);
18         System.out.println("Net Pay: " + netPay);
19         scanner.close();
20     }
21 }
```

```
Output
Enter Basic Pay: 25000
Gross Pay: 36250.0
Net Pay: 33125.0
```

7.4.3 Using Delimiters

The inputs to a program on a single line may not be of the same data types. For example, Figure 7.9 shows a data input which contains tokens of different data types – String, int, double, char. Moreover, the entered line may be delimited by one or more whitespaces.

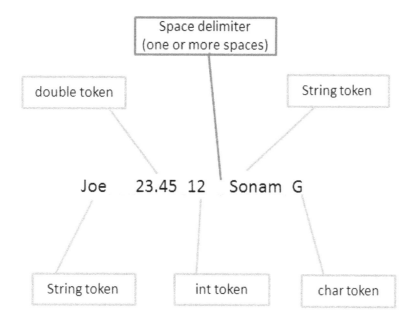

Figure 7.9: Mixed Input Tokens Delimited by Whitespaces

Let us consider an example where different types of data are entered on a single line, delimited by one or more whitespaces.

Write a program in Java to read the input as a single line "Joe 23.45 12 Sonam G" (delimited by one or more whitespaces) via the Scanner class and display the individual tokens.

Listing 7.7: WhitespaceDelimiter.java

```java
import java.util.Scanner;
public class WhitespaceDelimiter
{
    public static void main(String args[])
    {
        Scanner keyboard = new Scanner(System.in);

        System.out.print("Enter the input line: ");
        String str1Token = keyboard.next();           //Token1
        double dblToken = keyboard.nextDouble();       //Token2
        int intToken = keyboard.nextInt();             //Token3
        String str2Token = keyboard.next();            //Token4
```

```
13        char charToken = keyboard.next().charAt(0); //Token5
14        System.out.println("Token1 => String is: " + str1Token);
15        System.out.println("Token2 => double is: " + dblToken);
16        System.out.println("Token3 => int is: " + intToken);
17        System.out.println("Token4 => String is: " + str2Token);
18        System.out.println("Token5 => char is: " + charToken);
19
20        keyboard.close();
21    }
22 }
```

```
Output
Enter the input line: Joe 23.45 12 Sonam G
Token1 => String is: Joe
Token2 => double is: 23.45
Token3 => int is: 12
Token4 => String is: Sonam
Token5 => char is: G
```

Code Walkthrough:

◈ Line 9: Reads the first token as a **String** value.

◈ Line 10: Reads the next token as a **double** value. Automatically handles more than one space in the delimiter before reading the token.

Let us consider the following example where different types of data are entered on a single line, delimited by comma.

Write a program in Java to read the input as a single line "Joe, 23.45, 12, Sonam, G" (delimited by comma and one or more whitespaces) via the **Scanner** class and display the individual tokens.

Listing 7.8: CommaDelimiter.java

```
1  import java.util.Scanner;
2  public class CommaDelimiter
3  {
4      public static void main(String args[])
5      {
6          Scanner keyboard = new Scanner(System.in);
7          keyboard.useDelimiter("\n|, *");
8
9          System.out.print("Enter the input line: ");
10         String str1Token = keyboard.next();          //Token1
11         double dblToken = keyboard.nextDouble();      //Token2
12         int intToken = keyboard.nextInt();            //Token3
13         String str2Token = keyboard.next();           //Token4
14         char charToken = keyboard.next().charAt(0);   //Token5
15
16         System.out.println("Token1 => String is: " + str1Token);
17         System.out.println("Token2 => double is: " + dblToken);
18         System.out.println("Token3 => int is: " + intToken);
```

```
19        System.out.println("Token4 => String is: " + str2Token);
20        System.out.println("Token5 => char is: " + charToken);
21
22        keyboard.close();
23    }
24 }
```

Output

Enter the input line: Joe, 23.45, 12, Sonam, G
Token1 => String is: Joe
Token2 => double is: 23.45
Token3 => int is: 12
Token4 => String is: Sonam
Token5 => char is: G

Code Walkthrough:

◈ Line 7: The delimiter pattern "\n|, *" tells the Scanner to use either of the following patterns as the delimiter (here, the pipe character '|' denotes the or):

- an Enter key on the keyboard represented by '\n', or

- a comma and zero or more spaces represented by ", *".
  Note that character '*' here denotes any number of spaces after comma.

Note that while using the Scanner class for keyboard input, you can change the delimiters that separate keyboard input to almost any combination of characters.

7.5   Types of Errors

Errors are mistakes in a program that prevent it from its normal working. In programming terms, errors are often referred to as bugs.

It is very common to make mistakes while typing a program or developing its logic. There is no doubt that even well versed and highly experienced programmers make mistakes. If a program contains errors, it can lead to wrong results or sometimes no results at all. An error may abruptly terminate the execution of a program or sometimes may crash the system. It is, therefore, important to find and fix the errors so that programs can perform their specified tasks. The process of finding and eliminating errors is called debugging. Errors are broadly classified into three categories as defined in the following sub-sections.

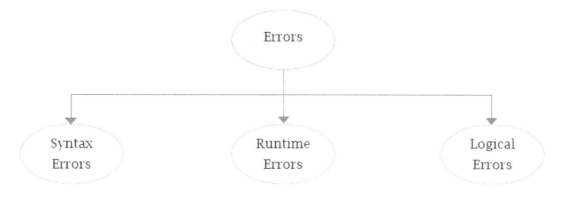

Figure 7.10: Types of Errors

7.5.1 Syntax Errors

As the name suggests, syntax errors occur due to the fact that the syntax of the programming language has not been followed correctly. Syntax errors are analogous to spelling or grammatical mistakes in a language such as English. These errors are reported by the compiler and prevent your program from running.

> **Definition**
>
> Syntax is the arrangement of tokens to create well-formed statements in a programming language.

Syntax errors are the easiest to find and fix. Over the years, language compilers have become so smart that they can catch errors at compile time which might otherwise turn out to be runtime errors.

Common syntax errors in Java include the following:

(i) Missing semicolon after a statement.

Syntax error	*Correct version*
| ```
int sum
sum++
``` | ```
int sum;
sum++;
``` |

(ii) Missing or unmatched brackets.

Syntax error	*Correct version*
| ```
public void DisplayMethod
{
    System.out.print("Java");
``` | ```
public void DisplayMethod
{
    System.out.print("Java");
}
``` |

(iii) Incorrect spelling of keywords or identifiers.
In this example, the keyword `static` is misspelled, and the identifier counter is spelled with zero (0) instead of o.

Syntax error	*Correct version*
| ```
public statc void Hello()
{
    int counter;
    c0unter++;
}
``` | ```
public static void Hello()
{
    int counter;
    counter++;
}
``` |

(iv) Using variables that have not been defined but are being used in the program. In this example, the compiler will report a syntax error because the variable `sum` has not been declared and initialised.

Syntax error

```
public void TestMethod()
{
    sum--;
}
```

Correct version

```
public void TestMethod()
{
    int sum = 0;
    sum--;
}
```

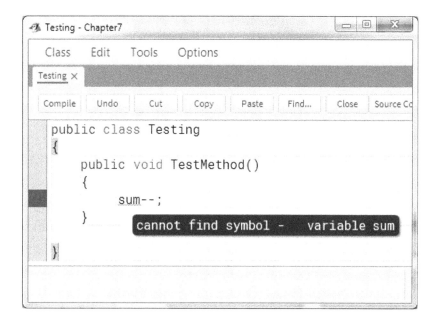

Figure 7.11: Syntax Error

(v) Missing double quotes in a string or single quotes in a character.

Syntax error

```
System.out.print("Hi there!);
System.out.print(K');
```

Correct version

```
System.out.print("Hi there!");
System.out.print('K');
```

(vi) Using an assignment operator (=) instead of an equality operator (==).

Syntax error

```
z = (x = y) ? x : y;
```

Correct version

```
z = (x == y) ? x : y;
```

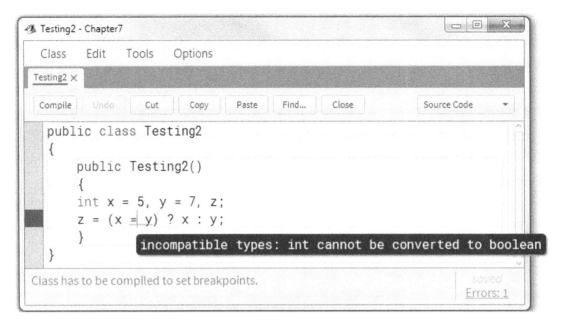

Figure 7.12: Syntax Error

(vii) Incompatible assignments, for example, assigning a string value "322" to an integer variable.

Syntax error	_Correct version_
`int myInt = "322";`	`int myInt = 322;`

(viii) Using uppercase characters in keywords, e.g., IF instead of if.

You might already have encountered a number of syntax errors while writing programs in Java so far. All syntax errors are detected and reported by the Java compiler at the time of compilation. Therefore, these types of errors are also referred to as compile-time errors.

7.5.2   Runtime Errors

A runtime error occurs during the execution of a program. The program may compile successfully but may not run properly as planned or may not execute at all. In programming terms, you say that the program has crashed. In some instances, the operating system may have to be rebooted. Such a program is syntactically correct, i.e., free from syntax errors, but a problem is detected when one of the statements is executed.

Consider the instruction in the English language Fly to New York. This instruction is structurally correct and is understandable, but it is not possible to follow it as it does not make a complete sense. Same is the case with the runtime errors, where the computer is unable to follow the given instruction.

These types of errors are not detected by compiler during the compilation process. Generally, detection and removal of runtime errors is a difficult task.

Definition

Runtime is when a program is running or being executed.

Some common runtime errors you may encounter are as follows:

(i) Divide by zero error.

```
int p = 13, q = 5, r = 10;
int result;
result = p/(q*2 - r); //division by zero error
```

(ii) Parsing an invalid string into a numeric value.

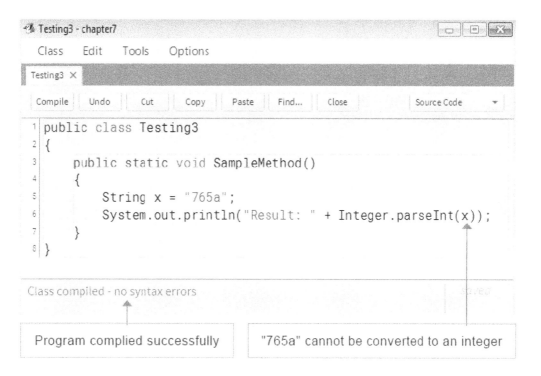

Figure 7.13: Invalid Parsing

(iii) Entering a string value where a numeric value is expected for the **Scanner** object.

```
Scanner keyboard = new Scanner(System.in);
System.out.println("Enter Roll Number: ");
int rollNumber = keyboard.nextInt();
```

Entering a non-integer value, R123 for the "Roll Number" will cause a runtime error as shown in Figure 7.14.

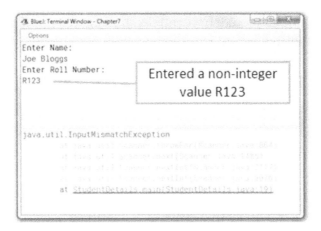

Figure 7.14: Runtime Error Example

(iv) Running out of memory during program execution.

(v) Trying to access a data file which does not exist.

7.5.3 Logical Errors

When a program compiles and runs without errors but produces an incorrect result, this type of error is known as logical error. It is caused by a mistake in the program logic which is often due to human error. Logical errors are the most difficult to fix because you do not get an error message as no syntax or runtime error has occurred.

Logical errors are also not detected by compiler. These errors occur due to:

(i) incorrect conversion of algorithm into the program,

(ii) poor understanding of the problem, and

(iii) a lack of clarity of precedence and associativity of operators.

Here are some examples of mistakes which lead to logical errors:

(i) Using the wrong variable name.

```java
public int FindMax()
{
    int x = 17, int y = 23;
    int max;
    max = (x > y) ? x : y;
    return x; //returning wrong variable, max should be returned
}
```

(ii) Using integer division by mistake instead of the floating-point division. For example, given x, y, and z are all int, using:

```
        (x + y + z)/3;
```
instead of:
```
        (x + y + z)/3.0;
```
to compute the average.

(iii) Using operators without understanding their precedence and associativity. For example, using:
```
        x + y / z;
```
instead of:
```
        (x + y) / z;
```

(iv) Displaying the wrong message.

Note that a program with logical errors may produce correct results for some input data and wrong results for other input data.

Multiple Choice Questions

1. A programmer wrote the following statement:
```
        netPay = grossPay + providentFund;
```
   instead of:
```
        netPay = grossPay - providentFund;
```

   Assuming all the unseen code is correct, what kind of error is it?

   A. Syntax error   C. Logical error

   B. Runtime error   D. None of the above

2. Which of the following might make the Java compiler report a syntax error in a particular line of a program?

   A. The program is typed in the wrong font.

   B. The line contains a comma (,) instead of a dot (.).

   C. It is caused by Java runtime.

   D. Program takes too long to compile.

3. Which of the following statement is true for logical errors?

   A. The compiler does not detect these errors.

   B. There is no indication of error when the program is executed.

   C. The program may produce correct results for some input data and wrong results for other input data.

   D. All of the above

4. Which keyword do you use to include a class in your program?

A. import   B. export   C. include   D. impart

5. Which of the following is not a valid method of the Scanner class?

     A. `next()`   C. `nextLong()`

     B. `nextInt()`   D. `NextNumber()`

6. Default delimiter used in the Scanner class is ....

     A. Comma   C. Colon

     B. Whitespace   D. There is no default delimiter.

7. Which package would you import to display the date and time?

     A. `java.util .*`   C. `java.io.*`

     B. `java .Date.*`   D. `java.lang.*`

8. Which package would you import for the Scanner class?

     A. `java.util .*`   C. `java.io.*`

     B. `java.awt.*`   D. `java.lang.*`

9. Errors occur in a program when ....

     A. Syntax of the programming language is not followed.

     B. The program does not run properly or does not execute at all.

     C. The program produces an incorrect result.

     D. All of the above

10. The Scanner class can be used to read input from ....

     A. A keyboard   C. A string

     B. A file   D. All of the above

Assignment Questions

1. Suppose you want to use the class `MyClass` of the package `MyPackage.UtilityLibrary` in a program you are writing. What do you need to do to make the following?

     (i) class MyClass available to your program

     (ii) all the classes of the package available to your program

2. Explain data input technique in a program using the `Scanner` class.

3. What are delimiters? Which is the default delimiter used in the `Scanner` class?

4. What are errors in a program?

5. Explain the following terms, giving an example of each.

(i) Syntax error   (iii) Logical error

(ii) Runtime error

6. If a student forgot to put a closing quotation mark on a string, what kind error would occur?

7. A program has compiled successfully without any errors. Does this mean the program is error free? Explain.

8. A program needed to read an integer, but the user entered a string instead, and an error occurred when the program was executed. What kind of error is this?

9. A student was asked to write a program for computing the area of a rectangle and he, mistakenly, wrote the program to compute the perimeter of a rectangle. What kind of error is this?

10. What is a java package? Give an example.

11. Explain the use of `import` statement with an example.

12. Distinguish between the following:

    (i) `next()` and `nextLine()`   (iii) `next()` and `hasNext()`

    (ii) `next()` and `next().charAt(0)`   (iv) `hasNext()` and `hasNextLine()`

13. Consider the following input:
```
one, two three, four, five
```

What values will the following code assign to the variables `input1` and `input2`?
```
String input1 = keyboard.next();
String input2 = keyboard.next();
```

14. Write a line of code that:

    (i) Creates a `Scanner` object named `scanner` to be used for taking keyboard input.

    (ii) Uses the object `scanner` to read a word from the keyboard and store it in the `String` variable named `stg`.

15. Write a code that creates a `Scanner` object and sets its delimiter to the dollar sign.

16. Write a statement to let the user enter an integer or a `double` value from the keyboard.

17. Write a program in Java that takes input using the `Scanner` class to calculate the Simple Interest and the Compound Interest with the given values:

    (i) Principle Amount = $1,00,000

    (ii) Rate = 3.5%

    (iii) Time = 5 years

Display the following output:

(i) Simple interest

(ii) Compound interest

(iii) Absolute value of the difference between the simple and compound interest.

18. Write a program to compute the Time Period (T) of a Simple Pendulum as per the following formula:

$$T = 2\pi\sqrt{\frac{L}{g}}$$

Input the value of L (Length of Pendulum) and g (gravity) using the **Scanner** class.

19. Write a program that takes the distance of the commute in kilometres, the car fuel consumption rate in kilometre per gallon, and the price of a gallon of petrol as input. The program should then display the cost of the commute.

20. Write a program in Java that accepts the seconds as input and converts them into the corresponding number of hours, minutes and seconds. A sample output is shown below:

```
Output
Enter Total Seconds:
5000
1 Hour(s) 23 Minute(s) 20 Second(s)
```

21. Write a program in Java, using the Scanner methods, to read and display the following details:

  Name - as a **String** data type
  Roll Number - as an **integer** data type
  Marks in 5 subjects - as a **float** data type
  Compute and display the percentage of marks.

22. Write a Java program that reads a line of text separated by any number of whitespaces and outputs the line with correct spacing, that is, the output has no space before the first word and exactly one space between each pair of adjacent words.

Answers To Objective Questions

Multiple Choice Questions

1. C	3. D	5. D	7. A	9. D
2. B	4. A	6. B	8. A	10. D

Chapter 8

Mathematical Library Methods

Mathematical Library Methods

THE Java environment has a huge library of built-in classes that contain pre-defined methods to support a number of operations. Such classes are available to all Java programmers in the form of packages. The built-in package, `java.lang` contains many useful classes, and one of them is the `Math` class, usually referred to as the maths library. This class contains many useful methods for performing common mathematical functions. In this chapter, you will learn about the maths library and how to use its methods in your program.

8.1 Methods of the Math Class

The `java.lang` package contains classes and interfaces that are fundamental to the Java programming language. Usually, you have to import packages into your program to access the classes defined in them, but `java.lang` package is imported, by default, by the Java compiler because it is the frequently used package. The `Math` class of the `java.lang` package contains a lot of generic mathematical functions, including geometric and trigonometric functions. The generic syntax to access a member method is:

```
Math.MethodName(arguments);
```

> **Note**
>
> All members (methods and variables) of the `Math` class are defined as static members. Therefore, you can invoke them with the class name directly, without creating an instance of the class.

Some basic methods of the Math class are described below.

| | Math Class Methods | | |
Method	Syntax	Return Type	Short Description
pow	Math.pow(x, y)	double	Returns the value of the first argument, raised to the power of the second argument (x^y).
sqrt	Math.sqrt(x)	double	Returns the square root of a double value ($\sqrt{x}$).
cbrt	Math.cbrt(x)	double	Returns the cube root of a double value ($\sqrt[3]{x}$).
ceil	Math.ceil(x)	double	Returns the smallest integer that is greater than or equal to the argument.

Math Class Methods Contd...			
Method	*Syntax*	*Return Type*	*Short Description*
floor	Math.floor(x)	double	Returns the largest integer that is less than or equal to the argument.
round	Math.round(x)	If the argument type is double, the return type is long. If the argument type is float, the return type is int.	Returns the closest int or long (as per the argument).
abs	Math.abs(a)	Same as the argument.	Returns the absolute value of the argument.
max	Math.max(a, b)	Same as the argument.	Returns the largest of the two arguments.
min	Math.min(a, b)	Same as the argument.	Returns the smallest of the two arguments.
random	Math.random()	double	Returns a double value greater than or equal to 0.0 and less than 1.0.

8.2 Java Mathematical Expressions

You can use Math class methods to compute simple expressions, such as:

Square root: $\sqrt{x}$ using Math.sqrt(x) method

Power: z^3 using Math.pow(z, 3) method

Cube root: $\sqrt[3]{z}$ using Math.cbrt(z, 3) method

Absolute value: $|x|$ using Math.abs(x) method

Similarly, you can use the Math class methods to build complex mathematical expressions.

Table 8.1 lists various examples of converting mathematical expression to its equivalent Java expression.

Mathematical Expression	Java Expression

$r = a^2 + b^2$	r = Math.pow(a, 2) + Math.pow(b, 2);
	OR
	r = a*a + b*b;

$y = ax^3 + bx + c$	y = a*x*x*x + b*x + c;
	OR
	y = a*Math.pow(x, 3) + b*x + c;

$c = \sqrt{a^2 + b^2}$	c = Math.sqrt(a*a + b*b);
$z = x * 2^y$	z = x * Math.pow(2, y);
$x = \dfrac{-b - \sqrt{(b^2 - 4ac)}}{2a}$	x = (-b - Math.sqrt(b*b − 4.0*a*c))/(2.0*a);
$\sqrt[3]{x^y + x}$	Math.cbrt(Math.pow(x, y) + x);
$area = \sqrt{s(s-a)(s-b)(s-c)}$	area = Math.sqrt(s*(s-a)*(s-b)*(s-c));
$v(1 - e^{-t})$	v * (1 − Math.exp(-t));
$area = \pi r^2 + 2\pi rh$	area = Math.PI * r*r + 2 * Math.PI * r * h;
$|m| + |n|$	Math.abs(m) + Math.abs(n);
$|p^y - y|$	Math.abs(Math.pow(p,y) - y);
$\dfrac{4}{3}\pi r^3$	4.0/3 * Math.PI * Math.pow(r, 3);
$\dfrac{2m_1 * m_2}{m_1 + m_2} * g$	2.0 * m1 *m2)/(m1 + m2) * g;

Table 8.1: Java Expressions

Let us now apply this knowledge in some programming examples.

Write a program to read a number via the Scanner class and display its square, cube, square root and cube root.

Listing 8.1: PowerAndRoots.java

```
1  import java.util.Scanner;
2  public class PowerAndRoots
3  {
4     public static void main(String args[])
5     {
6        Scanner scan = new Scanner(System.in);
7
8        System.out.print("Enter the number: ");
9        int number = scan.nextInt();
10
11       System.out.println ("Square of " + number + " is " + ↵
              ↪ Math.pow(number, 2));
12       System.out.println ("Cube of " + number + " is " + ↵
              ↪ Math.pow(number, 3));
13       System.out.println ("Square root of " + number + " is " + ↵
              ↪ Math.sqrt(number));
14       System.out.println ("Cube root of " + number + " is " + ↵
              ↪ Math.sqrt(number));
15
16       scan.close();
17    }
18 }
```

```
Output
Enter the number: 8
Square of 8 is 64.0
Cube of 8 is 512.0
Square root of 8 is 2.8284271247461903
Cube root of 8 is 2.0
```

Write a program to read two numbers via the **Scanner** class and demonstrate various mathematical library methods.

Listing 8.2: VariousMethods.java

```
1  import java.util.Scanner;
2  public class VariousMethods
3  {
4     public static void main(String args[])
5     {
6        Scanner scan = new Scanner(System.in);
7
8        System.out.print("Enter the first number: ");
9        double firstNumber = scan.nextDouble();
10
11       System.out.print("Enter the second number: ");
12       double secondNumber = scan.nextDouble();
13
```

```
14        System.out.println ("\n*** " + firstNumber + " ***");
15        System.out.println ("Absolute value: " + Math.abs(firstNumber));
16        System.out.println ("Rounded value: " + Math.round(firstNumber));
17        System.out.println ("Ceiling: " + Math.ceil(firstNumber));
18        System.out.println ("Floor: " + Math.floor(firstNumber));
19
20        System.out.println ("\n*** " + secondNumber + " ***");
21        System.out.println ("Absolute value: " + Math.abs(secondNumber));
22        System.out.println ("Rounded value: " + Math.round(secondNumber));
23        System.out.println ("Ceiling: " + Math.ceil(secondNumber));
24        System.out.println ("Floor: " + Math.floor(secondNumber));
25
26        System.out.println ("\n*** Min/Max ***");
27        System.out.println ("Min value: " + Math.min(firstNumber, ↵
              ↪ secondNumber));
28        System.out.println ("Max value: " + Math.max(firstNumber, ↵
              ↪ secondNumber));
29
30        scan.close();
31    }
32 }
```

Output

```
Enter the first number: 8.79
Enter the second number: 17.49
*** 8.79 ***
Absolute value: 8.79
Rounded value: 9
Ceiling: 9.0
Floor: 8.0
*** 17.49 ***
Absolute value: 17.49
Rounded value: 17
Ceiling: 18.0
Floor: 17.0
*** Min/Max ***
Min value: 8.79
Max value: 17.49
```

Write a program to read the radius and height of a cylinder, and calculate its area using the following formula: $A = 2\pi rh + 2\pi r^2$

Listing 8.3: AreaOfCylinder.java

```
1 import java.util.Scanner;
2 public class AreaOfCylinder
3 {
4    public static void main(String args[])
5    {
6        Scanner scan = new Scanner(System.in);
```

```
 7          double area;
 8          System.out.print("Enter radius of cylinder: ");
 9          double radius = scan.nextDouble();
10          System.out.print("Enter height of cylinder: ");
11          double height = scan.nextDouble();
12
13          area = 2.0 * Math.PI * radius * height + 2.0 * Math.PI * ↵
              ↪ Math.pow(radius, 2);
14          System.out.println ("Area of cylinder is: " + area);
15
16          scan.close();
17      }
18  }
```

```
Output
Enter radius of cylinder: 5.1
Enter height of cylinder: 12.5
Area of cylinder is: 563.9787131724396
```

Multiple Choice Questions

1. What will be the output of `Math.cbrt(-125)`?

    A. 5.0

    B. 0.0

    C. -5.0

    D. Error – can't use `Math.cbrt()` on a negative number

2. Which Java package includes the `Math` class?

    A. `java.io`   C. `java.util`

    B. `java.lang`   D. `java.sys`

3. Give the output of `Math.sqrt(x);` when `x = 9.0`

    A. 3   C. 3.00

    B. 3.0   D. All of the above

4. Give the output of `Math.ceil(-0.6)`.

    A. -1.6   C. -1.0

    B. -1.5   D. -0.0

5. Give the output of `Math.ceil(-46.6)`.

    A. -46.6   C. -47.0

    B. -46.5   D. -46.0

6. Give the output of `Math.abs(x);` when x = -9.99

    A. -9.99   C. 0.99

    B. 9.99   D. None of the above

7. Which of the following is a method to find the square root of a number?

    A. `FindSquareroot(x)`   C. `Math.Square(x)`

    B. `Sqrt(x)`   D. `Math.sqrt(x)`

8. What will be the output of `Math.pow(3, 0)`?

    A. 0.0   C. 3.0

    B. 1.0   D. -1.0

9. `Math.random()` returns a double value r such that ....

    A. $0.0 \leq r < 1.0$ C. $0.0 < r \leq 1.0$

    B. $0.0 \leq r \leq 1.0$ D. $0.0 < r < 1.0$

10. What will be the output of `Math.floor(-20.10)`?

    A. -20.0   C. 20

    B. -21.0   D. 21

11. What will be the output of `Math.round(0.5)`?

    A. 0.0   C. 1

    B. 0   D. 1.0

12. What will be the output of `Math.abs(-0)`?

    A. 0.0   C. -0

    B. 0   D. +0

13. Given the following statements:

```
int min = 1, max = 10;
int range = max - min + 1;
int num = (int) (range * Math.random() + min);
```

The value of num will be in integer such that ....

A. $1 \leq num \leq 10$

B. $1 \leq num < 10$

C. $1 < num \leq 10$

D. $1 < num < 10$

Assignment Questions

---

1. How do user-defined methods differ from library methods?

2. Distinguish between `Math.ceil()` and `Math.floor()` methods.

3. What is wrong with the following statements? Explain.

    (i) `result = (5/10) * Math.sqrt( a );`

    (ii) `result = math.sqrt(b * b - 4 * a * c) / ( 2 * a );`

4. Explain the following Math functions in Java:

    (i) `Math.abs()`   (iii) `Math.cbrt()`   (v) `Math.round()`

    (ii) `Math.sqrt()`   (iv) `Math.random()`   (vi) `Math.ceil()`

5. Write Java expressions for the following:

    (i) The square root of $a + 5b^3$

    (ii) The cube root of $x^3 + y^3 + z^3$

    (iii) The square root of $b^2 + 4ac$

6. Write the following as Java expressions:

    (i) $\sqrt[3]{x^2 + 5y^3}$

    (ii) $|x + y|$

    (iii) $|x^3 + y2 - 2xy|$

    (iv) $\dfrac{\pi}{6}(z^4 - 2\pi)$

    (v) $\sqrt[3]{z^2 - \pi}$

    (vi) $\sqrt[4]{x^3 - y^3}$

    (vii) $\dfrac{amount * rate}{(1 - \dfrac{1}{(1 + rate)^n})}$

    (viii) $\dfrac{-b + \sqrt{b^2 - 4ac}}{2a}$

    (ix) $\sqrt[4]{\dfrac{1}{LC} - \dfrac{R^2}{4C^2}}$

7. Write valid statements for the following in Java:

    (i) Print the rounded off value of 14.49

    (ii) Print the absolute value of -0.09

    (iii) Print the largest of -67 and -50

    (iv) Print the smallest of -56 and -57.4

    (v) Print a random integer between 25 and 35

    (vi) Print 47.5 raised to the power 6.3

(vii) Print minimum of -4, -7

8. Write a program in Java to find the maximum of three numbers using `Math.max()` method.

9. Write a program to print:

    (i) x to the power y

    (ii) the square root of y

    The values of x and y are 81 and 3, respectively.

10. Write a program to compute and display the value of expression:
    $$\frac{1}{x^2} + \frac{1}{y^3} + \frac{1}{z^4}$$
    where, the values of x, y and z are entered by the user.

11. Write a program to generate random integers in the following ranges:

    (i) 10 to 20 (both inclusive).

    (ii) 25 to 50 (both inclusive)

12. Write a program that accepts a number x and then prints:
    $x^0, x^1, x^2, x^3, x^4, x^5$

13. Write the equivalent Java statements for the following, by using the mathematical functions:

    (i) Print the positive value of -999.

    (ii) Store the value -3375 in a variable and print its cube root.

    (iii) Store the value 999.99 in a variable and convert it into its closest integer that is greater than or equal to 999.99.

14. Write a program in Java to compute the final velocity of a vehicle using the following formula:

    $$v^2 = u^2 + 2as$$

    where, u = initial velocity, a = acceleration and s = distance covered; they are entered by the user.

Answers To Objective Questions

Multiple Choice Questions

1. C	3. B	5. D	7. D	9. A	11. C	13. A
2. B	4. D	6. B	8. B	10. B	12. B	

Chapter 9

Conditional Constructs in Java

Conditional Constructs in Java

THE programs written so far have been using simple statements such as declaring variables, assigning values to these variables and computing the sum. These statements were executed sequentially in the order in which they appear, including any method calls as shown in Figure 9.1. During the execution of a program with methods, the control is transferred to the method called. The method is then executed in a sequential order and the flow of control is transferred back to the calling program, continuing the sequential execution.

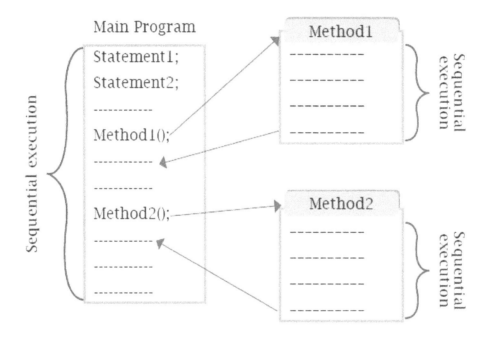

Figure 9.1: Sequential Execution

However, while programming you may have a number of situations where you need to change the order of execution based on a certain condition. For example:

- If the temperature is in Fahrenheit, then convert it into Celsius.

- If the year is a leap year, then there are 29 days in February.

- If the number is divisible by 2, then it is an even number.

In each of the scenarios mentioned above, an action is performed if the given condition is true. When a program breaks the sequential flow and jumps to another part of the code, it is known as *conditional branching*. On the other hand, if the branching takes place without any condition, it is known as *unconditional branching*. Java allows us to check a condition and execute certain instructions, depending on the outcome whether it is `true` or `false`. Such statements are called *conditional* or *decision* or *selection statements* as shown in Figure 9.2.

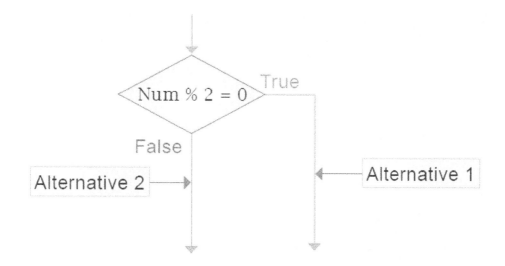

Figure 9.2: Conditional Statements

In Java, there are two forms of conditional statements:

- The `if` statement – to choose between two alternatives.

- The `switch` statement – to choose between multiple alternatives.

9.1 The if Statement

An `if` statement is the simplest form of the conditional statements that tests a particular condition. If the condition evaluates to `true`, the `statement-block` is executed; otherwise the `statement-block` is skipped.
Syntax:

```
if (condition)
{
    statement-block;
}
```

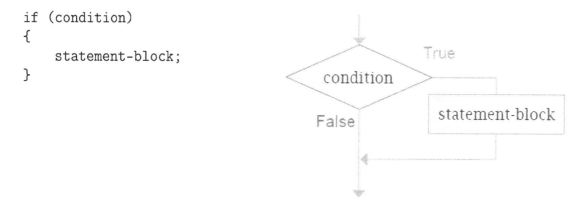

Figure 9.3: Flowchart of the if Statement

The `statement-block` may be a single statement or a block statement. The curly brackets may be omitted if the `statement-block` is a single statement. Let us consider the following code snippet:

```
if (num % 2 == 0)
    System.out.println("Even number");
```

The above statement checks if the value stored in the num variable is divisible by 2. If it is so, the message "Even number" is displayed in the Terminal window. If the condition evaluates to false, the statement to display the message "Even number" is skipped, and the execution continues with the next statement.

> **Note**
>
> Ensure that the condition is enclosed within the round brackets.

Write a program to accept three integers and find the largest among them using an if statement.

Listing 9.1: FindLargestOf3.java
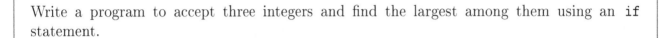

```
1  import java.util.Scanner;
2  public class FindLargestOf3
3  {
4      public static void main(String args[])
5      {
6          int maxNum;
7          Scanner scan = new Scanner(System.in);
8          System.out.print("Enter the first number: ");
9          int num1 = scan.nextInt();
10
11         System.out.print("Enter the second number: ");
12         int num2 = scan.nextInt();
13
14         System.out.print("Enter the third number: ");
15         int num3 = scan.nextInt();
16
17         maxNum = num1;
18
19         if (num2 > maxNum)
20             maxNum = num2;
21
22         if (num3 > maxNum)
23             maxNum = num3;
24
25         System.out.println("Largest of " + num1 + ", " + num2 + " and " + ↵
                ↪ num3 + " is: " + maxNum);
26         scan.close();
27     }
28 }
```

Output

Enter the first number: 12
Enter the second number: 56
Enter the third number: 34
Largest of 12, 56 and 34 is: 56

Code Walkthrough:

◈ Line 17: Stores the first number, num1 into the maxNum variable.

◈ Line 19: Checks if the second number, num2 is greater than maxNum.

◈ Line 20: If it is so, replaces the value of maxNum with num2.

◈ Line 22: Checks if the third number, num3 is greater than maxNum.

◈ Line 23: If it is so, replaces the value of maxNum with num3.

> Write a program in Java using an if statement to determine if a number num is divisible by two divisors div1 and div2.

Listing 9.2: Divisor.java

```java
import java.util.Scanner;
public class Divisor
{
    public static void main(String args[])
    {
        boolean result;
        Scanner input = new Scanner(System.in);

        System.out.print("Enter the an integer number: ");
        int num = input.nextInt();

        System.out.print("Enter the first divisor: ");
        int div1 = input.nextInt();

        System.out.print("Enter the second divisor: ");
        int div2 = input.nextInt();

        result = Check(num, div1, div2);
        System.out.println (num + " divisible by " + div1 + " and " + ↩
            ↪ div2 + " is: " + result);
        input.close();
    }

    static boolean Check(int x, int y, int z)
    {
        if ((x % y == 0) && (x % z == 0))
            return true;

        return false;
    }
}
```

```
Output
Enter the an integer number: 36
Enter the first divisor: 4
Enter the second divisor: 9
36 divisible by 4 and 9 is: true
```

Code Walkthrough:

◈ Line 18: Invokes the `Check()` method to find if `num` is divisible by `div1` and `div2`.
◈ Line 25: Checks if the remainder of division by `divisor1` and `divisor2` is zero.
◈ Line 26: If the remainder is zero in both the cases, the method returns `true`.
◈ Line 28: If the remainder is non-zero in any of the case, the statement at Line 26 is not executed. The program control moves to the next statement, i.e., Line 28, thus returning a `false` value.

9.2　The if-else Statement

The `if` statement you have seen so far allows you to execute a statement if the condition evaluates to `true`. However, there may be situations where you may want to execute a statement when the condition evaluates to `false`. For such scenarios, the `if-else` control structure is used which is an extension of the simple `if` statement. The statement that has to be executed when the condition evaluates to `false` is written under the *else-part*. The `if-else` statement has the following syntax:

```
if (condition)
{
    statement1-block;      ◄──── statement1-block is executed
                                 when the condition is true.
}
else
{
    statement2-block;      ◄──── statement2-block is executed
                                 when the condition is false.
}
```

If the condition evaluates to `true`, then `statement1-block` is executed and if the condition evaluates to `false`, then `statement2-block` is executed.

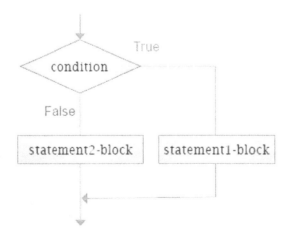

To understand the working of an `if-else` statement, let us consider the following example:

Write a program in Java to determine the nature of roots of the quadric equation $ax^2 + bx + c = 0$ where $discriminant = b^2 - 4ac$ determines the nature of the roots as follows:

$discriminant \geq 0$ Roots are real

$discriminant < 0$ Roots are imaginary

The roots are computed by the following formula:

$$root1 = \frac{-b + \sqrt{b^2 - 4ac}}{2a}$$

$$root2 = \frac{-b - \sqrt{b^2 - 4ac}}{2a}$$

Listing 9.3: Quadratic.java

```java
import java.util.Scanner;
public class Quadratic
{
    public static void main(String args[])
    {
        double discriminant, root1 = 0, root2 = 0;
        Scanner input = new Scanner(System.in);

        System.out.print("Enter the value of a: ");
        int a = input.nextInt();

        System.out.print("Enter the value of b: ");
        int b = input.nextInt();

        System.out.print("Enter the value of c: ");
        int c = input.nextInt();

        discriminant = Math.sqrt(b*b - 4*a*c);

        if (discriminant >= 0)
        {
            System.out.print("The roots are real.");
            root1 = (-b + discriminant)/(2.0 * a);
            root2 = (-b - discriminant)/(2.0 * a);
            System.out.print("The roots are " + root1 + " and " + root2);
        }
        else
        {
            System.out.print("The roots are imaginary.");
        }
        input.close();
```

```
32    }
33 }
```

```
                            Output
Enter the value of a: 1
Enter the value of b: 5
Enter the value of c: 6
The roots are real. The roots are -2.0 and -3.0
```

9.3 The if-else-if Ladder

The `if` statement variants you have seen so far allow you to check only one condition. If this condition evaluates to `true`, the *if-part* is executed. If this condition evaluates to `false`, the *else-part* is executed. However, in real life programming problems, there are situations where you have to check for a number of conditions. For example,

- evaluating grade of a student A, B, C, or D based on the percentage of marks.

- computing income tax according to the rate schedule.

Java provides an `if-else-if` ladder construct to program such cases. The `if-else-if` ladder construct takes the following generic syntax:

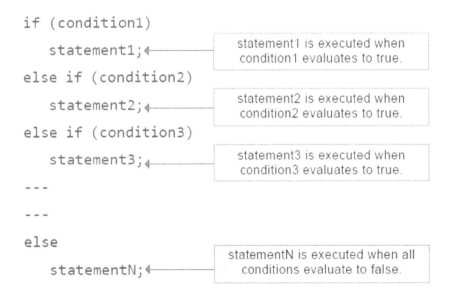

In such a ladder, the `if` statements are executed from the top (of the ladder) to bottom as per the following logic:

- As soon as one of the conditions becomes `true`, the statement associated with that `if` will be executed, skipping the rest of the ladder.

- If none of the `if` conditions evaluate to `true`, the final `else` statement will be executed.

- If there is no final `else` and all the other conditions are `false`, then no action will take place.

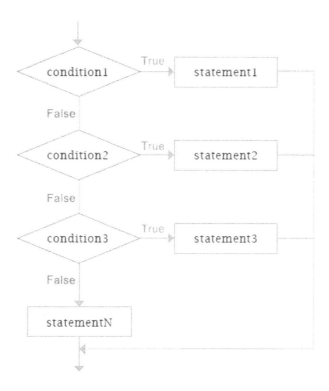

Figure 9.4: Flowchart of the if-else-if ladder

To understand the working of an `if-else-if` ladder, let us consider the following example:

Write a program in Java to input a student's name, class, roll number, and marks in 5 subjects. Compute the total marks, percentage, and grade as per the following table:

Percentage	Grade
Greater than or equal to 95	A*
Greater than or equal to 85 but less than 95	A
Greater than or equal to 75 but less than 85	B
Greater than or equal to 55 but less than 75	C
Greater than or equal to 40 but less than 55	D
Less than 40	E

Listing 9.4: StudentGrade.java

```java
import java.util.Scanner;
public class StudentGrade
{
    public static void main(String args[])
    {
        String studentName, studentClass;
        String studentGrade;
        int rollNumber, marksSub1, marksSub2, marksSub3, marksSub4, ↵
            ↪ marksSub5;
        double totalMarks, percentageMarks;

        Scanner input = new Scanner(System.in);

        System.out.print("Enter Student's Name: ");
        studentName = input.nextLine();

        System.out.print("Enter Class: ");
        studentClass = input.nextLine();

        System.out.print("Enter Roll Number: ");
        rollNumber = input.nextInt();

        System.out.print("Enter Marks in 5 subjects: ");
        marksSub1 = input.nextInt();
        marksSub2 = input.nextInt();
        marksSub3 = input.nextInt();
        marksSub4 = input.nextInt();
        marksSub5 = input.nextInt();

        totalMarks = marksSub1 + marksSub2 + marksSub3 + marksSub4 + ↵
            ↪ marksSub5;

        percentageMarks = (totalMarks/500.0) * 100;

        if (percentageMarks >= 95)
            studentGrade = "A*";
        else if ((percentageMarks >= 85) && (percentageMarks < 95))
            studentGrade = "A";
        else if ((percentageMarks >= 75) && (percentageMarks < 85))
            studentGrade = "B";
        else if ((percentageMarks >= 55) && (percentageMarks < 75))
            studentGrade = "C";
        else if ((percentageMarks >= 40) && (percentageMarks < 55))
            studentGrade = "D";
        else
```

```
44          studentGrade = "E";
45
46      System.out.println("Student's Name:    " + studentName);
47      System.out.println("Class:             " + studentClass);
48      System.out.println("Roll Number:       " + rollNumber);
49      System.out.println("Marks:             " + marksSub1 + ", " + ↵
            ↳ marksSub2 + ", " + marksSub3 + ", " + marksSub4 + ", " + ↵
            ↳ marksSub5);
50      System.out.println("Total Marks:       " + totalMarks);
51      System.out.println("Percentage Marks: " + percentageMarks);
52      System.out.println("Grade:             " + studentGrade);
53
54      input.close();
55    }
56 }
```

Output

Enter Student's Name: Nikky Varda
Enter Class: 10B
Enter Roll Number: 155
Enter Marks in 5 subjects: 99
98
97
94
96
Student's Name: Nikky Varda
Class: 10B
Roll Number: 155
Marks: 99, 98, 97, 94, 96
Total Marks: 484.0
Percentage Marks: 96.8
Grade: A*

Write a program in Java to display the season of the year based on the month entered by the user.

Listing 9.5: FourSeasons.java

```
1  import java.util.Scanner;
2  public class FourSeasons
3  {
4     public static void main(String args[])
5     {
6        Scanner scan = new Scanner(System.in);
7
8        System.out.print("Enter the month number: ");
```

```
9       int month = scan.nextInt();
10
11      if (month == 4 || month == 5 || month == 6)
12          System.out.println ("It is Summer Season");
13      else if (month == 7 || month == 8 || month == 9)
14          System.out.println ("It is Rainy Season");
15      else if (month == 10 || month == 11 || month == 12 || month == 1)
16          System.out.println ("It is Winter Season");
17      else if (month == 2 || month == 3)
18          System.out.println ("It is Spring Season");
19      else
20          System.out.println ("*** Invalid Month ***");
21
22      scan.close();
23    }
24 }
```

Output
Enter the month number: 6
It is Summer Season

9.4   Nested if Statement

Sometimes, within an if statement (*if-part* or *else-part*) you need to check another condition. For this, you can write another if statement in the *if-part* or *else-part* or both. An if statement that contains another if statement in its *if-part* or *else-part* or both is called a *nested if* statement as shown in Figures 9.5, 9.6, and 9.7 respectively.

> **Note**
>
> Nesting means having one statement inside another statement.

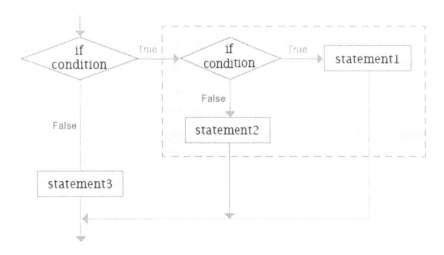

Figure 9.5: Nesting of if statement in the if-part

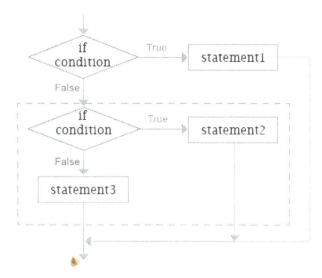

Figure 9.6: Nesting of if statement in the else-part

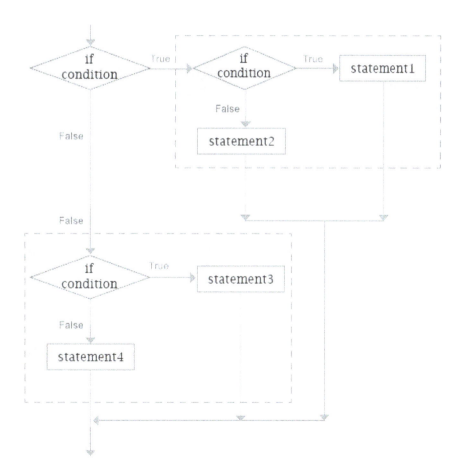

Figure 9.7: Nesting of if statement in both if-part and else-part

Let us consider the following program to understand the working of the nested if statement.

A hair saloon charges customers as per the following criteria:
Male customer:

> Boys (age ≤ 13): $200
> Men (age > 13): $300

Female customer:

> Girls (age ≤ 13): $250
> Women (age > 13): $350

Write a program in Java to read the gender code (M or F) and the age and print the price of the hair cut.

Listing 9.6: HairCutSaloon.java

```
1  import java.util.Scanner;
2  public class HairCutSaloon
3  {
4      public static void main(String args[])
5      {
6          int price = 0;
7          Scanner input = new Scanner(System.in);
8
9          System.out.print("Enter the Gender code (M or F): ");
10         char genderCode = input.next().charAt(0);
11
12         System.out.print("Enter the Age: ");
13         int age = input.nextInt();
14
15         if (genderCode == 'M' )
16         {
17             if (age <= 13)
18                 price = 200;
19             else
20                 price = 300;
21
22             System.out.println("Price is: " + price);
23         }
24         else if (genderCode == 'F' )
25         {
26             if (age <= 13)
27                 price = 250;
28             else
29                 price = 350;
30
31             System.out.println("Price is: " + price);
```

```
32        }
33        else
34            System.out.println("Invalid Gender code entered");
35
36        input.close();
37    }
38 }
```

```
┌─────────────Output──────────────┐      ┌─────────────Output──────────────┐
│ Enter the Gender code (M or F): F │      │ Enter the Gender code (M or F): a │
│ Enter the Age: 23                 │      │ Enter the Age: 23                 │
│ Price is: 350                     │      │ Invalid Gender code entered       │
└───────────────────────────────────┘      └───────────────────────────────────┘
```

9.5 Alternative to if-else Statement

Java has an operator that can be used as an alternative to the `if-else` statement. You have already learnt about this operator, the ternary (conditional) operator. The `if-else` statement works like the ternary operator. In fact, the conditional operator can be considered as a shorthand version of the `if-else` statement. The conditional operator form:

```
condition ? expression1 : expression2
```

is equivalent to the `if-else` form:

```
if (condition)
    expression1;
else
    expression2;
```

For example, assuming declaration `int min;` is in place, the following code snippet to find the minimum of two numbers:

```
min = (a < b) ? a : b;
```

is equivalent to the following `if-else` form:

```
if (a < b)
    min = a;
else
    min = b;
```

Although the two forms mentioned above are equivalent, there are some differences between the `if-else` statement and the ternary operator as listed in the Table 9.1.

	if-else statement	ternary operator
1.	The if-else statement code is very obvious about the logic it is implementing.	Although ternary operator code is neat and compact, the logic is less obvious.
2.	The if-else statement can have multiple statements (compound statements) in curly brackets in the if-part or else-part.	Only single expressions are allowed.
3.	A nested form of the if-else statement is easy to read and understand when proper indentation is used.	A nested form of the ternary operator is very difficult to read and understand.

Table 9.1: Difference between if-else Statement and Ternary Operator

9.6 Switch Statement

You have seen that when multiple conditions need to be checked, you can design a program using the various if statements. However, the complexity of the program increases when the number of conditions increases. The logic of the program becomes difficult to read and follow, even for the programmer who has written it. To deal with such situations, Java provides a `switch` statement that can be used when there is a requirement to check multiple conditions in a program. It provides an easy way to jump to different parts of the code in a program based on the value of an expression. It is a substitute for a large series of `if-else-if` ladder. Figure 9.8 shows the general syntax of a `switch` statement.

```
switch (expression)
{
    case <label-1>:
        statement block-1;
        break;


    case < label-2>:
        statement block2;
        break;
        .

        .
case label-n:
        statement block-n;
        break;


    default:
        statement block-default;
}
```

This statement block is executed when the *expression* evaluates to <label-1>.

This statement block is executed when the *expression* evaluates to <label-2>.

This statement block is executed when the *expression* evaluates to <label-n>.

This statement block is executed when the *expression* does not match any case label.

Figure 9.8: Switch Statement

The `switch` control structure has a switch *expression*, which stores a value. It also has multiple cases where every `case` has a unique label and a block of statements associated with it. The value of switch expression is compared to the labels of all the cases. If the value matches, the statements associated with that `case` get executed, i.e., the computer continues executing the program from that point. If none of the cases match, the computer executes the statements written in the `default` case.

The value stored in the *expression* should be of primitive type - `byte`, `short`, `int`, or `char`. The values defined in each `case` should be compatible with the value stored in *expression*. Each `case` value should be a unique literal (i.e., it should be a constant, not a variable). Duplicate `case` values are not allowed. The selection process of switch statement is illustrated in the flowchart shown in Figure 9.9.

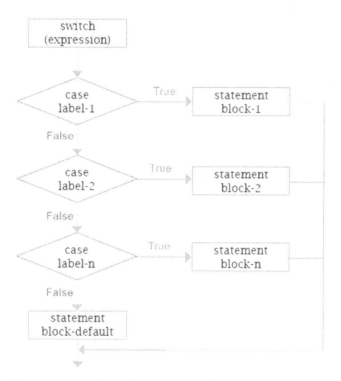

Figure 9.9: Flowchart of the Switch Statement

The `break` statement is used inside a `switch` statement to terminate a statement block. It brings the program control out of the `switch` statement. This process is illustrated in Figure 9.10.

The `default case` is the last statement of the `switch` statement. It is an optional statement. It executes only when the value stored in `switch` expression does not match with any `case` label.

> **Note**
>
> Duplicate `case` values are not allowed.

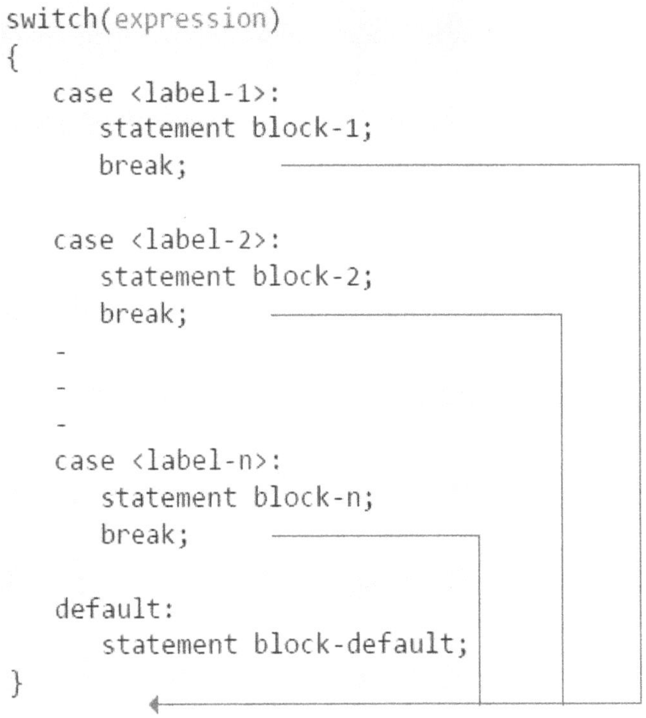

```
switch(expression)
{
    case <label-1>:
        statement block-1;
        break;

    case <label-2>:
        statement block-2;
        break;
    -
    -
    -
    case <label-n>:
        statement block-n;
        break;

    default:
        statement block-default;
}
```

Figure 9.10: Break in Switch Statement

Let us now understand the concept of switch statement using an example. The following is a code snippet to find out the colour-name using an `if-else-if` ladder.

```
if (code == 1)
    colour = "Violet";
else if (code == 2)
    colour = "Indigo";
else if (code == 3)
    colour = "Blue";
else if (code == 4)
    colour = "Green";
else if (code == 5)
    colour = "Yellow";
else if (code == 6)
    colour = "Orange";
else if (code == 7)
    colour = "Red";
else
    System.out.print("*** Invalid code entered ***");
```

The following program implements the same logic using a `switch` statement.

Listing 9.7: VIBGYOR.java

```java
1  import java.util.Scanner;
2  public class VIBGYOR
3  {
4      public static void main(String args[])
5      {
6          Scanner scan = new Scanner(System.in);
7          String colour = "";
8          System.out.print("Enter the colour code: ");
9          int code = scan.nextInt();
10
11         switch(code)
12         {
13             case 1:
14                 colour = "Violet";
15                 break;
16
17             case 2:
18                 colour = "Indigo";
19                 break;
20
21             case 3:
22                 colour = "Blue";
23                 break;
24
25             case 4:
26                 colour = "Green";
27                 break;
28
29             case 5:
30                 colour = "Yellow";
31                 break;
32
33             case 6:
34                 colour = "Orange";
35                 break;
36
37             case 7:
38                 colour = "Red";
39                 break;
40
41             default:
42                 System.out.println("*** Invalid code entered ***");
43         }
44
45         System.out.println("Colour for the code " + code + " is: " +
                ↪ colour);
46         scan.close();
```

```
47        }
48    }
```

You can see in the above-mentioned program that after every **case**, there is a **break** statement that signals the end of it and causes an exit from the **switch** statement. The **default case** is executed if the user enters a choice that does not match with any of the **case** values.

Omission of the break statement – the fall through

You know that the **break** statements in the **switch** statement are optional. The purpose of the **break** statement is to make the program jump to the end of the **switch** statement. If you do not specify the **break** statement, the program will just continue after completing the current **case** label and will execute the statements associated with the next **case** label until a **break** statement is encountered. In this case, it is said that a *fall through* has occurred. Sometimes, it is desirable to have multiple cases without **break** statements among them. Let us reconsider the following **FourSeasons** example that was discussed earlier, this time using a **switch** statement.

Listing 9.8: FourSeasonsWithSwitch.java

```java
1  import java.util.Scanner;
2  public class FourSeasonsWithSwitch
3  {
4      public static void main(String args[])
5      {
6          Scanner scan = new Scanner(System.in);
7          System.out.print("Enter month: ");
8          int month = scan.nextInt();
9
10         switch(month)
11         {
12             case 4:
13             case 5:
14             case 6:
15                 System.out.println ("It is Summer Season");
16                 break;
17
18             case 7:
19             case 8:
20             case 9:
21                 System.out.println ("It is Rainy Season");
22                 break;
23
24             case 10:
25             case 11:
26             case 12:
```

```
27          case 1:
28              System.out.println ("It is Winter Season");
29              break;
30
31          case 2:
32          case 3:
33              System.out.println ("It is Spring Season");
34              break;
35
36          default:
37              System.out.println("*** Invalid month entered ***");
38      }
39      scan.close();
40  }
41 }
```

```
Output
Enter month: 9
It is Rainy Season
```

The program given above illustrates two important features:

- It uses empty cases.

- There are no **break** statements after some cases.

Since there are no **break** statements after the cases 4 and 5, Java runtime starts executing statements from the matching case until a **break** statement is found at Line 16. Therefore, a fall through is said to have occurred. Similarly, there are other fall throughs in this switch statement.

9.7 The if Statement versus switch Statement

The if statement and the switch statement allow you to select an option out of many choices. However, there are some differences between their operations as given below:

	if statement	switch statement
1.	The if statement allows you to check all kinds of relational and logical conditions i.e. equal to, less than, greater than, AND, OR, etc.	The switch statement allows you to check for the equal to condition only.
2.	In the if statement, the selection can be based on different conditions or expressions.	In the switch statement, the selection is based on the evaluation of the same expression.
3.	The if statement can check multiple conditions in a single statement.	Each case label in a switch statement must be a single value.
4.	The if statement, in addition to other data types, can check conditions based on double and float data types.	The switch statement cannot check conditions based on double and float data types.
5.	A set of nested ifs are less efficient than a switch statement.	A switch statement is usually more efficient than a set of nested ifs.

9.8 Menu Driven Programs

A menu usually displays a list of options to the user. The user selects one of the options to carry out some action. The options are usually displayed in the form of a numbered list (e.g. 1, 2, 3...) or alphabetical list (e.g. A, B, C...). The chosen option can be used in a `switch` statement to carry out the corresponding action.

Let us consider an example to display a menu with the following options for a circle:

1. Calculate Diameter
2. Calculate Circumference
3. Calculate Area

On selecting a valid value, the computer should ask for the radius and compute the relevant measurement. If the user selects an invalid option, an error message should be displayed.

Listing 9.9: CircleMenu.java

```
1  import java.util.Scanner;
2  public class CircleMenu
3  {
4      public static void main(String args[])
5      {
6          Scanner scan = new Scanner(System.in);
7          double radius;
8
9          //display menu
10         System.out.println("\t\tCircle Menu");
11         System.out.println("\t\t===========");
12         System.out.println("\tA. Calculate Diameter");
13         System.out.println("\tB. Calculate Circumference");
14         System.out.println("\tC. Calculate Area");
15         System.out.println();
16
17         System.out.print("\tEnter your choice: ");
18         char choice = scan.next().charAt(0);
19
20         switch(choice)
21         {
22             case 'A':
23                 System.out.println ("Please enter radius:");
24                 radius = scan.nextDouble();
25                 System.out.println ("Diameter is: " + (2 * radius));
26                 break;
27
28             case 'B':
29                 System.out.println ("Please enter radius:");
30                 radius = scan.nextDouble();
```

```
31        System.out.println ("Circumference is: " + (2 * Math.PI * ↵
             ↪ radius));
32        break;
33
34    case 'C':
35        System.out.println ("Please enter radius:");
36        radius = scan.nextDouble();
37        System.out.println ("Area is: " + (Math.PI * radius * ↵
             ↪ radius));
38        break;
39
40    default:
41        System.out.println("*** Invalid option entered ***");
42    }
43    scan.close();
44  }
45 }
```

```
Output
     Circle Menu
     =======
A. Calculate Diameter
B. Calculate Circumference
C. Calculate Area

Enter your choice: C
Please enter radius:
4.6
Area is: 66.47610054996001
```

```
Output
     Circle Menu
     =======
A. Calculate Diameter
B. Calculate Circumference
C. Calculate Area

Enter your choice: Z
*** Invalid option entered ***
```

9.9   Terminating the Program

Sometimes, you may want to purposely terminate (end) a program depending on some event happening in the code, for example, user entered a wrong menu option and you want to end the program. Let us examine the output of Program 9.7 `VIBGYOR.java` when an invalid colour code was entered. You can see in the output that the line "Colour for the code 8 is:" is displayed, which does not seem right. In fact, the program should have terminated once the message "*** Invalid code entered ***" had displayed.

```
Output
Enter the colour code: 8
*** Invalid code entered***
Colour for the code 8 is:
```

Java provides a feature to terminate the currently running program (Java Virtual Machine) via the exit() method of the System class. It takes the following form:

    System.exit(n);

The argument n serves as a status code. A non-zero status code indicates *abnormal termination*, and a zero status code indicates a *normal termination*. Let us recapitulate the VIBGYOR program and see how you can fix the issue that is just discussed.

Listing 9.10: VIBGYORWithExit.java

```java
import java.util.Scanner;
public class VIBGYORWithExit
{
    public static void main(String args[])
    {
        Scanner scan = new Scanner(System.in);
        String colour = "";

        System.out.print("Enter the colour code: ");
        int code = scan.nextInt();

        switch(code)
        {
            case 1:
                colour = "Violet";
                break;

            case 2:
                colour = "Indigo";
                break;

            case 3:
                colour = "Blue";
                break;

            case 4:
                colour = "Green";
                break;

            case 5:
                colour = "Yellow";
                break;

            case 6:
                colour = "Orange";
                break;
```

```
38          case 7:
39              colour = "Red";
40              break;
41
42          default:
43              System.out.println("*** Invalid code entered ***");
44              System.exit(0);
45      }
46
47      System.out.println("Colour for the code " + code + " is: " + ←
            ↪ colour);
48      scan.close();
49  }
50 }
```

> **Output**
> Enter the colour code: 8
> *** Invalid code entered ***

During the execution of the program, as soon as the statement `System.exit(0);` is encountered, it terminates the execution, ignoring any remaining statements. This time the program terminates gracefully without displaying the unnecessary message.

Solved Programming Exercises

Write a program to accept a two-digit number. Add the sum of its digits to the product of its digits. If the value is equal to the input number, display the message "Special 2-digit number"; otherwise, display the message "Not a Special 2-digit number".

Listing 9.11: SpecialNumber.java

```
1  import java.util.Scanner;
2  public class SpecialNumber
3  {
4
5     public static void main(String[] args)
6     {
7        Scanner scanner = new Scanner(System.in);
8        System.out.print("Enter a two-digit number: ");
9        int number = scanner.nextInt();
10
11       if (number < 10 || number > 99)
12       {
13          System.out.println("Entered number is not a two-digit number.");
14          System.out.println("Exiting...");
15          System.exit(0);
16       }
17
```

```
18        int firstDigit = number % 10;   //Get remainder
19        int secondDigit = number / 10;  //Get quotient
20
21        int sumOfDigits = firstDigit + secondDigit;
22        int productOfDigits = firstDigit * secondDigit;
23
24        int newNumber = sumOfDigits + productOfDigits;
25
26        if (newNumber == number)
27            System.out.println("Special 2-digit number");
28        else
29            System.out.println("Not a Special 2-digit number");
30    }
31 }
```

Output
Enter a two-digit number: 59
Special 2-digit number

Output
Enter a two-digit number: 45
Not a Special 2-digit number

Write a program in Java to input year in four digit format (yyyy) and determine if it is a leap year.

Listing 9.12: LeapYear.java

```
1  import java.util.Scanner;
2  public class LeapYear
3  {
4      public static void main(String args[])
5      {
6          int largest;
7          Scanner scan = new Scanner(System.in);
8
9          System.out.print("Enter year in yyyy format: ");
10         int year = scan.nextInt();
11
12         if (IsLeapYear(year))
13             System.out.println (year + " is a leap year");
14         else
15             System.out.println (year + " is not a leap year");
16
17         scan.close();
18     }
19
20     static boolean IsLeapYear(int year)
21     {
```

```
22        boolean leapYear = false;
23
24        if (((year % 4 == 0) &&  !(year % 100 == 0)) || (year % 400 == 0))
25            leapYear = true;
26        else
27            leapYear = false;
28
29        return leapYear;
30    }
31 }
```

Output
Enter year in yyyy format: 2020 2020 is a leap year

Output
Enter year in yyyy format: 2200 2200 is not a leap year

Using the switch statement, write a menu driven program to calculate the maturity amount of a Bank Deposit. The user is given the following options:

(i) Term Deposit

(ii) Recurring Deposit

For option (i) accept principal(P), rate of interest(r) and time period in years(n). Calculate and output the maturity amount(A) receivable using the formula:

$$A = P(1 + \frac{r}{100})^n$$

For option (ii) accept monthly installment (P), rate of interest(r) and time period in months (n). Calculate and output the maturity amount(A) receivable using the formula:

$$A = P * n + P * \frac{n(n+1)}{2} * \frac{r}{100} * \frac{1}{12}$$

For an incorrect option, an appropriate error message should be displayed.

Listing 9.13: BankDeposit.java

```
1 import java.util.Scanner;
2 public class BankDeposit
3 {
4    public static void main(String[] args)
5    {
6        double P, r, maturityAmount;
7        int n;
8        Scanner scanner = new Scanner(System.in);
9
```

```
10          System.out.println("   ** Menu **");
11          System.out.println("1. Term Deposit");
12          System.out.println("2. Recurring Deposit");
13          System.out.print("Enter your choice: ");
14          int choice = scanner.nextInt();
15
16          switch (choice)
17          {
18              case 1:
19                  System.out.print("Enter principal amount: ");
20                  P = scanner.nextDouble();
21                  System.out.print("Enter rate of interest: ");
22                  r = scanner.nextDouble();
23                  System.out.print("Enter period in years: ");
24                  n = scanner.nextInt();
25
26                  maturityAmount = P * Math.pow(1 + r / 100.0, n);
27
28                  System.out.println("Maturity amount receivable is: " + ↵
                        ↪ maturityAmount);
29                  break;
30
31              case 2:
32                  System.out.print("Enter monthly installment: ");
33                  P = scanner.nextDouble();
34                  System.out.print("Enter rate of interest: ");
35                  r = scanner.nextDouble();
36                  System.out.print("Enter period in months: ");
37                  n = scanner.nextInt();
38
39                  maturityAmount = P * n + P * (n * (n + 1) / 2.0) * (r / ↵
                        ↪ 100.0) * (1.0 / 12);
40
41                  System.out.println("Maturity amount receivable is: " + ↵
                        ↪ maturityAmount);
42                  break;
43
44              default:
45                  System.out.println("Invalid choice entered.");
46          }
47
48          scanner.close();
49      }
50  }
```

```
        Output
     ** Menu **
1. Term Deposit
2. Recurring Deposit
Enter your choice: 1
Enter principal amount: 50000
Enter rate of interest: 8
Enter period in years: 3
Maturity    amount    receivable    is:
62985.600000000006
```

```
        Output
     ** Menu **
1. Term Deposit
2. Recurring Deposit
Enter your choice: 2
Enter monthly installment: 3000
Enter rate of interest: 9
Enter period in months: 24
Maturity amount receivable is: 78750.0
```

Write a program in Java to determine if an entered alphabet is a vowel or a consonant.

Listing 9.14: VowelOrConsonant.java

```java
import java.util.Scanner;
public class VowelOrConsonant
{
    public static void main(String args[])
    {
        Scanner scan = new Scanner(System.in);

        System.out.print("Enter a character: ");
        char myChar = scan.next().charAt(0);

        if ((myChar >= 'a' && myChar <= 'z') || (myChar >='A' && myChar
            <= 'Z'))
            CheckVowelOrConsonant(myChar);
        else
            System.out.print(myChar + " is not an alphabet");

        scan.close();
    }

    static void CheckVowelOrConsonant(char ch)
    {
        if(ch == 'a' || ch == 'e' || ch == 'i' || ch == 'o' || ch == 'u' ||
            ch == 'A' || ch == 'E' || ch == 'I' || ch == 'O' || ch == 'U')
                System.out.print("Character " + ch + " is a Vowel");
        else
            System.out.print("Character " + ch + " is a Consonant");
    }
}
```

Output
Enter a character: a
Character a is a Vowel

Output
Enter a character: %
% is not an alphabet

Write a program in Java to determine if an entered number is a Buzz number.

Hint: A number is said to be a Buzz number if it ends with 7 or is divisible by 7.

Examples: 1007 is a Buzz number as it ends with 7; 343 is also a Buzz Number as it is divisible by 7; but 978 is not a buzz number as it is not divisible by 7.

Listing 9.15: BuzzNumber.java

```java
import java.util.Scanner;
public class BuzzNumber
{
    public static void main(String args[])
    {
        Scanner input = new Scanner(System.in);

        System.out.print("Enter a number: ");
        int num = input.nextInt();

        if ((num % 10 == 7) || (num % 7 == 0))
            System.out.println (num + " is a Buzz number");
        else
            System.out.println (num + " is not a Buzz number");

        input.close();
    }
}
```

Output
Enter a number: 343
343 is a Buzz number

Output
Enter a number: 978
978 is not a Buzz number

Write a program to print the given values in an ascending order. For example, if the inputs are 9, 18, and 5, your program should print 5, 9, 18.

Listing 9.16: AscendingOrder.java

```java
import java.util.Scanner;
public class AscendingOrder
{
    public static void main (String args [])
```

```
5      {
6          Scanner keyboard = new Scanner(System.in);
7
8          System.out.print("Please enter the first number:");
9          int a = keyboard.nextInt();
10         System.out.print("Please enter the second number:");
11         int b = keyboard.nextInt();
12         System.out.print("Please enter the third number:");
13         int c = keyboard.nextInt();
14
15         System.out.println("The numbers in ascending order are: ");
16
17         if (a < b)
18             if (a < c)
19                 if (b < c)
20                     System.out.println(a + ", " + b + ", " + c);
21                 else
22                     System.out.println(a + ", " + c + ", " + b);
23             else
24                 System.out.println(c + ", " + a + ", " + b);
25         else
26             if (b < c)
27                 if (a < c)
28                     System.out.println(b + ", " + a + ", " + c);
29                 else
30                     System.out.println(b + ", " + c + ", " + a);
31             else
32                 System.out.println(c + ", " + b + ", " + a);
33     }
34 }
```

Output

```
Please enter the first number:9
Please enter the second number:18
Please enter the third number:5
The numbers in ascending order are:
5, 9, 18
```

Write a program in Java, using the `switch` statement, to determine if an entered alphabet is a vowel or a consonant.

Listing 9.17: CheckChar.java

```
1 import java.util.Scanner;
2 public class CheckChar
3 {
4     public static void main(String args[])
5     {
```

```
6        Scanner scanner = new Scanner(System.in);
7
8        System.out.print("Enter a character: ");
9        char myChar = scanner.next().charAt(0);
10
11       if ((myChar >= 'a' && myChar <= 'z') || (myChar >='A' && myChar ↵
            ↪ <= 'Z'))
12           CheckVowelOrConsonant(myChar);
13       else
14           System.out.print(myChar + " is not an alphabet");
15
16       scanner.close();
17   }
18
19   static void CheckVowelOrConsonant(char ch)
20   {
21       switch(ch)
22       {
23           case 'a': case 'e': case 'i': case 'o': case 'u':
24           case 'A': case 'E': case 'I': case 'O': case 'U':
25               System.out.print("Character " + ch + " is a Vowel");
26               break;
27
28           default:
29               System.out.print("Character " + ch + " is a Consonant");
30       }
31   }
32 }
```

Output
Enter a character: u
Character u is a Vowel

Output
Enter a character: T
Character T is a Consonant

Create a Menu driven program to perform the following operations:

1. Addition
2. Subtraction
3. Multiplication
4. Division
5. Remainder
6. Exit

After making a selection, the program should ask the user to input two numbers and perform the requested operation. An appropriate message should be displayed for an invalid choice.

Listing 9.18: Calculator.java

```
1  import java.util.Scanner;
2  public class Calculator
3  {
4      public static void main(String args[])
5      {
6          double num1, num2, result = 0;
7          Scanner scan = new Scanner(System.in);
8
9          System.out.println("  Calculator Menu");
10         System.out.println("  ===============");
11         System.out.println("    1.Addition");
12         System.out.println("    2.Subtraction");
13         System.out.println("    3.Multiplication");
14         System.out.println("    4.Division");
15         System.out.println("    5.Remainder");
16         System.out.println("    6.Exit");
17         System.out.println();
18
19         System.out.print("  Enter your choice (1-6) ");
20         int choice = scan.nextInt();
21
22         switch(choice)
23         {
24             case 1:
25                 num1 = AcceptInput(1);
26                 num2 = AcceptInput(2);
27                 result = num1 + num2;
28                 break;
29
30             case 2:
31                 num1 = AcceptInput(1);
32                 num2 = AcceptInput(2);
33                 result = num1 - num2;
34                 break;
35
36             case 3:
37                 num1 = AcceptInput(1);
38                 num2 = AcceptInput(2);
39                 result = num1 * num2;
40                 break;
41
42             case 4:
43                 num1 = AcceptInput(1);
44                 num2 = AcceptInput(2);
45                 result = num1 / num2;
```

```
46                    break;
47
48            case 5:
49                    num1 = AcceptInput(1);
50                    num2 = AcceptInput(2);
51                    result = num1 % num2;
52                    break;
53
54            case 6:
55                    System.out.println ("Thanks for using the Calculator!");
56                    System.exit(0);
57
58            default:
59                    System.out.println("*** Invalid option entered ***");
60                    System.exit(0);
61        }
62
63        System.out.println ("Result is: " + result);
64        scan.close();
65    }
66
67    public static double AcceptInput(int i)
68    {
69        Scanner scan = new Scanner(System.in);
70        System.out.println ("Please enter number " + i + ":");
71        double num = scan.nextDouble();
72        scan.close();
73        return num;
74    }
75 }
```

```
                    Output
          Calculator Menu
          ==========
             1.Addition
             2.Subtraction
             3.Multiplication
             4.Division
             5.Remainder
             6.Exit
          Enter your choice (1-6) 5
        Please enter number 1:
        625
        Please enter number 2:
        3
        Result is: 1.0
```

Zen Computers is a seller of personal computers. The staff works on a commission basis. At the end of each month, each sales person's commission is calculated according to the table listed below. The staff is also paid an advance amount Rs.1000 every month. When the sales commission is calculated, the advance amount is subtracted from the commission. If any salesperson's commission is less than the amount, he or she must pay back the difference.

Write a program in Java to compute the commission at the end of each month.

Total Sales (current month)	Commission Rate
Less than Rs. 20,000	Nil
Rs. 20,000 – Rs. 39,999	3%
Rs. 40,000 – Rs. 59,999	5%
Rs. 60,000 – Rs. 79,999	8%
Rs. 80,000 or more	10%

Listing 9.19: CommissionCalculator.java

```java
import java.util.Scanner;
public class CommissionCalculator
{
    public static void main(String args[])
    {
        double totalSales, commissionRate, commissionAmount,
            advanceAmount, payAmount;

        Scanner input = new Scanner(System.in);

        System.out.print("Enter total sales this month: ");
        totalSales = input.nextDouble();

        System.out.print("Enter advance amount: ");
        advanceAmount = input.nextDouble();

        if (totalSales < 20000)
            commissionRate = 0.0;
        else if (totalSales < 40000)
            commissionRate = 0.03;
        else if (totalSales < 60000)
            commissionRate = 0.05;
        else if (totalSales < 80000)
            commissionRate = 0.08;
        else
            commissionRate = 0.10;
```

```
26
27        commissionAmount = totalSales * commissionRate;
28        payAmount = commissionAmount - advanceAmount;
29
30        System.out.println("Commission Rate : " + (commissionRate * 100) ↵
              ↳ + "%");
31        System.out.println("Amount Payable   : " + payAmount);
32    }
33 }
```

Output

Enter total sales this month: 55950
Enter advance amount: 1000
Commission Rate : 5.0%
Amount Payable : 1797.5

City Electronics company gives a discount on the total amount of goods sold as per the following table. Write a program in Java which accepts the product price and the number of units sold. Calculate the amount of discount applicable and the amount payable.

Total Cost	Discount Rate
>= Rs. 100,000	5.0%
>= Rs. 75,000 and < Rs. 100,000	3.5%
>= Rs. 50,000 and <Rs. 75,000	2.5%
>= Rs. 20,000 and <Rs. 50,0000	1.5%
< Rs. 20,000	1.0%

Listing 9.20: DiscountCalculator.java

```
1  import java.util.Scanner;
2  public class DiscountCalculator
3  {
4      public static void main(String args[])
5      {
6          double producePrice, unitsSold, totalAmount, discountRate, ↵
                 ↳ discountAmount, payAmount;
7
8          Scanner input = new Scanner(System.in);
9
10         System.out.print("Enter the Product Price: ");
11         producePrice = input.nextDouble();
12
13         System.out.print("Enter Units Sold: ");
14         unitsSold = input.nextDouble();
```

```
15
16          totalAmount = producePrice * unitsSold;
17
18      if (totalAmount >= 100000)
19          discountRate = 0.05;
20      else if ((totalAmount >= 75000) && (totalAmount < 100000))
21          discountRate = 0.035;
22      else if ((totalAmount >= 50000) && (totalAmount < 75000))
23          discountRate = 0.025;
24      else if ((totalAmount >= 20000) && (totalAmount < 50000))
25          discountRate = 0.015;
26      else
27          discountRate = 0.01;
28
29      discountAmount = totalAmount * discountRate;
30      payAmount = totalAmount - discountAmount;
31
32      System.out.println("*******************************");
33      System.out.println("Product Price      : " + producePrice);
34      System.out.println("Units Sold         : " + unitsSold);
35      System.out.println("Total Amount       : " + totalAmount);
36      System.out.println("Discount Rate      : " + (discountRate * 100) + ↵
            ↪ "%");
37      System.out.println("Discount Amount    : " + discountAmount);
38      System.out.println("Amount Payable     : " + payAmount);
39      System.out.println("*******************************");
40  }
41 }
```

Output

```
Enter the Product Price: 25700
Enter Units Sold: 2
****************************
Product Price : 25700.0
Units Sold : 2.0
Total Amount : 51400.0
Discount Rate : 2.5%
Discount Amount : 1285.0
Amount Payable : 50115.0
****************************
```

Write a program in Java that reads month number and the year in yyyy format and displays number of days in that month.

Listing 9.21: DaysInMonth.java

```
1 import java.util.Scanner;
```

```java
2  public class DaysInMonth
3  {
4      public static void main(String args[])
5      {
6          int numberOfDays = 0;
7          Scanner keyboard = new Scanner(System.in);
8
9          System.out.print("Enter month number: ");
10         int month= keyboard.nextInt();
11
12         System.out.print("Enter year in the yyyy format: ");
13         int year = keyboard.nextInt();
14
15         switch(month)
16         {
17             case 1:
18             case 3:
19             case 5:
20             case 7:
21             case 8:
22             case 10:
23             case 12:
24                 numberOfDays = 31;
25                 break;
26
27             case 4:
28             case 6:
29             case 9:
30             case 11:
31                 numberOfDays = 30;
32                 break;
33
34             case 2:
35                 if (IsLeapYear(year))
36                     numberOfDays = 29;
37                 else
38                     numberOfDays = 28;
39
40                 break;
41
42             default:
43                 System.out.print("Invalid month " + month);
44                 System.exit(0);
45         }
46
47         System.out.println ("Number of days is " + numberOfDays);
48         keyboard.close();
49     }
```

```
50
51    static boolean IsLeapYear(int year)
52    {
53        boolean leapYear = false;
54
55        if (((year % 4 == 0) &&  !(year % 100 == 0)) || (year % 400 == 0))
56            leapYear = true;
57        else
58            leapYear = false;
59
60        return leapYear;
61    }
62 }
```

```
Output
Enter month number: 4
Enter year in the yyyy format: 2015
Number of days is 30
```

Multiple Choice Questions

1. Which of the following are conditional constructs?

   A. if-else

   B. if-else-if ladder

   C. switch statement

   D. All of the above

2. Which operator cannot be used with if-else statement?

   A. <=   B. || C. &&   D. ?:

3. What will be the output of the following code?

   ```
   int size = 2;
   if (size < 0)
       System.out.println("Small");
   else if (size == 0)
       System.out.println("Medium");
   else
       System.out.println("Large");
   ```

   A. Small

   B. Large

   C. Medium

   D. Runtime error

4. What will be the output of the following code?

   ```
   int fruit = 3;
   switch (fruit + 1)
   {
       case 1:
           System.out.println("Banana");
           break ;
       case 2:
   ```

```
            System.out.println("Apple");
            break ;
        case 3:
            System.out.println("Orange");
            break ;
        default :
            System.out.println("Fruitless");
    }
```

    A. Orange   B. Banana   C. Apple   D. Fruitless

5. Predict the output of the following code snippet:

```
int a = 1;
int b = 2;
if (a == b)
    System.out.println ("Both values are equal");
else
    System.out.println ("Values are not equal");
```

  A. Both values are equal   C. Values are not equal

  B. Incorrect use of the == operator   D. No output

6. Consider the following code snippet:

```
if ( c > d)
    x = c;
else
    x = d;
```

Choose the correct option if the code mentioned above is rewritten using the ternary operator:

  A. x = (c >d) ? c : d;   C. x = (c >d) ? c : c;

  B. x = (c >d) ? d : c;   D. x = (c >d) ? d : d;

7. if ((a > b) && (a > c)), then which of the following statements is **true**?

  A. a is the largest number.   C. c is the largest number.

  B. b is the largest number.   D. b is the smallest number.

8. Consider the following code snippet:

```
int val = 2;
switch (val)
{
    case 1: "System.out.println("Case 1");
        break;
    case 2: "System.out.println("Case 2");
```

```
        break;
    default: "System.out.println("No match found");
        break;
}
```

Which of the following statements is correct?

A. case 1 will be executed.   C. default will be executed.

B. case 2 will be executed.   D. both case 1 and 2 will be executed.

9. A sequence of statements enclosed between a pair of curly brackets is called ....

A. a compound statement   C. a null statement

B. an empty statement   D. a void statement

10. Which clause is optional in the switch statement?

A. `default`   C. `switch`

B. `case`   D. None of the above

11. Which of the following statements involves a fall-through?

A. `if-else`   C. `if-else-if` ladder

B. `for` loop   D. `switch`

12. Which of the following causes a fall-through in the switch statement?

A. the omission of fall   C. the omission of break

B. the omission of continue   D. the omission of loop

13. Which of the following is mandatory in the switch statement?

A. `break`   B. `continue`   C. `case`   D. `default`

14. Which of the following statement is a valid combination?

A. `if` inside `switch`   C. `else` inside `switch`

B. `switch` inside `if`   D. `default` inside `if`

Assignment Questions

1. What is sequential flow of control? Explain with an example.

2. What is conditional flow of control? Explain with an example.

3. Explain the significance of **break** statement in the **switch** statement.

4. What is a fall through? Give an example.

---

5. Explain the significance of the `default` label in the `switch` statement.

6. Explain the use of `System.exit(n)` method in Java.

7. Format the following `if` statements with indentation:

(i) `if (x == y) if (x == z) x = 1; else y = 1; else z = 1;`

(ii) `if (x == y) {if (y == z) x = 1; y = 2; } else z = 1;`

(iii)
```
if (num1 != num2) {
    if (num2 >= num3) x = 1; y = 2; }
    else {x = 1; if (num1 == num2) z = 3;}
```

8. Rewrite the following `if` statement, using the `switch` statement:
```
if (choice == 1)
    System.out.println("You selected One");
else if (choice == 2)
    System.out.println("You selected Two");
else if (choice == 3)
    System.out.println("You selected Three");
else if (choice == 4)
    System.out.println("You selected Four");
else if (choice == 5)
    System.out.println("You selected Five");
else if (choice == 6)
    System.out.println("You selected Six");
else
    System.out.println("Invalid choice");
```

9. Write the following `switch` statement by using nested `if` statements:
```
switch (choice)
{
    case 0:
    case 1:
        x = 111;
        y = 222;
        break;
    case 2:
        x = 333;
        y = 444;
        break;
    case 3:
        x = -11;
        y = -22;
        break;
    default:
        y = 555;
}
```

10. Write an `if` statement to find the smallest of the three given integers using the `min()` method of the `Math` class.

11. Find the error in the given statement:

    ```
    int x= (a => b)? "a" : "b";
    ```

12. Find the error, if any, in the following code. Write the correct statement.

    ```
    int a=5, b=10;
    int x = (a>b)>true:false;
    ```

13. Rewrite the following statement using `if else`:

    ```
    int max=215, min=323;
    String str=(max>min) ? "Max greater than Min" : "Min Greater than Max";
    ```

14. What will be the value of 'n' after the execution of the code given below?

    ```
    int x=2, m=1, c=-1;
    int n = x + c;
    n = n - c +x;
    System.out.println(n);
    ```

15. What will be the output of the following code?

    ```
    int x=2,y=5,a=0;
    a=x;
    x=y;
    y=a;
    System.out.println("x=" + x + " y=" + y);
    ```

16. Find the errors in the following code and rewrite the correct version:

    ```
    char m="A";
    Switch("A");
    {
        Case 'a';
            System.out.println("A");
            break;
        Case 'b';
            System.out.println("B");
            break;
        Default:
            System.out.println("Not a valid option");
    }
    ```

17. Write a program to find the number of and sum of all integers greater than 500 and less than 1000 that are divisible by 17.

18. Create a program to find out if the number entered by the user is a two, three or four digits number.
    Sample input: 1023
    Sample output: 1023 is a four digit number.

19. Write a program in Java that reads a word and checks whether it begins with a vowel or not.

20. Write a program in Java to read three integers and display them in descending order.

21. Using the ternary operator, create a program to find the largest of three numbers.

22. Write a program that reads a month number and displays it in words.

23. Admission in a professional course is subject to the following criteria:

    (i) Marks in Physics $>= 70$

    (ii) Marks in Chemistry $>= 60$

    (iii) Marks in Mathematics $>= 70$

    (iv) Total marks in all subjects $>= 225$

    Or

    Total marks in Physics and Mathematics $>= 150$

    Write a program in Java to accept marks in these 3 subjects (Physics, Chemistry, and Mathematics) and display if a candidate is eligible.

24. Using the `switch` statement in Java, write a program to display the name of the city according to the user's choice. D – Delhi, M – Mumbai, K – Kolkata, C – Chennai

25. Write a program that will read the value of x and compute the following function:
$$y = \begin{cases} 7, & \text{if } x > 0 \\ 0, & \text{if } x = 0 \\ -7, & \text{if } x < 0 \end{cases}$$

26. Employees at Arkenstone Consulting earn the basic hourly wage of $15. In addition to this, they also receive a commission on the sales they generate while tending the counter. The commission given to them is calculated according to the following table:

Total Sales	Commission Rate
$100 to less than $1000	1.0%
$1000 to less than $10000	2.0%
$10000 to less than $25000	3.0%
$25000 and above	3.5%

Write a program in Java that inputs the number of hours worked and the total sales. Compute the wages of the employees.

27. Write a program in Java to compute the perimeter and area of a triangle, with its three sides given as a, b, and c using the following formulas:

$Perimeter = a + b + c$

$Area = \sqrt{s(s-a)(s-b)(s-c)}$

Where $s = \dfrac{a+b+c}{2}$

28. Mayur Transport Company charges for parcels as per the following tariff:

Weight	Charges
Upto 10 Kg.	£30 per Kg.
For the next 20 Kg.	£20 per Kg.
Above 30 Kg.	£15 per Kg.

Write a program in Java to calculate the charge for a parcel, taking the weight of the parcel as an input.

29. Create a program in Java to find out if a number entered by the user is a Duck Number. A Duck Number is a number which has zeroes present in it, but there should be no zero present in the beginning of the number. For example, 6710, 8066, 5660303 are all duck numbers whereas 05257, 080009 are not.

30. The electricity board charges the bill according to the number of units consumed and the rate as given below:

Units Consumed	Rate Per Unit
First 100 units	80 Pence per unit
Next 200 units	£1 per unit
Above 300 units	£2.50 per unit

Write a program in Java to accept the total units consumed by a customer and calculate the bill. Assume that a meter rent of £50 is charged from the customer.

31. Write a menu driven program to accept a number from the user and check whether it is a Buzz number or an Automorphic number.

   (i) Automorphic number is a number, whose square's last digit(s) are equal to that number. For example, 25 is an automorphic number, as its square is 625 and 25 is present as the last two digits.

   (ii) Buzz number is a number, that ends with 7 or is divisible by 7.

32. Write a Java program in which you input students name, class, roll number, and marks in 5 subjects. Find out the total marks, percentage, and grade according to the following table.

Percentage	Grade
>=90	A+
>=80 and <90	A
>=70 and <80	B+
>=60 and <70	B
>=50 and <60	C
>=40 and <50	D
<40	E

33. Write a program in Java to accept three numbers and check whether they are Pythagorean Triplet or not. The program must display the message accordingly. [Hint: $h^2 = p^2 + b^2$]

34. Using switch case, write a program to convert temperature from Fahrenheit to Celsius and Celsius to Fahrenheit.

   Fahrenheit to Celsius formula: $(F - 32) \times 5/9$
   Celsius to Fahrenheit formula: $(C \times 9/5) + 32$

35. Star mall is offering discount on various types of products purchased by its customers. Following table shows different type of products and their respective code along with the discount offered. Based on the code entered, the mall is calculating the total amount after deducting the availed discount. Create a program to calculate total amount to be paid by the customer.

Item	Item Code	Discount
Laptop	L	5%
LCD	D	7%
XBox	X	10%
Printer	P	11%

36. A cloth showroom has announced the following festival discounts on the purchase of items based on the total cost of the items purchased:

Total Cost	Discount Rate
Less than $2000	5%
$2001 to $5000	25%
$5001 to $10,000	35%
Above $10,000	50%

Write a program to input the total cost and to compute and display the amount to be paid by the customer after availing the discount.

37. A cloth manufacturing company offers discounts to the dealers and retailers. The discount is computed using the total length of the cloth as per the following table:

Length of cloth	Dealer's Discount	Retailer's Discount
Up to 1000 meters	20%	15%
Above 1000 meters but less than 2000 meters	25%	20%
More than 2000 meters	35%	25%

Write a program in Java to input the length of the cloth and the total amount of purchase. The program should display a menu to accept type of customer – Dealer (D) or Retailer (R) and print the amount to be paid. Display a suitable error message for a wrong choice.

38. Using switch case statement in Java, create a program to convert rupee into dollar and dollar into rupee according to the user's choice. Assume conversion price: 1 Dollar = Rs.77.

39. A box of cookies can hold 24 cookies, and a container can hold 75 boxes of cookies. Write a program that prompts the user to enter the total number of cookies, the number of cookies in each box, and the number of cookies boxes in a container. The program then outputs the number of boxes and the number of containers required to ship the cookies.

40. Write a menu driven program to display the following menu:

Conversion Table
==========
1. Milliseconds to Seconds
2. Milliseconds to Minutes
3. Seconds to Milliseconds
4. Seconds to Minutes
5. Minutes to Milliseconds
6. Minutes to Seconds

For an incorrect choice, display an appropriate error message.
Hint: 1 second = 1000 milliseconds

41. Using the switch statement, write a menu driven program:

(i) To check and display whether a number input by the user is a composite number or not.
A number is said to be composite, if it has one or more than one factors excluding 1 and the number itself. Example: 4, 6, 8, 9...

(ii) To find the smallest digit of an integer that is input:
Sample input: 6524
Sample output: Smallest digit is 2
For an incorrect choice, an appropriate error message should be displayed.

42. A new taxi service based on electric vehicles is offering services within a metro city. Following is the fare chart including the type of taxi used to commute and price per kilometer. Create a program to calculate total fare depending on the distance travelled in kilometers.

Type	Fare
Micro	10.05/Km
Macro	15.05/Km
Shared	7.05/Km

43. The City Library charges late fine from members if the books were not returned on time as per the following table:

Number of days late	Magazines fine per day	Text books fine per day
Up to 5 days	£1	£2
6 to 10 days	£2	£3
11 to 15 days	£3	£4
15 to 20 days	£5	£6
More than 20 days	£6	£7

Using the switch statement, write a program in Java to input name of person, number of days late and type of book – 'M' for Magazine and 'T' for Text book. Compute the total fine and display it along with the name of the person.

Answers To Objective Questions

Multiple Choice Questions

1. D	3. B	5. C	7. A	9. A	11. D	13. C
2. D	4. D	6. A	8. B	10. A	12. C	14. A

Chapter 10

Iterative Constructs in Java

Iterative Constructs in Java

IN the previous chapters, you have learnt how to use the sequencing constructs to execute a set of statements in sequence and selection constructs to execute certain set of statements only if a condition is met. In this chapter, you will learn about the looping or iterative constructs that allow a set of instructions to be executed repeatedly until a condition is met.

Java provides three kinds of looping constructs – `for` loop, `while` loop and `do-while` loop. All three loops repeat a set of instructions as long as the underlying condition remains true. The underlying condition is termed as the test condition. The test condition may be evaluated before the start of the loop or at the end of the loop. Accordingly, the loop is termed as an *entry-controlled loop* or *exit-controlled loop*, respectively. Let us understand various segments of a looping construct.

10.1 Segments of a loop

A *loop* is a set of instructions that is continually repeated until a certain condition is met. The set of instructions may be repeated any number of times, as per your requirement. The loop consists of a number of segments as explained below:

10.1.1 Initialisation

This segment initialises the loop control variable[1] before starting the loop. This segment is executed only once at the beginning of the loop. An example of initialisation is:

```
int counter = 0; //initialise the loop control variable
```

> **Note**
>
> In the above statement, counter is a loop control variable.

10.1.2 Test-condition

The test-condition is the expression that is evaluated at the beginning of each iteration. Its value determines whether the body of the loop is to be executed or the loop is to be terminated. If the test-condition evaluates to **true**, the body of the loop (set of instructions) gets executed. If the test-condition evaluates to **false**, the loop terminates. An example of the test-condition is:

```
counter <= 50; //check condition
```

---

[1]A loop control variable (also known as a counter variable) is used to keep the record of the number of times the loop has been executed.

10.1.3 Update - the next step

This is the increment or decrement operation of the control variable. This operation is performed at the end of each iteration. An example of update statement is:

```
counter++; //update the loop control variable
```

10.1.4 Body of the loop

The body of the loop contains the set of instructions that is executed repeatedly. The statements are usually grouped together between a pair of curly brackets. For example,

```
{
    System.out.println("Iteration: " + counter);
    sum = sum + counter;
}
```

The body of the loop is repeated as long as the test-condition remains `true`. As soon as the condition becomes `false`, the loop terminates. The process of executing the body of the loop once is called an *iteration*.

10.2 The for loop

The `for` loop is an *entry-controlled loop* and performs a fixed number of iterations. This loop is generally used when the user knows in advance how many times the set of instructions is to be repeated. It's syntax is:

```
for (initialisation; test-condition; update)
{
    body-of-the-loop;
}
```

Here,

- The `initialisation` part is executed once before the loop begins, such as `counter = 0` or `i = 1`. The variables `counter` and `i` are known as loop control variables.

- The `test-condition` is evaluated before each iteration of the loop, such as `counter < 10`. The loop terminates when this condition evaluates to `false`.

- The `update` part is executed at the end of each iteration of the loop, such as `counter++`.

> **Note**
>
> The curly brackets {} are optional if the body of the loop contains a single statement.

Let us consider a simple program to understand how the for loop works.

Listing 10.1: NaturalNumbersForLoop.java

```
1  public class NaturalNumbersForLoop
2  {
3      public static void main(String args[])
4      {
5          for ( int i = 1;  i <= 5;  i++ )
6          {
7              System.out.println(i);
8          }
9      }
10 }
```

Initialisation

Test-condition

Update

Body of the loop

The execution of the for loop takes place as given below (see Figure 10.1):

(i) First of all, the initialisation ① of the control variable occurs giving it the initial value, i.e., i = 1.

(ii) Next, the test-condition i < = 5 is evaluated ②. Since i = 1 at this stage, the test-condition evaluates to true.

(iii) Since the test-condition is true, the body of the loop is executed printing ③ the value of i.

(iv) Once the body of the loop is executed, the update segment increments the value of the control variable i ④ using expression i++ giving it a value of 2.

(v) Now, the test-condition i <= 5 is evaluated again ② and the statements are repeated until the test condition evaluates to false.

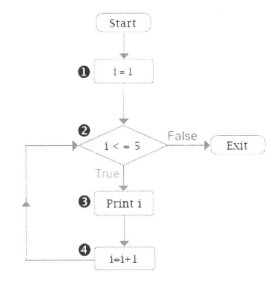

Figure 10.1: Flowchart - for loop

Iteration	Initialisation ❶	Test-condition ❷	Body-of-the-loop ❸	Update ❹
1	i = 1	i <= 5 evaluates to true	Executed	i = 2
2		i <= 5 evaluates to true	Executed	i = 3
3		i <= 5 evaluates to true	Executed	i = 4
4		i <= 5 evaluates to true	Executed	i = 5
5		i <= 5 evaluates to true	Executed	i = 6
6		i <= 5 evaluates to false	Not executed. Loop terminates.	

Figure 10.2: Various Iterations in the for Loop

```
Output
1
2
3
4
5
```

Write a program to display first 10 odd numbers starting with 51.

Listing 10.2: PrintOddNumbers.java

```
1  public class PrintOddNumbers
2  {
3     public static void main(String args[])
4     {
5        int oddNum = 51;
6
7        for (int n = 1; n <= 10; n++)
8        {
9           System.out.println(oddNum);
10          oddNum += 2;
11       }
12    }
13 }
```

```
Output
51
53
55
57
59
61
63
65
67
69
```

In the above example, variable `oddNum` has been used to store the odd numbers for printing. The `for` loop is just used to control the number of odd numbers you want to display.

Listing 10.3: PrintTable.java

```
1  import java.util.Scanner;
2  public class PrintTable
3  {
4     public static void main(String args[])
5     {
6        Scanner input = new Scanner(System.in);
7        System.out.println("Enter a number: ");
8        int number = input.nextInt();
9
10       System.out.println("*** Table of " + number + " ***");
11
12       for (int i = 1; i <= 10; i++)
13       {
14          System.out.println(number + " x " + i + " = " + (i * number));
```

```
15        }
16
17        input.close();
18    }
19 }
```

Output

```
Enter a number:
8
*** Table of 8 ***
8 x 1 = 8
8 x 2 = 16
8 x 3 = 24
8 x 4 = 32
8 x 5 = 40
8 x 6 = 48
8 x 7 = 56
8 x 8 = 64
8 x 9 = 72
8 x 10 = 80
```

Write a program in Java to display the natural numbers from 20 to 10, i.e., in the reverse order.

Listing 10.4: ReverseOrder.java

```
1  public class ReverseOrder
2  {
3      public static void main(String args[])
4      {
5          for (int i = 20; i >= 10; i--)
6          {
7              System.out.println(i);
8          }
9      }
10 }
```

Output

```
20
19
18
17
16
15
14
13
12
11
10
```

Write a program in Java to display the number pattern as shown below.
```
1 9
3 7
5 5
7 3
9 1
```

Listing 10.5: NumberPattern.java

```
1  public class NumberPattern
2  {
3     public static void main(String args[])
4     {
5        for (int i = 1, j = 9; i <= 9; i += 2, j -= 2)
6        {
7           System.out.println(i + "   " + j);
8        }
9     }
10 }
```

Output	
1	9
3	7
5	5
7	3
9	1

Code Walkthrough:

◈ Line 5:

- Initialises two control variables i and j, one for each column. The control variable i has been initialised with value 1 and the control variable j has been initialised with value 9.

- In the update segment of the for loop, value of the first control variable i has been incremented by 2 whereas value of the second control variable j has been decremented by 2.

◈ Line 7: Prints the value of control variables i and j, separated by a space.

10.2.1 Variations in the for loop

Java offers a number of variations of the for loop that increase its power and applicability. These variations are detailed below:

(i) Control variable data type: The control variable may be of any data type, for example, char, float and double. Program 10.6 is an example where the control variable is of double data type.

Listing 10.6: DoubleCVForLoop.java

```
1  public class DoubleCVForLoop
2  {
3     public static void main(String args[])
4     {
5        for (double d = 10.0; d <= 20; d += 2.5)
6        {
7           System.out.println(d);
8        }
9     }
10 }
```

Output
10.0
12.5
15.0
17.5
20.0

(ii) Multiple initialisation and updates: The `for` loop may contain multiple initialisations and updates, separated by commas.

Listing 10.7: NumberPattern.java

```
1  public class NumberPattern
2  {
3      public static void main(String args[])
4      {
5          for ( int i = 1, j = 9;  i <= 9;  i += 2, j -= 2 )
6          {
7              System.out.println(i + "   " + j);
8          }
9      }
10 }
```

Multiple Initialisation

Multiple Update

Notice that in this program, two initialisations `i=1` and `j=9` are used. Both initialisations will be executed at the start of the for loop. However, the `for` loop will be dependent on the control variable `i` for iterations as that is the only variable used in the test-condition.

Output	
1	9
3	7
5	5
7	3
9	1

(iii) Control variable independence: The test-condition need not be limited to use only control variables. In fact, the test-condition controlling the `for` loop can be any boolean expression. For example, let us look at the following program code:

Listing 10.8: ConditionForLoop.java

```
1  public class ConditionForLoop
2  {
3      public static void main(String args[])
4      {
5          boolean finished = false;
6          for (int counter = 11; !finished; counter++)
7          {
8              System.out.println(counter);
9
10             if (counter % 7 == 0)
11             {
12                 finished = true;
13                 System.out.println("Condition met...");
14             }
15         }
16     }
17 }
```

Output
11
12
13
14
Condition met...

In this example, the `for` loop continues to run until the boolean variable finished is set to `true`. It does not test the value of `i`.

(iv) Optional segments: In the `for` loop, the initialisation, the test-condition, and the update segment are optional. That means, you can create the `for` loop without any or all of these segments. The following code is an example where the initialisation and the update segment are omitted.

Listing 10.9: OptionalForLoop.java

```
1  public class OptionalForLoop
2  {
3     public static void main(String args[])
4     {
5        int n = 5;
6        for (; n <= 10; )
7        {
8           System.out.println(n);
9           n++;
10       }
11    }
12 }
```

```
Output
5
6
7
8
9
10
```

Note that even if the initialisation and update segments are omitted, the semicolon (;) following initialisation must still be present. The Java compiler takes the current value of the variable as the start value for the loop.

(v) Infinite for loop: A loop that never terminates is called an *infinite loop*.The following is an example where all the three segments have been omitted. Such a for statement will create an infinite loop.

Listing 10.10: InfiniteForLoop.java

```
1  public class InfiniteForLoop
2  {
3     public static void main(String args[])
4     {
5        for ( ; ; )
6        {
7           System.out.println("Hello there!");
8        }
9     }
10 }
```

This loop will run forever displaying the message "Hello there!" because there is no test-condition under which it will terminate.

(vi) Empty for loop: A for loop can just contain a null statement, i.e., just a semicolon (;). Such a loop is called an empty loop. Program 10.11 shows the code for an empty loop. The program just waits until the loop completes.

Listing 10.11: EmptyForLoop.java

```
1  public class EmptyForLoop
2  {
3      public static void main(String args[])
4      {
5          for (int i = 1; i <= 50000; i++) ;
6      }
7  }
```

Pitfall of a for loop

Sometimes, you may expect a for loop to perform a certain action a number of times, but the result is not as you expected. To understand this, consider the following for loop statement:

```
for (int i = 1; i <= 10; i++);   ◀──────  Problematic semicolon
    system.out.printIn("Hello");
```

You might expect this for loop to write the message "Hello" 10 times. However, if you execute this loop in a complete program, only one "Hello" will be displayed instead of 10. The reason for this is that placing a semicolon, just on its own, is treated as an *empty statement*. Java compiler considered this empty statement as the body of the loop and executed it. The System.out.println("Hello"); was not considered as the part of the body of the loop. Hence, when the loop finished, it was executed only once.

10.3   The while loop

The while loop is an *entry-controlled loop* that repeats a statement or a block of statements until its test-condition remains true. Its sytax is:

```
while (condition)
{
    body-of-the-loop;
}
```

During execution of while loop, first of all, the condition is evaluated. If it is true, the body of the loop is executed, and the value of the condition is then re-evaluated. The body of the loop is re-executed until the condition remains true. As soon as the condition becomes false, the control comes out of the loop and executes the statement following the loop. A loop control variable is generally used to control the number of iterations of the while loop. In that sense, the while loop has the following syntax:

```
initialisation;
while (condition)
{
    Body-of-the-loop;
    update;
}
```

The loop control variable is initialised before the loop begins. The loop control variable is updated inside the body of the loop in such a way that the condition becomes false. This causes the loop to terminate.

> **Note**
>
> The curly brackets {} are optional if the body of the loop contains a single statement.

Let us consider an example of a simple while loop to display natural numbers from 1 to 5.

Listing 10.12: NaturalNumbersWhileLoop.java

```
1  public class NaturalNumbersWhileLoop
2  {
3      public static void main(String args[])
4      {
5          int i = 1;              <---------------------- Initialisation
6
7          while ( i <= 5 )        <-------------------- Test-condition
8          {
9              System.out.println(i);
10             i++;                              <---- Body of the loop
11         }
12     }                    <---------------- Update
13 }
```

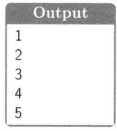

Output
1
2
3
4
5

(i) First of all, the initialisation (1) of the control variable occurs giving it the initial value, i.e., `i=1`.

(ii) Next, the test-condition `i <= 5` is evaluated (2). Since `i=1` at this stage, the test-condition evaluates to `true`.

(iii) Since the test-condition is `true`, the body of the loop is executed (3) printing the value of `i`.

(iv) Once the body of the loop is executed, the update segment increments the value of the control variable `i` (4) using expression `i++` giving it a value of 2.

(v) Now, the test-condition `i <= 5` is evaluated again (5) and the statements are repeated until the test condition evaluates to `false`.

Note that the flow of control is exactly similar to the `for` loop. Figure fig:WhileItr lists various iterations in the `while` loop.

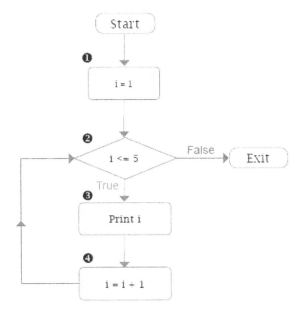

Figure 10.3: Flowchart - while loop

Iteration	Initialisation ❶	Test-condition ❷	Body of the loop ❸	Update ❹
1	i = 1	i <= 5 evaluates to true	Executed	i = 2
2		i <= 5 evaluates to true	Executed	i = 3
3		i <= 5 evaluates to true	Executed	i = 4
4		i <= 5 evaluates to true	Executed	i = 5
5		i <= 5 evaluates to true	Executed	i = 6
6		i <= 5 evaluates to false	Not executed. Loop terminates.	

Figure 10.4: Various Iterations in the while Loop

Write a program using `while` loop to calculate the sum of first 100 even and odd integers.

Listing 10.13: SumOddEven.java

```
1  public class SumOddEven
2  {
3      public static void main(String args[])
4      {
5          int num = 1;
6          int sumEven = 0, sumOdd = 0;
```

```
 7          while (num <= 100)
 8          {
 9              if (num % 2 == 0)
10              sumEven += num;
11              else
12              sumOdd += num;
13
14              num++;
15          }
16
17          System.out.println("The sum of even numbers is " + sumEven);
18          System.out.println("The sum of odd numbers is " + sumOdd);
19      }
20  }
```

Output

The sum of even numbers is 2550
The sum of odd numbers is 2500

Write a program that will display the Fibonacci series between 1 and 200 using a **while** loop. Hint: Fibonacci series is a series of numbers in which each number is the sum of the two preceding numbers. For example: 0 1 1 2 3 5 8 and so on.

Listing 10.14: FibonacciSeries.java

```
 1  public class FibonacciSeries
 2  {
 3      public static void main(String args[])
 4      {
 5          int num = 0, numNext = 1;
 6          int sum = 0;
 7
 8          System.out.println("Fibonacci series is: ");
 9          System.out.print(num + " ");
10          System.out.print(numNext + " ");
11          sum = num + numNext;
12
13          while (sum <= 200)
14          {
15              System.out.print(sum + " ");
16              num = numNext;
17              numNext = sum;
18              sum = num + numNext;
19          }
20      }
21  }
```

Output

Fibonacci series is:
0 1 1 2 3 5 8 13 21 34 55 89 144

Listing 10.15: FindFactorial.java

```java
import java.util.Scanner;
public class FindFactorial
{
   public static void main(String args[])
   {
      Scanner keyboard = new Scanner(System.in);
      int factorial = 1;
      System.out.print("Enter a number: ");
      int num = keyboard.nextInt();
      System.out.print("Factorial of " + num + " is: ");

      while (num > 0)
      {
         factorial *= num;
         num--;
      }

      System.out.println(factorial);
      keyboard.close();
   }
}
```

```
Output
Enter a number: 10
Factorial of 10 is: 3628800
```

10.3.1   Variations in the while loop

Just like the `for` loop, the `while` loop in Java also supports a number of variations. Let us look at some examples of these variations.

(i) Control variable data type: The control variable may be of any data type, including `char`, `double` or `float`.

Listing 10.16: DoubleCVWhileLoop.java

```java
public class DoubleCVWhileLoop
{
   public static void main(String args[])
   {
      double controlVariable = 15;
      while (controlVariable <= 30.5)
      {
         System.out.println(controlVariable);
         controlVariable += 2.5;
      }
   }
}
```

```
Output
15.0
17.5
20.0
22.5
25.0
27.5
30.0
```

(ii) Control variable independence: The test-condition controlling the `while` loop can be any boolean expression and need not be limited to use the control variables only.

Listing 10.17: ConditionWhileLoop.java

```
1  public class ConditionWhileLoop
2  {
3     public static void main(String args[])
4     {
5        boolean finished = false;
6        int counter = 1;
7
8        while (!finished)
9        {
10           System.out.println(counter);
11
12           if (counter % 7 == 0)
13           {
14              finished = true;
15              System.out.println("Condition met...");
16           }
17
18           counter++;
19        }
20     }
21  }
```

```
Output
1
2
3
4
5
6
7
Condition met...
```

(iii) Infinite while loop: Just like the infinite `for` loop, you can also create an infinite `while` loop that never terminates. In such a `while` loop, the condition always remains `true` as shown in the example.

Listing 10.18: InfiniteWhileLoop.java

```
1  public class InfiniteWhileLoop
2  {
3     public static void main(String args[])
4     {
5        while (true)
6        {
7           System.out.println("Hello there!");
8        }
9     }
10 }
```

This loop will run forever, displaying the message "Hello there!" because there is no test-condition under which it will terminate.

(iv) Empty while loop: When a `while` loop just contains a null statement i.e. just a semicolon (;), such a loop is called an empty loop. In the following example, the program just waits until the loop completes.

Listing 10.19: EmptyWhileLoop.java

```java
public class EmptyWhileLoop
{
    public static void main(String args[])
    {
        int n = 1;

        while (++n <= 100);
    }
}
```

10.4   The do-while loop

The `while` loop that we have just discussed in the previous section evaluates the test condition before the loop is executed. Therefore, the body of the loop may not execute at all if the condition is not satisfied in the beginning. On certain occasions, it may be desirable to execute the body of the loop before the test condition is evaluated. In these circumstances, you can use a `do-while` loop. Unlike the `for` and `while` loop, the `do-while` loop is an *exit-controlled loop* that repeats a statement or a block of statements until its test-condition remains `true`. It has the following syntax:

```
do
{
    body-of-the-loop;
}
while (condition);
```

During execution of `do-while` loop, the body of the loop is executed and then the value of the condition is evaluated. If the condition is `true`, the body of the loop is re-executed. As soon as the condition becomes `false`, the loop is terminated. A loop control variable is usually used to control the number of iterations of the `do-while` loop. In that sense, the `do-while` loop has the following syntax:

```
initialisation;
do
{
    body-of-the-loop;
    update;
}
while (condition);
```

Here, the loop control variable is initialised before the loop begins and is updated inside the body of the loop. Since the test-condition to end the loop is evaluated only after the body of the loop has been executed, the body of the `do-while` loop is always executed at least once even if the condition is `false`. The `do-while` loop is especially useful when you present a menu for the user selection. In this case, you would usually want the menu to be displayed at least once. Note that the curly brackets {} are optional if the body of the loop contains a single statement. Let us consider the following example to illustrate the working of `do-while` loop. The program displays natural numbers from 1 to 5.

Listing 10.20: NaturalNumbersDoWhile.java

```
1  public class NaturalNumbersDoWhile
2  {
3      public static void main(String args[])
4      {
5          int i = 1;  <--------------------- Initialisation
6
7          do
8          {
9              System.out.println(i);
10             i++;  <-------- Update          } <--- Body of the loop
11         }
12         while ( i <= 5 );  <--------------------- Test-condition
13     }
14 }
```

Output
1
2
3
4
5

The execution of do-while loop takes place as given below (see Figure 10.5):

(i) First of all, the initialisation ① of the control variable occurs giving it the initial value, i.e., i=1.

(ii) The body of the loop is executed ② printing the value of i.

(iii) The update segment increments the value of the control variable i ③ using the expression i++ giving it a value of 2.

(iv) Next, the test-condition i <= 5 is evaluated ④. Since i=2 at this stage, the test-condition evaluates to true. So, the body of the loop is re-executed. The statements are repeated until the test condition evaluates to false.

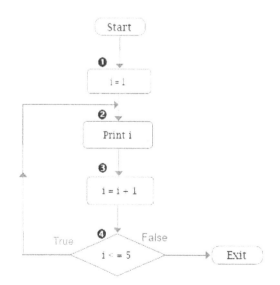

Figure 10.5: Flowchart – do while loop

Table 3 lists various iterations in the `do-while` loop.

Iteration	Initialisation ❶	Body-of-the-loop ❷	Update ❸	Test-condition ❹
1	i = 1	Executed	i = 2	i <= 5 evaluates to true
2		Executed	i = 3	i <= 5 evaluates to true
3		Executed	i = 4	i <= 5 evaluates to true
4		Executed	i = 5	i <= 5 evaluates to true
5		Executed	i = 6	i <= 5 evaluates to false Loop terminates

Figure 10.6: Various Iterations in the do-while Loop

Listing 10.21: ComputeSumOfFactors.java

```java
import java.util.Scanner;
public class ComputeSumOfFactors
{
    public static void main(String args[])
    {
        int sum = 0;
        int n = 1;
        Scanner keyboard = new Scanner(System.in);
        System.out.println("Enter an integer");
        int num = keyboard.nextInt();

        do
        {
            if (num % n == 0)
            {
                System.out.println("Found factor: " + n);
                sum += n;
            }

            n++;
        }
        while (n <= num);

        System.out.println("Sum of factors is: " + sum);
        keyboard.close();
    }
}
```

```
Output
Enter an integer
76
Found factor: 1
Found factor: 2
Found factor: 4
Found factor: 19
Found factor: 38
Found factor: 76
Sum of factors is: 140
```

10.4.1 Variations in the do-while loop

Just like the `for` and `while` loop, the `do-while` loop in Java also supports a number of variations. Let us look at some examples of these variations.

(i) Control variable data type: The control variable may be of any data type. You can have control variable of the `double`, `float` or `char` type, too, as shown in the following example.

Listing 10.22: DoubleCVDoWhile.java

```java
public class DoubleCVDoWhile
{
    public static void main(String args[])
    {
        double n = 15;

        do
        {
            System.out.println(n);
            n += 2.5;
        }
        while (n <= 25.5);
    }
}
```

```
Output
15.0
17.5
20.0
22.5
25.0
```

(ii) Control variable independence: The test-condition controlling the `do-while` loop can be any boolean expression as shown in the following example.

Listing 10.23: ConditionDoWhile.java

```java
public class ConditionDoWhile
{
    public static void main(String args[])
    {
        boolean finished = false;
        int n = 75;

        do
        {
            System.out.println(n);

            if (n % 7 == 0)
            {
                finished = true;
                System.out.println("Condition met...");
            }
```

```
17              n++;
18          }
19          while (!finished);
20      }
21  }
```

Output
75
76
77
Condition met...

(iii) Infinite do-while loop: Just like the infinite `while` loop, you can also create an infinite `do-while` loop that never terminates. In such a `do-while` loop, the condition always remains `true` as shown in the following example.

Listing 10.24: InfiniteDoWhileLoop.java

```java
1  public class InfiniteDoWhileLoop
2  {
3      public static void main(String args[])
4      {
5          do
6          {
7              System.out.println("Hello there!");
8          }
9          while (true);
10      }
11  }
```

This loop will run forever, displaying the message "Hello there!" because there is no test-condition under which it will terminate.

(iv) Empty do-while loop: A `do-while` loop can just contain a null statement. Such a loop is called an empty loop. In the following example, the program just waits until the loop completes.

Listing 10.25: VolumeOverload.java

```java
1  public class EmptyDoWhileLoop
2  {
3      public static void main(String args[])
4      {
5          int i = 1;
6
7          do
8          {
9          }
10          while (++i <= 50);
11      }
12  }
```

10.5   Jump statements

Loops execute a set of instructions repeatedly until the test condition evaluates to `false`. Sometimes, while executing a loop it becomes desirable to skip a part of the loop or to leave the loop as soon as a certain condition occurs. For example, consider the case of finding a particular number if it is a prime number. The program loop written for such scenario should be terminated as soon a factor greater than or equal to 2 is found. Java has features that allow you to unconditionally transfer program control within a method, i.e., without depending on the evaluation of the condition. Such statements are referred to as *jump statements*. These statements are flow control statements that cause a jump to another part of your program. Java supports three jump statements: `return`, `break` and `continue`. The return statement has already been covered in Section 6.5. Let us examine the other two jump statements in this section.

10.5.1   The break statement

The `break` statement terminates the current loop or `switch` statement. The execution then continues from the statement immediately following the current loop or `switch` statement. The `break` statement consists of the keyword `break` followed by a semicolon.

> break;

Programs 10.26, 10.27, and 10.28 show the use of break statement in `for`, `while`, and `do-while` loops.

Listing 10.26: ForLoopBreak.java

```
1  public class ForLoopBreak
2  {
3     public void ForLoopWithBreak()
4     {
5        int sum = 0;
6
7        for (int i = 1; i <= 10; i++)
8        {
9           //statement1;
10          if (sum > 100)
11              break;
12
13          //statement2;
14          sum += 25;
15       }
16
17       System.out.println("Out of the loop");
18    }
19 }
```

Listing 10.27: WhileLoopBreak.java

```
1  public class WhileLoopBreak
2  {
3     public void WhileLoopWithBreak()
4     {
5        int sum = 0;
6        int i = 1;
7
8        while (i <= 10)
9        {
10          //statement1;
11          if (sum > 100)
12             break;
13
14          //statement2;
15          //statement3;
16          sum += 25;
17       }
18
19       System.out.println("Out of the loop");
20    }
21  }
```

Listing 10.28: DoWhileLoopBreak.java

```
1   public class DoWhileLoopBreak
2   {
3      public void DoWhileLoopWithBreak()
4      {
5         int sum = 0;
6         int i = 0;
7
8         do
9         {
10           //statement1;
11           if (sum > 100)
12              break;
13
14           //statement2;
15           //statement3;
16           sum += 25;
17        }
18        while (i <= 10);
19
20        System.out.println("Out of the loop");
21     }
22  }
```

In each of the above-mentioned programs, as soon as the **break** statement is encountered, the loop is terminated, and the execution then continues from the statement immediately following the loop. In each case, as soon as the value of sum is greater than 100, the **break** statement skips the rest of the loop and jumps over to the statement following the loop.

A **break** statement used in a **switch** statement will terminate only the **switch** statement it appears in. If the **switch** is inside a loop, that loop remains unaffected. Let us consider the following program to understand the concept better.

Listing 10.29: SwitchInLoop.java

```java
1  public class SwitchInLoop
2  {
3      public static void main(String args[])
4      {
5          for (int i = 1; i <= 5; i++)
6          {
7              System.out.print(i);
8
9              switch (i)
10             {
11                 case 1:
12                 case 3:
13                 case 5:
14                     System.out.print(" => Odd number");
15                     break;
16
17                 case 2:
18                 case 4:
19                     System.out.print(" => Even number");
20                     break;
21             }
22
23             System.out.println();
24         }
25     }
26 }
```

The break statment will terminate the switch statement only.

Output
1 => Odd number
2 => Even number
3 => Odd number
4 => Even number
5 => Odd number

Notice that the **break** statement used in Lines 15 and 20 causes the termination of the **switch** statement only. The loop continues until the loop control variable i reaches a value of 5.

10.5.2   The continue statement

The **continue** statement in Java instructs the computer to skip the rest of the current iteration of the loop. However, instead of jumping out of the loop completely, it jumps back to the beginning of the loop and continues with the next iteration. This includes the evaluation of the loop controlling condition to check whether any further iterations are required. The **continue** statement consists of the keyword **continue** followed by a semicolon.

```
continue;
```

> **Note**
>
> Unlike the **break** statement which forces termination of the loop, the **continue** statement forces the next iteration of the loop to take place, skipping any instructions in between.

Programs 10.30, 10.31, and 10.32 show the use of continue statement in **for**, **while**, and **do-while** loops.

Listing 10.30: ForLoopContinue.java

```java
1   public class ForLoopContinue
2   {
3       public void ForLoopWithContinue()
4       {
5           int sum = 0;
6
7           for ( int i = 1; i <= 10; i++)
8           {
9               sum += 20;
10              if (sum > 100)
11                  continue;
12
13              //statement2;
14              //statement3;
15          }
16
17          System.out.println("Out of the loop");
18      }
19  }
```

Listing 10.31: WhileLoopContinue.java

```
1   public class WhileLoopContinue
2   {
3      public void WhileLoopWithContinue()
4      {
5         int sum = 0;
6         int i = 1;
7         while (i <= 10)
8         {
9            sum += 20;
10           if (sum > 100)
11               continue;
12
13           //statement;
14           //statement;
15           //statement;
16        }
17
18        System.out.println("Out of the loop");
19     }
20  }
```

Listing 10.32: DoWhileLoopContinue.java

```
1   public class DoWhileLoopContinue
2   {
3      public void DoWhileLoopWithContinue()
4      {
5         int sum = 0;
6         int i = 0;
7
8         do
9         {
10           sum += 20;
11           if (sum > 100)
12               continue;
13
14           //statement;
15           //statement;
16           //statement;
17        }
18        while (i <= 10);
19
20        System.out.println("Out of the loop");
21     }
22  }
```

Write a Java program to display the following series: 1, 2, 4, 5, 7, 8, 10, ... 19
Hint: Skip numbers divisible by 3.

Listing 10.33: ContinueDemo.java

```
1  public class ContinueDemo
2  {
3     public static void main(String args[])
4     {
5        for (int i = 1; i <= 19; i++)
6        {
7           if (i % 3 == 0)
8                continue;
9
10          System.out.print(i + " ");
11       }
12    }
13 }
```

Output

1 2 4 5 7 8 10 11 13 14 16 17 19

In the above-mentioned example, when the loop control variable `i` gets a value divisible by 3 (Line 7), the `continue` statement at Line 8 skips the rest of the iteration, i.e., statement at Line 10.

10.6 Interconversion of loops

You have studied three types of loops provided by Java, namely `for`, `while`, and `do-while` loops. So, while writing a computer program in Java, there is always a flexibility to choose the type of loop. You can convert one type of loop into another, e.g., program written using a `for` loop can be converted into a `while` loop or `do-while` loop. There could be a number of factors in deciding the loop construct that you may want to choose to implement a particular functionality, such as:

- Ease of converting logic to program code

- Ease of readability

- Demand of the logic. For example:

  ⋆ for loop is better suited for programs when you know in advance how many iterations you need.

  ⋆ while loop should be preferred when you may not want to execute the body of the loop even once depending on the condition under test.

  ⋆ do-while loop should be preferred when you want to execute the body of the loop at least once, such as for displaying menu options.

You have seen a number of examples in this chapter where different loops have been used to implement the same logic. For example, Programs 10.1, 10.12, and 10.20 have implemented the same logic to display first 5 natural numbers using different loops. So in Java, three iterative constructs (`for` loop, `while` loop, and `do-while` loop) are available to you, and anyone of them can be used in your program, based on what best fits your requirement.

Solved Programming Exercises

Write a program in Java to display the star pattern shown below.
```
1 *
2 * *
3 * * *
4 * * * *
5 * * * * *
```

Listing 10.34: DisplayStarPattern.java

```
1  public class DisplayStarPattern
2  {
3     public static void main(String args[])
4     {
5        String star = "*";
6        int i;
7
8        for (i = 1; i <= 5; i++, star = star + "*")
9        {
10           System.out.println(i + " " + star);
11       }
12    }
13 }
```

Output
1 *
2 * *
3 * * *
4 * * * *
5 * * * * *

Code Walkthrough:

◈ Line 5: Declares a `String` variable star to hold the stars.

◈ Line 6: Declares the control variable i outside the for loop. Yes, you can do it, and it is legal to do so in Java!

◈ Line 8:

(i) Initialisation: As usual, provide the initial value of the control variable, i.e., `i = 1`.

(ii) Update: In the update segment of the `for` loop, something different has been done this time! In addition to the usual increment of the control variable (`i++`), the existing value of the star variable has been updated. The update concatenates another star (`"*"`) to its existing value. Again yes, you can do it, and it is legal to do so in Java!

◈ Lines 9 - 11: The body of the loop prints the value of the control variable, followed by a space and finally, the current value of the star variable.

Write a program in Java to display the powers of 2 from 1 to 10.

Listing 10.35: PowersOfTwo.java

```java
public class PowersOfTwo
{
   public static void main(String args[])
   {
      int power = 2;

      for (int i = 1; i <= 10; i++, power *= 2)
      {
         System.out.println("2^" + i + " = " + power);
      }
   }
}
```

Output
2^1 = 2
2^2 = 4
2^3 = 8
2^4 = 16
2^5 = 32
2^6 = 64
2^7 = 128
2^8 = 256
2^9 = 512
2^10 = 1024

Write a program to calculate and print the sum of each of the following series:

(i) $Sum(S) = 2 - 4 + 6 - 8 + \ldots \cdots - 20$

(ii) $Sum(S) = x/2 + x/5 + x/8 + \ldots \cdots + x/20$

(Value of x to be input by the user.)

Listing 10.36: SumSeries.java

```java
import java.util.Scanner;
public class SumSeries
{
   public static void SumSeriesOne()
   {
      int sum = 0;

      for (int i = 2; i <= 20; i += 2)
      {
         if (i % 4 == 0)
             sum = sum - i;
         else
             sum = sum + i;
      }

      System.out.println("Sum of series1 = " + sum);
   }
```

```
19      public static void SumSeriesTwo(double x)
20      {
21          double sum = 0;
22
23          for (int i = 2; i <= 20; i += 3)
24          {
25              sum = sum + (x/i);
26          }
27
28          System.out.println("Sum of series2 = " + sum);
29      }
30
31      public static void main(String args[])
32      {
33          Scanner keyboard = new Scanner(System.in);
34          System.out.println("Enter the value of x:");
35          int x = keyboard.nextInt();
36
37          SumSeriesOne();
38          SumSeriesTwo(x);
39
40          keyboard.close();
41      }
42  }
```

```
Output
Enter the value of x:
10
Sum of series1 = -10
Sum of series2 = 10.961611917494269
```

Write a program to input a number and print whether the number is a special number or not. (A number is said to be a special number, if the sum of the factorial of the digits of the number is same as the original number).

For example, 145 is a special number because $1! + 4! + 5! = 1 + 24 + 120 = 145$.
Similarly, 40585 is special number because $4! + 0! + 5! + 8! + 5! = 24 + 1 + 120 + 40320 + 120 = 40585$.

Listing 10.37: SpecialNumber.java

```
1   import java.util.Scanner;
2
3   public class SpecialNumber
4   {
5       //Compute factorial
6       public static long Factorial(int n)
7       {
8           long fact = 1;
9
10          for (int i = 1; i <= n; i++)
11          {
```

```
12              fact = fact * i;
13          }
14
15          return fact;
16      }
17
18      //Compute sum of factorials of digits
19      public static long sumOfFactOfDigits(int num)
20      {
21          long sumDigits = 0;
22
23          while (num > 0)
24          {
25              int digit = num % 10;
26              sumDigits = sumDigits + Factorial(digit);
27              num = num / 10;
28          }
29
30          return sumDigits;
31      }
32
33      public static void main(String args[])
34      {
35          Scanner scanner = new Scanner(System.in);
36          System.out.print("Enter a number: ");
37          int num = scanner.nextInt();
38
39          long sum = sumOfFactOfDigits(num);
40
41          if (sum == num)
42              System.out.println(num + " is a special number");
43          else
44              System.out.println(num + " is Not a special number");
45
46          scanner.close();
47      }
48 }
```

Output
Enter a number: 145
145 is a special number

Output
Enter a number: 40585
40585 is a special number

Output
Enter a number: 121
121 is Not a special number

Write a program using while loop to print the sum of digits of a given number.

Listing 10.38: SumOfDigits.java

```java
import java.util.Scanner;
public class SumOfDigits
{
    public static void main(String args[])
    {
        int sum = 0, digit;
        Scanner keyboard = new Scanner(System.in);

        System.out.print("Enter a number: ");
        int num = keyboard.nextInt();

        while (num > 0)
        {
            digit = num % 10;
            sum = sum + digit;
            num = num / 10;
        }

        System.out.println("The sum of digits is " + sum);
        keyboard.close();
    }
}
```

Output

Enter a number: 12345
The sum of digits is 15

Write a program using while loop to print the divisors of a given number.

Listing 10.39: Divisors.java

```java
import java.util.Scanner;
public class Divisors
{
    public static void main(String args[])
    {
        Scanner keyboard = new Scanner(System.in);
        int divisor = 1;
        int count = 0;

        System.out.print("Enter a number: ");
        int num = keyboard.nextInt();

```

```
13        System.out.println("Divisors of " + num + " are");
14
15        while (divisor <= num/2)
16        {
17            if (num % divisor == 0)
18            {
19                System.out.println(divisor);
20                count++;
21            }
22
23            divisor++;
24        }
25
26        //Number itself is also a divisor so display it
27        System.out.println(num);
28        //Increment the counter too
29        count++;
30
31        System.out.println("Number of divisors = " + count);
32        keyboard.close();
33    }
34 }
```

Output

Enter a number: 38
Divisors of 38 are
1
2
19
38
Number of divisors = 4

Write a program to read the number n using the Scanner class and compute the sum of series:
$1/1! + 2/2! + 3/3! + \ldots n/n!$

Listing 10.40: SumSeriesWithFactorials.java

```
1  import java.util.Scanner;
2  public class SumSeriesWithFactorials
3  {
4      public static void main(String args[])
5      {
6          Scanner keyboard = new Scanner(System.in);
7          int i = 1;
8          double sum = 0;
9
10         System.out.print("Enter the number of terms in the series: ");
11         int n = keyboard.nextInt();
12
13         while (i <= n)
14         {
15             sum = sum + (double)i / (Factorial(i));
16             i++;
17         }
```

```
18
19      System.out.println("Sum of series is: " + sum);
20      keyboard.close();
21   }
22
23   static long Factorial(int num)
24   {
25      long factorial = 1;
26
27      for (int i = 1; i <= num; i++)
28      {
29         factorial *= i;
30      }
31
32      return factorial;
33   }
34 }
```

> **Output**
>
> Enter the number of terms in the series: 50
> Sum of series is: 2.718281828459045

Write a program to input some positive and negative numbers and compute the sum of positive numbers and the product of negative numbers. The program should exit when a 0 (zero) is entered.

Listing 10.41: SumProduct.java

```
1  import java.util.Scanner;
2  public class SumProduct
3  {
4     public static void main(String args[])
5     {
6        int num;
7        int sum = 0;
8        int product = 1;
9        Scanner keyboard = new Scanner(System.in);
10
11       do
12       {
13          System.out.println("Enter +ve or -ve number (zero to exit)");
14          num = keyboard.nextInt();
15
16          if (num > 0)
17              sum += num;
18          else if (num < 0)
19              product *= num;
20       }
21       while (num != 0);
```

```
22
23        System.out.println("Sum of +ve numbers is: " + sum);
24        System.out.println("Product of -ve numbers is: " + product);
25        keyboard.close();
26    }
27 }
```

Write a program to check whether a number is a perfect number or not using a do-while loop. Hint: A number is said to be perfect if sum of all its factors (excluding the number itself) is equal to the number.

Listing 10.42: PerfectNumber.java

```java
1  import java.util.Scanner;
2  public class PerfectNumber
3  {
4      public static void main(String args[])
5      {
6          int sum = 0;
7          int i = 1;
8          Scanner keyboard = new Scanner(System.in);
9          System.out.println("Enter an integer");
10         int num = keyboard.nextInt();
11
12         do
13         {
14             if (num % i == 0)
15             sum += i;
16
17             i++;
```

```
18          }
19          while (i <= num/2);
20
21          if (sum == num)
22              System.out.println(num + " is a Perfect number");
23          else
24              System.out.println(num + " is NOT a Perfect number");
25
26          keyboard.close();
27      }
28 }
```

Output
Enter an integer
8128
8128 is a Perfect number

Output
Enter an integer
1729
1729 is NOT a Perfect number

Write a program to accept a long integer and check if it is an Armstrong number.

Hint: Armstrong number is a number which is equal to the sum of digits raise to the power total number of digits in the number.

For example, 8208 is an Armstrong number because $8208 = 8^4+2^4+0^4+8^4 = 4096+16+0+4096 = 8208$.

Listing 10.43: ArmstrongNumber.java

```
1  import java.util.Scanner;
2  public class ArmstrongNumber
3  {
4      public static void main(String args[])
5      {
6          Scanner keyboard = new Scanner(System.in);
7          long numOrginal, sumOfCubes = 0;
8          int totalDigits = 0;
9
10         System.out.print("Enter a number: ");
11         long num = keyboard.nextInt();
12
13         //Save the original number for later use
14         numOrginal = num;
15
16         // Count number of digits in the number
17         while (num != 0)
18         {
19             totalDigits++;
20             num = num/10;
21         }
```

```
22
23        num = numOrginal;
24
25        while (num > 0)
26        {
27            //Ger the last digit
28            int digit = (int)num % 10;
29            //Find the cube of digit
30            long digitCube = (int)Math.pow(digit, totalDigits);
31            //add to the sum
32            sumOfCubes = sumOfCubes + digitCube;
33            //Remove the used last digit from num
34            num = num / 10;
35        }
36
37        if (numOrginal == sumOfCubes)
38            System.out.println(numOrginal + " is an Armstrong number");
39        else
40            System.out.println(numOrginal + " is Not an Armstrong number");
41
42        keyboard.close();
43    }
44 }
```

Output
Enter a number: 8208
8208 is an Armstrong number

Output
Enter a number: 1234
1234 is Not an Armstrong number

Write a program to check whether a number is a Spy number or not.

Hint: A number is said to be a Spy number if the sum of all the digits is equal to the product of all the digits.

For example, 1124 is a Spy number. The sum of its digits (1+1+2+4=8) is the same as product of its digits (1*1*2*4=8).

Listing 10.44: SpyNumber.java

```
1  import java.util.Scanner;
2  public class SpyNumber
3  {
4      static boolean isSpy( int num)
5      {
6          int sum=0;
7          int product = 1;
8          int saveNum = num;
9          while (num != 0)
10         {
```

```
11              int digit = num % 10;
12              sum = sum + digit;
13              product = product * digit;
14              num = num / 10;
15          }
16
17          return(sum == product) ;
18      }
19      public static void main(String args[])
20      {
21          Scanner keyboard = new Scanner(System.in);
22
23          System.out.println("Enter an integer (-1 to exit)");
24          int number = keyboard.nextInt();
25
26          while (number != -1)
27          {
28              if (isSpy(number))
29                  System.out.println(number + " is a Spy number");
30              else
31                  System.out.println(number + " is NOT a Spy number");
32
33              System.out.println("Enter an integer (-1 to exit)");
34              number = keyboard.nextInt();
35          }
36
37          System.out.println("Exiting...");
38          keyboard.close();
39      }
40  }
```

```
Output
Enter an integer (-1 to exit)
1124
1124 is a Spy number
Enter an integer (-1 to exit)
1234
1234 is NOT a Spy number
Enter an integer (-1 to exit)
-1
Exiting...
```

Code Walkthrough:

◈ Line 11: Gets the last digit.

◈ Line 12: Adds the digit to the accumulator sum.

◈ Line 13: Multiplies the digit with the accumulator product.

◈ Line 14: Removes the last used digit.

Write a program to check whether a number is a Niven number or not.

Hint: Any positive integer which is divisible by the sum of its digits is a Niven number or Harshad number. For example:

$\frac{111}{1 + 1 + 1} = 37$ is a Niven number.

Listing 10.45: NivenNumber.java

```java
import java.util.Scanner;
public class NivenNumber
{
    static boolean isNiven(int num)
    {
        int sumOfDigits=0;
        int temp = num;

        while(temp != 0)
        {
            int digit = temp % 10;
            sumOfDigits = sumOfDigits + digit;
            temp = temp / 10;
        }

        return(num % sumOfDigits == 0) ;
    }
    public static void main(String args[])
    {
        Scanner keyboard = new Scanner(System.in);
        System.out.println("Enter an integer (0 to exit)");
        int number = keyboard.nextInt();

        while (number != 0)
        {
            if (isNiven(number))
                System.out.println(number + " is a Niven number");
            else
                System.out.println(number + " is NOT a Niven number");

            System.out.println("Enter an integer (0 to exit)");
            number = keyboard.nextInt();
        }

        System.out.println("Exiting...");
        keyboard.close();
    }
}
```

```
Output
Enter an integer (0 to exit)
37
37 is NOT a Niven number
Enter an integer (0 to exit)
111
111 is a Niven number
Enter an integer (0 to exit)
300
300 is a Niven number
Enter an integer (0 to exit)
0
Exiting...
```

Write a program to accept a number and check whether the number is a Palindrome or not. Hint: A palindrome number is a number that remains the same when its digits are reversed. For example, 18381.

Listing 10.46: PalindromeNumber.java

```java
1  import java.util.Scanner;
2  public class PalindromeNumber
3  {
4      public static void main(String args[])
5      {
6          Scanner keyboard = new Scanner(System.in);
7          int numOrginal, numReverse = 0;
8
9          System.out.print("Enter a number: ");
10         int num = keyboard.nextInt();
11
12         //Save the original number for later use
13         numOrginal = num;
14
15         while (num > 0)
16         {
17             //Get the last digit
18             int digit = ( int )num % 10;
19             //Append it to the reverse number
20             numReverse = numReverse * 10 + digit;
21             //Remove the last digit from num
22             num = num / 10;
23         }
24
25         if (numReverse == numOrginal)
26             System.out.println(numOrginal + " is a Palindrome number");
27         else
28             System.out.println(numOrginal + " is a not Palindrome number");
29
30         keyboard.close();
31     }
32 }
```

Output

Enter a number: 1831
1831 is a not Palindrome number

Output

Enter a number: 1221
1221 is a Palindrome number

Write a program to find the Greatest Common Denominator (GCD) of two numbers.

Listing 10.47: FindGCD.java

```
1  import java.util.Scanner;
2  public class FindGCD
3  {
4     public static void main(String args[])
5     {
6        Scanner keyboard = new Scanner(System.in);
7
8        System.out.print("Enter the first number: ");
9        int n1 = keyboard.nextInt();
10
11       System.out.print("Enter the second number: ");
12       int n2 = keyboard.nextInt();
13
14       System.out.println ("The Greatest Common Divisor is: " + GCD(n1, ←
              ↪ n2));
15       keyboard.close();
16    }
17
18    static int GCD(int num1, int num2)
19    {
20       while (num1 != num2)
21       {
22          if (num1 > num2)
23             num1 = num1 - num2;
24          else
25             num2 = num2 - num1;
26       }
27
28       return num1;
29    }
30 }
```

```
Output
Enter the first number: 68
Enter the second number: 16
The Greatest Common Divisor is: 4
```

Write a program to find the Lowest Common Multiple (LCM) of two numbers.

Listing 10.48: FindLCM.java

```
1  import java.util.Scanner;
2  public class FindLCM
3  {
4     public static void main(String args[])
```

```
5     {
6         Scanner keyboard = new Scanner(System.in);
7
8         System.out.print("Enter the first number: ");
9         int n1 = keyboard.nextInt();
10
11        System.out.print("Enter the second number: ");
12        int n2 = keyboard.nextInt();
13
14        System.out.println ("The Lowest Common Multiple is: " + LCM(n1, ↵
              ↪ n2));
15        keyboard.close();
16    }
17
18    static int LCM(int num1, int num2)
19    {
20        int lcm = (num1 > num2) ? num1 : num2;
21
22        while(true)
23        {
24            if (lcm % num1 == 0 && lcm % num2 == 0)
25            break;
26
27            lcm++;
28        }
29
30        return lcm;
31    }
32 }
```

```
Output
Enter the first number: 36
Enter the second number: 48
The Lowest Common Multiple is: 144
```

Write a Java program that reads two positive integer numbers (a and b) and calculates a^b using only addition and multiplication operations.

Listing 10.49: ComputePower.java

```
1  import java.util.Scanner;
2  public class ComputePower
3  {
4      public static void main(String args[])
5      {
6          int power = 1;
7          int counter = 1;
8
9          Scanner keyboard = new Scanner(System.in);
10
11         System.out.print("Enter the first number: ");
```

```
12          int a = keyboard.nextInt();
13
14          System.out.print("Enter the second number: ");
15          int b = keyboard.nextInt();
16
17          while (counter <= b)
18          {
19             power = power * a;
20             counter++;
21          }
22
23          System.out.println (a + "^" + b + " = " +power);
24          keyboard.close();
25       }
26  }
```

> **Output**
>
> Enter the first number: 3
> Enter the second number: 6
> 3^6 = 729

Write a program to roll a dice until a six comes up. Display the outcomes except when a one comes up. Also, display the number of iterations it takes.

Listing 10.50: DiceGame.java

```
1  public class DiceGame
2  {
3     public static void main(String args[])
4     {
5        int min = 1, max = 6;
6        int range = max - min + 1;
7        int counter = 0;
8
9        while (true)
10       {
11          counter++;
12          int num = (int) (range * Math.random() + min);
13
14          if (num == 6)
15          {
16             System.out.println(num);
17             break;
18          }
19
20          if (num == 1)
21          {
22             System.out.println("Skipped");
23             continue;
```

> **Output**
>
> 4
> 4
> 2
> 3
> 5
> Skipped
> 2
> Skipped
> 5
> Skipped
> Skipped
> 2
> 5
> Skipped
> 6
> Total iterations: 15

```
24          }
25
26          System.out.println(num);
27      }
28
29      System.out.println("Total iterations: " + counter);
30    }
31 }
```

Write a Java program to check whether the given number is a prime number or not. While doing so, demonstrate the use of the break statement in Java.

Listing 10.51: PrimeNumberWithBreak.java

```java
1  import java.util.Scanner;
2  public class PrimeNumberWithBreak
3  {
4     static boolean IsPrime(int num)
5     {
6        boolean prime = true;
7
8        for (int i = 2; i <= num/2; i++)
9        {
10          if (num % i == 0)
11          {
12             prime = false;
13             break; //Factors exists, so no need to continue further.
14          }
15       }
16
17       return prime;
18    }
19    public static void main(String args[])
20    {
21       Scanner keyboard = new Scanner(System.in);
22
23       System.out.println("Enter an integer (0 to exit)");
24       int number = keyboard.nextInt();
25
26       while (number != 0)
27       {
28          if (IsPrime(number))
29             System.out.println(number + " is a prime number");
30          else
31             System.out.println(number + " is NOT a prime number");
32
```

```
33          System.out.println("Enter an integer (0 to exit)");
34          number = keyboard.nextInt();
35        }
36
37        System.out.println("Exiting...");
38        keyboard.close();
39    }
40 }
```

```
Output
Enter an integer (0 to exit)
96
96 is NOT a prime number
Enter an integer (0 to exit)
97
97 is a prime number
Enter an integer (0 to exit)
0
Exiting...
```

Write a program to check whether the given number is a composite number or not.
Hint: A composite number is a positive integer that has factors other than 1 and itself.

Listing 10.52: CompositeNumber.java

```
1  import java.util.Scanner;
2  public class CompositeNumber
3  {
4     static boolean IsComposite(int num)
5     {
6        boolean composite = false;
7
8        for (int i = 2; i <= num/2; i++)
9        {
10           if (num % i == 0)   //factors exist
11           composite = true;
12        }
13
14        return composite;
15     }
16     public static void main(String args[])
17     {
18        Scanner keyboard = new Scanner(System.in);
19
20        System.out.println("Enter an integer (0 to exit)");
21        int number = keyboard.nextInt();
22
23        while (number != 0)
24        {
25           if (IsComposite(number))
26           System.out.println(number + " is a Composite number");
27           else
28           System.out.println(number + " is NOT a Composite number");
```

```
29
30          System.out.println("Enter an integer (0 to exit)");
31          number = keyboard.nextInt();
32      }
33
34      System.out.println("Exiting...");
35      keyboard.close();
36   }
37 }
```

```
Output
Enter an integer (0 to exit)
47
47 is NOT a Composite number
Enter an integer (0 to exit)
94
94 is a Composite number
Enter an integer (0 to exit)
0
Exiting...
```

Write a Java program to check whether the given number is a Neon number or not.

Hint: A number is said to be a Neon number if the sum of digits of the square of the number is equal to the number itself.

For example, if the input number is 9, its square is $9 * 9 = 81$ and sum of the digits is also $9(= 8 + 1)$.

Listing 10.53: NeonNumber.java

```java
1  import java.util.Scanner;
2  public class NeonNumber
3  {
4     static boolean isNeon(int num)
5     {
6        int squareOfNum = num * num;
7        int sum=0;
8
9        while (squareOfNum != 0)
10       {
11          int digit = squareOfNum % 10;
12          sum = sum + digit;
13          squareOfNum = squareOfNum / 10;
14       }
15
16       return(sum == num) ;
17    }
18    public static void main(String args[])
19    {
20       Scanner keyboard = new Scanner(System.in);
21
22       System.out.println("Enter an integer (-1 to exit)");
23       int number = keyboard.nextInt();
24
```

```
25        while (number != -1)
26        {
27            if (isNeon(number))
28            System.out.println(number + " is a Neon number");
29            else
30            System.out.println(number + " is NOT a Neon number");
31
32            System.out.println("Enter an integer (-1 to exit)");
33            number = keyboard.nextInt();
34        }
35
36        System.out.println("Exiting...");
37        keyboard.close();
38    }
39 }
```

```
Output
Enter an integer (-1 to exit)
9
9 is a Neon number
Enter an integer (-1 to exit)
15
15 is NOT a Neon number
Enter an integer (-1 to exit)
-1
Exiting...
```

Multiple Choice Questions

1. Which of the following segment can be omitted in a for loop?

    A. Initialisation   C. Update expression

    B. Test condition   D. All of the above

2. Which of the following loop executes at least once?

    A. while   C. do-while

    B. for   D. None of the above

3. Which of the following is an exit-controlled loop?

    A. while   C. for

    B. do-while   D. None of the above

4. Which of the following is an invalid loop?

    A. repeat   C. do-while

    B. for   D. while

5. Which of the following statement causes complete termination of the loop?

A. continue   C. break

B. jump   D. terminate

6. Which of the following is an empty loop?

    A. `for (i = 0; i < 5; i++);`   C. `do i++; while (i < 5);`

    B. `while (i < 5) i++;`   D. All of the above

7. Which of the following is not a jump statement in Java?

    A. `break`   C. `return`

    B. `jump`   D. `continue`

8. How many times will the following code print "Java"?

```
for (int i = 1; i <= 5; i ++);
{
    System.out.println("Java");
}
```

    A. 0   C. 5

    B. 1   D. 4

9. What will be the output of the following code?

```
int sum = 0;
for (int i = 1; i <= 5; i ++)
{
    sum = i;
}
System.out.println(sum);
```

    A. 15   C. 5

    B. 21   D. 0

10. How many times will the following loop execute?

```
public static void main(String args[])
{
    int sum = 0;
    for (int i = 10; i > 5; i++)
    {
        sum += i;
    }
    System.out.println(sum);
}
```

A. 5
C. 15

B. 0
D. Infinite loop

11. Which of the following for loops will cause the body of the loop to be executed 10 times?

A. `for (int i = 0; i <= 10; i++)`
C. `for (int i = 10; i > 1; i--)`

B. `for (int i = 1; i < 10; i++)`
D. `for (int i = 0; i < 10; i++)`

12. How many times will the following loop execute?

```java
public static void main(String args[])
{
    int i = 1;
    while (i < 10)
        if (i++ % 2 == 0)
            System.out.println(i);
}
```

A. 4
C. 0

B. 5
D. 10

State whether the given statements are True or False:

☐ The `while` loop is an exit-controlled loop.

☐ To execute a `do-while` loop, the condition must be `true` in the beginning.

☐ The `while` part of a `do-while` statement must be terminated by a semicolon.

☐ All types of loops in Java (`for`, `while`, and `do-while`) can be infinite loops.

☐ The `continue` statement terminates the current loop and then continues from the statement immediately following the current loop.

☐ The `return` statement is a jump statement.

☐ The `for` loop may contain multiple initialisations and updates.

☐ A loop that never terminates is called an empty loop.

☐ The `do-while` loop executes at least once even if the condition is `false`.

☐ The `do-while` loop is an exit-controlled loop.

☐ An infinite loop can be constructed using a `while` loop only.

☐ The statements that facilitate unconditional transfer of control are called jump statements.

Assignment Questions

1. What are loop control structures? What are the essential segments of a loop control structure?

2. How are these statements different from each other?

   (i) `break`   (ii) `continue`   (iii) `System.exit(0)` (iv) `return`

3. Identify all the errors in the following statements.

   (i)
   ```
   for (int i = 5; i > 0; i++)
   {
       System.out.println("Java is fun!");
   }
   ```

   (ii)
   ```
   while (x < 1 && x > 50)
   {
       a = b;
   }
   ```

   (iii)
   ```
   while (x == y) ;
   {
       xx = yy;
       x = y;
   }
   ```

4. What is an empty statement? Explain its usefulness.

5. Convert the following `for` loop statement into the corresponding `while` loop and `do-while` loop:

   ```
   int sum = 0;
   for (int i = 0; i <= 50; i++)
       sum = sum + i;
   ```

6. What are the differences between `while` loop and `do-while` loop?

7. How many times are the following loop bodies repeated? What is the final output in each case?

   (i)
   ```
   int x = 2;
   while (x < 20)
       if (x % 2 == 0)
           System.out.println(x);
   ```

   (ii)
   ```
   int y = 2;
   while (y < 20)
       if (y % 2 == 0)
           System.out.println(y++);
   ```

(iii)
```
        int z = 2;
        while (z < 20)
            if ((z++) % 2 == 0)
                System.out.println(z);
```

8. What is the output produced by the following code?

```
        int n = 20;
        do
        {
            System.out.println(n);
            n = n - 3;
        } while (n > 0);
```

9. What is the output produced by the following code?

```
        int num = 20;
        while (num > 0)
        {
            num = num - 2;
            if (num == 4)
                break ;
            System.out.println(num);
        }
        System.out.println("Finished");
```

10. What is the output produced by the following code?

```
        int num = 10;
        while (num > 0)
        {
            num = num - 2;
            if (num == 2)
                continue ;
            System.out.println(num);
        }
        System.out.println("Finished");
```

11. Write a program to input **n** number of integers and find out:

   (i) Number of positive integers

   (ii) Number of negative integers

   (iii) Sum of positive numbers

   (iv) Product of negative numbers

   (v) Average of positive numbers

12. Write a program using `do-while` loop to compute the sum of the first 500 positive odd integers.

13. Write three different programs using `for`, `while` and `do-while` loops to find the product of series 3, 9, 12,..., 30.

14. Write a program to convert kilograms to pounds in the following tabular format (1 kilogram is 2.2 pounds):

Kilograms	Pounds
1	2.2
2	4.4
20	44.0

15. Write a program that displays all the numbers from 150 to 250 that are divisible by 5 or 6, but not both.

16. Write a program in Java to read a number and display its digits in the reverse order. For example, if the input number is 2468, then the output should be 8642.

```
Output
Enter a number: 2468
Original number: 2468
Reverse number: 8642
```

17. Write a program in Java to read a number, remove all zeros from it, and display the new number. For example,

Sample Input: 45407703
Sample Output: 454773

18. Write a program to read the number n using the Scanner class and print the Tribonacci series: 0, 0, 1, 1, 2, 4, 7, 13, 24, 44, 81 ... and so on.
Hint: The Tribonacci series is a generalisation of the Fibonacci sequence where each term is the sum of the three preceding terms.

19. Write a program to calculate the value of Pi with the help of the following series:
$Pi = (4/1) - (4/3) + (4/5) - (4/7) + (4/9) - (4/11) + (4/13) - (4/15)...$
Hint: Use `while` loop with 100000 iterations.

20. Write a program to display the following patterns as per user's choice.

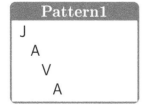

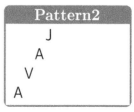

21. Write a program to input a number and check and print whether it is a Pronic number or not. (Pronic number is a number which is the product of two consecutive integers.)
Example:

$$12 = 3 \times 4$$
$$20 = 4 \times 5$$
$$42 = 6 \times 7$$

22. Write a program to accept a number and check and display whether it is a spy number or not.
(A number is called a spy number if the sum of its digits equals the product of the digits.)
Example:

Consider the number 1124.
Sum of the digits $= 1 + 1 + 2 + 4 = 8$.
Product of the digits $= 1 * 1 * 2 * 4 = 8$.

23. Write a program to accept a number and check and display whether it is a Niven number or not. (Niven number is a number which is divisible by the sum of its digits).
Example:

Consider the number 126.
Sum of its digits is $1 + 2 + 6 = 9$ and 126 is divisible by 9.

24. Using the switch statement, write a menu driven program to:

(i) Generate and display the first 10 terms of the Fibonacci series 0, 1, 1, 2, 3, 5.... The first two Fibonacci numbers are 0 and 1, and each subsequent number is the sum of the previous two.

(ii) Find the sum of the digits of an integer that is input.
Sample Input: 15390
Sample Output: Sum of the digits $= 18$

For an incorrect choice, an appropriate error message should be displayed.

25. Write a menu driven program to accept a number and check and display whether (i) it is a Prime Number or not (ii) it is an Automorphic Number or not. (Use switch-case statement).

(i) Prime number: A number is said to be a prime number if it is divisible only by 1 and itself and not by any other number.
Example: 3, 5, 7, 11, 13 etc.

(ii) Automorphic number: An automorphic number is the number which is contained in the last digit(s) of its square.
Example: 25 is an automorphic number as its square is 625 and 25 is present as the last two digits.

26. Write a menu driven program to accept a number from the user and check whether it is a BUZZ number or to accept any two numbers and to print the GCD of them.

(i) A BUZZ number is the number which either ends with 7 or is divisible by 7.

(ii) GCD (Greatest Common Divisor) of two integers is calculated by continued division method. Divide the larger number by the smaller; the remainder then divides the previous divisor. The process is repeated till the remainder is zero. The divisor then results the GCD.

27. Write a program to read the number x using the Scanner class and compute the series:

$$Sum = x/2 + x/5 + x/8 + x/11 + \ldots + x/20$$

The output should look like as shown below:

Output
Enter a value of x: 10
Sum of the series is: 10.961611917494269

28. Write a program in Java to compute and display factorial of numbers up to a number entered via the Scanner class. The output should look like as shown below when 7 is input.

Output
Enter a number: 7
1! (=1) = 1
2! (=1 × 2) = 2
3! (=1 × 2 × 3) = 6
4! (=1 × 2 × 3 × 4) = 24
5! (=1 × 2 × 3 × 4 × 5) = 120
6! (=1 × 2 × 3 × 4 × 5 × 6) = 720
7! (=1 × 2 × 3 × 4 × 5 × 6 × 7) = 5040

29. Write a program in Java to find the sum of the given series:

(i) $x^1 + x^2 + x^3 + x^4 \cdots + x^n$

(ii) $x^1 - x^2 + x^3 - x^4 \cdots - x^n$, where x = 3

(iii) $\dfrac{1}{x^1} + \dfrac{2}{x^2} + \dfrac{3}{x^3} + \cdots + \dfrac{n}{x^n}$

(iv) $\dfrac{1}{2} + \dfrac{2}{3} + \dfrac{3}{4} + \cdots + \dfrac{49}{50}$

(v) $\dfrac{1}{\sqrt{1}} + \dfrac{2}{\sqrt{2}} + \dfrac{3}{\sqrt{3}} + \cdots + \dfrac{10}{\sqrt{10}}$

(vi) $\dfrac{x+1}{3} + \dfrac{x+2}{5} + \dfrac{x+3}{7} + \ldots$ to n terms

(vii) $\dfrac{x}{2!} + \dfrac{x}{3!} + \dfrac{x}{4!} + \cdots + \dfrac{x}{20!}$

(viii) $\dfrac{x^2}{2!} + \dfrac{x^3}{3!} + \dfrac{x^4}{4!} + \cdots + \dfrac{x^n}{n!}$, where n=10

(ix) $1 + 3 + 7 + 15 + 31 + \cdots + (2^{20} - 1)$

(x) $1 * 2 * 4 * 8 * \cdots * 2^{20}$

30. Write a menu driven class to accept a number from the user and check whether it is Palindrome or a Perfect number.

   (i) Palindrome number: A number is a Palindrome which when read in reverse order is same as read in the right order.
   Example: 11, 101, 151, etc.

   (ii) Perfect number: A number is called Perfect if it is equal to the sum of its factors other than the number itself.
   Example: 6 = 1+2+3

31. Write a program to print the sum of negative numbers, sum of positive even numbers and sum of positive odd numbers from a list of n numbers entered by the user. The program terminates when the user enters a zero.

Answers To Objective Questions

Multiple Choice Questions

1. D	3. B	5. C	7. B	9. C	11. D
2. C	4. A	6. A	8. B	10. D	12. A

True or False

1. False	3. True	5. False	7. True	9. True	11. False
2. False	4. True	6. True	8. False	10. True	12. True

Chapter 11

Nested for loops

Nested for loops

Y OU have learnt that a loop repeats a set of instructions a fixed number of times or depending on the outcome of a condition. In problem solving, you often face situations where you need to repeat the action of a loop, a number of times. So, what should you do? You might have already guessed it. Repeat the loop by placing it inside another loop. When one loop is inside the body of another loop, it is called a nested loop. This process allows us to create a loop within a loop as shown in Figure 11.1. The contained loop is referred to as the *inner loop*. The container loop is referred to as the *outer loop*.

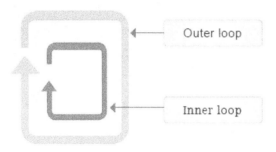

Figure 11.1: Nested loop

Nested loops are used to solve a wide variety of programming problems and are an essential part of programming. When you nest two loops, the outer loop takes control of the repetitions of the inner loop. If the outer loop is not executed, the inner loop will not get executed at all. However, if the outer loop is executed, the inner loop may or may not get executed, depending on the test-condition it is evaluating.

11.1   Nested for loop

When one **for** loop is inside the body of another for loop, it is called a nested **for** loop. The inner loop must have a different name for its loop control variable so that it does not conflict with the outer loop. To understand the nested for loops, let us consider Program 11.1 that displays a rectangular pattern.

For each iteration of the outer loop, the inner loop is repeated. For example, when the outer loop control variable i takes the value as 1, the inner loop control variable j is repeated with values 1, 2, 3, 4, and 5. The output produced by this is five hash signs (#) followed by the New Line character. This process is repeated until the outer loop completes.

Listing 11.1: HashPattern.java

```
1  public class HashPattern
2  {
3     public static void main(String args[])
4     {
5        for (int i = 1; i <= 5; i++)
6        {
7           for (int j = 1; j <= 5; j++)
8           {
9              System.out.print("# ");
10          }
11
12          System.out.println();
13       }
14    }
15 }
```

Outer loop

Inner loop

Output
```
# # # # #
# # # # #
# # # # #
# # # # #
# # # # #
```

Outer Loop Control variable i	Inner Loop Control variable j	Output
1	1, 2, 3, 4, 5	# # # # # followed by New Line
2	1, 2, 3, 4, 5	# # # # # followed by New Line
3	1, 2, 3, 4, 5	# # # # # followed by New Line
4	1, 2, 3, 4, 5	# # # # # followed by New Line
5	1, 2, 3, 4, 5	# # # # # followed by New Line

Write a program to display the following star pattern.
```
*
* *
* * *
* * * *
* * * * *
```

Listing 11.2: HalfStarPyramid.java

```
1  public class HalfStarPyramid
2  {
3     public static void main(String args[])
4     {
5        for (int i = 1; i <= 5; i++)
6        {
7           for (int j = 1; j <= i; j++)
```

```
8              {
9                  System.out.print("* ");
10             }
11 .
12             System.out.println();
13         }
14     }
15 }
```

```
Output
*
* *
* * *
* * * *
* * * * *
```

Write a program to display the following pattern.
```
* * * * *
* * * *
* * *
* *
*
```

Listing 11.3: InvertedStarPyramid.java

```
1  public class InvertedStarPyramid
2  {
3      public static void main(String args[])
4      {
5          for (int i = 1; i <= 5; i++)
6          {
7              for (int j = i; j <= 5; j++)
8              {
9                  System.out.print("* ");
10             }
11
12             System.out.println();
13         }
14     }
15 }
```

```
Output
* * * * *
* * * *
* * *
* *
*
```

Write a program to display the following pattern.
```
5 4 3 2 1
4 3 2 1
3 2 1
2 1
1
```

Listing 11.4: ReverseNumberPyramid.java

```
1  public class ReverseNumberPyramid
2  {
3     public static void main(String args[])
4     {
5        for (int i = 5; i >= 1; i--)
6        {
7           for (int j = i; j >= 1; j--)
8           {
9              System.out.print(j + " ");
10          }
11
12          System.out.println();
13       }
14    }
15 }
```

Output
5 4 3 2 1
4 3 2 1
3 2 1
2 1
1

Write a program to display the following pattern.
5
5 4
5 4 3
5 4 3 2
5 4 3 2 1

Listing 11.5: ReverseNumberPyramid2.java

```
1  public class ReverseNumberPyramid2
2  {
3     public static void main(String args[])
4     {
5        for (int i = 5; i >= 1; i--)
6        {
7           for (int j = 5; j >= i; j--)
8           {
9              System.out.print(j + " ");
10          }
11
12          System.out.println();
13       }
14    }
15 }
```

Output
5
5 4
5 4 3
5 4 3 2
5 4 3 2 1

Write a program to display the following pattern. The program should accept number of rows to be printed using the **Scanner** class. For example, if the user enters 10 the following pattern gets printed.

1
2 3
4 5 6
7 8 9 10
11 12 13 14 15
16 17 18 19 20 21
22 23 24 25 26 27 28
29 30 31 32 33 34 35 36
37 38 39 40 41 42 43 44 45
46 47 48 49 50 51 52 53 54 55

Listing 11.6: AccendingNumberPyramid.java

```java
import java.util.Scanner;
public class AccendingNumberPyramid
{
    public static void main(String args[])
    {
        Scanner scan = new Scanner(System.in);
        System.out.print ("Please enter number of rows:");
        int rows = scan.nextInt();

        int myNum = 1;

        for (int i = 1; i <= rows; i++)
        {
            for (int j = 1; j <= i; j++)
            {
                System.out.print(myNum + " ");
                myNum++;
            }

            System.out.println();
        }
    }
}
```

```
                            Output
1
2 3
4 5 6
7 8 9 10
11 12 13 14 15
16 17 18 19 20 21
22 23 24 25 26 27 28
29 30 31 32 33 34 35 36
37 38 39 40 41 42 43 44 45
46 47 48 49 50 51 52 53 54 55
```

Write a program to display tables from 1 to 9 in a fancy format.

Listing 11.7: Table1To9.java

```
1  public class Table1To9
2  {
3      public static void main(String args[])
4      {
5          int max = 9;
6          for (int i = 1; i <= max; i++)
7          {
8              if (i==1)
9              {
10                 System.out.print ("* |\t");
11
12                 for (int k = 1; k <= max; k++)
13                     System.out.print(k + "\t");
14
15                 System.out.println();
16
17                 for (int k = 1; k <= max; k++)
18                     System.out.print("--------");
19
20                 System.out.println("---");
21             }
22
23             for (int j = 1; j <= max; j++)
24             {
25                 if (j == 1)
26                 {
27                     System.out.print(i + " |\t");
28                 }
29
30                 System.out.print((i*j) + "\t");
31             }
32
33             System.out.println();
34         }
35     }
36 }
```

Output								
*	1	2	3	4	5	6	7	8	9
1	1	2	3	4	5	6	7	8	9
2	2	4	6	8	10	12	14	16	18
3	3	6	9	12	15	18	21	24	27
4	4	8	12	16	20	24	28	32	36
5	5	10	15	20	25	30	35	40	45
6	6	12	18	24	30	36	42	48	54
7	7	14	21	28	35	42	49	56	63
8	8	16	24	32	40	48	56	64	72
9	9	18	27	36	45	54	63	72	81

11.2 Nested for loop with break statement

You know that the **break** statement terminates the execution of a loop. You can also use the **break** statement in a nested for loop. However, the **break** statement will terminate only the loop it is part of. That means, the **break** statement in an inner loop causes termination of the inner loop only and the outer loop is unaffected. Similarly, when the **break** statement is used in the outer loop, it causes the termination of the outer loop and in that case, the inner loop will automatically not execute. The flow of control then transfers to the statement that follows the outer for loop. In general, remember that the **break** statement will terminate only a single loop, i.e., the enclosing loop.

```
for (...)
{
    //loop statements
    for (...)
    {
        break;
    }
}
```

Let us, first of all, consider an example where the **break** statement has been used in the inner loop.

The following program generates Prime numbers using a nested **for** loop.

Listing 11.8: PrimeNumberGenerator.java

```
1  import java.util.Scanner;
2  public class PrimeNumberGenerator
3  {
4      public static void main(String args[])
5      {
6          Scanner keyboard = new Scanner(System.in);
7
8          System.out.print("Enter the start number: ");
9          int start = keyboard.nextInt();
10
11          System.out.print("Enter the end number: ");
12          int end = keyboard.nextInt();
13          System.out.println("Prime numbers between " + start + " and "+ end
14          + " are:");
15
16          for (int num = start; num <= end; num++)
17          {
18              boolean prime = true;
19
20              for (int i = 2; i <= num/2; i++)
21              {
```

```
22              if (num % i == 0)
23              {
24                  prime = false;
25                  //factors exist, no need to continue further
26                  break;
27              }
28          }
29
30          if (prime)
31              System.out.print(num + " ");
32      }
33  }
34 }
```

> The break statement in the inner loop causes termination of inner loop only.

Output

Enter the start number: 20
Enter the end number: 50
Prime numbers between 20 and 50 are:
23 29 31 37 41 43 47

In the above-mentioned program, the outer loop generates a set of numbers between the **start** and **end** range entered by the user. The inner loop checks if a factor of the number exists that is greater than 2 and less than **num/2**. As soon as the factor is found, the inner loop terminates indicating the fact the number is not a prime. Let us consider an example where the **break** statement has been used in the outer loop.

Listing 11.9: BreakOuterLoop.java

```
1  public class BreakOuterLoop
2  {
3      public static void main(String args[])
4      {
5          for ( int i = 1; i <= 5; i++)
6          {
7              for ( int j = 1; j <= 5; j++)
8              {
9                  System.out.print(i + " ");
10             }
11
12             System.out.println();
13             System.out.println("Inner loop complete");
14
15             if (i ==3)
16                  break;
17         }
18
19         System.out.println("Outer loop complete");
20     }
21 }
```

Output

1 1 1 1 1
Inner loop complete
2 2 2 2 2
Inner loop complete
3 3 3 3 3
Inner loop complete
Outer loop complete

> The break statement in the outer loop causes termination of the outer loop.

In the above program, the **break** statement has been used in the outer loop. The outer loop terminates during the third iteration, and the inner loop does not execute anymore. Note that in this example, once the outer loop terminates, the inner loop also terminates.

11.3   Nested for loop with continue statement

You have learnt that the **continue** statement skips the rest of the statements in the current iteration, and transfers the control to the next iteration of the loop. The **continue** statement can also be used in a nested for loop. The **continue** statement in an inner loop causes skipping the rest of the current iteration of the inner loop only and the outer loop is unaffected.

Similarly, the **continue** statement in the outer loop causes skipping the rest of the current iteration of the outer loop. This includes any inner loops if they appear after the **continue** statement. In the case of for loop, the **continue** statement causes the update segment of the loop to be executed before the test condition is evaluated. However, in **while** and **do-while** loops, the continue statement causes the control to go directly to the test condition and then to continue the iteration process.

Let us consider an example where the **continue** statement has been used in the inner loop.

Listing 11.10: ContinueInInner.java

```
1   public class ContinueInInner
2   {
3      public static void main(String args[])
4      {
5         for ( int i = 1; i <= 4; i++)
6         {
7            for ( int j = 1; j <= 4; j++)
8            {
9               if (i == j)
10              {
11                 continue;
12              }
13
14              System.out.println("(" + i + "," + j + ")");
15           }
16           System.out.println("Inner loop complete");
17        }
18
19        System.out.println("Outer loop complete");
20     }
21  }
```

Skips the rest of the current iteration of the loop it is part of.

In this program, the `continue` statement has been used in the inner loop. As soon as the outer loop control variable reaches a value that is equal to the value of the inner loop control variable, the `continue` statement is executed. This causes skipping of the rest of the current iteration of the inner loop only, i.e., no values of control variables are printed when their values match, i.e., (1, 1), (2, 2), (3, 3), and (4, 4).

Output
(1,2)
(1,3)
(1,4)
Inner loop complete
(2,1)
(2,3)
(2,4)
Inner loop complete
(3,1)
(3,2)
(3,4)
Inner loop complete
(4,1)
(4,2)
(4,3)
Inner loop complete
Outer loop complete

Let us consider an example where the `continue` statement has been used in the outer loop.

Listing 11.11: ContinueOuterLoop.java

```
1   public class ContinueOuterLoop
2   {
3       public static void main(String args[])
4       {
5           for ( int i = 1; i <= 5; i++)
6           {
7               if (i ==3)
8                   continue;
9
10              for (int j = 1; j <= 5; j++)
11              {
12                  System.out.print(i + " ");
13              }
14
15              System.out.println();
16              System.out.println("Inner loop complete");
17          }
18
19          System.out.println("Outer loop complete");
20      }
21  }
```

Skips the rest of the current iteration of the loop it is part of, i.e., when i = 3.

Output
1 1 1 1 1
Inner loop complete
2 2 2 2 2
Inner loop complete
4 4 4 4 4
Inner loop complete
5 5 5 5 5
Inner loop complete
Outer loop complete

Note that in this example, when the outer loop control variable reaches a value of 3, the rest of the statements are skipped by the outer loop after the `continue` statement. The inner loop is also skipped in this case, as it can be observed in the output that the values 3 3 3 3 3 are not displayed.

Write a program to display the following pattern.

```
* * * * * * 1
* * * * * 2 *
* * * * 3 * *
* * * 4 * * *
* * 5 * * * *
* 6 * * * * *
7 * * * * * *
```

Listing 11.12: RectangularPattern2.java

```java
 1  import java.util.Scanner;
 2
 3  public class RectangularPattern2
 4  {
 5      public static void main(String args[])
 6      {
 7          Scanner input = new Scanner(System.in);
 8          System.out.print ("Please enter number of rows:");
 9          int numRows = input.nextInt();
10
11          for (int i = 1; i <= numRows; i++)
12          {
13              for (int j = i; j <= numRows; j++)
14              {
15                  if (j == numRows)
16                      System.out.print(i + " ");
17                  else
18                      System.out.print("* ");
19              }
20
21              for (int k = 1; k < i; k++)
22              {
23                  System.out.print("* ");
24              }
25
26              System.out.println();
27          }
28
29          input.close();
30      }
31  }
```

```
                      Output
          Please enter number of rows:7
          * * * * * * 1
          * * * * * 2 *
          * * * * 3 * *
          * * * 4 * * *
          * * 5 * * * *
          * 6 * * * * *
          7 * * * * * *
```

Write a program to display the following pattern.

```
@@@@@@@
@@@@@@
@@@@@
@@@
@@
@
@@
@@@
@@@@
@@@@@
@@@@@@
@@@@@@@
```

Listing 11.13: RightAngledTrianglePattern.java

```java
public class RightAngledTrianglePattern
{
    public static void main(String args[])
    {
        for (int i = 1; i <= 7; i++)
        {
            for (int j = i; j <= 7; j++)
            {
                System.out.print ("@ ");
            }

            System.out.println ();
        }

        for (int i = 2; i <= 7; i++)
        {
            for (int j = 1; j <= i; j++)
            {
                System.out.print ("@ ");
            }

            System.out.println ();
        }
    }
}
```

Output

```
Please enter number of rows:7
@ @ @ @ @ @ @
@ @ @ @ @ @
@ @ @ @ @
@ @ @ @
@ @ @
@ @
@
@ @
@ @ @
@ @ @ @
@ @ @ @ @
@ @ @ @ @ @
@ @ @ @ @ @ @
```

Write a program to display the following pattern.

```
@@@@@@@ 7
@@@@@@ 6
@@@@@@5
@@@@ 4
@@@ 3
@@ 2
@ 1
0
```

Listing 11.14: RightAngledTrianglePattern2.java

```java
1  import java.util.Scanner;
2
3  public class RightAngledTrianglePattern2
4  {
5      public static void main(String args[])
6      {
7          Scanner input = new Scanner(System.in);
8          System.out.println ("Please enter number of rows:");
9          int numRows = input.nextInt();
10
11         for (int i = 1; i <= numRows; i++)
12         {
13             for (int j = i; j <= numRows; j++)
14             {
15                 if (j == numRows)
16                     System.out.print((numRows-i) + " ");
17                 else
18                     System.out.print("@ ");
19             }
20
21             System.out.println();
22         }
23
24         input.close();
25     }
26 }
```

```
Output
Please enter number of rows:
8
@ @ @ @ @ @ @ 7
@ @ @ @ @ @ 6
@ @ @ @ @ 5
@ @ @ @ 4
@ @ @ 3
@ @ 2
@ 1
0
```

Write a program to accept an input and display the following pattern:
Please enter the value of n:8

```
\ . . . . . . /
. \ . . . . / .
. . \ . . / . .
. . . \ / . . .
. . . / \ . . .
. . / . . \ . .
. / . . . . \ .
/ . . . . . . \
```

Listing 11.15: PatternWithContinue.java

```java
1  import java.util.Scanner;
2  public class PatternWithContinue
3  {
4      public static void main(String args[])
5      {
6          Scanner input = new Scanner(System.in);
7          System.out.print ("Please enter the value of n:");
8          int n = input.nextInt();
9          for (int i = 1; i <= n; i++)
10         {
11             for (int j = 1; j <= n; j++)
12             {
13                 if (i == j)
14                 {
15                     System.out.print("\\ ");
16                     continue;
17                 }
18                 if (i + j == n + 1)
19                 {
20                     System.out.print("/ ");
21                     continue;
22                 }
23                 System.out.print(". ");
24             }
25             System.out.println();
26         }
27         input.close();
28     }
29 }
```

Output

Please enter the value of n:8

```
\ . . . . . . /
. \ . . . . / .
. . \ . . / . .
. . . \ / . . .
. . . / \ . . .
. . / . . \ . .
. / . . . . \ .
/ . . . . . . \
```

Write a program to display the following menu:

Pattern Menu
========
1. Triangle
2. Inverted Triangle
3. Exit
Enter your choice:

Let the user select an option. For option 1 and 2, accept the number of rows to be printed using the Scanner class.

Listing 11.16: PatternWithMenu.java

```java
import java.util.Scanner;

public class PatternWithMenu
{
    public static void main(String args[])
    {
        int choice;
        int numRows;
        Scanner scan = new Scanner(System.in);

        System.out.println("   Pattern Menu");
        System.out.println("   ============");
        System.out.println("1. Triangle");
        System.out.println("2. Inverted Triangle");
        System.out.println("3. Exit");
        System.out.println();

        System.out.print("Enter your choice: ");
        choice = scan.nextInt();

        switch(choice)
        {
            case 1:
                numRows = AcceptInput();

                for (int i = 1; i <= numRows; i++)
                {
                    for (int j = 1; j <= i; j++)
                    {
                        System.out.print ("@ ");
                    }
```

```
32
33                      System.out.println ();
34            }
35         break;
36
37      case 2:
38         numRows = AcceptInput();
39
40         for (int i = 1; i <= numRows; i++)
41         {
42            for (int j = i; j <= numRows; j++)
43            {
44               System.out.print ("@ ");
45            }
46
47            System.out.println ();
48         }
49         break;
50
51      case 3:
52         System.out.println ("Goodbye!");
53         break;
54
55      default:
56         System.out.println("*** Invalid option entered ***");
57      }
58      scan.close();
59   }
60
61   static int AcceptInput()
62   {
63      Scanner input = new Scanner(System.in);
64      System.out.println ("Please enter number of rows:");
65      int rows = input.nextInt();
66      input.close();
67
68      return rows;
69   }
70 }
```

```
                    Output
          Pattern Menu
          ========
          1. Triangle
          2. Inverted Triangle
          3. Exit
          Enter your choice: 1
          Please enter number of rows:
          7
          @
          @ @
          @ @ @
          @ @ @ @
          @ @ @ @ @
          @ @ @ @ @ @
          @ @ @ @ @ @ @
```

```
                    Output
          Pattern Menu
          ========
          1. Triangle
          2. Inverted Triangle
          3. Exit
          Enter your choice: 2
          Please enter number of rows:
          7
          @ @ @ @ @ @ @
          @ @ @ @ @ @
          @ @ @ @ @
          @ @ @ @
          @ @ @
          @ @
          @
```

Write a program called NumberGuessingGame to play a number guessing game. The program shall generate a random number between 1 and 100. The player inputs his/her guess, and the program shall response with "Try a higher number", "Try a lower number" or "You guessed it in n tries!" accordingly. Also display the random number in the end.

Listing 11.17: NumberGuessingGame.java

```java
1  import java.util.Scanner;
2
3  public class NumberGuessingGame
4  {
5      public static void main(String args[])
6      {
7          Scanner scan = new Scanner(System.in);
8          int secretNumber = (int) (100 * Math.random() + 1);
9          int guessNumber, count = 0;
10
11         System.out.print ("Please guess the number (enter 0 to quit): ");
12         guessNumber = scan.nextInt();
13
14         while ((guessNumber != secretNumber) && (guessNumber != 0))
15         {
16             if (guessNumber > secretNumber)
17                 System.out.print("Try a lower number ");
18             else if (guessNumber < secretNumber)
19                 System.out.print("Try a higher number ");
```

```
20              else
21                  break;
22
23          count++;
24          guessNumber = scan.nextInt();
25      }
26
27      if (guessNumber == 0)
28      {
29          System.out.println("You tried " + count + " times!");
30          System.out.println("The secret number was " + secretNumber);
31      }
32      else
33      {
34          System.out.println("You guessed it in " + count + " tries!");
35          System.out.println("Yes! The secret number is " + secretNumber);
36      }
37
38      scan.close();
39  }
40 }
```

Output

Please guess the number (enter 0 to quit): 55
Try a lower number 42
Try a higher number 47
Try a higher number 49
Try a higher number 51
Try a lower number 50
You guessed it in 5 tries!
Yes! The secret number is 50

Assignment Questions

1. Write a program to generate the following output.

```
@
@ #
@ # @
@ # @ #
@ # @ # @
```

---

2. Write a program in Java to display the following patterns.

(i) 1
  2 3
  4 5 6
  7 8 9 10
  11 12 13 14 15

(ii) #
  * *
  # # #
  * * * *
  # # # # #

(iii) $ $ $ $ 5
  $ $ $ 4
  $ $ 3
  $ 2
  1

(iv) 5 4 3 2 1
  4 3 2 1
  3 2 1
  2 1
  1

(v) 1 2 3 4 5
  1 2 3 4
  1 2 3
  1 2
  1
  1 2
  1 2 3
  1 2 3 4
  1 2 3 4 5

(vi) 1 * * * *
  * 2 * * *

* * 3 * *
* * * 4 *
* * * * 5

(vii) 1 * * * *
  2 2 * * *
  3 3 3 * *
  4 4 4 4 *
  5 5 5 5 5

(viii) A B C D E
  A B C D
  A B C
  A B
  A

(ix) B
  B L
  B L U
  B L U E
  B L U E J

(x) 1 2 3 4 5
  2 3 4 5
  3 4 5
  4 5
  5
  4 5
  3 4 5
  2 3 4 5
  1 2 3 4 5

3. Write a program to print the series given below.

8 88 888 8888 88888 888888

4. What will be the value of **sum** after each of the following nested loops is executed?

(i)
```
    int sum = 0;
    for (int i = 0; i <= 10; i++)
        for (int j = 0; j <= 10; j++)
            sum += i ;
```

(ii)
```
    int sum = 0;
    for (int i = 1; i <= 3; i++)
        for (int j = 1; j <= 3; j++)
            sum = sum + (i + j);
```

5. Write a program to generate a triangle or an inverted triangle till **n** terms based upon the user's choice of triangle to be displayed.

Example 1
Input: Type 1 for a triangle and type 2 for an inverted triangle
1
Enter the number of terms
5

Output
1
2 2
3 3 3
4 4 4 4
5 5 5 5 5

Example 2
Input: Type 1 for a triangle and type 2 for an inverted triangle
2
Enter the number of terms
6

Output
6 6 6 6 6 6
5 5 5 5 5
4 4 4 4
3 3 3
2 2
1

6. Write a program to compute and display factorials of numbers between p and q where p > 0, q > 0, and p > q.

7. Write a program to determine if an entered number is a Happy Number. A happy number is defined by the following process:

Starting with any positive integer, replace the number by the sum of the squares of its digits, and repeat the process until the number is equal to 1. For example, 19 is a happy number, as per the following calculation:

$$1^2 + 9^2 = 82,$$
$$8^2 + 2^2 = 68,$$
$$6^2 + 8^2 = 100,$$
$$1^2 + 0^2 + 0^2 = 1$$

8. Write a menu driven program that prompts the user to select one of the four triangle patterns (a, b, c, or d). The program then accepts number of rows and prints the selected pattern as shown below:

Enter the size: 8

```
*                    * * * * * * * *      * * * * * * * *      *
* *                  * * * * * * *        * * * * * * *        * *
* * *                * * * * * *          * * * * * *          * * *
* * * *              * * * * *            * * * * *            * * * *
* * * * *            * * * *              * * * *              * * * * *
* * * * * *          * * *                * * *                * * * * * *
* * * * * * *        * *                  * *                  * * * * * * *
* * * * * * * *      *                    *                    * * * * * * * *
      (a)                  (b)                  (c)                  (d)
```

9. Write a menu driven program that prompts the user to select one of the four triangle patterns (a, b, c, or d). The program then accepts number of rows and prints the selected pattern as shown below:

   Enter the size: 8

```
1                    1 2 3 4 5 6 7 8      1                    8 7 6 5 4 3 2 1
1 2                  1 2 3 4 5 6 7        1 2                  7 6 5 4 3 2 1
1 2 3                1 2 3 4 5 6          1 2 3                6 5 4 3 2 1
1 2 3 4              1 2 3 4 5            1 2 3 4              5 4 3 2 1
1 2 3 4 5            1 2 3 4              1 2 3 4 5            4 3 2 1
1 2 3 4 5 6          1 2 3                1 2 3 4 5 6          3 2 1
1 2 3 4 5 6 7        1 2                  1 2 3 4 5 6 7        2 1
1 2 3 4 5 6 7 8      1                    1 2 3 4 5 6 7 8      1
      (a)                  (b)                  (c)                  (d)
```

10. Write a program that computes `sinx` and `cosx` by using the following power series:

$$sinx = x - \frac{x^3}{3!} + \frac{x^5}{5!} - \frac{x^7}{7!} + \ldots$$

$$cosx = 1 - \frac{x^2}{2!} + \frac{x^4}{4!} - \frac{x^6}{6!} + \ldots$$

Chapter 12

Constructors

Constructors

You have learnt that an object of a class contains instance variables. You may often want to initialise the instance variables when you create the object. For example, consider the scenario of a BankAccount class that contains an instance variable balanceAmount. When you create an object of the BankAccount class, you may want to set the instance variable balanceAmount to an initial value of £100. That is because every newly created account should have a minimum initial balance.

There are a number of approaches to initialise instance variables, but initialising instance variables via a special kind of method called constructor is the most common form of initialisation. In this chapter, you will understand how to define and use such constructors.

12.1   Constructors and Their Use

A constructor is a member method of a class that is used to initialise the instance variables. Let us have a look at a statement that creates an object:

```
Student student = new Student();
```

The above statement creates a new object called student of the Student class type. The code following the new keyword looks very much like a method call. In fact, it is a call to a special kind of method called a constructor. Every class has at least one constructor method. The purpose of a constructor is to create an instance of the class.

The new operator creates an empty object[1] of the given class and then calls the constructor method, which can initialise the instance variables of the object. Let us now have a look at the Student class with a constructor method.

```
class Student //Class name
{
    int rollNumber;
    char grade;
    public Student() //Constructor
    {
        rollNumber = 17;
        grade = 'B';
    }
    //statement1
    //statement2
}
```

---

[1]An object without any values assigned to the instance variables is known as an empty object.

Note the following characteristics of the constructor:

(i) The constructor has exactly the same name as its defining class, i.e., the constructor name **Student** is the same as that of the class.

(ii) The constructor method does not have a return type - not even **void**.

(iii) The constructor can be invoked only via the **new** operator. You cannot invoke them like a normal method call.

In the above example, whenever the computer creates an object of the **Student** type, the constructor method **Student()** is called automatically. The constructor assigns default values of **17** and 'B' to the member variables **rollNumber** and **grade**, respectively.

So, why do you use constructors?
A constructor instructs the computer to perform the start-up tasks of a new object. These can be like assigning default values to instance variables, aligning all the buttons on a screen when a new window object is created, or moving the cursor to a specific data entry field for the user input.

12.2 Types of Constructors

There are two types of constructors in Java.

12.2.1 Default Constructor

The class name followed by parentheses specifies a constructor for the class. The constructor defines what happens when an object of the class is created. However, it is not compulsory to define the constructor explicitly in the class. If no constructor has been defined for the class, then the Java compiler automatically includes a default constructor. The default constructor is a constructor that does not accept any arguments and has no statements in its body. For example, if you omit the constructor from the **Student** class you defined earlier, the default constructor will be added to the class by the compiler.

```
Class Student //Class name
{
    int rollNumber;
    Char grade;

    //Default Constructor
    public Student()
    {
    }

    //statement1
    //statement2
}
```

Once a programmer has added a constructor to the class, no default constructor will be added by the compiler. A constructor that does not contain any parameters is called a non-parameterised constructor. Since the default constructor has no parameters, it is also known as a non-parameterised constructor.

Let us consider an example in which no constructor has been defined, and the Java compiler automatically includes a default constructor.

Listing 12.1: Student1.java

```
1  class Student1 //Class name
2  {
3     int rollNumber;
4     char grade;
5
6     public void DisplayData()
7     {
8        System.out.println("Roll Number: " + rollNumber);
9        System.out.println("Grade: " + grade);
10    }
11
12    public static void main(String args[])
13    {
14       Student1 student1 = new Student1();
15       student1.DisplayData();
16    }
17 }
```

Output
Roll Number: 0
Grade:

Here, notice that both the instance variables `rollNumber` and `grade` are printed with the default values of 0 and `null`, respectively, assigned by the compiler.

Let us now consider an example where a constructor has been defined in the class.

Listing 12.2: Student2.java

```
1  class Student2 //Class name
2  {
3     int rollNumber;
4     char grade;
5
6     public Student2()  //Constructor
7     {
8        System.out.println("Inside Constructor");
9        rollNumber = 17;
10       grade = 'Z';
```

Constructor defined in the class with the same name as the class name. It initialises the member variables.

```
11      }
12
13      public void DisplayData()
14      {
15          System.out.println("Roll Number: " + rollNumber);
16          System.out.println("Grade: " + grade);
17      }
18
19      public static void main(String args[])
20      {
21          Student2 student2 = new Student2();
22          student2.DisplayData();
23      }
24  }
```

> **Output**
>
> Inside Constructor
> Roll Number: 17
> Grade: Z

12.2.2 Parameterised Constructor

A constructor with parameters is called a parameterised constructor. The parameterised constructor allows the programmer to initialise objects with different values. This is achieved by passing the required values as arguments to the constructor method. Let us reconsider the previous example and create a parameterised constructor.

Listing 12.3: Student3.java

```
1   class Student3 //Class name
2   {
3       int rollNumber;
4       char grade;
5
6       public Student3(int roll, char grd)
7       {
8           System.out.println("Inside Constructor");
9           rollNumber = roll;
10          grade = grd;
11      }
12
13      public void DisplayData()
14      {
15          System.out.println("Roll Number: " + rollNumber);
16          System.out.println("Grade: " + grade);
17      }
18
19      public static void main(String args[])
20      {
21          Student3 studentA = new Student3(23, 'D');
```

> Constructor defined in the class with the same name as the class name. It initialises the member variables with the argument values.

```
22        studentA.DisplayData();
23
24        Student3 studentB = new Student3(27, 'A');
25        studentB.DisplayData();
26    }
27 }
```

Output
Inside Constructor
Roll Number: 23
Grade: D
Inside Constructor
Roll Number: 27
Grade: A

Note that with a parameterised constructor, you must provide initial values while instantiating the object; otherwise, the compiler will report an error as shown in Figure 12.1.

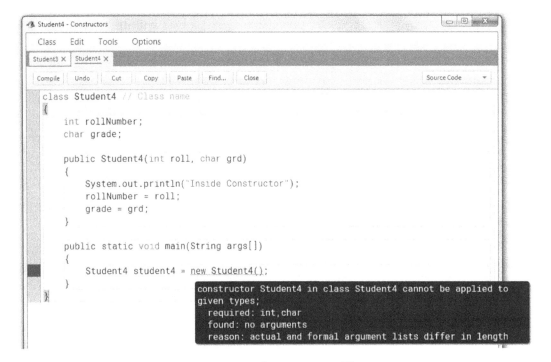

Figure 12.1: Constructor Error

12.3 Constructor Overloading

Just like methods, the constructor of a class can also be overloaded, that is, a class can have multiple constructors with the same name but different signatures. The process of creating more than one constructor with the same name but with different parameter declarations is called constructor overloading.

The signature of all versions of the constructor should be different for the constructor overloading purpose, i.e., they should have different type of parameters or different number of parameters or both.

Let us understand the concept by creating a class Cuboid to compute the volume of a cuboid. The class has four different versions of the Cuboid() constructor as explained below:

(i) The first version has no parameters.

(ii) The second version has one parameter.

(iii) The third version has two parameters.

(iv) The fourth version has three parameters.

The versions of the constructor should be designed in the following way:

- **Type 1**: If the constructor is called with no arguments (default constructor), then the integer values 20, 15, and 10 should be assigned to the `length`, `width`, and the `height` variable, respectively.

- **Type 2**: If the constructor is called with only one argument, this value is assigned to the `length` variable, and the other variables `width` and `height` should be assigned the integer values 15 and 10, respectively.

- **Type 3**: If the constructor is called with two arguments, the passed values are assigned to the `length` and `width` variable, respectively. The height variable is initialised with the integer value 10.

- **Type 4**: If the constructor is called with three arguments, these values are assigned to all the three variables in the same order they are passed.

Listing 12.4: Cuboid.java

```java
public class Cuboid //Class name
{
    int length;
    int width;
    int height;

    //Constructor without any parameter
    public Cuboid()
    {
        System.out.println("Invoking constructor with no parameters");
        length = 20;
        width = 15;
        height = 10;
    }

    //Constructor with one parameter
    public Cuboid(int len)
    {
        System.out.println("Invoking constructor with one parameter");
        length = len;
        width = 15;
        height = 10;
    }
```

```
24
25      //Constructor with two parameters
26      public Cuboid(int len, int wd)
27      {
28         System.out.println("Invoking constructor with two parameters");
29         length = len;
30         width = wd;
31         height = 10;
32      }
33
34      //Constructor with three parameters
35      public Cuboid(int len, int wd, int ht)
36      {
37         System.out.println("Invoking constructor with three parameters");
38         length = len;
39         width = wd;
40         height = ht;
41      }
42
43      void Volume()
44      {
45         int volume;
46         volume = length * width * height;
47         System.out.println("Dimensions of the cuboid are:");
48         System.out.println("Length: " + length);
49         System.out.println("Width:  " + width);
50         System.out.println("Height: " + height);
51         System.out.println("Volume of the cuboid is: " + volume);
52         System.out.println();
53      }
54
55      public static void main(String args[])
56      {
57         Cuboid cuboid1 = new Cuboid();
58         cuboid1.Volume();
59
60         Cuboid cuboid2 = new Cuboid(50);
61         cuboid2.Volume();
62
63         Cuboid cuboid3 = new Cuboid(102, 40);
64         cuboid3.Volume();
65
66         Cuboid cuboid4 = new Cuboid(46, 30, 14);
67         cuboid4.Volume();
68      }
69 }
```

Code Walkthrough:

◈ Line 20: Assigns the provided value to the `length` member variable.

◈ Lines 29 - 30: Assign the provided values to the `length` and `width` member variables.

◈ Lines 38 - 40: Assign the provided values to the `length`, `width` and `height` member variables.

◈ Line 57: Creates an instance without any parameter passed to the constructor method.

◈ Line 60: Creates an instance with one parameter passed to the constructor method.

◈ Line 63: Creates an instance with two parameters passed to the constructor method.

◈ Line 66: Creates an instance with three parameters passed to the constructor method.

```
                              Output
Invoking constructor with no parameters
Dimensions of the cuboid are:
Length: 20
Width: 15
Height: 10
Volume of the cuboid is: 3000
Invoking constructor with one parameter
Dimensions of the cuboid are:
Length: 50 } Parameter value assigned to the length member variable.
Width: 15
Height: 10
Volume of the cuboid is: 7500
Invoking constructor with two parameters
Dimensions of the cuboid are:
Length: 102 } Parameter value assigned to the length and width member
Width: 40    variables.
Height: 10
Volume of the cuboid is: 40800
Invoking constructor with three parameters
Dimensions of the cuboid are:
Length: 46  } Parameter value assigned to the length, width and height
Width: 30     member variables.
Height: 14
Volume of the cuboid is: 19320
```

12.4 Difference between Constructor and Method

Although a constructor is also a member method of the class just like other methods, yet there are certain differences between the constructor and the method, as shown in Table on the next page.

	Constructor	Method
1.	The constructor name must be the same as the class name.	The method name must be different from the class name.
2.	A constructor has no return type - not even void.	A method must have a return type. If it does not return a value, it must return void.
3.	Constructors are called only via the new operator at the time of object creation. You cannot invoke them as normal method calls.	Methods can be called directly by an object that has already been created. The method calls are specified by the programmer.
4.	Execution of at least one constructor is a must when an object of the class is created.	All the methods defined in a class may or may not execute, depending on the calls specified by the programmer.

12.5   The this Keyword

Within a constructor or a method, this is a reference to the current object - the object whose constructor or method is being invoked. Consider the following program to understand the use of the this keyword.

Listing 12.5: Area.java

```
1  class Area
2  {
3      int length, breadth;
4
5      public Area(int length, int breadth)
6      {
7          length = length;
8          breadth = breadth;
9      }
10
11     public void Display()
12     {
13         int area = length * breadth;
14         System.out.println("Area is " + area);
15     }
16
17     public static void main(String args[])
18     {
19         Area area = new Area(2, 3);
20         area.Display();
21     }
22 }
```

Inside the constructor, length, and breadth are local variables.

Output
Area is 0

Note that the output of the program is zero. Here is the reason why it is so.

Both the parameters `length` and `breadth` are local variables inside the constructor `Area()`. The instance variables also have the same name, i.e., `length` and `breadth`. Therefore, in Line 8, when you assigned the value of parameter `length` to the instance variable `length`, you actually assigned the parameter value to itself, i.e.,

```
parameter variable length = parameter variable length;
```

Although the intention was:

```
instance variable length = parameter variable length;
```

Due to this, the instance variables `length` and `breadth` were not assigned any value at all! Because no values were assigned to the instance variables `length` and `breadth`, they were initialised with the default value of `int`, i.e., 0 (zero) when the constructor was invoked. This resulted in an area equal to zero.

Now the question is how do you specify the intended variable name when the instance variable and the local variable have the same name? In such a scenario, you can use the `this` keyword that would refer to the instance variable instead of the argument variable. Program 12.6 shows the modified code using the `this` keyword.

Listing 12.6: AreaNew.java

```
1  class AreaNew
2  {
3     int length , breadth ;
4
5     public AreaNew(int length , int breadth)
6     {
7        this.length = length ;
8        this.breadth = breadth ;
9     }
10
11    public void Display ()
12    {
13       int area = length * breadth ;
14       System.out.println("Area is " + area);
15    }
16
17    public static void main(String args[])
18    {
19       AreaNew area = new AreaNew(2, 3);
20       area.Display ();
21    }
22 }
```

> The this keyword is used to assign values to the instance variables.

Output
Area is 6

Solved Programming Exercises

Write a class **MyDate** in Java with the following details:

Instance Variables/Data Members:

day: stores the day

month: stores the month

year: stores the year

Constructor Methods:

Default constructor: initialises instance variables as **day = 1**, **month = 1**, **year = 1900**

Parameterised constructor: initialises instance variables with the provided initial values

Write a main method to create an object of the class and call the above member methods.

Listing 12.7: MyDate.java

```java
1  class MyDate //Class name
2  {
3     int day, month, year;
4     //Default constructor
5     public MyDate()
6     {
7        day = 1;
8        month = 1;
9        year = 1900;
10    }
11
12    //Parameterised constructor
13    public MyDate(int dy, int mn, int yr)
14    {
15       day = dy;
16       month = mn;
17       year = yr;
18    }
19
20    public static void main(String args[])
21    {
22       MyDate myDate1 = new MyDate();
23       System.out.println("Date is: " + myDate1.day + "/" +
             ↪ myDate1.month + "/" + myDate1.year);
24
25       MyDate myDate2 = new MyDate(25, 12, 2020);
26       System.out.println("Date is: " + myDate2.day + "/" +
             ↪ myDate2.month + "/" + myDate2.year);
27    }
```

```
28  }
```

> Define a class **Student** described as below:
>
> Data Members/Instance Variables:
>
> name, age, m1, m2, m3 (marks in 3 subjects), maximum, average
>
> Member Methods:
>
>   (i) A parameterised constructor to initialise the data members
>
> (ii) To accept the details of a student
>
> (iii) To compute the average and the maximum out of three marks
>
> (iv) To display the name, age, and marks in three subjects, maximum marks and average marks
>
> Write a main method to create an object of a class and call the above member methods.

Listing 12.8: Student.java

```java
1   import java.util.Scanner;
2   public class Student
3   {
4      String name;
5      int age;
6      int m1, m2, m3, maximum;
7      double average;
8
9      public Student()
10     {
11     }
12
13     public Student(String nm, int ag, int mks1, int mks2, int mks3)
14     {
15        name = nm;
16        age = ag;
17        m1 = mks1;
18        m2 = mks2;
19        m3 = mks3;
20        maximum = 0;
21        average = 0;
22     }
23
24     public void AcceptDetails()
25     {
26        Scanner scanner = new Scanner(System.in);
27        System.out.print("Enter Name: ");
```

```
28          name = scanner.nextLine();
29          System.out.print("Enter Age: ");
30          age = scanner.nextInt();
31          System.out.print("Enter Marks in Subject1: ");
32          m1 = scanner.nextInt();
33          System.out.print("Enter Marks in Subject2: ");
34          m2 = scanner.nextInt();
35          System.out.print("Enter Marks in Subject3: ");
36          m3 = scanner.nextInt();
37
38          scanner.close();
39      }
40
41      public void Compute()
42      {
43          average = (m1 + m2 + m3) / 3.0;
44          maximum = Math.max(m1, (Math.max(m2, m3)));
45      }
46
47      public void DisplayDetails()
48      {
49          System.out.println("Name: " + name);
50          System.out.println("Age: " + age);
51          System.out.println("Marks in Subject1: " + m1);
52          System.out.println("Marks in Subject2: " + m2);
53          System.out.println("Marks in Subject3: " + m3);
54          System.out.println("Maximum Marks: " + maximum);
55          System.out.println("Average Marks: " + average);
56      }
57
58      public static void main(String[] args)
59      {
60          Student student1 = new Student();
61          student1.AcceptDetails();
62          student1.Compute();
63          System.out.println("Student1 details *** With default ←
                → constructor");
64          student1.DisplayDetails();
65
66          Student student2 = new Student("Rekha Batra", 15, 94, 99, 92);
67          System.out.println("Student2 details *** With parameterised ←
                → constructor");
68          student2.Compute();
69          student2.DisplayDetails();
70      }
71  }
```

```
                    Output
Enter Name: Ronit Singh
Enter Age: 16
Enter Marks in Subject1: 90
Enter Marks in Subject2: 98
Enter Marks in Subject3: 85
Student1 details *** With default constructor
Name: Ronit Singh
Age: 16
Marks in Subject1: 90
Marks in Subject2: 98
Marks in Subject3: 85
Maximum Marks: 98
Average Marks: 91.0
Student2 details *** With parameterised constructor
Name: Rekha Batra
Age: 15
Marks in Subject1: 94
Marks in Subject2: 99
Marks in Subject3: 92
Maximum Marks: 99
Average Marks: 95.0
```

Define a class **BankAccount** as described below:

Data Members/Instance Variables:

holdersName: to store the name of the account holder

accountNumber: to store the account number

balanceAmount: to store the balance amount

Member Methods:

(i) A constructor to initialise the data members. Initialise the balanceAmount with balance of £100 on creation of the account.

(ii) To deposit money into account.

(iii) To withdraw money from the account. Ensure that there is enough balance before withdrawal.

Write a main method to create an object of the class and call the above member methods.

Listing 12.9: BankAccount.java

```
1  class BankAccount
2  {
```

```
3     String holdersName;
4     long accountNumber;
5     double balanceAmount;
6
7     public BankAccount(String name, long number)
8     {
9         holdersName = name;
10        accountNumber = number;
11        balanceAmount = 100.0;
12    }
13
14    public void Deposit(double amount)
15    {
16        balanceAmount += amount;
17    }
18
19    public void Withdraw(double amount)
20    {
21        if (amount <= balanceAmount)
22            balanceAmount -= amount;
23    }
24
25    public void Display()
26    {
27        System.out.println("Name of the Account Holder: " + holdersName);
28        System.out.println("Account Number: " + accountNumber);
29        System.out.println("Balance Amount: " + balanceAmount);
30    }
31
32    public static void main(String args[])
33    {
34        BankAccount objAccount = new BankAccount("Joe Bloggs", 1122334455);
35        objAccount.Deposit(20000);
36        objAccount.Withdraw(11750);
37        objAccount.Display();
38    }
39 }
```

Output
Name of the Account Holder: Joe Bloggs
Account Number: 1122334455
Balance Amount: 8350.0

Multiple Choice Questions

1. A member method having the same name as that of the class is called ....

   A. an alias   C. a constructor

   B. a friendly method   D. a protected method

2. A constructor has .... return type.

   A. a void   C. String[] args

   B. more than one   D. no

3. A constructor is used when an object is ....

   A. created   C. assigned a value

   B. destroyed   D. abstracted

4. A default constructor has ....

   A. no parameters   C. two parameters

   B. one parameter   D. multiple parameters

5. Pick the correct answer.

   A. A constructor has exactly the same name as its defining class.

   B. A constructor method does not have a return type.

   C. A constructor can be invoked only via the new operator.

   D. All of the above

6. In constructor overloading, ...

   A. All constructors must have the same name as that of the class.

   B. All constructors must have the same number of arguments.

   C. All constructors must have arguments of type String[] args.

   D. All constructors must have no arguments.

Assignment Questions

1. What is a constructor? Why do you need a constructor?

2. If the constructor is automatically generated by the compiler, why do you need to define your own constructor?

3. Explain the statement, "you cannot invoke constructors as normal method calls".

4. Describe the importance of parameterised constructors.

5. If a class is named `DemoClass`, what names are allowed as constructor names in the class `DemoClass`?

6. Explain the concept of constructor overloading with an example.

7. What is the use of the keyword `this`?

8. What is a no-argument constructor? Does every class have a no-argument constructor?

9. Create a class named `Pizza` that stores details about a pizza. It should contain the following:
   Instance Variables:
   `String pizzaSize` - to store the size of the pizza (small, medium, or large)
   `int cheese` - the number of cheese toppings
   `int pepperoni` - the number of pepperoni toppings
   `int mushroom` - the number of mushroom toppings

   Member Methods:
   `Constructor` - to initialise all the instance variables
   `CalculateCost()` - A `public` method that returns a `double` value, that is, the cost of the pizza.
   Pizza cost is calculated as follows:

   - Small: £5 + £1 per topping
   - Medium: £6.5 + £1 per topping
   - Large: £8 + £1 per topping

   `PizzaDescription()` - A `public` method that returns a `String` containing the pizza size, quantity of each topping, and the pizza cost as calculated by `CalculateCost()`.

Answers To Objective Questions

Multiple Choice Questions

1. C   2. D   3. A   4. A   5. D   6. A

Chapter 13

Library Classes

Library Classes

IT is now evident to you that everything in Java exists in the form of classes and objects. In object-oriented programming, a class library is a collection of pre-written classes or coded templates which simplify the job of a programmer. In the previous chapters, you have used many built-in methods of Java, such as `println()` and `print()`. While using these methods, you have used the keyword, `System` before the method call.

```
System.out.println();
System.out.print();
```

As per their syntax, you can interpret that all these methods are members of the `System` class. The `System` class is predefined in Java and is automatically included in the programs.

The Java environment has a huge library of built-in classes that contain pre-defined methods to support the input/output operations and `String` handling operations. They also provide various methods for the development of network and graphical user interface.

These library classes are an integral part of their respective packages. A Java package is a collection of similar types of built-in classes (library classes), and sub packages, which provide most of the functionality that comes with Java, so it is extremely important to learn the art of using them. Some most commonly used classes are the wrapper classes contained in the `java.lang` package. In this chapter, let us learn how to use these wrapper classes.

13.1   Primitive Data Type

Primitive data types are pre-defined by the language and form the basic building blocks of representing data. A primitive type stores a single value of a specific declared type at a time. For example, a variable defined as `int` can store an integer at a time. When another value is stored in the variable, the initial value is replaced by the new one. The eight built-in primitive data types supported by the Java programming language are `byte`, `short`, `int`, `long`, `float`, `double`, `boolean`, and `char`.

13.2   Composite Data Type

A composite data type is a data type which can be constructed in a program using the programming language's primitive data types. In other words, it is a collection of primitive data types. For example, the `String` data type you use in Java is actually a class which is a collection of `char` data types.

13.3 User Defined Data Type

The data type defined by the user to perform some specific task is known as a user-defined data type. The classes created by the user are user-defined data types.

13.4 Class as a Composite Type

In a class, you can assemble items of different data types to create a composite data type. The class can also be considered as a new data type created by the user, that has its own functionality. The classes allow these user-defined types to be used in programs. Let us see an example of this.

Listing 13.1: Calculator.java

```java
public class Calculator
{
   int num1, num2;

   public int Add()
   {
      int result;

      result = num1 + num2;
      return result;
   }

   public int Sub()
   {
      int result;

      result = num1 - num2;
      return result;
   }
}
```

The above class, Calculator, is a user-defined data type (as it is defined by the user) which uses a collection of two primitive data type variables - int num1 and num2. Thus, the class Calculator is a composite data type. Variables num1 and num2 are called its member variables.

The Calculator class has two member methods - Add() and Sub(). The member method Add() provides the functionality to add two numbers, and the member method Sub() provides the functionality to subtract two numbers.

13.4.1 Creating Objects of the Class

Since a class is an object factory, let us see how to create an object of the `Calculator` class. You can use the **new** operator to create an object of the `Calculator` class as shown below:

```
Calculator myCalculator = new Calculator();
```

Here, `myCalculator` object is a variable of `Calculator` data type and can also be called a reference type as it stores reference to the memory location where the object is stored.

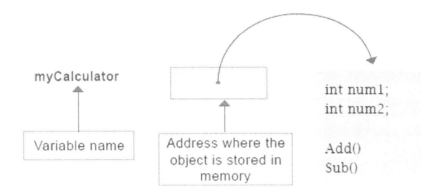

Figure 13.1: Memory Allocation

13.4.2 Accessing Member Variables

After creating an object (or instance), you can access its member variables via the dot (.) operator. For example, you can access member variable `num1` as `myCalculator.num1`. Similarly, you can access member variable `num2` as `myCalculator.num2`. You can also assign values to member variables as follows:

```
myCalculator.num1 = 9;
myCalculator.num2 = 8;
```

13.4.3 Accessing Member Methods

You can access the functionality provided by the `Calculator` class using its member methods. For example, in order to invoke the addition operation, you can use the following statement:

```
myCalculator.Add();
```

Let us define a `main()` method in the class that creates an object of the `Calculator` class type and demonstrates its functionality. Here is the complete code:

Listing 13.2: Calculator.java

```
1  public class Calculator
2  {
3     int num1, num2;
4
5     public int Add()
6     {
7        int result;
8
9        result = num1 + num2;
10       return result;
11    }
12
13    public int Sub()
14    {
15       int result;
16
17       result = num1 - num2;
18       return result;
19    }
20
21    public static void main(String args[])
22    {
23       int sum, diff;
24
25       Calculator myCalculator = new Calculator();
26
27       myCalculator.num1 = 9;
28       myCalculator.num2 = 8;
29       sum = myCalculator.Add();
30       diff = myCalculator.Sub();
31
32       System.out.println("Sum is: " + sum);
33       System.out.println("Difference is: " + diff);
34    }
35 }
```

Output
```
Sum is: 17
Difference is: 1
```

Code Walkthrough:

◈ Line 3: Declares member variables **num1** and **num2**.

◈ Lines 5 - 11: Define a member method **Add** to compute the sum of two numbers.

◈ Lines 13 - 19: Define a member method **Sub** to compute the difference between two numbers.

◈ Line 25: Instantiates an object **myCalculator** of the **Calculator** class type.

◈ Line 27: Assigns value 9 to the member variable **num1**.

◇ Line 28: Assigns value 8 to the member variable `num2`.

◇ Line 29: Invokes the member method `Add()` to compute the sum.

◇ Line 30: Invokes the member method `Sub()` to compute the difference.

13.4.4 Difference between Primitive and Composite Data Types

Table 13.1 shows the difference between primitive data type and composite data type.

	Primitive Data Type	Composite Data Type
1.	Primitive data type represents a single value. For example, int and char.	Composite type is a collection that holds zero or more primitive values or objects. For example, class and arrays.
2.	When primitive data is copied to a variable, that variable gets its own unique copy of the data, stored separately in memory.	When composite data is copied to a variable, only a reference to the data is stored in the variable.
3.	If two variables contain data that is primitive, they compare by value. This means that if they both contain the same values, they are equal.	If two variables contain data that is composite, they compare by reference. This means that they are equal if they refer to the same object.
4.	In a method call, primitive data is passed by value.	In a method call, composite data is passed by reference.

Table 13.1: Difference between Primitive and Composite Data Types

13.5 Wrapper Classes

A wrapper class allows you to convert a primitive data type into an object type. Each of Java's eight primitive data types has a wrapper class dedicated to it. These are known as *wrapper classes* because they wrap the primitive data type into an object of that class. Thus, there is an `Integer` class that wraps an `int` variable, a `Double` class that wraps a `double` variable, and so on. These wrapper classes in Java serve three primary purposes:

(i) To store primitive data types as an object.

(ii) To allow primitive data types to have functionality like conversion from one type to another. For example, converting a numeric string value to an integer.

(iii) To allow primitive data types to do activities reserved for the objects such as being added to an array list and hash map.

Eight wrapper classes used to wrap primitive data types in Java are given below:

Primitive Type	Wrapper Class
byte	Byte
short	Short
int	Integer
long	Long
float	Float
double	Double
boolean	Boolean
char	Character

Note that the names of primitive data types are all in lowercase whereas the first letters of the wrapper classes are in uppercase. For example, `float` is a data type whereas `Float` is a wrapper class. These wrapper classes are defined in the `java.lang` package and are hierarchically structured as follows:

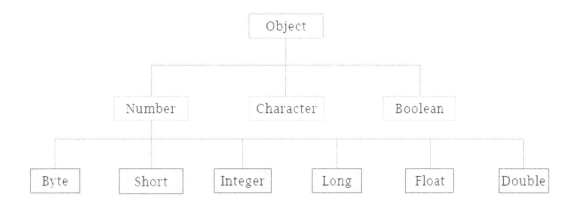

Figure 13.2: Hierarchical Structure of Wrapper Classes

Listing 13.3: WrapperClasses.java

```java
public class WrapperClasses
{
    public static void main(String args[])
    {
        Byte varByte = 100;
        Short varShort = 3200;
        Integer varInteger = 77777;
        Long varLong = 123455L;
        Float varFloat = 123.34F;
        Double varDouble = 2233.33;
        Character varCharacter = 'K';
```

```
12       Boolean varBoolean = true;
13
14       System.out.println("varByte: " + varByte);
15       System.out.println("varShort: " + varShort);
16       System.out.println("varInteger: " + varInteger);
17       System.out.println("varLong: " + varLong);
18       System.out.println("varFloat: " + varFloat);
19       System.out.println("varDouble: " + varDouble);
20       System.out.println("varCharacter: " + varCharacter);
21       System.out.println("varBoolean: " + varBoolean);
22    }
23 }
```

Output
varByte: 100
varShort: 3200
varInteger: 77777
varLong: 123455
varFloat: 123.34
varDouble: 2233.33
varCharacter: K
varBoolean: true

13.6   Autoboxing

Autoboxing is the automatic conversion of the primitive types into their corresponding object wrapper classes. For example, automatic conversion from an `int` to an `Integer` and from a `double` to a `Double`. Consider the following statement:

```
Integer myInteger = 20;
```

It is a simple example of autoboxing where the `int` value 20 is autoboxed into the wrapper class `Integer`.

Listing 13.4: Autoboxing.java

```
1  public class Autoboxing
2  {
3     public static void main(String args[])
4     {
5        int myInt = 20;
6        Integer myInteger = myInt;        int value autoboxed into
                                            the wrapper class Integer
7
8        System.out.println("Primitive type int value is: " + myInt);
9        System.out.println("Wrapper class Integer value is: " + myInteger);
10    }
11 }
```

Output
Primitive type int value is: 20
Wrapper class Integer value is: 20

13.7 Auto-unboxing

Auto-unboxing is the reverse process of Autoboxing. That means it is the automatic conversion of a wrapper class object into its corresponding primitive type. For example, automatic conversion from an `Integer` to an `int` and from a `Long` to a `long`. Consider the following statements:

```
Integer myInteger = 20;
int myInt = myInteger;
```

Here, the object `myInteger` is automatically unboxed into primitive type `int` when the assignment `myInt = myInteger` takes place.

Listing 13.5: Autounboxing.java

```java
1  public class Autounboxing
2  {
3      public static void main(String args[])
4      {
5          Integer myInteger = 20;
6          int myInt = myInteger;          Object myInteger is automatically
7                                          unboxed into primitive type int
8          System.out.println("Wrapper class Integer value is: " + myInteger);
9          System.out.println("Primitive type int value is: " + myInt);
10     }
11 }
```

```
Output
Wrapper class Integer value is: 20
Primitive type int value is: 20
```

With autoboxing and auto-unboxing, the conversion between primitive types and their corresponding objects occurs automatically. Autoboxing converts primitive types into wrapper objects, and auto-unboxing takes place when an object is converted into its corresponding primitive type.

Let us understand some of the methods provided by the wrapper classes of numeric and character data type.

13.8 Parsing String Value to Numeric

The wrapper classes `Integer`, `Long`, `Float`, and `Double` have corresponding methods to parse a string argument as a numeric value.

	Method Name	Wrapper Class	Description
1	parseInt(string)	Integer	Parses the string argument as a signed integer. The characters in the string must be digits or digits separated with a decimal. The first character may be a minus sign (-) to indicate a negative value or a plus sign (+) to indicate a positive value. Syntax: int parseInt(String s)
2	parseLong(string)	Long	Parses the string argument as a signed long. The characters in the string must be digits or digits separated with a decimal. The first character may be a minus sign (-) to indicate a negative value or a plus sign (+) to indicate a positive value. Syntax: long parseLong(String s)
3	parseFloat(string)	Float	Returns a float value represented by the specified string. Syntax: float parseFloat(String s)
4	parseDouble(string)	Double	Returns a double value represented by the specified string. Syntax: double parseDouble(String s)5

Let us understand this with the following program that demonstrates the parsing of all four types.

Listing 13.6: VolumeOverload.java

```java
public class Parsing
{
    public static void main(String args[])
    {
        String strInt = "-1234";
        int numInt = Integer.parseInt(strInt);
        System.out.println("Integer value is: " + numInt);

        String strLong = "1234567890";
        long numLong = Long.parseLong(strLong);
        System.out.println("Long value is: " + numLong);

        String strFloat = "-345.56";
        float numFloat = Float.parseFloat(strFloat);
        System.out.println("Float value is: " + numFloat);

        String strDouble = "1.02E23";
```

```
18        double numdouble = Double.parseDouble(strDouble);
19        System.out.println("Double value is: " + numdouble);
20    }
21 }
```

```
                                              Output
                              Integer value is: -1234
                              Long value is: 1234567890
                              Float value is: -345.56
                              Double value is: 1.02E23
```

13.9   Checking Character Methods

The `Character` class wraps a value of the primitive type `char` into an object. It has a number of useful methods as described below:

	Method Name	Wrapper Class	Description
1	isDigit(char)	Character	Returns true if the specified character is a digit; returns false otherwise. Syntax: boolean isDigit(char ch)
2	isLetter(char)	Character	Returns true if the specified character is a letter; returns false otherwise. Syntax: boolean isLetter(char ch)
3	isLetterOrDigit(char)	Character	Returns true if the specified character is a letter or a digit; returns false otherwise. Syntax: boolean isLetterOrDigit(char ch)
4	isWhitespace(char)	Character	Returns true if the specified character is whitespace; returns false otherwise. Syntax: boolean isWhitespace(char ch)

The following program demonstrates these methods.

Listing 13.7: LetterOrDigit.java

```
1 public class LetterOrDigit
2 {
3    public static void main(String args[])
4    {
5        char ch1 = '9';
6        char ch2 = 'Z';
7        char ch3 = '%';
```

```
 8          char ch4 = ' ';
 9
10      if (Character.isDigit(ch1))
11          System.out.println(ch1 + " is a digit");
12      else
13          System.out.println(ch1 + " is not a digit");
14
15      if (Character.isLetter(ch2))
16          System.out.println(ch2 + " is a letter");
17      else
18          System.out.println(ch2 + " is not a letter");
19
20      if (Character.isLetterOrDigit(ch3))
21          System.out.println(ch3 + " is a letter or digit");
22      else
23          System.out.println(ch3 + " is not a letter or digit");
24
25      if (Character.isWhitespace(ch4))
26          System.out.println(ch4 + " is a whitespace character");
27      else
28          System.out.println(ch4 + " is not a whitespace character");
29      }
30 }
```

```
Output
9 is a digit
Z is a letter
% is not a letter or digit
   is a whitespace character
```

13.10   Determining Character Case Methods

The wrapper class **Character** has a number of useful methods to determine the case (upper or lower) of a character as described below:

	Method Name	Wrapper Class	Description
1	isLowerCase(char)	Character	Returns true if the specified character is a lowercase character; returns false otherwise. Syntax: boolean isLowerCase(char ch)
2	isUpperCase(char)	Character	Returns true if the specified character is an uppercase character; returns false otherwise. Syntax: boolean isUpperCase(char ch)

Let us consider an example program that demonstrates these methods.

Listing 13.8: LowerOrUpper.java

```java
public class LowerOrUpper
{
    public static void main(String args[])
    {
        char ch1 = 'a';
        char ch2 = 'B';

        if (Character.isLowerCase(ch1))
            System.out.println(ch1 + " is a lowercase letter");
        else
            System.out.println(ch1 + " is not a lowercase letter");

        if (Character.isUpperCase(ch2))
            System.out.println(ch2 + " is an uppercase letter");
        else
            System.out.println(ch2 + " is not an uppercase letter");
    }
}
```

```
Output
a is a lowercase letter
B is an uppercase letter
```

13.11 Changing Character Case Methods

The wrapper class Character has the following methods to change the case (upper or lower) of a character:

	Method Name	Wrapper Class	Description
1	toLowerCase(char)	Character	Converts the character argument into lowercase. Syntax: char toLowerCase(char ch)
2	toUpperCase(char)	Character	Converts the character argument into uppercase. Syntax: char toUpperCase(char ch)

Listing 13.9: ChangeCase.java

```java
public class ChangeCase
{
    public static void main(String args[])
    {
        char ch1 = 'G';
        char ch2 = 'd';
```

```
7
8       System.out.println("Original letter : " + ch1);
9       System.out.println("Letter after converting to lowercase: " + ↵
            ↪ Character.toLowerCase(ch1));
10
11      System.out.println("Original letter : " + ch2);
12      System.out.println("Letter after converting to uppercase: " + ↵
            ↪ Character.toUpperCase(ch2));
13    }
14  }
```

Output
Original letter : G
Letter after converting to lowercase: g
Original letter : d
Letter after converting to uppercase: D

Solved Programming Exercises

Write a program in Java to accept a string in lowercase and change the first letter of every word to uppercase. Display the new string.
Sample INPUT: we are in cyber world
Sample OUTPUT: We Are In Cyber World

Listing 13.10: Capitalise.java

```
1   import java.util.Scanner;
2   public class Capitalise
3   {
4      public static void main(String args[])
5      {
6         Scanner scanner = new Scanner(System.in);
7
8         System.out.print("Enter a string: ");
9         String input = scanner.nextLine();
10
11        String output = "";
12
13        for (int i = 0; i < input.length(); i++)
14        {
15           char currentChar = input.charAt(i);
16
17           if (i == 0 || input.charAt(i - 1) == ' ')
18               output += Character.toUpperCase(currentChar);
19           else
20               output += currentChar;
```

```
21        }
22
23        System.out.println("New string is: " + output);
24        scanner.close();
25    }
26 }
```

```
Output
Enter a string: we are in cyber world
New string is: We Are In Cyber World
```

Code Walkthrough:

◈ Line 11: Initialises the String variable **output**.

◈ Line 15: Stores the character at i^{th} position in the **currentChar** variable.

◈ Line 17: Checks if it is the first character of the input string (**i == 0**) or if the previous character was a space character.

◈ Line 18: Converts the **currentChar** to uppercase and appends it to the output string.

◈ Line 20: Otherwise, just appends the **currentChar** to the output string.

The International Standard Book Number (ISBN) is a unique numeric book identifier which is printed on every book. The ISBN is based upon a 10-digit code. The ISBN is legal if:
1 x digit1 + 2 x digit2 + 3 x digit3 + 4 x digit4 + 5 x digit5 + 6 x digit6 + 7 x digit7 + 8 x digit8 + 9 x digit9 + 10 x digit10
is divisible by 11
Example: For an ISBN 1401601499
Sum=$1\times1 + 2\times4 + 3\times0 + 4\times1 + 5\times6 + 6\times0 + 7\times1 + 8\times4 + 9\times9 + 10\times9 = 253$ which is divisible by 11.
Write a program to:

(i) input the ISBN code as a 10-digit integer.

(ii) If the ISBN is not a 10-digit integer, output the message **"Illegal ISBN"** and terminate the program.

(iii) If the number is 10-digit, extract the digits of the number and compute the sum as explained above.
If the sum is divisible by 11, output the message, **"Legal ISBN"**. If the sum is not divisible by 11, output the message, **"Illegal ISBN"**.

Listing 13.11: CheckISBN.java

```
1 import java.util.Scanner;
2
3 public class CheckISBN
4 {
5    public static void main(String[] args)
6    {
7        Scanner scanner = new Scanner(System.in);
8        int sumOfDigits = 0;
```

```
 9
10        System.out.print("Enter ISBN code: ");
11        long inputNumber = scanner.nextLong();
12
13        String isbnNumber = inputNumber + "";
14
15        if (isbnNumber.length() != 10)
16        {
17            System.out.println("Ilegal ISBN");
18            System.exit(0);
19        }
20
21        for (int i = 0; i < 10; i++)
22        {
23            String stringDigit = isbnNumber.charAt(i) + "";
24            int numericDigit = Integer.parseInt(stringDigit);
25            sumOfDigits = sumOfDigits + ((i + 1) * numericDigit);
26        }
27
28        if (sumOfDigits % 11 == 0)
29            System.out.println("Legal ISBN");
30        else
31            System.out.println("Illegal ISBN");
32
33        scanner.close();
34    }
35 }
```

Output
Enter ISBN code: 1401601499
Legal ISBN

Output
Enter ISBN code: 1401601498
Illegal ISBN

Code Walkthrough:

◇ Line 13: Converts the inputNumber into a String by appending "" in the end.

◇ Line 15: Checks if the input number is of 10 digits.

◇ Line 23: Stores the character at the ith position into the stringDigit variable.

◇ Line 24: Parses the string value of stringDigit into an integer value and stores it in the numericDigit variable.

◇ Line 25: Computes the required sum and adds it to the accumulator variable sumOfDigits.

◇ Line 28: Checks if the sum of digits is divisible by 11.

Define a class Rectangle with the following specification:

Member Variables: length and width

Member Methods:

AcceptInput => To accept the length and width of the rectangle

Compute => To compute the area, perimeter and diagonal of the rectangle

DisplayData => To display the results

Write a main() method in the class that creates an object of the Rectangle class and demonstrates its functionality.

Listing 13.12: Rectangle.java

```java
1  import java.util.Scanner;
2
3  public class Rectangle
4  {
5      int length, width;
6      int area, perimeter;
7      double diagonal;
8
9      public void AcceptInput()
10     {
11         Scanner keyboard = new Scanner(System.in);
12
13         System.out.print("Enter length: ");
14         length = keyboard.nextInt();
15
16         System.out.print("Enter width: ");
17         width = keyboard.nextInt();
18
19         keyboard.close();
20     }
21
22     public void Compute()
23     {
24         area = length * width;
25         perimeter = 2 * (length + width);
26         diagonal = Math.sqrt(length * length + width * width);
27     }
28
29     public void DisplayData()
30     {
31         System.out.println("The area of rectangle is: " + area);
32         System.out.println("The perimeter of rectangle is: " + perimeter);
33         System.out.println("The diagonal of rectangle is: " + diagonal);
34     }
35
36     public static void main(String args[])
37     {
38         Rectangle myRectangle = new Rectangle();
39         myRectangle.AcceptInput();
40         myRectangle.Compute();
41         myRectangle.DisplayData();
42     }
43 }
```

Output

```
Enter length: 6
Enter width: 5
The area of rectangle is: 30
The perimeter of rectangle is: 22
The diagonal of rectangle is: 7.810249675906654
```

Define a class **Salary** as described below:

Data Members: Name, Address, Phone, Subject, Specialisation, Monthly Salary, Income Tax

Member Methods:

(i) To accept the details of a teacher including the monthly salary

(ii) To display the details of the teacher

(iii) To compute the annual income tax at 5% of the annual salary above Rs. 1,75,000.

Write a **main()** method to create an object of the class and call the above member methods.

Listing 13.13: Salary.java

```java
import java.util.Scanner;

public class Salary
{
    String name, address, subject, special;
    long phone;
    double monthlySalary, incomeTax;

    public void AcceptInput()
    {
        Scanner keyboard = new Scanner(System.in);

        System.out.print("Enter Name: ");
        name = keyboard.nextLine();

        System.out.print("Enter Address: ");
        address = keyboard.nextLine();

        System.out.print("Enter Phone: ");
        phone = keyboard.nextLong();

        System.out.print("Enter Subject: ");
        subject = keyboard.next();

        System.out.print("Enter Specialisation: ");
        special = keyboard.next();

        System.out.print("Enter Monthly Salary: ");
        monthlySalary = keyboard.nextDouble();

        keyboard.close();
    }
```

```
33
34    public void Compute()
35    {
36        double annualSalary = 12 * monthlySalary;
37        if (annualSalary > 175000)
38        incomeTax = annualSalary * 0.05;
39        else
40        incomeTax = 0;
41    }
42
43    public void DisplayData()
44    {
45        System.out.println("Name: " + name);
46        System.out.println("Address: " + address);
47        System.out.println("Phone: " + phone);
48        System.out.println("Subject: " + subject);
49        System.out.println("Specialisation: " + special);
50        System.out.println("Monthly Salary: Rs." + monthlySalary);
51        System.out.println("Income Tax: Rs." + incomeTax);
52    }
53
54    public static void main(String args[])
55    {
56        Salary objSalary = new Salary();
57        objSalary.AcceptInput();
58        objSalary.Compute();
59        objSalary.DisplayData();
60    }
61 }
```

Output

```
Enter Name: Ram Prasad
Enter Address: 101, Sector 55, Noida
Enter Phone: 08433345908
Enter Subject: Computers
Enter Specialisation: Java
Enter Monthly Salary: 20000
Name: Ram Prasad
Address: 101, Sector 55, Noida
Phone: 8433345908
Subject: Computers
Specialisation: Java
Monthly Salary: Rs.20000.0
Income Tax: Rs.12000.0
```

Define a class called **Library** with the following description:
Instance variables/Data members:
int acc_num: stores the accession number of the book
String title: stores the title of the book
String author: stores name of the author
Member Methods:

(i) void input() : to input and store accession number, title and author.

(ii) void compute() : to accept the number of days late, calculate and display the fine charge at the rate of Rs. 2 per day

(iii) void display() : to display the details in the following format:
Accession Number   Title   Author

Write a **main()** method to create an object of the class and call the above member methods.

Listing 13.14: Library.java

```java
import java.util.Scanner;

public class Library
{
    int acc_num;
    String title, author;

    public void input()
    {
        Scanner keyboard = new Scanner(System.in);

        System.out.println("Enter Accession Number: ");
        acc_num = keyboard.nextInt();
        keyboard.nextLine();

        System.out.println("Enter Title: ");
        title = keyboard.nextLine();

        System.out.println("Enter Author's Name: ");
        author = keyboard.nextLine();

        keyboard.close();
    }

    public void compute()
    {
        int numDays, fineAmount;
        Scanner keyboard = new Scanner(System.in);
```

```
29
30        System.out.println("Enter number of days late: ");
31        numDays = keyboard.nextInt();
32        fineAmount = 2 * numDays;
33        System.out.println("Fine to be paid is: " + fineAmount);
34
35        keyboard.close();
36    }
37
38    public void display()
39    {
40        System.out.println("Accession Number\tTitle\tAuthor");
41        System.out.println(acc_num + "\t" + title + "\t" + author);
42    }
43
44    public static void main(String args[])
45    {
46        Library objLibrary = new Library();
47        objLibrary.input();
48        objLibrary.compute();
49        objLibrary.display();
50    }
51 }
```

> **Output**
>
> Enter Accession Number:
> 1122334455
> Enter Title:
> Malgudi Days
> Enter Author's Name:
> R. K. Narayan
> Enter number of days late:
> 5
> Fine to be paid is: 10
> Accession Number Title Author
> 1122334455 Malgudi Days R. K. Narayan

Note

Notice the additional **keyboard.nextLine();** at Line 14. It is needed because when you enter a number followed by the Enter key at Line 13, the **keyboard.nextInt()** consumes only the number, not the "end of line" character. The additional **keyboard.nextLine();** at Line 14 then consumes the "end of line" character.

Define a class `ParkingLot` with the following description:
Instance variables/Data members:
`int vno`: to store the vehicle number
`int hours`: to store the number of hours the vehicle is parked in the parking lot
`double bill`: to store the bill amount
Member Methods:

  (i) `void input()`: to input and store vno and hours

 (ii) `void calculate()`: to compute the parking charge at the rate of Rs. 3 for the first hour or part thereof, and Rs.1.50 for each additional hour or part thereof.

(iii) `void display()`: to display the detail

Write a `main()` method to create an object of the class and call the above methods.

Listing 13.15: ParkingLot.java

```java
import java.util.Scanner;
public class ParkingLot
{
    int vno;
    int hours;
    double bill;

    public void input()
    {
        Scanner keyboard = new Scanner(System.in);

        System.out.print("Enter Vehicle Number: ");
        vno = keyboard.nextInt();

        System.out.print("Enter Number of hours: ");
        hours = keyboard.nextInt();

        keyboard.close();
    }

    public void calculate()
    {
        bill = 3 + (hours -1 ) * 1.50;
    }

    public void display()
    {
        System.out.println("Vehicle Number: " + vno);
        System.out.println("Hours Parked   : " + hours);
```

```
30          System.out.println("Bill Amount    : Rs." + bill);
31      }
32
33      public static void main(String args[])
34      {
35          ParkingLot objParkingLot = new ParkingLot();
36          objParkingLot.input();
37          objParkingLot.calculate();
38          objParkingLot.display();
39      }
40  }
```

```
Output
Enter Vehicle Number : 1729
Enter Number of hours : 5
Vehicle Number : 1729
Hours Parked : 5
Bill Amount : Rs.9.0
```

Define a class named BookFair with the following description:

Instance variables/Data members:

String Bname: stores the name of the book.

double price: stores the price of the book.

Member Methods:

(i) BookFair(): default constructor to initialise data members.

(ii) void Input(): to input and store the name and the price of the book.

(iii) void calculate(): to calculate the price after discount. Discount is calculated based on the following criteria:

Price	Discount
Less than or equal to Rs 1000	2% of price
More than Rs 1000 and less than or equal to Rs 3000	10% of price
More than Rs 3000	15% of price

(iv) void display(): to display the name and price of the book after discount.

Write a main() method to create an object of the class and call the above methods.

Listing 13.16: BookFair.java

```
1  import java.util.Scanner;
2  public class BookFair
3  {
4      String Bname;
5      double price;
```

```
 6      double priceDiscounted;
 7
 8      public BookFair()
 9      {
10         Bname = "";
11         price = 0;
12      }
13
14      public void input()
15      {
16         Scanner keyboard = new Scanner(System.in);
17         System.out.print("Enter Book Name: ");
18         Bname = keyboard.nextLine();
19         System.out.print("Enter Book Price: ");
20         price = keyboard.nextDouble();
21         keyboard.close();
22      }
23
24      public void calculate()
25      {
26         double discountPercentage = 0;
27
28         if (price <= 1000)
29            discountPercentage = 2;
30         else if (price > 1000 && price <= 3000)
31            discountPercentage = 10;
32         else if (price > 3000)
33            discountPercentage = 15;
34
35         priceDiscounted = price - (price * discountPercentage / 100);
36      }
37
38      public void display()
39      {
40         System.out.println("Book name: " + Bname);
41         System.out.println("Price after discount: " + priceDiscounted);
42      }
43
44      public static void main(String args[])
45      {
46         BookFair objBookFair = new BookFair();
47         objBookFair.input();
48         objBookFair.calculate();
49         objBookFair.display();
50      }
51   }
```

```
Output
Enter Book Name: The Lord of the Rings
Enter Book Price: 2500
Book name: The Lord of the Rings
Price after discount: 2250.0
```

Define a class called `FruitJuice` with the following description:

Instance variables/Data members:

`int product_code`: stores the product code number

`String flavour`: stores the flavour of the juice.(orange, apple, etc.)

`String pack_type`: stores the type of packaging (tetra-pack, bottle, etc.)

`int pack_size`: stores package size (200ml, 400ml, etc.)

`int product_price`: stores the price of the product

Member Methods:

`FriuitJuice()` – default constructor to initialise integer data members to zero and string data members to "".

`void input()` – to input and store the product code, flavour, pack type, pack size, and product price.

`void discount()` – to reduce the product price by 10.

`void display()` – to display the product code, flavour, pack type, pack size, and product price.

Listing 13.17: FruitJuice.java

```java
import java.util.Scanner;
public class FruitJuice
{
    int product_code;
    String flavour;
    String pack_type;
    int pack_size;
    int product_price;

    public FruitJuice()
    {
        product_code = 0;
        flavour = "";
        pack_type = "";
        pack_size = 0;
        product_price = 0;
    }

    public void input()
    {
        Scanner keyboard = new Scanner(System.in);

        System.out.print("Enter Product Code: ");
        product_code = keyboard.nextInt();
        System.out.print("Enter Flavour: ");
        flavour = keyboard.next();
        System.out.print("Enter Pack Type: ");
        pack_type = keyboard.next();
```

```
29          System.out.print("Enter Pack Size (in ml): ");
30          pack_size = keyboard.nextInt();
31          System.out.print("Enter Product Price: ");
32          product_price = keyboard.nextInt();
33          keyboard.close();
34      }
35
36      public void discount()
37      {
38          product_price = (int) (0.9 * product_price);
39      }
40
41      public void display()
42      {
43          System.out.println("Product Code: " + product_code);
44          System.out.println("Flavour: " + flavour);
45          System.out.println("Pack Type: " + pack_type);
46          System.out.println("Pack Size (in ml): " + pack_size);
47          System.out.println("Product Price: " + product_price);
48      }
49  }
```

Multiple Choice Questions

1. Which of the following is a primitive data type?

   A. int   C. char

   B. float   D. All of the above

2. Which of the following is a composite data type?

   A. int   C. char

   B. float   D. String

3. The return type of the isLowerCase() method is ....

   A. int   C. char

   B. boolean   D. String

4. The return type of the toLowerCase() method is ....

   A. int   C. char

   B. boolean   D. String

5. The value returned by `Integer.parseInt("-321")` is ....

    A. -321   C. 321.0

    B. 321   D. "321"

6. Name the method that can convert a string into its integer equivalent.

    A. `Integer.parseInteger()`   C. `Integer.parseInt()`

    B. `Integer.getInt()`   D. `Integer.readInt()`

7. What will be the result when the following statement is executed?

```
int count = new Integer(12);
```

    A. Variable `count` will be initialised with value 12.

    B. Variable `count` will be initialised with default value of int, i.e., zero (0).

    C. An array `count` will be initialised with 12 elements, all having a default value of zero (0).

    D. Value of `count` will be unknown as no value has been assigned yet.

8. In which package is the wrapper class Integer available?

    A. `java.io`   C. `java.awt`

    B. `java.util`   D. `java.lang`

Assignment Questions

1. What are the library classes in Java? What is their use?

2. Define the following terms:

    (i) Primitive data type

    (ii) Composite data type

    (iii) User-defined data type

3. Why is a class called a composite data type? Explain.

4. What is a wrapper class? Name three wrapper classes in Java.

5. Explain the terms, Autoboxing and Auto-unboxing in Java.

6. How do you convert a numeric string into a double value?

7. Describe wrapper class methods available in Java to parse string values to their numeric equivalents.

8. How can you check if a given character is a digit, letter or a space?

9. Distinguish between the following methods:

    (i) `isLowerCase()` and `toLowerCase()`

    (ii) `isUpperCase()` and `toUpperCase()`

    (iii) `isDigit()` and `isLetter()`

    (iv) `pasrseFloat()` and `parseDouble()`

10. Define a class (using the Scanner class) to generate a pattern of a word in the form of a triangle or in the form of an inverted triangle, depending upon user's choice.

Sample Input:

Enter a word: CLASS
Enter your choice: 1

Sample Output:

C
C L
C L A
C L A S
C L A S S

Enter your choice: 2

Sample Output:

C L A S S
C L A S
C L A
C L
C

11. Define a class called `mobike` with the following description:

Instance variables/Data members:

`int bno` – to store the bike's number

`int phno` – to store the phone number of the customer

`String name` – to store the name of the customer

`int days` – to store the number of days the bike is taken on rent

`int charge` – to calculate and store the rental charge

Member Methods: `void input()` – to input and store the details of the customer

`void computer()` – to compute the rental charge

    The rent for a mobike is charged on the following basis:

        First five days £50 per day;

        Next five days £40 per day;

        Rest of the days £20 per day

`void display()` – to display the details in the following format:

    Bike No.   Phone No.   No. of days Charge

Answers To Objective Questions

Multiple Choice Questions

1. D	3. B	5. A	7. A
2. D	4. C	6. C	8. D

Chapter 14

Encapsulation and Inheritance

Encapsulation and Inheritance

IN this chapter, you will learn in detail about the two principles of OOP that result in well-designed and reusable class definitions. These are encapsulation and inheritance.

The dictionary meaning of the word capsule is "a sealed gelatine case that holds a dose of medication". A capsule protects its contents from outside contaminants. To encapsulate something is to place it into a capsule.

One of the most important goals of designing a class is to protect its contents from being damaged by the actions of external code. If the contents of a class can be changed only through a well-defined interface, then it is much easier to fix errors in an application.

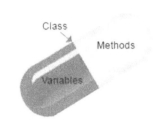

Figure 14.1: Encapsulation

You might have studied the term heredity in biology, which means children inheriting characteristics of their parents. For example, hair colour, nose shape and eye colour. Similarly, Java allows one class to inherit attributes and behaviour from the other. Thus, the classes developed in Java are much closer to the real world. Inheritance is an important and powerful feature for reusing software.

Figure 14.2: Inheritance

Let us now understand how Java helps in implementing encapsulation and inheritance.

14.1 Encapsulation

You know that a class consists of:

- Member variables (data) that contain the necessary attributes to represent the class

- Member methods that perform operations on the member variables

Encapsulation refers to the process wherein the data and the operations are combined together into a single unit (in OOP terms, a class), and the details of the implementation are hidden. If a class is well designed, the programmer who uses the class does not need to know all the implementation details (coding) of the class but need only a much simpler description of how to use the class.

Note that in larger software development projects, it is not necessary you are the developer of the class you are using. The class may have been developed by some other programmer, and you are only using it just as you use methods present in the Math class. For example, `sqrt()`, `pow()`, and `round()`. The creator of a class describes the methods of the class and lets the user know how the class can be used.

As a real-life example, consider getting a loan for your car. A specific loan can be regarded as an object of a **Loan** class. Its member variables (data) are:

- loan amount

- interest rate

- loan duration

Its member methods are:

- calculate monthly payment

- calculate total payment

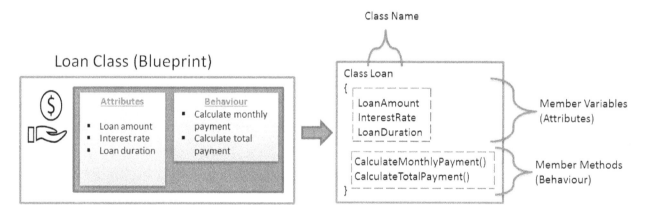

Figure 14.3: The Loan Class

```
Loan carLoan = new Loan(500000, 8, 10);
```

When you buy a car, a loan object is created by instantiating the **Loan** class with your loan amount, loan interest rate, and loan duration. You can then use the member methods to find the monthly payment and total payment of your loan. As a user of the **Loan** class, you do not need to know how these methods are implemented. Here, the details of the **Loan** class implementation are said to be encapsulated and hidden from the user.

14.2 Access Specifiers

In Java, encapsulation is achieved via the access specifiers. The property which controls the accessibility of member variables (data) and member methods in a class is known as access specifier. There are three types of access specifiers in Java – public, private and protected. Let us learn about these in detail.

14.2.1 The public specifier

The class members (variables and methods) declared with the public access specifier can be accessed from outside the class. When no access specifier is mentioned, then by default that member (variable or method) of a class is public within the package.

Let us see an example where you create a class Student and use it in another class TestStudent.

Listing 14.1: Student.java

```
1  public class Student
2  {
3     public int rollNumber;
4     char grade;
5
6     public void DisplayData()
7     {
8        System.out.println("Roll Number: " + rollNumber);
9        System.out.println("Grade: " + grade);
10    }
11 }
```

Code Walkthrough:
◈ Line 1: Defines the Student class.
◈ Line 4: Defines the member variable grade without an access specifier, therefore, by default it will be public.

Listing 14.2: TestStudent.java

```
1  public class TestStudent
2  {
3     public static void main(String args[])
4     {
5        Student student = new Student();
6        student.rollNumber = 34;
7        student.grade = 'A';
8        student.DisplayData();
9     }
10 }
```

Code Walkthrough:

◈ Line 1: Defines the TestStudent class.

◈ Line 5: Creates an instance student of the Student class.

◈ Line 6: Assigns a value to the rollNumber member variable using the instance named student.

◈ Line 7: Assigns a value to the grade member variable using the instance named student.

◈ Line 8: Invokes the DisplayData() member method using the instance named student.

Executing the program:

- Save and compile both the classes.

- BlueJ's Project window will look like as shown in Figure 14.4. The arrow indicates that the class TestStudent instantiates an object of the class Student.

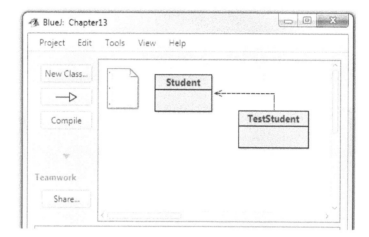

Figure 14.4: Encapsulation Example

- Right-click on the TestStudent icon in BlueJ window and select void main(String[] args).

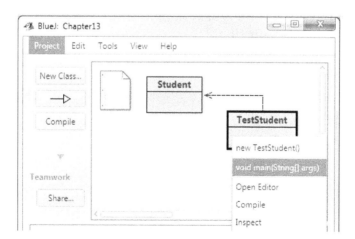

Figure 14.5: Execute Method

- Click on the OK button.

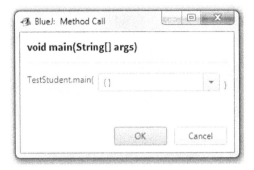

Figure 14.6: BlueJ Method Call

- A Terminal Window as shown in Figure 14.7 appears displaying the Roll Number and Grade of the student.

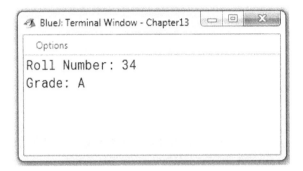

Figure 14.7: Terminal Window

You have successfully accessed class members (variables and methods) of the **Student** class, which had the **public** access specifier, from outside the class, i.e., via the **TestStudent** class.

Note that the **main()** method of a class is always preceded by the **public** specifier. That is why, it is accessible by the code that is outside the program, i.e., the Java run-time environment.

> **Note**
>
> When no access specifier is mentioned, then by default that member (variable or method) of a class is **public** within the package.

14.2.2 The private specifier

The class members (variables and methods) declared with the `private` access specifier can be accessed within the same class only.

Let us see an example where you create a class `Student1` with a `private` member variable `grade` and try to use it in another class `TestStudent1`.

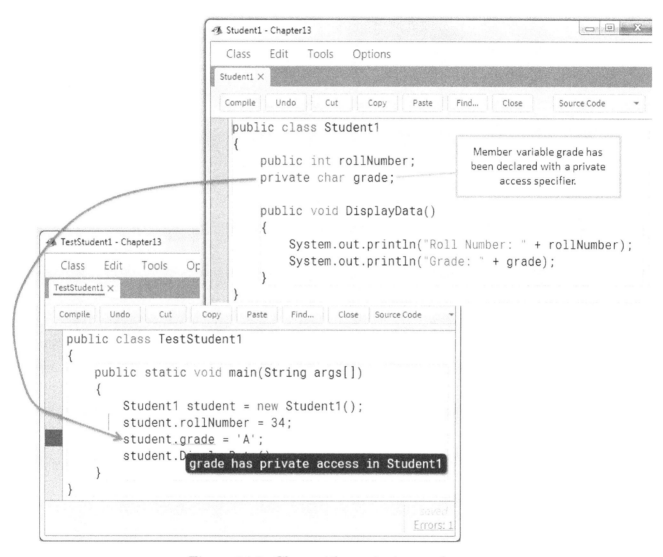

Figure 14.8: Class with a private member

When you try to use the `private` member variable `grade` of class `Student1` in another class `TestStudent1`, BlueJ throws an error stating that `grade` has `private` access in `Student1` class and therefore, cannot be used in `TestStudent1` class. Here, the member variable `grade` is said to be well encapsulated from the outside code.

> **Note**
>
> It is considered a good programming practice to make all instance variables `private`.

14.2.3   The protected specifier

The class members (variables and methods) declared with the **protected** access specifier can be accessed within the same package only. They are not accessible from outside the package.

Let us see an example where you create a class **Student2** with a **protected** member variable **grade** and try to use it in another class **TestStudent2**.

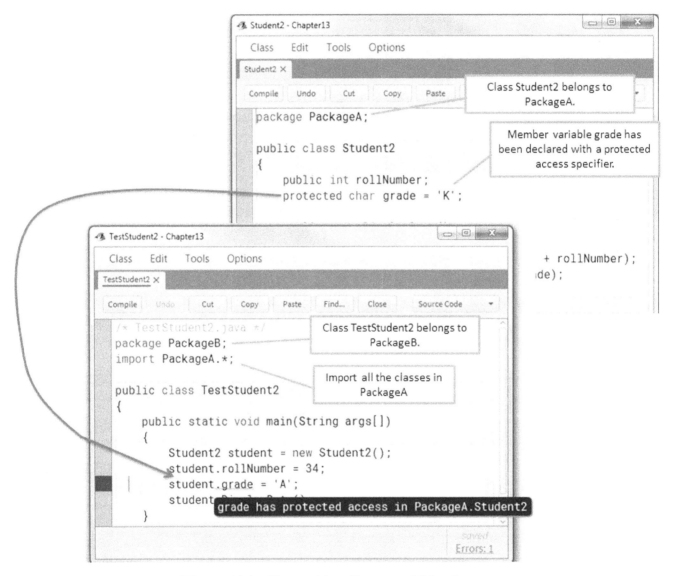

Figure 14.9: Class with a Protected Member

Here, **Student2** class belongs to **PackageA** and the **TestStudent2** class belongs to **PackageB**. The **import** statement brings all the classes in **PackageA** into the **TestStudent2.java** program.

When you try to use the **protected** member variable **grade** of class **Student2** in class **TestStudent2**, BlueJ throws an error stating that **grade** has **protected** access in **PackageA.Student2** and therefore, cannot be used in class **TestStudent2**. In this illustration, the member variable **grade** declared with the `protected` access specifier is not accessible from outside the package and is said to be well-encapsulated. Note that `rollNumber` being a `public` member is accessible in `TestStudent2` class.

> **Note**
>
> A class that is not defined in a named package is in an unnamed package called `default` package.

14.2.4 Visibility Rules of Access Specifiers

You have seen some examples of how Java provides three levels of protection to allow fine-grained control over the visibility of variables and methods. The term visibility refers to the accessibility of member variables and methods within classes, subclasses, and packages. Table 14.1 shows the access to members permitted by each modifier. In addition to the three access specifiers, `public`, `private`, and `protected`, the table also lists no modifier when a member does not have an explicit access specifier.

Visibility Rules				
Access Modifier	*Same class*	*Other class same package*	*Subclass other package*	*Any class*
Public	Yes	Yes	Yes	Yes
Private	Yes	No	No	No
Protected	Yes	Yes	Yes	No
<no modifier>	Yes	Yes	No	No

Table 14.1: Visibility Rules of Access Specifiers

Here:

- Column *Same class* indicates whether the class itself has access to the member declared with the access modifier or not. Observe that a class always has access to its own members no matter what the modifier is.

- Column *Other class same package* indicates whether classes in the same package as the class have access to its member or not. Clearly, the `private` members of the class are not accessible to other classes in the same package.

- Column *Subclass other package* indicates whether subclasses of the class declared outside this package have access to the class member or not. Again, the `private` members of the class (and members declared with no modifier) are not accessible to other classes.

- Column *Any class* indicates whether all other classes have access to the class member. Only members declared with `public` access modifier are accessible.

14.3   Scope of Variables

You know that a variable is a name given to a memory location. It is the basic unit of storage in a program. The scope of a variable refers to that part of the program in which the variable is accessible. The variables used in a class can be any of the following types:

14.3.1   Local Variables

The variables declared inside a method or "block" are called *local variables*. A *block* is a set of statements enclosed in curly brackets . The scope of local variables is limited to the method or the block they are declared in. So, local variables are accessible only to the method or block in which they are declared; they are not accessible to the rest of the class.

14.3.2   Argument (Parameter) Variables

The variables used as arguments in the method heading are called *argument variables*. Their scope is limited to the method where they are being used. Therefore, parameter variables are visible only to the method in which they are used; they are not accessible to the rest of the class.

14.3.3   Instance Variables (Non-Static)

The member variables in a class that are used to store the individual states (attributes and behaviour) of an object are called *instance variables*. These variables are called instance variables because their values are unique to each instance of the class. These variables are declared without the `static` keyword, hence are non-static.

14.3.4   Class Variables (Static)

A variable declared in a class with the `static` modifier is called a *class variable*. The static variable will be available as a single copy to all instances of the class.

> **Note**
>
> The scope of a variable refers to that part of the program in which the variable is accessible or where it is legal to reference (use) the variable.

Let us understand all these variables with the help of an example. Given the value of radius, program 14.3 computes the area of a circle using the following formula:

$$Area\ of\ circle = \pi * radius^2$$

All four types of variables are marked in the program.

Listing 14.3: Circle.java

```
1   public class Circle                              ┌─────────────────────────────┐
2   {                          ┌──────────────────── │ Class variable              │
3       static double  PI = 3.1415;            │     │ (declared with the static keyword). │
4       private int  radius ;                        └─────────────────────────────┘
5                           ▲                  ┌─────────────────────────────┐
6       public void setRadius(int  r )         │ Instance variable           │
7       {                             │        │ (declared without the static keyword). │
8           radius = r;               │        └─────────────────────────────┘
9       }                             │    ┌─────────────────────────────┐
10                                    └─── │ Argument variable r,        │
11      public double calculateArea()        │ local to the setRadius() method. │
12      {                                    └─────────────────────────────┘
13          double  area = PI * (radius * radius);
14          return  area;
15      }
16
17      public static void  main(String  args[]) ┌─────────────────────────────┐
18      {                   ┌──────────────────── │ Local variables rad and result, │
19          int  rad  = 4;                        │ local to the main() method. │
20          double result;                        └─────────────────────────────┘
21
22          Circle myCircle = new Circle();
23          myCircle.setRadius(rad);
24          result = myCircle.calculateArea();
25          System.out.println("Value of PI is: " + Circle.PI);
26          System.out.println("Radius of circle is: " + myCircle.radius);
27          System.out.println("Area of circle is: " + result);
28      }
29  }
```

```
Output
Value of PI is: 3.1415
Radius of circle is:  4
Area of circle is: 50.264
```

Code Walkthrough:

◈ Line 3: Declares a `static` variable named PI with a value of 3.1415. Since conceptually the same value of PI will apply to all instances of the `Circle` class, you can declare it as a `static` variable. (Note: Additionally, you can add the keyword `final` to indicate that the value of PI will never change.)

◈ Line 4: Declares an instance variable named `radius`.

◈ Line 8: Assigns the value of parameter variable `r` to the member variable `radius`.

◈ Lines 11 - 15: Calculate and return the value of `area` using the instance and class variables.

◈ Line 22: Creates an instance of the `Circle` class.

◈ Line 23: Invokes the `setRadius()` member method and passes the `rad` value as its parameter.

◈ Line 24: Invokes the `calculateArea()` member method to calculate the area.

◈ Line 25: Accesses the `static` (class) variable `PI` using the class name. Note that an instance is not required to access the `static` variable.

◈ Line 26: Accesses the instance variable `radius` using the instance name. Note that an instance is required to access the instance variable.

Let us summarise the key points you have just learnt:

- An instance is required to access a non-static variable (also known as an instance variable). In order to create an instance of the class, you use the following generic syntax:

  ```
  ClassName objectName = new ClassName();
  ```

  And in order to access the non-static variable, you use the following generic syntax:

  ```
  objectName.Non-staticVariableName
  ```

- An instance is not required to access a `static` variable. When you declare a variable with the `static` modifier, it belongs to the class rather than to the objects of that class. Hence, it is also called a *class variable*. In order to access the static variable, you use the following generic syntax:

  ```
  ClassName.StaticVariableName
  ```

14.3.5   Difference between Static and Non-Static Variables

The table given below summarises the difference between static and non-static variables:

	Static Variable	Non-Static Variable
1.	These variables are preceded by static keyword in the declaration.	These variables are not preceded by static keyword in the declaration.
2.	They are also known as class variables.	They are also known as instance variables.
3.	Static variables are accessed via the class name, for example, ClassName.StaticVariableName	Non-static variables are accessed via the object name, for example, objectName.Non-staticVariableName

14.3.6   Scope of Variables in a Block

Let us explore the scope of variables in a block. A *block* (also called a *compound statement*) consists of a sequence of statements enclosed between a pair of curly brackets. The statements in the block are executed in a sequential order. A block statement usually occurs inside other statement. The purpose of the block is to group together several statements into a unit. You might have already noticed that the main() method of a program and the definition of the method are a block because they include a sequence of statements enclosed within a pair of curly brackets.

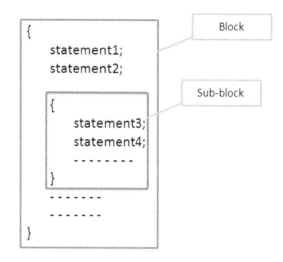

The block may contain another block known as a *sub-block*. A block of statements can also contain variable declarations. A variable declared in a block is visible (accessible) in the block and in all the sub-blocks. However, it is not visible outside the block. Let us consider an example of variables declared in blocks.

Figure 14.10: Block with a Sub-block

Listing 14.4: ScopeInBlock.java

```java
import java.util.Scanner;
public class ScopeInBlock
{
    public static void main(String args[])
    {
        //Main block
        int x = 10;

        //Block 1
        {
            int y = 20;
            System.out.println ("Block 1: x is visible here: " + x);
            x++;
            y++;

            //z is not visible here (z is not accessible)
            //Block 2
            {
                int z = 30;
                System.out.println ("Block 2: x is visible here: " + x);
                System.out.println ("Block 2: y is visible here: " + y);
            }
        }
        //y is not visible here (y is not accessible)
        //z is not visible here (z is not accessible)
    }
}
```

Output

Block 1: x is visible here: 10
Block 2: x is visible here: 11
Block 2: y is visible here: 21

Let us examine the visibility of variables x, y, and z.

- Variable x is declared in the main block, so it is accessible in the main block and the sub-blocks: Block 1 and 2.

- Variable y is declared in Block 1, so it is visible in Block 1 and its sub-block, Block 2.

- Variable z is declared in Block 2, so it is visible in Block 2 only.

- None of the variables is visible outside the block in which it is declared.

- Note that a variable is local to the block it is declared in.

14.4 Inheritance

The biological meaning of inheritance is the transfer of characteristics from parent to child. Likewise in Java, inheritance can be defined as the process where one class acquires the properties of another class. It implements the feature of reusability. Inheritance enables you to create new classes that reuse, extend, and modify the behaviour that is defined in other classes.

Inheritance is a mechanism of deriving a new class from an existing class. The process is called *derivation*. The derived class inherits the state and behaviour from the base class. The derived class is also called *sub class* or *child class*, and the base class is also known as *super class* or *parent class*. The derived class can add its own additional variables and methods, which differentiate it from the base class.

Let us understand this property with the given example.

Consider a base class `Vehicle`. Different vehicles have different features and properties. However, some features are common to all, such as speed, colour, fuel capacity, and size. Hence, we can create a `Vehicle` class with attributes and behaviour that are common to all the vehicles. The derived class of this base class can be any type of vehicle. For example, the `Car` class has all the features of a vehicle. But it has its own attributes, which make it different from other derived classes. By using inheritance, we need not rewrite the code that we have already used with the `Vehicle` class. The derived class can also be extended. We can make a class, `Racing Car`, which extends the class `Car`. It inherits the features of both `Vehicle` and `Car`.

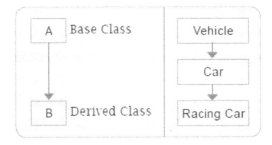

Figure 14.11: Inheritance Example

Let us write a simple program to demonstrate the use of inheritance.

Listing 14.5: Car.java

```
1   class Vehicle
2   {
3      String vehicleType;
4
5      Vehicle()
6      {
7         vehicleType = "N/A";
8      }
9
10     void set(String vt)
11     {
12        vehicleType = vt;
13     }
14
15     void show()
16     {
17        System.out.println ("The vehicle type is: " + vehicleType);
18     }
19  }
20
21  public class Car extends Vehicle
22  {
23     String modelType;
24
25     Car()
26     {
27        modelType = "N/A";
28     }
29
30     void set(String vt, String mt)
31     {
32        super.set (vt);
33        modelType = mt;
34     }
35
36     void show()
37     {
38        super.show ();
39        System.out.println("The model type is: " + modelType);
40     }
41
42     public static void main(String args[])
43     {
44        Vehicle objVehicle1 = new Vehicle();
45        System.out.println("Vehicle with N/A values");
```

```
46        objVehicle1.show();
47        System.out.println();
48
49        Vehicle objVehicle2 = new Vehicle();
50        System.out.println("Vehicle with assigned values");
51        objVehicle2.set("Car");
52        objVehicle2.show();
53        System.out.println();
54
55        Car objCar1 = new Car();
56        System.out.println("Car with N/A values");
57        objCar1.show();
58        System.out.println();
59
60        Car objCar2 = new Car();
61        System.out.println("Car with assigned values");
62        objCar2.set("Car", "Mercedes C Class");
63        objCar2.show();
64    }
65 }
```

```
Output
Vehicle with N/A values
The vehicle type is: N/A

Vehicle with assigned values
The vehicle type is: Car

Car with N/A values
The vehicle type is: N/A
The model type is: N/A
Car with assigned values

The vehicle type is: Car
The model type is: Mercedes C Class
```

14.4.1   Types of Inheritance

You know now that a new class can be derived from an existing class using the concept of inheritance. The inheritance mechanism makes it possible for an object to be a specific instance of a more generic object. If you did not apply inheritance, each object would need to define all of its characteristics explicitly. However, using inheritance, an object needs to define only those qualities that make it unique within its class. The rest of the general qualities are inherited from the parent class.Inheritance may take place in many forms as described below:

14.4.1.1 Single Inheritance

When a class is derived from only one base class, it is known as single inheritance. Figure 13.11 shows the subclass B is derived from the single base class A.

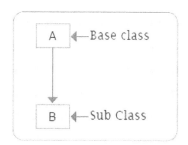

Figure 14.12: Single Inheritance

14.4.1.2 Multiple Inheritance

When a sub class is inherited from multiple base classes, it is known as multiple inheritance. Figure 13.12 shows the subclass C is inherited from the two base classes A and B.

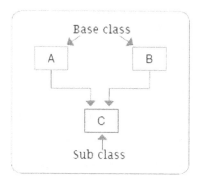

Figure 14.13: Multiple Inheritance

14.4.1.3 Hierarchical Inheritance

When many sub classes are inherited from a single base class, it is known as hierarchical inheritance. Figure 13.13 shows the subclasses B, C and D are inherited from the same base class A.

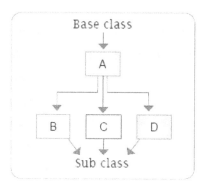

Figure 14.14: Hierarchical Inheritance

14.4.1.4 Hybrid Inheritance

When more than one type of inheritance forms are used together, it is known as hybrid inheritance. Figure 13.14 shows an example where the hierarchical and multiple inheritances are used together.

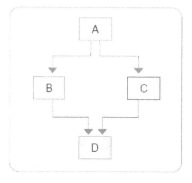

Figure 14.15: Hybrid Inheritance

14.4.1.5 Multilevel Inheritance

When a sub class is inherited from a class that itself is being inherited from another class, it is known as multilevel inheritance. Figure 13.15 shows that the sub class C is derived from class B, which in turn is derived from the base class A.

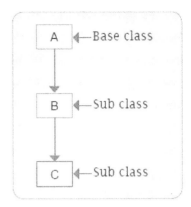

Figure 14.16: Multilevel Inheritance

> **Note**
>
> In Java, only single inheritance is allowed. This means a child class can have only one parent class.

14.4.2 Need for Inheritance

Inheritance is a wonderful feature of the object-oriented languages. There are a number of reasons for using inheritance, but some of the main reasons are as follows:

(i) Inheritance divides a program into useful and reusable set of classes.

(ii) Changes made in the original class are reflected in all the inherited classes.

(iii) The transitive nature of inheritance ensures the closeness with the real world objects.

Multiple Choice Questions

1. .... is the technique of binding both data and methods together to keep them safe from unauthorised access and misuse.
   - A. Abstraction
   - B. Inheritance
   - C. Encapsulation
   - D. Polymorphism

2. Which of the following is an access specifier?
   - A. public
   - B. protected
   - C. private
   - D. All of the above

3. A member variable declared with a public access specifier has visibility in ....
   - A. Class
   - B. Package
   - C. Subclass
   - D. All of the above

4. A member variable declared with a private access specifier has visibility only in the ....

    A. Class   C. Subclass

    B. Package   D. All of the above

5. A member variable declared with no access specifier has visibility in ....
    A. Class and package only

    B. Class, package and subclass only

    C. Class and subclass only

    D. Class and subclass only

6. An instance variable ....
    A. needs an instance to access it

    B. does not need an instance to access it

    C. can be accessed using the class name

    D. is declared with the static keyword

7. A static variable ....
    A. is preceded by static keyword in the declaration

    B. is accessed via the class name

    C. is also known as a class variable

    D. all of the above

8. .... is the feature by means of which one class acquires the properties of another class.
    A. Abstraction   C. Encapsulation

    B. Inheritance   D. Encapsulation

9. The class that gets inherited is known as ....
    A. Parent class   C. Super class

    B. Base class   D. All of the above

10. When many sub classes are inherited from a single base class, it is known as ....
    A. Hierarchical inheritance   C. Single inheritance

    B. Multiple inheritance   D. Multilevel inheritance

Assignment Questions

1. How does a class encapsulate state and behaviour?

2. Name the access specifiers available in Java.

3. Explain visibility in terms of the following access modifiers:

(i) `public`   (iii) `protected`

(ii) `private`   (iv) no modifier specified

4. Why is it a good idea to make all instance variables private?

5. What do you mean by the scope of variables in Java?

6. Explain the scope of the following variables in Java:

(i) Local variables   (iii) Instance variables

(ii) Parameter variables   (iv) Class variables

7. Explain the scope of variables in blocks and sub-blocks.

8. Is it legal to define local variables with the same identifier in nested blocks?

9. Why do you need to use `static` variables in Java?

10. What is the mechanism that allows one class to extend another class?

11. What do you call a class that is an extension of another class?

12. What does the inheritance mechanism allow one class to acquire from another?

13. How is inheritance transitive? Explain.

14. Explain various types of inheritance.

15. Why do you need to use inheritance? Give two reasons.

16. Declare a public class `CoolClass`.

(i) Write the header for a `public` member method `CoolMethodA`.

(ii) Write the header for an integer member method `CoolMethodB` that should be accessible to the classes in the package but not to derived classes.

(iii) Write the header for an integer member method `CoolMethodC` that should be accessible only to other methods in the class.

(iv) Write the header for a character member method `CoolMethodD` that should be accessible to the classes in the package and any derived classes.

Answers To Objective Questions

Multiple Choice Questions

1. C	3. D	5. A	7. D	9. D
2. D	4. A	6. A	8. B	10. A

Chapter 15

Arrays

Arrays

TILL now, you have learnt about variables that can hold a single value. However, there may be situations where lots of variables are needed to hold similar and related data. For example, you need to store marks of 100 students. How would you do that? In this situation, using an array can simplify a program by storing all related data under one name. This means that a program can be written to search through an array of data much more quickly than having to write a new line of code for every variable.

Arrays are commonly used reference data types in Java programming. Using an array makes the programming task much more convenient than using the traditional primitive data types. In this chapter, let us delve into the details of single and double dimensional arrays.

15.1　Arrays

So far, you have used a single variable to store data. For example, in a school, if you want to store the number of students a room can accommodate, you can then declare a variable like:

```
int room;
```

This variable is enough to store the number of students a room can accommodate, for example, 30. If you need to store the number of students for three rooms, you could use three variables like:

```
int room0, room1, room2;
```

Note that we have numbered the variables starting with a 0 (zero) because starting with a 0 makes the examples in this chapter more sensible. Now, if you want to print the number of students in each room, you could use the following print statements:

```
System.out.println(room0);
System.out.println(room1);
System.out.println(room2);
```

Now, consider the scenario where we had one hundred rooms. We would have to declare 100 variables like room0, room1,..., room99 and need to write 100 individual statements to print the capacity of each room.

```
int room0, room1,..., room99;
- - -
System.out.println(room0);
System.out.println(room1);
- - -
System.out.println(room2);
```

There are better ways in Java to code the above scenario, such as by using an Array. An array is a structure created in the computer memory to represent a number of values of the same data type. To visualise an array, consider all the rooms lined up next to one another as shown in Figure 15.1.

Now, assume the entire row of rooms as an array. Each room in the array is called an element of the array. Each room (element) has two components associated with it:

(i) The room number 0 to 99. This is called the index or subscript of the array.

(ii) The number of students a room can accommodate. This is the value stored in the element of the array.

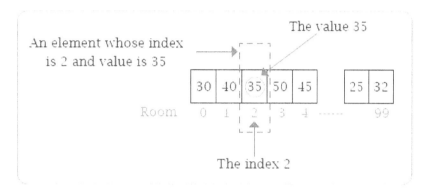

Figure 15.1: An Abstract Representation of Rooms

Figure 15.2 shows a memory representation of the room array. Observe that a single name, room, can reference the entire array. Note that the array's indices start with 0 and end with the number that is one less than the total number of elements.

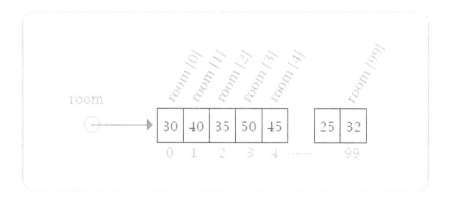

Figure 15.2: Memory Representation of the Array

As shown in Figure 14.3, you can access an element of the array by referring to its name along with its index (subscript) enclosed in square brackets. The syntax of the same is:

```
arrayName[index];
```

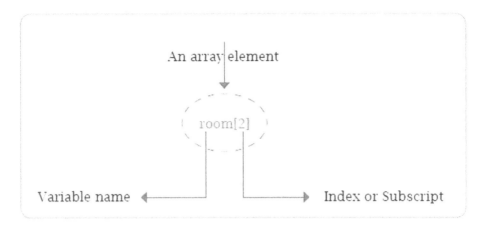

Figure 15.3: An Array Element

Having understood the concept of an array, let us formally define it:

An array is an ordered collection or numbered list of values that are stored in contiguous memory locations. The values stored in an array can be of primitive or non-primitive data types. However, all the values must be of the same data type.

Note: An array can store objects as well.

15.2 Creating an Array

Like other variables in Java, arrays must be declared before they can be used. The syntax to declare an array is:

```
type arrayName[] = new type[size];
```

or

```
type[] arrayName = new type[size];
```

In the above declaration, the type declares the base type of the array, which is the data type of each element. The arrayName specifies the name by which the array would be referenced in the program and the size defines the number of elements contained in the array.

For example, you can declare the room array which can store the capacity of 100 rooms as shown below (see Figure 15.4):

```
int room[] = new int[100];
```

Alternatively, you can rewrite the above single statement in two separate statements as shown below:

```
int room[];
room = new int[100];
```

In both the code snippets, the value 100 instructs the computer to define a room array that can have 100 elements. Each element of the array has its own index. Therefore, the starting element will be `room[0]`, the next will be `room[1]`, and so on. The last element in the array will be `room[99]`. Since the size of the array was specified as 100, therefore the last index will be one less than the size, i.e., 100 - 1 = 99.

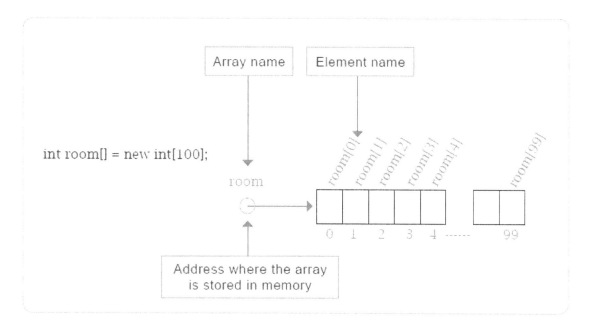

Figure 15.4: Creating an Array

Note

While creating an array, you can put the square brackets after or before the variable name. For example, you can write `int room[]` or `int[] room`. The computer treats both forms in the same way.

When the elements of an array are specified using a single index, the array is called a single dimensional array or a 1-D array. In a single dimensional array, the elements are stored in contiguous memory locations in the order of their index. Figure 14.4 is an example of a single dimensional array.

15.3 Types of Arrays

The type of an array is the type of values it holds. For example, you can have arrays of `byte`, `int`, `float`, etc., as shown in Table 15.1.

Array type	Data type	Data type
An array of bytes	byte	byte[] arrayOfBytes;
An array of integers	int	int[] arrayOfInts;
An array of floating point numbers	float	float[] arrayOfFloats;
An array of characters	char	char[] arrayOfChars;

Table 15.1: Types of Arrays

You can choose to use the type of array depending on the requirement of your program logic. For example, to store the roll number of 100 students, you would need an array of integers and to store the percentage marks, you would need an array of `float` or `double`. You will learn about the array of `Strings` to store names in the next chapter.

15.4   Storing Values in a Single Dimensional Array

In the earlier sections, you have already learnt that each element can hold a specific value. Let us now learn the different ways of assigning values to the array elements.

15.4.1   Direct Assignment

In this assignment technique, you assign the value to an element using its indexed name. For example, to store value 35 in an element with index 2, you can write a statement like:

```
room[2] = 35;
```

Let us see an example where you store and print the marks of 3 students via direct assignment.

Listing 15.1: DirectStore.java

```
1  public class DirectStore
2  {
3      public static void main(String args[])
4      {
5          int marks[] = new int[3];
6
7          marks[0] = 92;
8          marks[1] = 85;
9          marks[2] = 95;
10
11         System.out.println("marks[0] " + marks[0]);
12         System.out.println("marks[1] " + marks[1]);
13         System.out.println("marks[2] " + marks[2]);
```

Output
marks[0] 92
marks[1] 85
marks[2] 95

```
14      }
15  }
```

15.4.2   Using an Array Initialiser

You can use an array initialiser to assign values to array elements. In fact, when you use an array initialiser, you do not need to instruct the computer how many elements the array has. The computer figures this out for you. Let us see an example to create an array with 5 rooms and assign the capacity values through the array initialiser.

Listing 15.2: ArrayInit.java

```
1   public class ArrayInit
2   {
3       public static void main(String args[])
4       {
5           int room[] = {35, 30, 20, 25, 45};
6
7           System.out.println("Room No.\tCapacity");
8           System.out.println("********\t********");
9
10          for (int i = 0; i < 5; i++)
11          {
12              System.out.println(i + "\t\t" + room[i]);
13          }
14      }
15  }
```

Output	
Room No.	Capacity
********	********
0	35
1	30
2	20
3	25
4	45

15.4.3   Using Method Argument in BlueJ

Using this technique, the values are entered by the user and saved in an array at the runtime. Let us understand this concept by the following program which stores a set of five characters in an array. The characters are entered during program execution.

Listing 15.3: UsingMethod.java

```
1   public class UsingMethod
2   {
3       public static void main(char inputChars[])
4       {
5           System.out.println("Input characters are:");
6
7           for(int i = 0; i < 5; i++)
```

```
8          {
9              System.out.println(inputChars[i]);
10         }
11     }
12 }
```

Steps to execute the program

(i) Compile the program.

(ii) As shown in Figure 15.5, right-click on the class icon `UsingMethod` and select `void main(char[] inputChars)`.

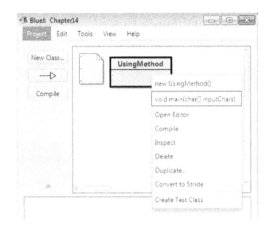

Figure 15.5: Invoking Method

(iii) Enter characters within curly brackets enclosed in single quotes, i.e., 'H','E','L','L','O' as shown in Figure 15.6.

Figure 15.6: Input using Method Call

(iv) Click on the OK button. The output will be shown in the Terminal Window as shown in Figure 15.7.

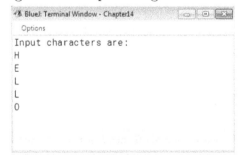

Figure 15.7: Terminal Window

15.4.4   Using the Scanner Class

Using this technique, the values are entered by the user and saved in an array at the runtime. Let us understand this concept by writing a simple program that accepts 5 floating point numbers, stores them in an array and prints them in the reverse order of input.

Listing 15.4: ArrayUsingScanner.java

```java
import java.util.*;

public class ArrayUsingScanner
{
    public static void main(String args[])
    {
        Scanner keyboard = new Scanner(System.in);

        float numbers[] = new float[5];

        System.out.println("Enter 5 floating point numbers:");
        for (int i = 0; i < 5; i++)
            numbers[i] = keyboard.nextFloat();

        System.out.println("Numbers in reverse order are:");
        for (int i = 4; i >= 0; i--)
            System.out.println(numbers[i]);

        keyboard.close();
    }
}
```

```
Output
Enter 5 floating point numbers:
34.7
45.5
66.0
99
125.9
Numbers in reverse order are:
125.9
99.0
66.0
45.5
34.7
```

15.5   Out of Bound Indices

Each element of an array is accessed using the name of the array and its index 0, 1, 2, ... n-1, where n is the number of elements in the array. For example, if the array is marks[5] then the valid array elements will be:

    marks[0], marks[1], marks[2], marks[3], marks[4]

The indices which are less than 0 or greater than 4 will be invalid for this array. Therefore, accessing elements with the following indices will be invalid:

    marks[-5], marks[-1], marks[5], marks[7], etc.

These indices are said to be out of bound as they are outside the valid range of indices, i.e., 0 to 4. When you access an element that is outside its valid index, an out of bound runtime error occurs.

To understand the concept better, let us consider the following program. Here, the elements of an array are printed using a for loop. However, the loop continues beyond its valid indices, i.e., 0 to 4. Therefore, as soon as the element `marks[5]` is accessed, an out of bound runtime error occurs as shown in Fugure 15.8.

Listing 15.5: OutOfBoundArray.java

```
1  public class OutOfBoundArray
2  {
3      public static void main(String args[])
4      {
5          int marks[] = {75, 85, 95, 55, 78};
6
7          for(int i = 0; i <= 5; i++)
8          {
9              System.out.println("marks[" + i + "] = " + marks[i]);
10         }
11     }
12 }
```

When i=5, marks[5] will refer to an invalid element.

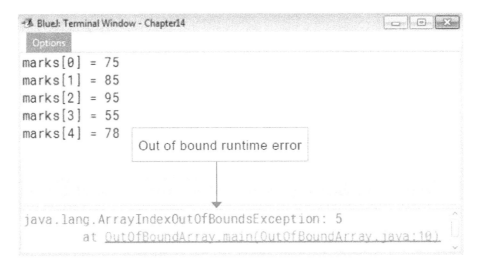

Figure 15.8: Out of Bound Indices

15.6   Double Dimensional Arrays

Let us reconsider the room example, which stores the number of students a room can accommodate in your school. Let us assume that there are five storeys in the school building, and each storey has five rooms. We can store the capacity of each room in a distinct location by using a double dimensional array as shown in Figure 15.9. The first dimension in this illustration denotes the floor number, and the second dimension denotes the room number.

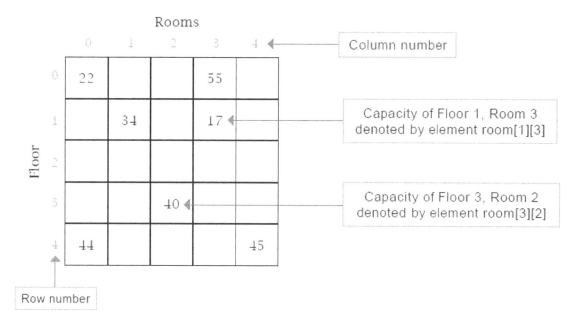

Figure 15.9: A Double Dimensional Array of Rooms

Such double dimensional array can be declared as:

```
int room[][] = new int[5][5];
```

The above declaration creates a two-dimensional array, consisting of 5 rows (0-4) and 5 columns (0-4). Thus, this array can store 5 x 5 = 25 elements. The total number of elements an array can store is calculated by a simple formula:

```
Total elements in array = Number of rows x Number of columns
```

Figure 15.10 shows the location of each element in the matrix form.

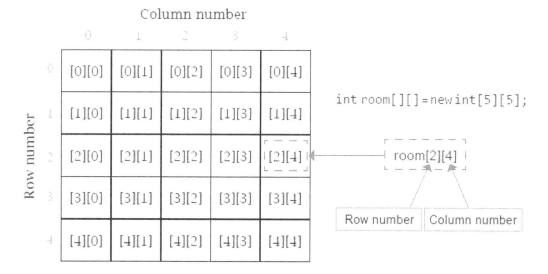

Figure 15.10: Two-dimensional Array Matrix

Let us now understand the generic syntax to define a double dimensional array.

```
type arrayName[][] = new type[rows][columns];
```

or

```
type[][] arrayName = new type[rows][columns];
```

In the above declaration, the type declares the base type of the array, which is the data type of each element. The **arrayName** specifies the name by which the array would be referenced in the program. The first index, **rows** refers to the number of rows in the array. The second index, **columns** refers to the number of columns in the array.

15.7 Storing Values in a Double Dimensional Array

Just like the single dimensional arrays, you can also store values in a two-dimensional array in the following ways.

15.7.1 Direct Assignment

In this assignment technique, you assign the value to an element using its indexed name. Thus to store a value 55 in the element at row index 2 and column index 3, you can use a direct assignment statement like:

```
room[2][3] = 55;
```

You can use this stored value using the element **room[2][3]** in your program.

Listing 15.6: Array2D.java

```
1  public class Array2D
2  {
3      public static void main(String args[])
4      {
5          int room[][] = new int[5][5];
6
7          room[1][4] = 30;
8          room[2][3] = 55;
9          room[3][3] = 48;
10
11         System.out.println("room[1][4] = " + room[1][4]);
12         System.out.println("room[2][3] = " + room[2][3]);
13         System.out.println("room[3][3] = " + room[3][3]);
14     }
15 }
```

```
Output
room[1][4] = 30
room[2][3] = 55
room[3][3] = 48
```

15.7.2 Using an Array Initialiser

You can use an array initialiser to assign values to a two-dimensional array. Just like the single dimensional arrays, when you use an array initialiser, you do not need to instruct the computer how many elements the array has. The computer figures this out for you. Let us see an example to create an array with 3 rows and 4 columns, and assign values through the array initialisation.

Listing 15.7: ArrayInit2D.java

```
1  public class ArrayInit2D
2  {
3     public static void main(String args[])
4     {
5        int array2D[][] =   {{1, 2, 3, 4},
6                             {1, 3, 5, 9},
7                             {2, 4, 6, 8}};
8
9        for(int i = 0; i < 3; i++)
10       {
11          for (int j = 0; j < 4; j++)
12          {
13             System.out.print(array2D[i][j] + " ");
14          }
15          System.out.println();
16       }
17    }
18 }
```

Values for each row in curly brackets separated by comma

Row 0
Row 1
Row 2

Output
```
1 2 3 4
1 3 5 9
2 4 6 8
```

15.7.3 Using Method Argument in BlueJ

Using this technique, the values are entered by the user and saved in a two-dimensional array at the runtime. The following program uses the two-dimensional array to store two rows of data, with each row containing three characters. The characters are entered during program execution.

Listing 15.8: UsingMethod2D.java

```
1  public class UsingMethod2D
2  {
3     public static void main(char array2D[][])
4     {
5        System.out.println("Two dimensional matrix is:");
6
7        for(int i = 0; i < 2; i++)
8        {
9           for (int j = 0; j < 3; j++)
10          {
```

Double dimensional array as an argument to the method

```
11              System.out.print(array2D[i][j] + " ");
12          }
13          System.out.println();
14      }
15    }
16 }
```

Steps to execute the program

(i) Compile the program.

(ii) As shown in Figure 15.11, right-click on the icon UsingMethod2D and select void main(char[][] array2D).

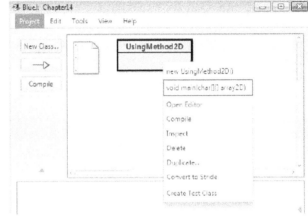

Figure 15.11: Invoking Method

(iii) Enter data as 'a', 'b', 'c', 'x', 'y', 'z' as shown in Figure 15.12.

Figure 15.12: Input using Method Call

(iv) Click on the OK button. The output will be shown in the Terminal Window as shown in Figure 15.13.

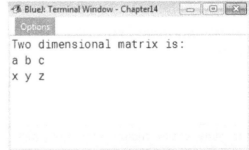

Figure 15.13: Terminal Window

15.7.4 Using the Scanner Class

In this technique, the values are entered by the user and saved in a two-dimensional array at runtime using the Scanner class. Let us write a simple program that accepts the number of rows and columns in a double dimensional matrix, reads and stores the numbers in the two-dimensional array, and prints them in the matrix form.

Listing 15.9: Array2DUsingScanner.java

```java
import java.util.*;
public class Array2DUsingScanner
{
    public static void main(String args[])
    {
        Scanner keyboard = new Scanner(System.in);

        System.out.println("Enter number of rows:");
        int rows = keyboard.nextInt();

        System.out.println("Enter number of columns:");
        int columns = keyboard.nextInt();

        int array2D[][] = new int[rows][columns];
        System.out.println("Enter " + (rows * columns) + " numbers");

        for(int i = 0; i < rows; i++)
        {
            for (int j = 0; j < columns; j++)
            {
                array2D[i][j] = keyboard.nextInt();
            }
        }

        System.out.println("Two dimensional array is:");

        for(int i = 0; i < rows; i++)
        {
            for (int j = 0; j < columns; j++)
            {
                System.out.print(array2D[i][j] + " ");
            }
            System.out.println();
        }

        keyboard.close();
    }
}
```

Code Walkthrough:

◈ Line 9: Accepts the number of rows from the user.

◈ Line 12: Accepts the number of columns from the user.

◈ Line 14: Declares a double dimensional array for the number of rows and columns entered by the user.

◈ Line 15: Computes the total number of elements required and prints a message for input.

◈ Line 21: Accepts array elements into the double dimensional array.

◈ Line 31: Prints the double dimensional array elements.

```
Output
Enter number of rows:
2
Enter number of columns:
4
Enter 8 numbers
1
3
5
7
2
4
6
8
Two dimensional array is:
1 3 5 7
2 4 6 8
```

15.8   Finding the Length of an Array

The length or size of an array is the number of elements contained in it. You can use the length property to determine the size of an array. You can use this property to iterate through the elements of an array. Let us see an example to find the length of a single dimensional array.

Listing 15.10: ArrayLength.java

```
1  public class ArrayLength
2  {
3      public static void main(String args[])
4
5          char chars[]={'C','O','M','P','U','T','E','R'};
6
7          System.out.println("Array length is: " + chars.length);
8
9          for (int i = 0; i < chars.length; i++)
10             System.out.println(chars[i]);
11     }
12 }
```

```
Output
Array length is: 8
C
O
M
P
U
T
E
R
```

Code Walkthrough:

◈ Line 5: Declares a single dimensional array chars of characters.

◈ Line 7: Prints the length of the array using the length property.

◈ Lines 9 - 10: Print the elements of the array using a for loop.

The following program illustrates how to find the number of rows and columns of a two-dimensional array.

Listing 15.11: ArrayLength2D.java

```
1  public class ArrayLength2D
2  {
3      public static void main(String args[])
4      {
5          char array2D[][]= {{'S','U','N','D','A','Y'}, ↵
               ↪ {'M','O','N','D','A','Y'}};
6
7          int rows = array2D.length;
8          int columns = array2D[0].length;
9
10         System.out.println("Number of rows are: " + rows);
11         System.out.println("Number of columns are: " + columns);
12     }
13 }
```

Output
Number of rows are: 2
Number of columns are: 6

Code Walkthrough:

◈ Line 5: Declares a double dimensional array array2D of characters.

◈ Line 7: Uses the length property on double dimensional array and assigns its value to the rows variable.

◈ Line 8: Uses the length property on single dimensional array and assigns its value to the columns variable.

15.9 Searching

Searching is one of the most important uses of arrays. It is used to find out whether an item is part of the array or not. There are a number of techniques to perform the search operation, but the two most common techniques are the linear search and the binary search. Let us now learn about these techniques.

15.9.1 Linear Search

This is one of the simplest search techniques to search a value within an array. Starting with the first element (0th element), it sequentially checks each element of the list for the search value until a match is found or all the elements have been searched. As soon as the search value is found, the algorithm quits and returns the position (index) of the target value in the array. This search technique is also known as Sequential Search.

> **Definition**
>
> The search technique that traverses the array sequentially to locate a given value is known as linear or sequential search.

There are two possible outcomes while performing a search: either you find the search value in the array or you do not. You call the former, a *successful search* and the latter, an *unsuccessful search*. The example shown in Figure 15.14 searches a value, 99, in the array.

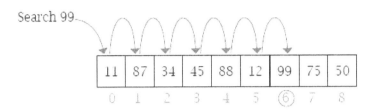

Figure 15.14: Linear Search

The array is searched from the first position to the last position, in a linear progression. As can be seen, the search value 99 is located at index 6, resulting in a successful search. The search returns 6 as the output. It is so because the value 99 exists at the 6th index of the array.

If you search for a value 76, obviously it is not present in the array, resulting in an unsuccessful search. An unsuccessful search is usually represented by a return value of -1.

> **Note**
>
> A linear search can be used with both sorted[a] and unsorted[b] arrays.
>
> ---
> [a]A sorted array is an array whose values are arranged in ascending or descending order.
> [b]An unsorted array is an array whose values are not arranged in ascending or descending order.

Let us now write a program to input a number and perform a linear search to check if it exists in the array.

Listing 15.12: LinearSearch.java

```java
1  import java.util.*;
2
3  public class LinearSearch
4  {
5      public static void main(String args[])
6      {
7          Scanner keyboard = new Scanner(System.in);
8          int searchNumber;
9          int foundIndex = -1;
10
11         int list[] = {11, 87, 34, 45, 88, 12, 99, 75, 50};
12
13         System.out.println("Enter a number to search:");
14         searchNumber = keyboard.nextInt();
```

```
15
16        for (int i = 0; i < list.length; i++)
17        {
18            if (list[i] == searchNumber)
19            {
20                foundIndex = i;
21                break;
22            }
23        }
24
25        if (foundIndex >= 0)
26            System.out.println("Number " + searchNumber + " found at ↵
                 ↪ index " + foundIndex);
27        else
28            System.out.println("Number " + searchNumber + " not found");
29
30        keyboard.close();
31    }
32 }
```

Code Walkthrough:

◇ Line 9: Initialises the `foundIndex` variable with a default value of -1 (i.e., search value not found).

◇ Line 14: Accepts the number to search for and stores it in the `searchNumber` variable.

◇ Line 16: Iterates through the array using the `length` property.

◇ Line 18: Checks if the `searchNumber` matches any of the array elements.

◇ Line 20: Assigns the index value to the `foundIndex` variable.

◇ Line 21: As soon as the search value is found, the loop is terminated with the `break` statement.

◇ Line 25: Checks if the `foundIndex` variable was assigned a value in the loop.

◇ Line 26: Displays the index where the `searchNumber` was found in the array.

◇ Line 28: Otherwise, displays a message for the unsuccessful search.

Output
Enter a number to search:
33
Number 33 not found

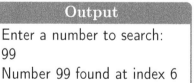

Output
Enter a number to search:
99
Number 99 found at index 6

15.9.2 Binary Search

Binary search is another technique which is used to find an element in an array, but the array needs to be sorted. This technique finds the presence of an element quicker than the linear search. In this search, the sorted array is divided into two halves. The search element can either be in the first half or the second half. Depending on which half the element is present, that half is further divided into two halves and the process is repeated until the search element is found or not found.

Since in this technique we divide the array elements continuously into two halves, this search is termed as *binary search* or *half-interval search*.

> **Note**
>
> A binary search can be used with sorted arrays only.

Let us understand this technique with the help of an example. Assume that we have a sorted array as shown in Figure 14.14.

0	1	2	3	4	5	6	7	8
11	33	40	45	68	72	89	95	99

Figure 15.15: Sorted Array with Indices

Let us name the array as `list[]` so that we can refer it in our discussion. Suppose you want to search for number 72 in this array. Let us call it the `searchNumber`. Since you need to divide the sorted array into two halves, you would need three variables as given below:

`start` – stores the start index of the array
`end` – stores the end index of the array
`mid` – stores the middle value of the index (to divide into two halves)

Pass 1: To begin with, the array has a starting index of 0 and the ending index of 8; therefore, the values of the three variables will be:

```
start = 0
end = 8
mid = (start + end) / 2 = (0 + 8) / 2 = 4
```

0	1	2	3	4	5	6	7	8	Pass 1
11	33	40	45	68	72	89	95	99	72 > 68

start = 0   mid = 4   end = 8

Figure 15.16: Binary Search Pass 1

Now, the `searchNumber` is compared with the element at the `mid` position 4 (i.e., `list[mid]`). Three possibilities arise when this comparison is made:

(i) The searchNumber is equal to the value at `list[mid]`. In this case, you have found the number at index denoted by `mid`. The search is complete.

(ii) The `searchNumber` is less than the value at `list[mid]`. In this case, the number you are looking for exists in the first half. Therefore, you adjust your `end` variable to one less than `mid` as given below:

```
end = mid - 1
```

(iii) The `searchNumber` is greater than the value at `list[mid]`. In this case, the number you are looking for exists in the second half. Therefore, you adjust your `start` variable to one more than `mid` as given below:

```
start = mid + 1
```

In this case, the `searchNumber` (i.e., 72) is greater than `list[4]` (i.e., 68); therefore, you adjust your `start` variable as per Point (iii) mentioned above. Hence, its updated value will be:

```
start = mid + 1, i.e., 4 + 1 = 5
```

Pass 2: Figure 15.17 shows the updated values of the three variables as per the following calculations:

```
start = 5
end = 8
mid = (start + end) / 2 = (5 + 8)/2 = 6
```

Note that *integer division* has taken place in calculating the value of `mid`.

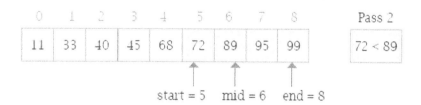

Figure 15.17: Binary Search Pass 2

Now, the `searchNumber` is again compared with the element at the `mid` position 6 (i.e., `list[mid]`). In this case, the `searchNumber` (i.e., 72) is less than the value of `list[6]` (i.e., 89) therefore, you adjust your `end` variable as per Point (ii) mentioned above. Hence, its updated value will be:

```
end = mid - 1 = 6 - 1 = 5
```

Pass 3: Figure 15.18 shows the updated values of the three variables as per the following calculations:

```
start = 5
end = 5
mid = (start + end) / 2 = (5 + 5) / 2 = 5
```

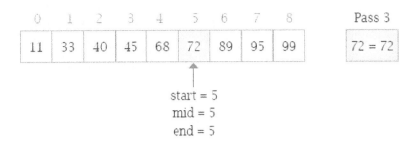

Figure 15.18: Binary Search Pass 3

Now, the searchNumber is again compared with the element at the mid position (i.e., list[mid]). In this case, the searchNumber (i.e., 72) is equal to the value at list[5] (i.e., 72). Hence, you found the number at the index denoted by mid, i.e., 5. The search is complete now. Figure 15.19 shows the three passes in one diagram.

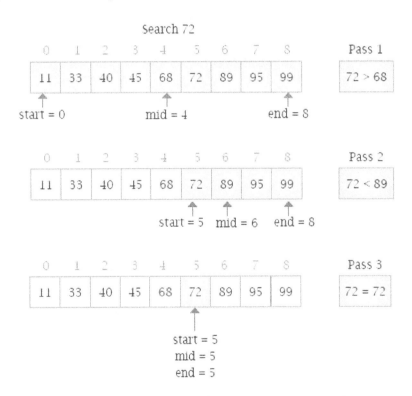

Figure 15.19: Binary Search Pass 1, 2, and 3

The following program shows the Java implementation of the binary search algorithm.

Listing 15.13: BinarySearch.java

```java
1  import java.util.*;
2
3  public class BinarySearch
4  {
5      public static void main(String args[])
```

```
6      {
7          Scanner keyboard = new Scanner(System.in);
8          int searchNumber;
9          int foundIndex = -1;
10         int start, mid, end;
11
12         int list[] = {11, 33, 40, 45, 68, 72, 89, 95, 99};
13
14         System.out.println("Enter a number to search:");
15         searchNumber = keyboard.nextInt();
16
17         start = 0;
18         end = list.length - 1;
19
20         while (start <= end)
21         {
22             mid = (start + end) / 2;
23
24             if (searchNumber == list[mid])
25             {
26                 foundIndex = mid;
27                 break;
28             }
29             else if (searchNumber < list[mid])
30                 end = mid - 1;
31             else
32                 start = mid + 1;
33         }
34
35
36         if (foundIndex >= 0)
37             System.out.println("Number " + searchNumber + " found at ←
                    ↪ index " + foundIndex);
38         else
39             System.out.println("Number " + searchNumber + " not found");
40
41         keyboard.close();
42     }
43 }
```

Code Walkthrough:

◈ Line 12: Declares a sorted array list[] with 9 elements.

◈ Line 17: Initialises the **start** variable with the first index, i.e., 0.

◈ Line 18: Initialises the **end** variable with the last index, i.e., length of the array minus one.

◈ Line 20: Loops through until **start** is less than or equal to **end**.

◈ Line 22: Calculates the value of the **mid** variable, i.e., mid index.

◈ Line 24: Checks if the **searchNumber** matches with the array element at the **mid** index.

◈ Line 26: Updates the **foundIndex** variable with the index value at the **mid** location.

◈ Line 27: Stops searching any further.

◈ Lines 29 - 30: If the **searchNumber** is present in the first half, it adjusts the **end** variable.

◈ Line 32: Otherwise, adjusts the **start** variable.

Output
Enter a number to search: 72 Number 72 found at index 5

Output
Enter a number to search: 55 Number 55 not found

15.10 Sorting

Sorting is the process of arranging array elements in ascending[1] or descending[2] order. There are a number of ways to perform the sorting operation, but the two most common techniques are selection sort and bubble sort. Let us delve into the details of these techniques.

15.10.1 Selection Sort

The selection sort is a combination of searching and sorting. During each pass, the unsorted element with the smallest (or the largest) value is moved to its final position in the array. In other words, the process repeatedly finds the smallest (or the largest) value from the unsorted part and moves it to its final position in the array.

Let us understand this technique with the help of an example. Assume that we have an unsorted array as shown in Figure 15.20.

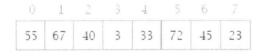

Figure 15.20: Unsorted Array with Indices

> **Note**
>
> An unsorted array is an array whose values are not arranged in ascending or descending order.

Pass 1: To begin with, the smallest number (3) in the unsorted list is selected and swapped with the number at the 0th index (55) as shown in Figure 15.21. This results in the element at the 0th index in its final position.

---

[1]Ascending means smallest to largest, i.e., 0 to 9 for numbers and A to Z for letters/words.

[2]Descending means largest to smallest, i.e., 9 to 0 for numbers and Z to A for letters/words.

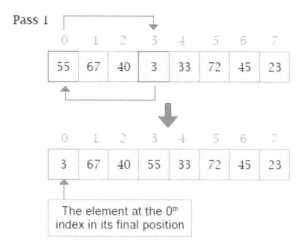

Figure 15.21: Selection Sort - Pass 1

Pass 2: Now as the index 0 is filled with its final value, the starting index shifts to index 1. The next smallest number (23), from index 1 onwards, is found and swapped with the number at the 1st index (67) as shown in Figure 15.22. This results in placing the element at the 1st index in its final position.

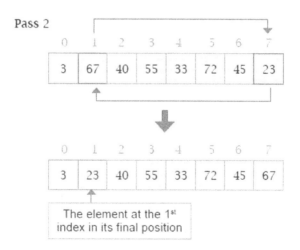

Figure 15.22: Selection Sort - Pass 2

Pass 3: As the index 1 is filled with its final value, the starting index shifts to index 2. The next smallest number (33), from index 2 onwards, is found and swapped with the number at the 2nd index (40) as shown in Figure 15.23. This results in placing the element at the 2nd index in its final position.

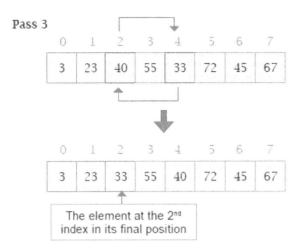

Figure 15.23: Selection Sort - Pass 3

Pass 4: As the index 2 is filled with its final value, the starting index shifts to index 3. The next smallest number (40), from index 3 onwards, is found and swapped with the number at the 3rd index (55) as shown in Figure 15.24. This results in placing the element at the 3rd index in its final position.

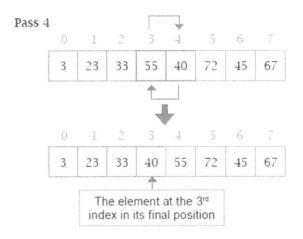

Figure 15.24: Selection Sort - Pass 4

Pass 5: As the index 3 is filled with its final value, the starting index shifts to index 4. The next smallest number (45), from index 4 onwards, is found and swapped with the number at the 4th index (55) as shown in Figure 15.25. This results in placing the element at the 4th index in its final position.

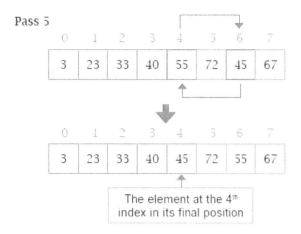

Figure 15.25: Selection Sort - Pass 5

Pass 6: As the index 4 is filled with its final value, the starting index shifts to index 5. The next smallest number (55), from index 5 onwards, is found and swapped with the number at the 5th index (72) as shown in Figure 15.26. This results in placing the element at the 5th index in its final position.

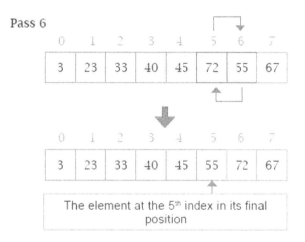

Figure 15.26: Selection Sort - Pass 6

Pass 7: As the index 5 is filled with its final value, the starting index shifts to index 6. The next smallest number (67), from index 6 onwards, is found and swapped with the number at the 6th index (72) as shown in Figure 15.27. This results in placing the element at the 6th index in its final position. This automatically results in placing the last element in its final position. Now, the whole array is sorted in ascending order.

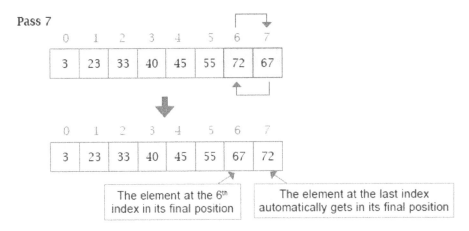

Figure 15.27: Selection Sort - Pass 7

The following program shows the Java implementation of the Selection Sort algorithm.

Listing 15.14: SelectionSort.java

```java
public class SelectionSort
{
   public static void main(String args[])
   {
      int list[] = {55, 67, 40, 3, 33, 72, 45, 23};
      int len = list.length;

      //The outer loop tells which position in array list[] to fill next
      for (int i = 0; i < len-1; i++)
      {
         //Find the minimum element in the unsorted part of the array
         int minIndex = i;
         for (int j = i+1; j < len; j++)
         {
            if (list[j] < list[minIndex])
               minIndex = j;
         }

         //Swap the minimum element with the position to fill
         System.out.println("Pass "+ (i+1) + " => Swap " + list[i] + " ↵
              ↪ and " + list[minIndex]);
         int tmp = list[i];
         list[i] = list[minIndex];
         list[minIndex] = tmp;
      }

      //Print the sorted array
      System.out.println("Sorted array is:");
```

```
28        for (int i = 0; i < len; i++)
29        {
30            System.out.println(list[i]);
31        }
32    }
33 }
```

Code Walkthrough:

◈ Line 5: Declares an unsorted array list of integers.

◈ Line 6: Stores the number of elements in list in the `len` variable.

◈ Line 9: The outer loop tells the next position in the array to fill.

◈ Lines 12 - 17: Determine the smallest element in the unsorted part of the array (from i^{th} index onwards).

◈ Line 12: Sets the `minIndex` to the ith index.

◈ Line 15: Checks if the element at the jth index is less than the element at the `minIndex`.

◈ Line 16: Updates the `minIndex` with the jth index.

◈ Lines 21 – 23: Logic to swap the minimum number with the number in the position to fill.

◈ Line 21: Stores the value of the current element in a temporary variable.

◈ Line 22: Stores the value of the element at `minIndex` in the current element.

◈ Line 23: Stores the value of the temporary variable in the element at `minIndex`.

◈ Line 30: Displays the elements of sorted array.

Output
Pass 1 => Swap 55 and 3
Pass 2 => Swap 67 and 23
Pass 3 => Swap 40 and 33
Pass 4 => Swap 55 and 40
Pass 5 => Swap 55 and 45
Pass 6 => Swap 72 and 55
Pass 7 => Swap 72 and 67
Sorted array is:
3
23
33
40
45
55
67
72

15.10.2 Bubble Sort

The bubble sort is a sorting algorithm that works by repeatedly iterating through the array, comparing each pair of adjoining elements and swapping them if they are in the wrong order.

Let us understand this technique with the help of an example. Assume that we have an unsorted array as shown in Figure 15.28.

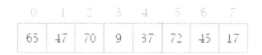

Figure 15.28: Unsorted Array with Indices

To begin with, the elements at the 0th and the 1st index are compared. Their positions are swapped if the element at the 0th index is greater than the element at the 1st index. Since $65 > 47$, a swap occurs.

```
                  Swap
   0   1   2   3   4   5   6   7
  65  47  70   9  37  72  45  17
```

Now, the elements at the 1st and the 2nd index are compared. Since $65 < 70$, no swap occurs.

```
                  No Swap
   0   1   2   3   4   5   6   7
  47  65  70   9  37  72  45  17
```

The elements at the 2nd and the 3rd index are compared. Since $70 > 9$, a swap occurs.

```
                  Swap
   0   1   2   3   4   5   6   7
  47  65  70   9  37  72  45  17
```

The elements at the 3rd and the 4th index are compared. Since $70 > 37$, a swap occurs.

```
                  Swap
   0   1   2   3   4   5   6   7
  47  65   9  70  37  72  45  17
```

The elements at the 4th and the 5th index are compared. Since $70 < 72$, no swap occurs.

```
                  No Swap
   0   1   2   3   4   5   6   7
  47  65   9  37  70  72  45  17
```

The elements at the 5th and the 6th index are compared. Since $72 > 45$, a swap occurs.

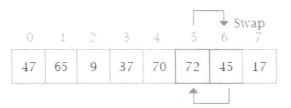

The elements at the 6th and the 7th index are compared. Since $72 > 17$, a swap occurs.

This results in a list with the highest element in the last position.

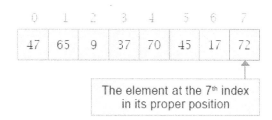

The element at the 7th index in its proper position

In the next pass, the second highest number is placed in the second last position and so on. This process is repeated until the entire array is sorted. The following program shows the Java implementation of the Bubble Sort algorithm.

Listing 15.15: BubbleSort.java

```
1  public class BubbleSort
2  {
3     public static void main(String args[])
4     {
5        int list[] = {65, 47, 40, 9, 37, 72, 45, 17};
6        int len = list.length;
7
8        for (int i = 0; i < len-1; i++)
9        {
10          for (int j = 0; j < len-i-1; j++)
11          {
12             if (list[j] > list[j+1])
13             {
14                //Swap the adjacent elements
15                int tmp = list[j];
16                list[j] = list[j+1];
17                list[j+1] = tmp;
18             }
19          }
20       }
21
22       //Print the sorted array
23       System.out.println("Sorted array is:");
```

```
24          for (int i = 0; i < len; i++)
25          {
26              System.out.println(list[i]);
27          }
28      }
29 }
```

Output
Sorted array is:
9
17
37
40
45
47
65
72

Code Walkthrough:

◈ Line 5: Stores the unsorted numbers into an array named list.

◈ Line 6: Stores the length of list in the len variable.

◈ Line 8: The outer loop iterates through the entire array.

◈ Line 10: The inner loop iterates through the remaining unsorted array only. This has been achieved by subtracting the value of counter variable i in the inner loop test condition (len-i-1).

◈ Line 12: Compares the two adjacent elements, i.e., element at j^{th} position and that at $(j+1)^{th}$ position.

◈ Line 15: Stores the value of the current element in a temporary variable.

◈ Line 16: Stores the value of the next element of the array in the current element.

◈ Line 17: Stores the value of the temporary variable in the next element.

Solved Programming Exercises

Write a program in Java to input 10 integers and save them in a single dimensional array. Perform the following tasks:

(i) Print the elements in the array on a single line followed by a space.

(ii) Compute and print the sum of elements at even indices.

(iii) Compute and print the product of elements at odd indices.

Listing 15.16: SumProduct.java

```
1  import java.util.*;
2
3  public class SumProduct
4  {
5      public static void main(String args[])
6      {
7          Scanner keyboard = new Scanner(System.in);
8
9          int numbers[] = new int[10];
10         int sumEven = 0;
11         long productOdd = 1;
12
```

```
13        System.out.println("Enter 10 integers:");
14        for (int i = 0; i < 10; i++)
15        numbers[i] = keyboard.nextInt();
16
17        for (int i = 0; i < 10; i++)
18        {
19            System.out.print(numbers[i] + " ");
20
21            if (i % 2 == 1)
22                productOdd = productOdd * numbers[i];
23            else
24                sumEven = sumEven + numbers[i];
25        }
26
27        System.out.println("\nSum of integers at even indices: " + ↵
              ↪ sumEven);
28        System.out.println("Product of integers at odd indices: " + ↵
              ↪ productOdd);
29
30        keyboard.close();
31    }
32 }
```

Code Walkthrough:

◈ Line 10: Defines an accumulator sumEven to store the sum of numbers at even indices.

◈ Line 11: Defines an accumulator productOdd to store the product of numbers at odd indices.

◈ Lines 21 - 22: If the index divided by 2 has a remainder of 1 (i.e., index is odd) then accumulates the product.

◈ Line 24: Otherwise, accumulates the sum.

Output
Enter 10 integers:
1
2
3
4
5
6
7
8
9
10
1 2 3 4 5 6 7 8 9 10
Sum of integers at even indices: 25
Product of integers at odd indices: 3840

Write a program to accept 10 different numbers in a single dimensional array. Display the greatest and smallest numbers of the array elements.

Listing 15.17: MinMax.java

```java
import java.util.*;
public class MinMax
{
    public static void main(String args[])
    {
        Scanner keyboard = new Scanner(System.in);

        int numbers[] = new int[10];
        int min, max;

        System.out.println("Enter 10 integers:");
        for (int i = 0; i < 10; i++)
            numbers[i] = keyboard.nextInt();

        min = numbers[0];
        max = numbers[0];

        for (int i = 1; i < 10; i++)
        {
            if (numbers[i] > max)
                max = numbers[i];

            if (numbers[i] < min)
                min = numbers[i];
        }

        System.out.println("The greatest of the array elements is: " + ←
            ↪ max);
        System.out.println("The smallest of the array elements is: " + ←
            ↪ min);

        keyboard.close();
    }
}
```

Code Walkthrough:

◈ Line 15: Stores the number at the 0th index as the **min** number.

◈ Line 16: Stores the number at the 0th index as the **max** number.

◈ Line 18: Notice that the loop starts from the 1st index rather than from the 0th index.

◈ Lines 20 - 21: If the element at the ith index is greater than the **max** then updates the value stored in **max** with the element.

◈ Lines 23 - 24: If the element at the ith index is less than the min then updates the value stored in min with the element.

```
Output
Enter 10 integers:
12
34
1
45
6
34
55
67
43
56
The greatest of the array elements is: 67
The smallest of the array elements is: 1
```

Write a program in Java to store the characters in word COMPUTER in a single dimensional array. Arrange and display all the characters in descending order using Bubble Sort.

Listing 15.18: BubbleSortDesc.java

```java
public class BubbleSortDesc
{
    public static void main(String args[])
    {
        char list[] = {'C', 'O', 'M', 'P', 'U', 'T', 'E', 'R'};
        int len = list.length;

        for (int i = 0; i < len-1; i++)
        {
            for (int j = 0; j < len-i-1; j++)
            {
                if (list[j] < list[j+1])
                {
                    //Swap the adjacent elements
                    char tmp = list[j];
                    list[j] = list[j+1];
                    list[j+1] = tmp;
                }
            }
        }

        //Print the sorted array
```

```
Output
Array in descending order is:
U
T
R
P
O
M
E
C
```

```
23        System.out.println("Array in descending order is:");
24        for (int i = 0; i < len; i++)
25        {
26            System.out.println(list[i]);
27        }
28    }
29 }
```

Write a program to input a string in uppercase and print the frequency of each character.

Listing 15.19: CharFrequency.java

```
1  import java.util.Scanner;
2  public class CharFrequency
3  {
4      public static void main(String args[])
5      {
6          Scanner keyboard = new Scanner(System.in);
7          //Declare an array to store frequence of each letter
8          int charFrequency[] = new int[26];
9
10         System.out.print("Enter a string: ");
11         String input = keyboard.nextLine();
12
13         //Ensure it is in uppercase
14         input = input.toUpperCase();
15
16         for (int i = 0; i < input.length(); i++)
17         {
18             //Extract the char at ith position
19             char ch = input.charAt(i);
20             //Ensure it is a letter
21             if (Character.isLetter(ch))
22                 charFrequency[ch - 'A']++;
23         }
24
25         System.out.println("Characters Frequency");
26         for (int i = 0; i < 26; i++)
27         {
28             //Display non-zero frequency only
29             if (charFrequency[i] != 0)
30             {
31                 //Display the character with its frequency
32                 System.out.println((char) (i + 'A') + "\t\t" + ↵
                       ↪ charFrequency[i]);
```

```
33              }
34          }
35
36          keyboard.close();
37      }
38 }
```

Output

```
Enter a string: COMPUTER HARDWARE
Characters Frequency
A          2
C          1
D          1
E          2
H          1
M          1
O          1
P          1
R          3
T          1
U          1
W          1
```

Write a program in Java to input a two-dimensional array of size n x m (rows=n; columns=m) and perform the following tasks:

(i) Print the array in matrix form (n x m).

(ii) Compute and print the sum of elements of each row.

Listing 15.20: SumRows.java

```java
1  import java.util.*;
2  public class SumRows
3  {
4      public static void main(String args[])
5      {
6          Scanner keyboard = new Scanner(System.in);
7          int sumRow = 0;
8
9          System.out.println("Enter number of rows:");
10         int rows = keyboard.nextInt();
11
12         System.out.println("Enter number of columns:");
13         int columns = keyboard.nextInt();
14
15         int array2D[][] = new int[rows][columns];
16
17         System.out.println("Enter " + (rows * columns) + " numbers");
18
19         for (int i = 0; i < rows; i++)
20         {
21             for (int j = 0; j < columns; j++)
```

```
22            {
23                array2D[i][j] = keyboard.nextInt();
24            }
25        }
26
27        System.out.println("Two dimensional array:");
28
29        for (int i = 0; i < rows; i++)
30        {
31            for (int j = 0; j < columns; j++)
32            {
33                System.out.print(array2D[i][j] + " ");
34            }
35            System.out.println();
36        }
37
38        System.out.println("Sum of rows:");
39        for (int i = 0; i < rows; i++)
40        {
41            sumRow = 0;
42
43            for (int j = 0; j < columns; j++)
44            {
45                sumRow = sumRow + array2D[i][j];
46            }
47            System.out.println("Sum of row with index " + i + " is " + ↵
                ↪ sumRow);
48        }
49
50        keyboard.close();
51    }
52 }
```

Output

```
Enter number of rows:
2
Enter number of columns:
3
Enter 6 numbers
1
2
3
4
5
6
Two dimensional array:
1 2 3
4 5 6
Sum of rows:
Sum of row with index 0 is 6
Sum of row with index 1 is 15
```

Write a program in Java to input a two-dimensional array of size n x m (rows=n; columns=m) and perform the following tasks:

  (i) Print the array in matrix form (n x m).

  (ii) Compute and print the sum of elements of each column.

Listing 15.21: SumColumns.java

```java
import java.util.*;
public class SumColumns
{
    public static void main(String args[])
    {
        Scanner keyboard = new Scanner(System.in);
        int sumColumn = 0;

        System.out.println("Enter number of rows:");
        int rows = keyboard.nextInt();

        System.out.println("Enter number of columns:");
        int columns = keyboard.nextInt();

        int array2D[][] = new int[rows][columns];

        System.out.println("Enter " + (rows * columns) + " numbers");
        for (int i = 0; i < rows; i++)
        {
            for (int j = 0; j < columns; j++)
            {
                array2D[i][j] = keyboard.nextInt();
            }
        }

        System.out.println("Two dimensional array:");
        for (int i = 0; i < rows; i++)
        {
            for (int j = 0; j < columns; j++)
            {
                System.out.print(array2D[i][j] + " ");
            }
            System.out.println();
        }

        System.out.println("Sum of columns:");
        for (int i = 0; i < columns; i++)
        {
```

```
39          sumColumn = 0;
40          for (int j = 0; j < rows; j++)
41          {
42              sumColumn = sumColumn + array2D[j][i];
43          }
44          System.out.println("Sum of columns with index " + i + " is " ↵
                ↪ + sumColumn);
45      }
46
47      keyboard.close();
48  }
49 }
```

```
┌────────────────────────────────────────┐
│                Output                  │
├────────────────────────────────────────┤
│ Enter number of rows:                  │
│ 2                                      │
│ Enter number of columns:               │
│ 3                                      │
│ Enter 6 numbers                        │
│ 1                                      │
│ 3                                      │
│ 5                                      │
│ 7                                      │
│ 9                                      │
│ 2                                      │
│ Two dimensional array:                 │
│ 1 3 5                                  │
│ 7 9 2                                  │
│ Sum of columns:                        │
│ Sum of columns with index 0 is 8       │
│ Sum of columns with index 1 is 12      │
│ Sum of columns with index 2 is 7       │
└────────────────────────────────────────┘
```

Write a program in Java to input a two-dimensional array of size n (rows=columns=n) and perform the following tasks:

(i) Print the array in matrix form (n x n).

(ii) Compute and print the sum of the elements at the left diagonal.

(iii) Compute and print the sum of the elements at the right diagonal.

A 4 x 4 matrix (size=4) takes the following form:

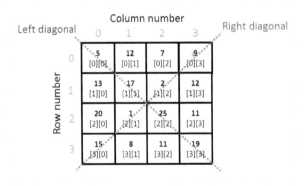

The left diagonal elements are present at locations where row index=column index, i.e., [0][0], [1][1], [2][2], and [3][3].

The right diagonal elements are present at locations where row index + column index = size of array - 1, i. e., $0 + 3 = 1 + 2 = 2 + 1 = 3 + 0 = 4 - 1 = 3$.

Listing 15.22: DiagonalSum.java

```java
import java.util.*;
public class DiagonalSum
{
    public static void main(String args[])
    {
        Scanner keyboard = new Scanner(System.in);

        System.out.println("Enter size of n x n array:");
        int size = keyboard.nextInt();

        int array2D[][] = new int[size][size];
        int sumLeftDiag = 0, sumRightDiag = 0;

        System.out.println("Enter " + (size * size) + " numbers");

        for(int i = 0; i < size; i++)
        {
            for (int j = 0; j < size; j++)
            {
                array2D[i][j] = keyboard.nextInt();
            }
        }

        System.out.println("Two dimensional array is:");

        for(int i = 0; i < size; i++)
        {
            for (int j = 0; j < size; j++)
            {
                System.out.print(array2D[i][j] + " ");

                //Sum of left diagonal
                if (i == j)
                    sumLeftDiag = sumLeftDiag + array2D[i][j];

                //Sum of right diagonal
                if ((i+j) == (size-1))
                    sumRightDiag = sumRightDiag + array2D[i][j];
```

```
39              }
40          System.out.println();
41      }
42
43      System.out.println("Left diagonal sum: " + sumLeftDiag);
44      System.out.println("Right diagonal sum: " + sumRightDiag);
45
46      keyboard.close();
47   }
48 }
```

Output

```
Enter size of n x n array:
4
Enter 16 numbers
1
2
3
4
5
6
7
8
9
8
7
6
5
4
3
2
Two dimensional array is:
1 2 3 4
5 6 7 8
9 8 7 6
5 4 3 2
Left diagonal sum: 16
Right diagonal sum: 24
```

Write a program in Java that computes the sum of two 3 x 3 matrices and displays their sum. Hint: For two 3 x 3 matrices, their sum is computed as:

$$\begin{bmatrix} a_{11} & a_{12} & a_{13} \\ a_{21} & a_{22} & a_{23} \\ a_{31} & a_{32} & a_{33} \end{bmatrix} + \begin{bmatrix} b_{11} & b_{12} & b_{13} \\ b_{21} & b_{22} & b_{23} \\ b_{31} & b_{32} & b_{33} \end{bmatrix} = \begin{bmatrix} a_{11}+b_{11} & a_{12}+b_{12} & a_{13}+b_{13} \\ a_{21}+b_{21} & a_{22}+b_{22} & a_{23}+b_{23} \\ a_{31}+b_{31} & a_{32}+b_{32} & a_{33}+b_{33} \end{bmatrix}$$

Listing 15.23: MatrixSum.java

```
1  public class MatrixSum
2  {
3     public static void main(String args[])
4     {
5        int matrixA[][] = {{1, 2, 3},
6                           {4, 5, 6},
7                           {7, 8, 9}};
8
9        int matrixB[][] = {{11, 12, 13},
10                           {14, 15, 16},
11                           {17, 18, 19}};
12
13        int matrixC[][] = new int[3][3];
14
15        for(int i = 0; i < 3; i++)
16        {
17           for (int j = 0; j < 3; j++)
18           {
19              matrixC[i][j] = matrixA[i][j] + matrixB[i][j];
20           }
21        }
22        for(int i = 0; i < 3; i++)
23        {
24           for (int j = 0; j < 3; j++)
25           {
26              System.out.print(matrixC[i][j] + " ");
27           }
28           System.out.println();
29        }
30     }
31  }
```

Output
```
12 14 16
18 20 22
24 26 28
```

If arrays M and M+N are as shown below, write a program in Java to find the array N.

$$M = \begin{bmatrix} -1 & 0 & 2 \\ -3 & -1 & 6 \\ 4 & 3 & -1 \end{bmatrix} \text{ and } M+N = \begin{bmatrix} -6 & 9 & 4 \\ 4 & 5 & 0 \\ 1 & -2 & -3 \end{bmatrix}$$

Listing 15.24: FindN.java

```
1  public class FindN
2  {
3    public static void main(String args[])
4    {
5      int matrixM[][] = {{-1, 0, 2},
6                         {-3, -1, 6},
7                         {4, 3, -1 }};
8
9      int matrixMN[][] = {{-6, 9, 4},
10                          {4, 5, 0},
11                          {1, -2, -3}};
12
13     int matrixN[][] = new int[3][3];
14     for(int i = 0; i < 3; i++)
15     {
16       for (int j = 0; j < 3; j++)
17       {
18         matrixN[i][j] = matrixMN[i][j] - matrixM[i][j];
19       }
20     }
21     for(int i = 0; i < 3; i++)
22     {
23       for (int j = 0; j < 3; j++)
24       {
25         System.out.print(matrixN[i][j] + " ");
26       }
27       System.out.println();
28     }
29   }
30 }
```

Output

```
-5 9 2
7 6 -6
-3 -5 -2
```

Multiple Choice Questions

1. The size of an array that signifies the number of elements it can store is given using .... brackets.

   A. {}   C. ( )

   B. [ ]   D. All of the above

2. Given array int x[] = 11, 22, 33, 44; the value of x[1] is ....

   A. 11   C. 33

   B. 22   D. Invalid value

3. Given array int x[] = 11, 22, 33, 44; the value of x[1+2] is ....

A. 11   B. 22   C. 33   D. 44

4. If `int arr[]` = 3, 5, 7, 9; what is the value of `arr.length`?

     A. 3   C. 4

     B. 5   D. Cannot be determined

5. Given array `int z[]` = 15, 16, 17; It will occupy .... bytes in memory.

     A. 3   B. 12   C. 24   D. 64

6. A linear search ....

     A. can be used with sorted arrays only

     B. can be used with unsorted arrays only

     C. can be used with both sorted and unsorted arrays

     D. cannot be used with arrays

7. A binary search ....

     A. can be used with sorted arrays only

     B. can be used with unsorted arrays only

     C. can be used with both sorted and unsorted arrays

     D. cannot be used with arrays

8. Which of the following statements is `true`?

     A. Binary search is less efficient than the sequential search.

     B. Binary search is less efficient than the linear search.

     C. Binary search is more efficient than the sequential search.

     D. Binary search is as efficient as the sequential search.

9. In .... search, the algorithm uses the middle value of the array for the search operation.

     A. Binary   B. Linear   C. Bubble   D. Selection

10. Which element is `num[9]` of the array num?

     A. 8th B. 9th C. 10th D. 11th

Assignment Questions

1. Write a program to initialise the given data in an array and find the minimum and maximum values along with the sum of the given elements.

Numbers: 2, 5, 4, 1, 3
Output:
Minimum value: 1
Maximum value: 5
Sum of the elements: 15

2. Differentiate between the following.

   (i) Array Declaration and Initialisation   (iv) Linear search and Binary search

   (ii) `int a[10]` and `char a[10]`

   (iii) Sorting and Searching   (v) Selection sort and Bubble sort

3. How does the linear search find an element in the array? Explain your answer with a suitable example.

4. Explain the technique of Bubble Sort with an example.

5. Explain the technique of Selection Sort with an example.

6. Why does Binary Search need a sorted array to perform the search operation?

7. How does the binary search find the presence of an element quicker than the linear search?

8. Write a program to input integer elements into an array of size 20 and perform the following operations:

   (i) Display largest number from the array   (iii) Display sum of all the elements of the array

   (ii) Display smallest number from the array

9. Declare and instantiate a one dimensional `int` array named `evenNums` with five elements. Use an initialiser list that contains the first five even integers, starting with 11.

10. Suppose `x` is an array of type `int[]` with 50 elements. Write a code segment that will count and print the frequency of number 42 in the array.

11. A student wrote the following code segment, intending to print 11 22 33 44:

```
int arr[] = {11, 22, 33, 44};
for (int i = 1; i <= 4; i++)
System.out.println(arr[i]);
```

However, the program crashed with a run-time error. Can you explain the reason for this?

12. Write a code segment to compute the sum of all positive real numbers stored in the following array.

```
double numb[] = new double[50];
```

13. Write a code segment that finds the largest integer in this two-dimensional array.

```
int data[][] = new int[5][5];
```

14. Given the following declarations:

```
final int SIZE = 20;
char[] name = new char[SIZE];
```

   (i) Write an assignment statement that stores 'D' into the first element of the array name.

  (ii) Write an output statement that prints the value of the tenth element of the array name.

 (iii) Write a for statement that fills the array name with spaces.

15. What happens in Java if you try to access an element that is outside the bounds of the array?

16. Write Java statements for the following:

   (i) Create an array to hold 15 double values.

  (ii) Assign the value 10.5 to the last element in the array.

 (iii) Display the sum of the first and the last element.

 (iv) Write a loop that computes the sum of all elements in the array.

17. Write a program to accept the year of graduation from school as an integer value from the user. Using the Binary Search technique on the sorted array of integers given below, output the message "Record exists" if the value input is located in the array. If not, output the message ''Record does not exist''. (1982, 1987, 1993. 1996, 1999, 2003, 2006, 2007, 2009, 2010)

18. Write a program that reads ten integers and displays them in the reverse order in which they were read.

19. Write a program that reads a long number, counts and displays the occurrences of each digit in it.

20. Write a program to input 10 integer elements in an array and sort them in descending order using bubble sort technique.

21. Write a program to perform binary search on a list of integers given below, to search for an element input by the user. If it is found display the element along with its position, otherwise display the message "Search element not found".
5, 7, 9, 11, 15, 20, 30, 45, 89, 97

22. The annual examination result of 50 students in a class is tabulated as follows.

```
Roll No.    Subject A    Subject B    Subject C
--------    ---------    ---------    ---------
```

Write a program to read the data, calculate and display the following:

  (i) Average marks obtained by each student

 (ii) Print roll number and average marks of the students whose average mark is above 80

(iii) Print roll number and average marks of the students whose average mark is below 40

23. Declare a double single dimensional array of size 28 to store daily temperatures for the month of February. Using this structure, write a program to find:

(i) The hottest day of the month

(ii) The coldest day of the month

(iii) The average temperature of the month

24. Repeat the above exercise using a double two-dimensional array with 4 rows and 7 columns to store daily temperatures for the month of February.

25. The weekly hours of all employees of ABC Consulting Ltd. are stored in a two-dimensional array. Each row records an employee's 7-day work hours with seven columns. For example, the following array stores the work hours of five employees. Write a program that displays employees and their total hours in decreasing order of the total hours.

Sr.No.	Mon	Tue	Wed	Thu	Fri	Sat	Sun
Employee 0	8	5	1	11	1	0	0
Employee 1	11	6	0	2	2	2	4
Employee 2	4	5	4	10	4	3	1
Employee 3	4	7	3	12	6	2	0
Employee 4	3	8	3	2	4	4	0

26. Write a program that computes the standard deviation of N real numbers. The standard deviation s is computed according to:

$$s = \sqrt{\frac{(x_1 - \bar{x})^2 + (x_2 - \bar{x})^2 + \cdots + (x_N - \bar{x})^2}{N}}$$

The variable $\bar{x}$ is the average of N input values x_1 through x_N. The program first prompts the user for N and then declares an array of size N.

Answers To Objective Questions

Multiple Choice Questions

1. B	3. D	5. B	7. A	9. A
2. B	4. C	6. C	8. C	10. C

Chapter 16

String Handling

16.1 String Handling

A string is a data type used to represent text. It is comprised of a set of characters enclosed within double quotes. The Java platform provides the `String` class to create and process strings. Java uses strings as built-in objects and provides a lot of features that ease the process of string handling.

16.2 Creating Strings

Strings in Java are represented as objects of the `String` class, which is defined in the `java.lang` package. These are created by declaring objects of string type class and initialising them with string constants. In Java, you can create string objects by using:

- The `String` literal (Implicitly)

- The `new` keyword (Explicitly)

16.2.1 Creating Strings Implicitly

Using this technique, the strings are formed by writing a series of characters and enclosing them in double quotes. After doing so, the Java compiler implicitly creates an object of the `String` class and assigns it the value written in double quotes. Syntax:

```
String objectName = "Series of characters that make the string";
```

For example, you can write a statement as:

```
String myCoffee = "Espresso";
```

Each string is stored in the computer memory as a sequence of characters as shown in Figure 16.1. Each character in a string has an index which denotes its position within the string. The first character has an index of 0, the second character has an index of 1, and the third character has an index of 2 and so on. This type of indexing is called *zero-based indexing* because the string indexes start at zero.

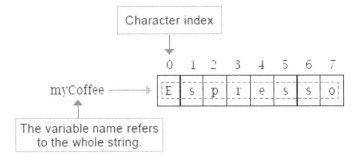

Figure 16.1: String – Memory Allocation

16.2.2 Creating Strings Explicitly

This technique uses the **new** keyword to create a string object. The objects of the **String** class are created in the same manner as you create objects of other classes. There is also a constructor in the **String** class that accepts a string as a parameter and creates a unique string. It has the syntax:

```
String objectName = new String();
```

For example, you can rewrite the earlier statement with the explicit use of the **new** operator as:

```
String myCoffee = new String ("Espresso");
```

This will create a variable named **myCoffee**, storing the address where the value **"Espresso"** is stored in the computer memory as shown in Figure 16.2.

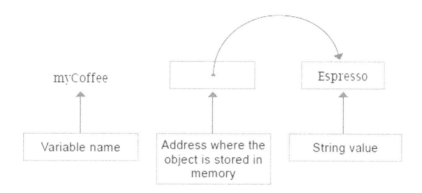

Figure 16.2: Creating a String Instance

Note that the variable **myCoffee** contains the address where the object is stored in memory. An arrow has been used in the above figure to indicate that the content is an address and not the value itself.

The **String** class offers a number of methods to support a range of operations. For example, examining individual characters in a string, comparing and searching strings, extracting substrings from a string, etc. Now, let us learn about these methods.

16.3   trim() method

The **trim()** method of the **String** class removes the leading and trailing spaces from a string. However, it does not remove the spaces present in between the string.
Syntax:

```
stringObject.trim()
```

Listing 16.1: TrimDemo.java

```
1  public class TrimDemo
2  {
3     public static void main(String args[])
4     {
5        String testString = "    String with leading and trailing spaces. ←
          ↪    ";
6
7        System.out.println("Trimmed string is:");
8        System.out.println(testString.trim());
9     }
10 }
```

Output

Trimmed string is:
String with leading and trailing spaces.

Note

Recall that you can access member methods of a class using the syntax `objectName.MethodName()`. As String is a class, its method `trim()` has been accessed in the same way using the object name, i.e., `testString.trim()`.

16.4 toLowerCase() method

The `toLowerCase()` method converts each character in a string to lowercase. However if the string contains any special character, it remains unchanged.

Syntax:

```
stringObject.toLowercase()
```

Listing 16.2: ToLowerCaseDemo.java

```
1  public class ToLowerCaseDemo
2  {
3     public static void main(String args[])
4     {
5        String testString = "Testing The toLowerCase() Method.";
6
7        System.out.println(testString.toLowerCase());
8     }
9  }
```

Output

testing the tolowercase() method.

16.5   toUpperCase() method

The toUpperCase() method converts each character in a string to uppercase. However if the string contains any special character, it remains unchanged.

Syntax:

```
stringObject.toUppercase()
```

Listing 16.3: ToUpperCaseDemo.java

```java
public class ToUpperCaseDemo
{
    public static void main(String args[])
    {
        String testString = "Testing The toUpperCase() Method.";

        System.out.println(testString.toUpperCase());
    }
}
```

Output

TESTING THE TOUPPERCASE() METHOD.

16.6   length() method

The length() method returns the length of a string. The length is equal to the number of characters present in the string including the white spaces.

Syntax:

```
stringObject.length()
```

Listing 16.4: LengthDemo.java

```java
public class LengthDemo
{
    public static void main(String args[])
    {
        String testString = "Arkenstone";
        System.out.println("Length of " + testString + " is " + ↵
            ↪ testString.length());
    }
}
```

Output

Length of Arkenstone is 10

16.7   charAt() method

The `charAt()` method accepts an index number as its argument and returns the character present at that particular index. The index of the string ranges from 0 to `length()` - 1.
Syntax:

```
stringObject.charAt(index)
```

Let us understand this method using the following example, where the testString stores a value `"ARKENSTONE"`. The method call `testString.charAt(5)` will return character 'S' at index 5.

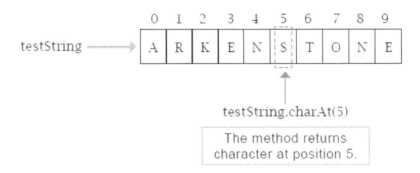

Listing 16.5: CharAtDemo.java

```
1  public class CharAtDemo
2  {
3      public static void main(String args[])
4      {
5          String testString = "ARKENSTONE";
6          System.out.println("testString.charAt(5) is " + ↵
               ↪ testString.charAt(5));
7      }
8  }
```

Output
The character at 5th position is S

16.8   indexOf() method

The `indexOf()` method returns the index (position) of the first occurrence of the specified character in a string. The character is specified as an argument to this method. If the character is present in the string, the method will return the index number; otherwise, it will return -1.
Syntax:

```
stringObject.indexOf(char)
```

Let us understand this method using the following example, where the testString stores a value "ARKENSTONE". The method call testString.indexOf('E') will return 3, i.e., the first occurrence of character 'E' in the testString.

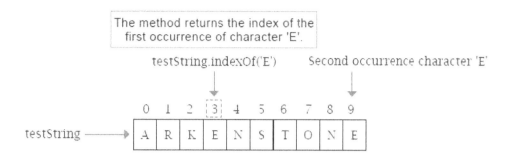

Listing 16.6: IndexOfDemo.java

```
1  public class IndexOfDemo
2  {
3      public static void main(String args[])
4      {
5          String testString = "ARKENSTONE";
6          System.out.println("testString.indexOf('E') is " + ↵
                  testString.indexOf('E'));
7          System.out.println("testString.indexOf('G') is " + ↵
                  testString.indexOf('G'));
8      }
9  }
```

Output

testString.indexOf('E') is 3
testString.indexOf('G') is -1

16.9   lastIndexOf() method()

The lastIndexOf() method returns the index (position) of the last occurrence of the specified character in a string. This means that if a character occurs more than once in the string, the lastIndexOf() method returns the index value of its last occurrence. If the character does not occur in the string, it returns -1.

Syntax:

    stringObject.lastIndexOf(char)

Let us understand this method using the following example, where the testString stores a value "ARKENSTONE". The method call testString.lastIndexOf('E') will return 9, i.e., the last occurrence of character 'E' in the testString.

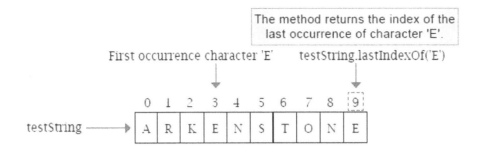

Listing 16.7: LastIndexOfDemo.java

```
1  public class LastIndexOfDemo
2  {
3      public static void main(String args[])
4      {
5          String testString = "ARKENSTONE";
6          System.out.println("testString.lastIndexOf('E') is " + ↵
                ↪ testString.lastIndexOf('E'));
7          System.out.println("testString.lastIndexOf('G') is " + ↵
                ↪ testString.lastIndexOf('G'));
8      }
9  }
```

Output

testString.lastIndexOf('E') is 9
testString.lastIndexOf('G') is -1

16.10   concat() method

The concat() method joins or concatenates two strings.
Syntax:

        string1.concat(string2)

Consider the following example, where **string1** stores a value **"SAVE"** and **string2** stores a value **"WATER"**. The value returned by **string1.concat(string2)** will be **"SAVE WATER"**.

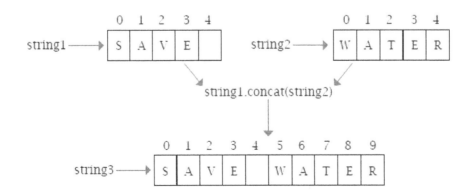

Listing 16.8: ConcatDemo.java

```
1  public class ConcatDemo
2  {
3     public static void main(String args[])
4     {
5        String string1 = "SAVE ";
6        String string2 = "WATER";
7        String string3 = string1.concat(string2);
8        System.out.println("Concatenated string is " + string3);
9     }
10 }
```

Output
Concatenated string is SAVE WATER

Note that you can also use the '+' operator to join two strings. For example, the following statements in the above program will also produce the same result.

```
String string4 = string1 + string2;
System.out.println("Concatenated string is " + string4);
```

16.11   equals() method

The equals() method compares two strings to check whether they are equal or not. The result is a boolean value true if they are equal, otherwise the result is false. For this method, the corresponding uppercase and lowercase characters are different. That means, 'G' and 'g' are not equal.

Syntax:

```
string1.equals(string2)
```

Listing 16.9: EqualsDemo.java

```
1  public class EqualsDemo
2  {
3     public static void main(String args[])
4     {
5        String string1 = "Computer";
6        String string2 = "Computer";
7
8        if (string1.equals(string2))
9            System.out.println("Both strings are equal");
10       else
11           System.out.println("Both strings NOT are equal");
12    }
13 }
```

Output
Both strings are equal

Difference between == and equals() when comparing strings

Let us grasp the concept by understanding the difference between

```
String word1, word2;
-----
if (word1 == word2) ...
```

and

```
if (word1.equals(word2)) ...
```

The equality test (==) is true if the contents of variables `word1` and `word2` are the same. For a primitive data type, the contents are the values themselves. However, for a reference data type, the contents are addresses where the strings are stored. Thus, for a reference data type, the equality test is true if both variables refer to the same address. The result of `equals()` method is `true` if the `String` objects these two variables refer to contain the same string value.

Figure 16.3 is the schematic representation of scenario where `word1` and `word2` refer to the same object. Therefore, the addresses stored in `word1` and `word2` are same. In this case:

```
word1 == word2 will evaluate to true
word1.equals(word2) will evaluate to true
```

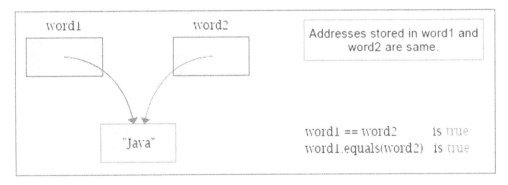

Figure 16.3: Referring to the Same Object

Figure 16.4 is the schematic representation of scenario where `word1` and `word2` refer to different objects with the same value `"Java"`. Therefore, the addresses stored in `word1` and `word2` are different. In this case:

```
word1 == word2 will evaluate to false
word1.equals(word2) will evaluate to true
```

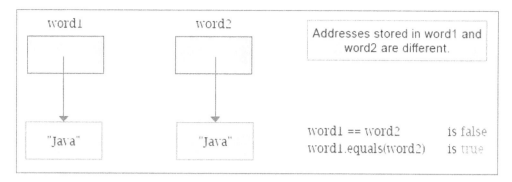

Figure 16.4: Referring to Different Objects with the Same Value

16.12 equalsIgnoreCase() method

The equalsIgnoreCase() method compares two strings to check whether they are equal or not after ignoring their case (uppercase or lowercase). The result is a boolean value **true** if they are equal, otherwise the result is **false**. For this method, the corresponding uppercase and lowercase characters are the same. That means, 'G' and 'g' are equal.

Syntax:

```
string1.equalsIgnoreCase(string2)
```

Listing 16.10: EqualsIgnoreDemo.java

```java
 1  public class EqualsIgnoreDemo
 2  {
 3      public static void main(String args[])
 4      {
 5          String string1 = "computer";
 6          String string2 = "COMPuter";
 7
 8          if (string1.equalsIgnoreCase(string2))
 9              System.out.println("Both strings are equal");
10          else
11              System.out.println("Both strings NOT are equal");
12      }
13  }
```

Output

Both strings are equal

16.13 compareTo() method

The compareTo() method compares two strings. It not only checks the equality of the strings but also checks whether a string is bigger or smaller than the other string.

Syntax:

```
string1.compareTo(string2)
```

The comparison of strings is based on the Unicode value of each character present in the strings. The character sequence represented by **string1** is compared lexicographically[1] to the character sequence represented by **string2** as per the following logic:

- if **string1** > **string2** the result will be a positive integer, i.e., result > 0

- if **string1** < **string2** the result will be a negative integer, i.e., result < 0

- if **string1** = **string2** the result will be 0, i.e., result $= 0$

Let us, first of all, consider an example where two strings differ in the first character, for example, **"CAT"** and **"FOX"** as shown in Figure 16.5.

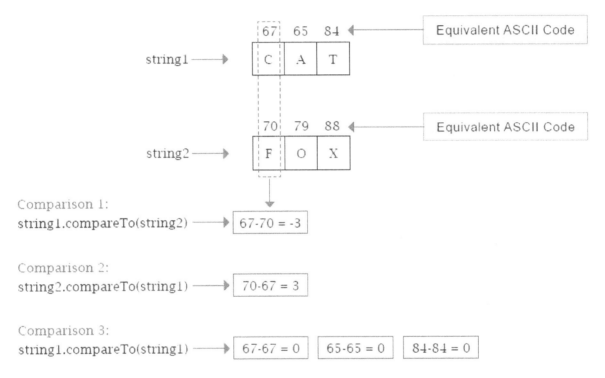

Figure 16.5: Two Strings Differ in the First Character

When the lexicographical comparison is performed, the result is the difference of the equivalent ASCII codes of the corresponding characters where they differ in the first occurrence. The following steps explain the logic behind the comparisons shown in Figure 16.5.

- **Comparison 1**: When you compare **"CAT"** with **"FOX"**, the first occurrence where these two strings differ is 'C' and 'F'. The result is -3 ($= 67$-70) which is the difference of their equivalent ASCII codes.

- **Comparison 2**: When you compare **"FOX"** with **"CAT"**, the first occurrence where these two strings differ is 'F' and 'C'. The result is 3 ($= 70$-67) which is the difference of their equivalent ASCII codes.

---

[1]Lexicographic order is same as the dictionary order, except that all the uppercase letters precede all the lowercase letters. That means, upper case 'A' comes before lowercase 'a'.

- **Comparison 3**: While comparing "CAT" with "CAT", there is no difference because the ASCII codes of the corresponding characters are same. Thus, the result is 0.

Listing 16.11: CompareToDemo1.java

```
1  public class CompareToDemo1
2  {
3      public static void main(String args[])
4      {
5          String string1 = "CAT";
6          String string2 = "FOX";
7
8          System.out.println(string1.compareTo(string2));
9          System.out.println(string2.compareTo(string1));
10         System.out.println(string1.compareTo(string1));
11     }
12 }
```

Output
-3
3
0

Let us now consider an example where two strings have the same first character but a different second character. For example, "CAT" and "COT" as shown in Figure 16.6.

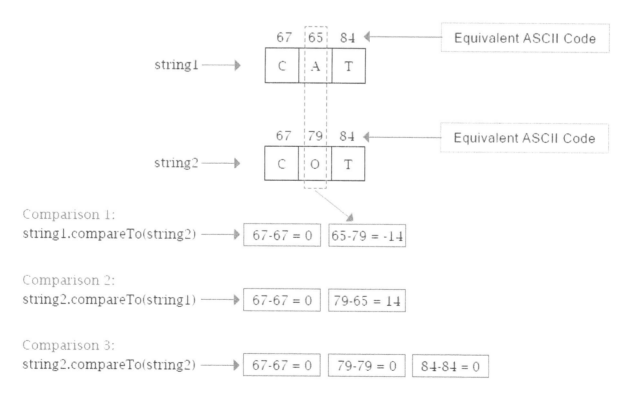

Figure 16.6: Two Strings Differ in the Second Character

The following steps explain the logic behind the comparisons shown in Figure 16.6.

- **Comparison 1**: When you compare "CAT" with "COT", the first occurrence where these two strings differ is 'A' and 'O'. The result is -14 (= 65-79) which is the difference of their equivalent ASCII codes.

- **Comparison 2**: When you compare "COT" with "CAT", the first occurrence where these two strings differ is 'O' and 'A'. The result is 14 (= 79-65) which is the difference of their equivalent ASCII codes.

- **Comparison 3**: While comparing "COT" with "COT", there is no difference because the ASCII codes of the corresponding characters are same. Thus, the result is 0.

Listing 16.12: CompareToDemo2.java

```
1  public class CompareToDemo2
2  {
3      public static void main(String args[])
4      {
5          String string1 = "CAT";
6          String string2 = "COT";
7
8          System.out.println(string1.compareTo(string2));
9          System.out.println(string2.compareTo(string1));
10         System.out.println(string1.compareTo(string1));
11     }
12 }
```

Output
```
-14
14
0
```

16.14 compareToIgnore() method

The `compareToIgnore()` method compares two strings lexicographically, ignoring case differences in the strings.

Syntax:

```
string1.compareToIgnoreCase(string2)
```

Ignoring case differences, the character sequence represented by **string1** is compared lexicographically to the character sequence represented by **string2** as per the following logic:

- if **string1** > **string2** the result will be a positive integer, i.e., result > 0

- if **string1** < **string2** the result will be a negative integer, i.e., result < 0

- if **string1** = **string2** the result will be 0, i.e., result = 0

Listing 16.13: CompareToIgnoreDemo.java

```
1  public class CompareToIgnoreDemo
```

```
 2  {
 3      public static void main(String args[])
 4      {
 5          String string1 = "SCHOOL";
 6          String string2 = "school";
 7
 8          System.out.println(string1.compareToIgnoreCase(string2));
 9      }
10  }
```

Output

```
0
```

16.15 replace() method

The `replace()` method replaces all occurrences of a character in a string with another character.
Syntax:

```
stringObject.replace(oldChar, newChar);
```

Listing 16.14: ReplaceDemo.java

```
1  public class ReplaceDemo
2  {
3      public static void main(String args[])
4      {
5          String string1 = "Jack and Jill went up the hill.";
6
7          System.out.println(string1.replace('J', 'Z'));
8      }
9  }
```

Output

```
Zack and Zill went up the hill.
```

16.16 substring() method

The `substring()` method returns a new string that is a substring of the given string.
Syntax:

```
stringObject.substring(startIndex)
```

The substring begins with the character at the specified `startIndex` and extends to the end of the string. Consider the following example where `string1` stores a value `"BLUE MOON"`. The value of `string1.substring(5)` will be `"MOON"` with a `startIndex` of 5 that extends to the end of `string1`.

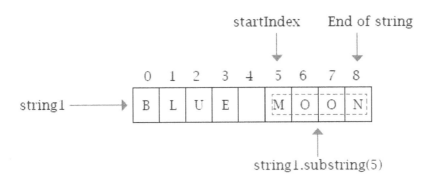

Figure 16.7: Substring of a String

Listing 16.15: SubstringDemo.java

```
1  public class SubstringDemo
2  {
3     public static void main(String args[])
4     {
5        String string1 = "BLUE MOON";
6
7        System.out.println(string1.substring(5));
8     }
9  }
```

Output
MOON

There is another variant of the substring() method that returns a new string which is a substring of the given string. However, the substring begins at the specified startIndex and extends to the character at index endIndex - 1 as per the following syntax:

```
stringObject.substring(int startIndex, int endIndex);
```

Consider the following example where string1 stores a value "RISE AND SHINE". The value of string1.substring (5, 8) will be "AND" with a startIndex of 5 that extends to endIndex-1, i.e., 7 (= 8-1) of string1.

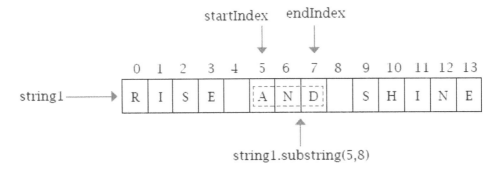

Figure 16.8: Substring with a Start and End Index

Listing 16.16: SubstringDemo2.java

```
1  public class SubstringDemo2
2  {
3     public static void main(String args[])
4     {
5        String string1 = "RISE AND SHINE";
6
7        System.out.println(string1.substring(5, 8));
8     }
9  }
```

Output

AND

16.17   startsWith() method

The `startsWith()` method checks whether a string starts with a particular string. The method returns `true` if the given string starts with the specified prefix, otherwise it returns `false`.
Syntax:

```
stringObject.startsWith(prefixStr)
```

Listing 16.17: StartsWithDemo.java

```
1   public class StartsWithDemo
2   {
3      public static void main(String args[])
4      {
5         String string1 = "One World";
6         String string2 = "One";
7
8         System.out.println(string1.startsWith(string2));
9      }
10  }
```

Output

true

16.18   endsWith() method

The `endsWith()` method checks whether a string ends with a particular string. The method returns `true` if the given string ends with the specified suffix, otherwise it returns `false`.
Syntax:

```
stringObject.endsWith(suffixStr)
```

Listing 16.18: EndsWithDemo.java

```
1  public class EndsWithDemo
2  {
3    public static void main(String args[])
4    {
5      String string1 = "One World";
6      String string2 = "World";
7      System.out.println(string1.endsWith(string2));
8    }
9  }
```

Output

true

16.19 valueOf() method

The valueOf() method returns the string representation of the argument.
Syntax:

```
String.valueOf(data)
```

There are a number of variants of this method as shown below:

1. public static String valueOf(boolean b)

2. public static String valueOf(char c)

3. public static String valueOf(int i)

4. public static String valueOf(long l)

5. public static String valueOf(float f)

6. public static String valueOf(double d)

7. public static String valueOf(char[] data)

8. public static String valueOf(char[] data, int offset, int count)

For example, when invoked with character 'Z' the valueOf() method returns a string value "Z".
When invoked with integer value 1234, the valueOf() method returns a string value "1234".

For variant 8, the offset argument is the index of the first character of the subarray. The count
argument specifies the length of the subarray. For example, if the char array is defined as

```
char[] myCharArray = {'S', 'U', 'N', 'D', 'A', 'Y'};
```

The subarray with offset = 3 and count = 3 will be 'D', 'A', 'Y' as shown in Figure 16.9.

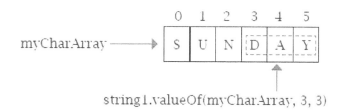

string1.valueOf(myCharArray, 3, 3)

Figure 16.9: Method valueOf() with offset and count

Listing 16.19: ValueOfDemo.java

```java
public class ValueOfDemo
{
    public static void main(String args[])
    {
        boolean myBoolean = true;
        char myChar = 'Z';
        int myInt = 1234;
        long myLong = 987654321;
        float myFloat = 343.55f;
        double myDouble = 34333.566665;
        char[] myCharArray = {'S', 'U', 'N', 'D', 'A', 'Y'};

        //String representation of the boolean argument.
        System.out.println(String.valueOf(myBoolean));

        //String representation of the char argument.
        System.out.println(String.valueOf(myChar));

        //String representation of the int argument.
        System.out.println(String.valueOf(myInt));

        //String representation of the long argument.
        System.out.println(String.valueOf(myLong));

        //String representation of the float argument.
        System.out.println(String.valueOf(myFloat));

        //String representation of the double argument.
        System.out.println(String.valueOf(myDouble));

        //String representation of the char array argument.
        System.out.println(String.valueOf(myCharArray));

        //String representation of the char array argument from an offset.
        System.out.println(String.valueOf(myCharArray, 3, 3));
    }
}
```

```
Output
true
Z
1234
987654321
343.55
34333.566665
SUNDAY
DAY
```

16.20 String Array

You have learnt in the previous sections that you can define and initialise a string using the String class. You can access any character of the string using the charAt() method as shown in Figure 15.10. In this illustration, a String named colour has been defined with a value "RED". The chartAt(1) method will give you the value 'E' at index1.

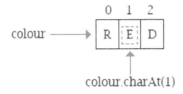

Figure 16.10: A String

Program 15.20 shows its code implementation.

Listing 16.20: StringDemo.java

```
1  public class StringDemo
2  {
3      public static void main(String args[])
4      {
5          String colour = "RED";
6
7          System.out.println("colour.charAt(1): " + colour.charAt(1));
8      }
9  }
```

Output

colour.charAt(1): E

Similar to defining a String, you can also define an array of strings called a String Array that can store multiple strings as shown in Figure 15.11. In this illustration:

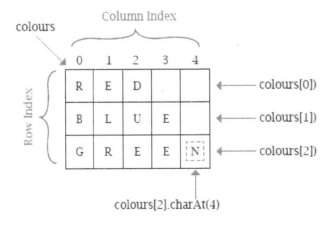

Figure 16.11: String Array

- A String Array named colours has been defined with values "RED", "BLUE", and "GREEN".

- Individual elements of the String Array can be accessed using the row index. For example, colours[2] will give you the value "GREEN" at row index2.

- You can access individual characters of element colours[2] using the chartAt() method. For example, colours[2].chartAt(4) method will give you the value 'N' at column index 4.

Program 16.21 shows its code implementation.

Listing 16.21: StringArray.java

```
1  public class StringArray
2  {
3      public static void main(String args[])
4      {
5          String colours[] = {"RED", "BLUE", "GREEN"};
6
7          System.out.println("colours[0]: " + colours[0]);
8          System.out.println("colours[1]: " + colours[1]);
9          System.out.println("colours[2]: " + colours[2]);
10
11         System.out.println("colours[0].charAt(1): " + ↵
                ↪ colours[0].charAt(1));
12         System.out.println("colours[1].charAt(2): " + ↵
                ↪ colours[1].charAt(2));
13         System.out.println("colours[2].charAt(4): " + ↵
                ↪ colours[2].charAt(4));
14     }
15 }
```

```
Output
colours[0]: RED
colours[1]: BLUE
colours[2]: GREEN
colours[0].charAt(1): E
colours[1].charAt(2): U
colours[2].charAt(4): N
```

Solved Programming Exercises

Write a program to display the given pattern for a string input.
Sample Input: SCHOOL
Sample Output:
S
SC
SCH
SCHO
SCHOO
SCHOOL

Listing 16.22: Pattern2.java

```
1  import java.util.*;
2
3  public class Pattern2
4  {
5      public static void main(String args[])
6      {
7          Scanner scan = new Scanner(System.in);
8          int length;
9
10         System.out.println("Enter a word:");
11         String word = scan.next();
12
13         length = word.length();
14
15         for (int i = 1; i <= length; i++)
16             System.out.println(word.substring(0,i));
17
18         scan.close();
19     }
20 }
```

```
Output
Enter a word:
SCHOOL
S
SC
SCH
SCHO
SCHOO
SCHOOL
```

Code Walkthrough:
◇ Line 15: Stores the length of the word in the length variable.
◇ Line 15: Loops through the number of characters in the word.
◇ Line 15: Displays the substring from the 0th position until the ith position.

> Write a program to display the given pattern for a string input.
> Sample Input: SCHOOL
> Sample Output:
> SCHOOL
>   SCHOO
>   SCHO
>   SCH
>   SC
>   S

Listing 16.23: Pattern3.java

```
1  import java.util.*;
2
3  public class Pattern3
4  {
```

```
5       public static void main(String args[])
6       {
7           Scanner scan = new Scanner(System.in);
8           int length;
9
10          System.out.print("Enter a word:");
11          String word = scan.next();
12
13          length = word.length();
14
15          for (int i = 0; i <= length; i++)
16          {
17              for (int j = 0; j < i; j++)
18              {
19                  System.out.print(" ");
20              }
21              System.out.println(word.substring(0,length-i));
22          }
23
24          scan.close();
25      }
26  }
```

```
Output
Enter a word:
SCHOOL
 SCHOO
  SCHO
   SCH
    SC
     S
```

Code Walkthrough:
◈ Lines 17 - 20: Display spaces until the value of the loop control variable i.
◈ Line 21: Displays the substring from the 0th position until the $(length - i)^{th}$ position.

Write a program to accept a string and display the number of vowels in it.

Listing 16.24: Vowels.java

```
1   import java.util.*;
2
3   public class Vowels
4   {
5       public static void main(String args[])
6       {
7           Scanner scan = new Scanner(System.in);
8           int length;
9           int vowels = 0;
10          char tmpChar;
11
12          System.out.println("Enter a word:");
13          String sentence = scan.nextLine();
14
```

```
15        length = sentence.length();
16
17        for (int i = 0; i < length; i++)
18        {
19            tmpChar = sentence.charAt(i);
20            if (tmpChar == 'a' || tmpChar == 'e' || tmpChar == 'i' ||
21                tmpChar == 'o' || tmpChar == 'u' || tmpChar == 'A' ||
22                tmpChar == 'E' || tmpChar == 'I' || tmpChar == 'O' ||
23                tmpChar == 'U' )
24                    vowels++;
25        }
26
27        System.out.println("Number of vowels are: " + vowels);
28        scan.close();
29    }
30 }
```

Output
Enter a word:
Amazing
Number of vowels are: 3

Write a program to accept a string and change the case of each letter of the string. Display the new string.
Sample Input: WelComE TO School
Sample Output: wELcOMe to sCHOOL

Listing 16.25: ChangeCase.java

```
1  import java.util.*;
2
3  public class ChangeCase
4  {
5      public static void main(String args[])
6      {
7          Scanner scan = new Scanner(System.in);
8          int length;
9          char tmpChar;
10         String newString  = "";
11
12         System.out.println("Enter a word:");
13         String string = scan.nextLine();
14
15         length = string.length();
16
17         for (int i = 0; i < length; i++)
18         {
19             tmpChar = string.charAt(i);
```

```
20            if (tmpChar >= 'a' && tmpChar <= 'z' )
21                newString = newString + Character.toUpperCase(tmpChar);
22            else if (tmpChar >= 'A' && tmpChar <= 'Z' )
23                newString = newString + Character.toLowerCase(tmpChar);
24            else
25                newString = newString + tmpChar;
26        }
27
28        System.out.println("New string after conversion is: ");
29        System.out.println(newString);
30        scan.close();
31    }
32 }
```

```
Output
Enter a string:
WelComE TO School
New string after conversion is:
wELcOMe to sCHOOL
```

Write a program to accept a string and display:

(i) The number of lower case characters

(ii) The number of upper case characters

(iii) The number of special characters

(iv) The number of digits present in the string

Listing 16.26: Counts.java

```
1  import java.util.*;
2
3  public class Counts
4  {
5      public static void main(String args[])
6      {
7          Scanner scan = new Scanner(System.in);
8          int length, ucase = 0, lcase = 0, special = 0, digits = 0;
9          char tmpChar;
10
11         System.out.println("Enter a word:");
12         String string = scan.nextLine();
13
14         length = string.length();
15
16         for (int i = 0; i < length; i++)
17         {
18             tmpChar = string.charAt(i);
19             if (tmpChar >= 'a' && tmpChar <= 'z' )
```

```
20                    lcase++;
21               else if (tmpChar >= 'A' && tmpChar <= 'Z' )
22                    ucase++;
23               else if (tmpChar >= '0' && tmpChar <= '9' )
24                    digits++;
25               else
26                    special++;
27          }
28
29          System.out.println("The number of lower case characters: " + ↵
               ↪ lcase);
30          System.out.println("The number of upper case characters: " + ↵
               ↪ ucase);
31          System.out.println("The number of special characters: " + special);
32          System.out.println("The number of digits: " + digits);
33
34          scan.close();
35     }
36 }
```

```
Output
Enter a string:
Victoria No. 203
The number of lower case characters: 8
The number of upper case characters: 2
The number of special characters: 3
The number of digits: 3
```

Code Walkthrough:

◈ Lines 19 - 20: If the `tmpChar` is in lowercase, increments the `lcase` accumulator.

◈ Lines 21 - 22: If the `tmpChar` is in uppercase, increments the `ucase` accumulator.

◈ Lines 23 - 24: If the `tmpChar` is a digit, increments the `digits` accumulator.

◈ Lines 25 - 26: Otherwise, increments the `special` accumulator.

Write a program that reads a string and a word separately. The program then finds the frequency of the word in the string.
Sample Input: The quick brown fox jumps over the lazy dog.
Sample Output: Frequency of the is: 2

Listing 16.27: WordCount.java

```
1  import java.util.*;
2
3  public class WordCount
4  {
5     public static void main(String args[])
6     {
7        Scanner scan = new Scanner(System.in);
8        int length, count = 0;
9        char tmpChar;
```

```
10        String tmpWord = "";
11
12        System.out.println("Enter a string:");
13        String searchString = scan.nextLine();
14
15        searchString = searchString.trim() + " ";
16
17        length = searchString.length();
18
19        System.out.println("Enter the word to search for:");
20        String searchWord = scan.next();
21
22        for (int i = 0; i < length; i++)
23        {
24            tmpChar = searchString.charAt(i);
25
26            if (tmpChar == ' ')
27            {
28                if (tmpWord.compareToIgnoreCase(searchWord) == 0)
29                {
30                    count++;
31                }
32
33                tmpWord = "";
34            }
35            else
36                tmpWord = tmpWord + tmpChar;
37        }
38
39        System.out.println("Frequency of " + searchWord + " is: " + count);
40        scan.close();
41    }
42 }
```

Output

```
Enter a string:
The quick brown fox jumps over the lazy dog.
Enter the word to search for:
the
Frequency of the is: 2
```

Code Walkthrough:

◈ Line 15: Removes any leading and trailing spaces and adds an extra trailing space.

◈ Line 26: Checks if it is a complete word.

◈ Lines 28 - 31: Check if the tmpWord and the searchWord are the same. If they are, increment the count variable.

◈ Line 33: Resets the tmpWord.

◈ Line 36: Appends the tmpChar to the tmpWord.

Write a program to accept a word and check if it is a Palindrome or not.
(Hint: A Palindrome is a word which reads the same backward as forward)
Sample Input: Radar
Sample Output: Radar is Palindrome

Listing 16.28: PalindromeString.java

```java
import java.util.*;
public class PalindromeString
{
    public static void main(String args[])
    {
        Scanner scan = new Scanner(System.in);
        int length;
        String reverseString = "";
        System.out.println("Enter a string:");
        String inputString = scan.nextLine();

        length = inputString.length();

        for (int i = length-1; i >= 0; i--)
        {
            reverseString = reverseString + inputString.charAt(i);
        }

        if (reverseString.equalsIgnoreCase(inputString))
            System.out.println(inputString + " is Palindrome");
        else
            System.out.println(inputString + " is not Palindrome");

        scan.close();
    }
}
```

Output

```
Enter a word:
Radar
Radar is Palindrome
```

Code Walkthrough:

◈ Line 14: Loops through the string in the reverse order, i.e., from `length-1` until 0.

Write a program that encodes a word in PigLatin. To translate a word into PigLatin word, convert the word into uppercase and then place the first vowel of the original word as a start of the new word along with the remaining alphabets. The alphabets present before the vowel being shifted towards the end followed by "AY".
Sample Input: London Sample Output: ONDONLAY
Sample Input: Olympics Sample Output: OLYMPICSAY

Listing 16.29: PigLatinWord.java

```java
import java.util.*;

public class PigLatinWord
{
    public static void main(String args[])
    {
        Scanner scan = new Scanner(System.in);
        int length;
        String pigLatinWord = "", preVowelWord = "", postVowelWord = "";
        char tmpChar;
        int posVowel = -1;

        System.out.println("Enter a string:");
        String inputString = scan.nextLine();

        inputString = inputString.toUpperCase();

        length = inputString.length();

        for (int i = 0; i < length; i++)
        {
            tmpChar = inputString.charAt(i);

            if (tmpChar=='A' || tmpChar=='E' || tmpChar=='I' || ↵
              ↪ tmpChar=='O' || tmpChar=='U')
            {
                posVowel = i;
                System.out.println("Position: " + posVowel);
                break;
            }
        }

        if (posVowel >= 0)
        {
            preVowelWord = inputString.substring(0, posVowel);
            postVowelWord = inputString.substring(posVowel);
            pigLatinWord = postVowelWord + preVowelWord + "AY";
            System.out.println("PigLatin of " + inputString + " is " + ↵
              ↪ pigLatinWord);
        }
        else
        {
            System.out.println("No vowels found");
        }
```

```
44          scan.close();
45      }
46  }
```

Code Walkthrough:

◈ Line 11: Sets the initial value of the position of vowel to -1.

◈ Line 16: Converts the input string to uppercase.

◈ Line 20: Loops through the length of the input string.

◈ Line 26: Stores the position of the first vowel.

◈ Line 28: Breaks out of the loop because the position of the first vowel has been found.

◈ Line 32: Checks if the position of vowel is greater than or equal to 0.

Output
Enter a string:
London
Position: 1
PigLatin of LONDON is ONDONLAY

Output
Enter a string:
Olympics
Position: 0
PigLatin of OLYMPICS is OLYMPICSAY

Write a program that accepts a word and checks if it Is Palindrome or just a Special word.
Hint: A Palindrome is a word which reads the same backward as forward. For example, MADAM, MALAYALAM, CIVIC, etc.
Special words are those which start and end with the same character. For example, COMIC, WINDOW, etc.

Listing 16.30: PalindromeSpecial.java

```java
1  import java.util.*;
2  public class PalindromeSpecial
3  {
4      public static void main(String args[])
5      {
6          Scanner scan = new Scanner(System.in);
7          int length;
8          String reverseString = "";
9
10         System.out.println("Enter a string:");
11         String inputString = scan.nextLine();
12
13         length = inputString.length();
14
15         for (int i = length-1; i >= 0; i--)
16         {
17             reverseString = reverseString + inputString.charAt(i);
18         }
```

```
19
20        if (reverseString.equalsIgnoreCase(inputString))
21            System.out.println(inputString + " is a Palindrome word");
22        else if (inputString.charAt(0) == inputString.charAt(length-1))
23            System.out.println(inputString + " is a Special word");
24        else
25            System.out.println(inputString + " is neither a Palindrome ←
                  ↪ nor a Special word");
26
27        scan.close();
28    }
29 }
```

Code Walkthrough:

◈ Line 22: Checks if the character at 0th position is the same as the character at the $(length-1)^{th}$ positon for it to start and end with the same character to be a special word.

Output
Enter a string:
WINDOW
WINDOW is a Special word

Output
Enter a string:
MALAYALAM
MALAYALAM is a Palindrome word

Write a program to accept a word and convert into lowercase if it is in uppercase, and display the new word by replacing only the vowels with the character following it.
Sample Input: computer
Sample Output: cpmpvtfr

Listing 16.31: ReplaceVowels.java

```
1  import java.util.*;
2  public class ReplaceVowels
3  {
4      public static void main(String args[])
5      {
6          Scanner scan = new Scanner(System.in);
7          int length;
8          String newWord = "";
9          char tmpChar;
10
11         System.out.println("Enter a string:");
12         String inputString = scan.nextLine();
13
14         length = inputString.length();
15
16         for (int i = 0; i < length; i++)
```

```
17          {
18              tmpChar = inputString.charAt(i);
19
20              if (Character.isUpperCase(tmpChar))
21                  tmpChar = Character.toLowerCase(tmpChar);
22
23              if (tmpChar=='a' || tmpChar=='e' || tmpChar=='i' || ↵
                  ↪ tmpChar=='o' || tmpChar=='u')
24                  tmpChar++;
25
26              newWord = newWord + tmpChar;
27          }
28
29          System.out.println("Encoded word is: " + newWord);
30          scan.close();
31      }
32 }
```

Output

Enter a word:
computer
Encoded word is: cpmpvtfr

Code Walkthrough:
Lines 20 - 21: Convert the character to lowercase only if it is in uppercase.

Write a program to assign a full path and file name as given below. Using library functions, extract and output the file path, file name and file extension separately as shown.
Sample Input: C:\Users\admin\Pictures\flower.jpg
Sample Output:
Path: C:\Users\admin\Pictures\
File Name: flower
File Extension: jpg

Listing 16.32: PathFileName.java

```
1  import java.util.*;
2  public class PathFileName
3  {
4      public static void main(String args[])
5      {
6          Scanner scan = new Scanner(System.in);
7          String filePath, fileName, fileExtn;
8          int posLastSlash, posDot;
9
10         System.out.println("Enter a string:");
11         String inputString = scan.nextLine();
12
13         posLastSlash = inputString.lastIndexOf('\\');
```

```
14        posDot = inputString.lastIndexOf('.');
15
16        filePath = inputString.substring(0, posLastSlash+1);
17        fileName = inputString.substring(posLastSlash+1, posDot);
18        fileExtn = inputString.substring(posDot+1);
19
20        System.out.println("Path: " + filePath);
21        System.out.println("File Name: " + fileName);
22        System.out.println("File Extension: " + fileExtn);
23
24        scan.close();
25    }
26 }
```

```
Output
Enter a string:
C:\Users\admin\Pictures\flower.jpg
Path: C:\Users\admin\Pictures\
File Name: flower
File Extension: jpg
```

Code Walkthrough:
◈ Line 13: Finds position of the last \ in the input string using escape sequence.
◈ Line 14: Finds position of the last dot (.) in the input string.

> Write a program to assign 5 names to an array of strings. Count and print number of lowercase letters in each name.

Listing 16.33: CountLowerLetters.java

```java
1  public class CountLowerLetters
2  {
3      public static void main(String args[])
4      {
5          String list[] = {"IndIA", "AMERica", "fRANce", "Canada", ↵
                ↪ "GerMANY"};
6          char tmpChar;
7          int length, count = 0;
8
9          System.out.println("Name \t\t Lower case count");
10         System.out.println("**** \t\t *****************");
11
12         for (int i = 0; i < 5; i++)
13         {
14             length = list[i].length();
15
16             for (int j = 0; j < length; j++)
17             {
18                 tmpChar = list[i].charAt(j);
19                 if (tmpChar >= 'a' && tmpChar <= 'z')
20                     count++;
```

```
21              }
22
23              System.out.println(list[i] + "\t\t\t" + count);
24              count = 0;  //reset counter
25          }
26      }
27 }
```

Output	
Name	Lower case count
*****	**************
IndIA	2
AMERica	3
fRANce	3
Canada	5
GerMANY	2

Code Walkthrough:

◈ Line 14: Stores the length of the ith array in the **length** variable.

◈ Line 18: Stores the character at the jth position of the **list[i]** into the **tmpChar**.

Write a program to initialise the seven wonders of the world along with their locations in two different arrays. Search for a name of the country input by the user. If found, display the name of the country along with its wonder, otherwise display "Sorry Not Found!".

Seven Wonders: CHICHEN ITZA, CHRIST THE REMEMBER, TAJMAHAL, GREAT WALL OF CHINA, MACHU PICCHU, PETRA COLOSSEUM
Locations: MEXICO, BRAZIL, INDIA, CHINA, PERU, JORDAN, ITALY
Examples: Country Name: INDIA Output: INDIA TAJMAHAL
Country Name: USA Output: Sorry Not Found!

Listing 16.34: Wonders.java

```
1  import java.util.*;
2  public class Wonders
3  {
4      public static void main(String args[])
5      {
6          String wonders[] = {"CHICHEN ITZA", "CHRIST THE ↵
                ↪ REMEMBER","TAJMAHAL",
7              "GREAT WALL OF CHINA", "MACHU PICCHU", "PETRA COLOSSEUM"};
8
9          String country[] = {"MAXICO", "BRAZIL", "INDIA", "CHINA", "PERU",
10             "JORDAN", "ITLAY"};
11
12         boolean found = false;
13         Scanner scan = new Scanner(System.in);
14         int length;
15
16         System.out.println("Enter a word:");
```

```
17        String searchCountry = scan.next();
18
19        length = searchCountry.length();
20
21        for (int i = 0; i < 7; i++)
22        {
23            if (searchCountry.equals(country[i]))
24            {
25                System.out.println(country[i] + "   " + wonders[i]);
26                found = true;
27                break;
28            }
29
30        }
31
32        if (!found)
33            System.out.println("Sorry Not Found!");
34
35        scan.close();
36    }
37 }
```

```
Output
Enter a name of the country:
INDIA
INDIA TAJMAHAL
```

Code Walkthrough:

◈ Line 23: Checks if the **searchCountry** equals any value in the country array.

◈ Line 26: Sets the **found** flag to true.

◈ Line 33: If the **searchCountry** is not found, displays an appropriate message.

> Write a program to assign 10 country names to an array of strings. Sort them in ascending order using Bubble Sort technique.

Listing 16.35: BubbleSort.java

```
1  public class BubbleSort
2  {
3      public static void main(String args[])
4      {
5          String list[] = {"India", "Canada", "Brazil", "America", "Peru",
6              "Zimbabwe", "South Africa", "Italy", "France", "Germany"};
7
8          int len;
9          String tmpStr = "";
10
11         len = list.length;
12
13         for (int i = 0; i < len-1; i++)
```

```
14        {
15            for (int j = 0; j < len-i-1; j++)
16            {
17                if (list[j].compareTo(list[j+1]) > 0)
18                {
19                    tmpStr = list[j];
20                    list[j] = list[j+1];
21                    list[j+1] = tmpStr;
22                }
23            }
24        }
25
26        System.out.println("Sorted list is:");
27
28        for (int i = 0; i < len; i++)
29            System.out.println(list[i]);
30    }
31 }
```

Output
Sorted list is:
America
Brazil
Canada
France
Germany
India
Italy
Peru
South Africa
Zimbabwe

Code Walkthrough:

◈ Line 17: Compares the two adjacent elements, i.e., element at j^{th} position and that at $(j+1)^{th}$ position.

◈ Line 19: Stores the value of the current element in a temporary variable.

◈ Line 20: Stores the value of the next element of the array in the current element.

◈ Line 21: Stores the value of the temporary variable in the next element.

Define a class `ElectricBill` with the following specifications:

Instance Variables/Data Member:

`String n` – to store the name of the customer

`int units` – to store the number of units consumed

`double bill` – to store the amount to be paid

Member Methods:

`void accept()` – to accept the name of the customer and number of units consumed

`void calculate()` – to calculate the bill as per the following tariff :

Number of units	Rate per unit
First 100 units	Rs.2.00
Next 200 units	Rs.3.00
Above 300 units	Rs.5.00

A surcharge of 2.5% charged if the number of units consumed is above 300 units.

`void print()` – to print the details as follows:

Name of the customer

Number of units consumed

Bill amount

Write a main method to create an object of the class and call the above member methods.

Listing 16.36: ElectricBill.java

```java
1  import java.util.Scanner;
2
3  public class ElectricBill
4  {
5     private String n;
6     private int units;
7     private double bill;
8
9     public void accept()
10    {
11       Scanner keyboard = new Scanner(System.in);
12
13       System.out.print("Enter Name: ");
14       n = keyboard.nextLine();
15
16       System.out.print("Enter Units: ");
17       units = keyboard.nextInt();
18
19       keyboard.close();
20    }
21
22    public void calculate()
23    {
24       double surcharge;
25
26       if (units <= 100)
27          bill = units * 2;
28       else if (units <= 300)
29          bill = 100 * 2 + (units - 100) * 3;
30       else
31       {
32          bill = 100 * 2 + 200 * 3 + (units - 300) * 5;
33          surcharge = bill * 2.5 / 100;
34          bill = bill + surcharge;
35       }
36    }
37
38    public void print()
39    {
40       System.out.println("Name of the customer: " + n);
41       System.out.println("Number of units consumed: " + units);
42       System.out.println("Bill amount: " + bill);
43    }
44
45    public static void main(String[] args)
```

```
46    {
47        ElectricBill electricBill = new ElectricBill();
48        electricBill.accept();
49        electricBill.calculate();
50        electricBill.print();
51    }
52 }
```

```
Output
Enter Name: Anil Verma
Enter Units: 250
Name of the customer: Anil Verma
Number of units consumed: 250
Bill amount: 650.0
```

Multiple Choice Questions

1. The **trim()** method of the **String** class removes ....

    A. leading spaces only   C. spaces in between words

    B. trailing spaces only   D. leading and trailing spaces

2. While using the **toLowerCase()** method on a string containing special characters, ...

    A. the special characters remain unaffected.

    B. the special characters are converted to spaces.

    C. the special characters are converted to null character.

    D. the special characters are removed from the string.

3. The index of a string ....

    A. ranges from 0 to the **length-1** of the string

    B. ranges from 0 to the **length** of the string

    C. ranges from 1 to the **length** of the string

    D. ranges from 1 to the **length-1** of the string

4. The **indexOf()** method returns the position of the ....

    A. first occurrence of the specified character

    B. last occurrence of the specified character

    C. **null** character

    D. '\n'

5. The return type of the **equals()** method is ....

    A. **int**   B. **char**   C. **boolean**   D. **void**

6. Which one of the given statements is **true** for the following statement?

string1.compareTo(string2)

    A. if string1 > string2 the result will be a negative integer i.e. < 0.

    B. if string1 > string2 the result will be a positive integer i.e. > 0.

    C. if string1 > string2 the result will be 0.

    D. None of the above

7. Which one of the given statements is **true** for the following statement?

string1.compareTo(string2)

    A. if string1 > string2 the result will be a positive integer i.e. > 0.

    B. if string1 < string2 the result will be a negative integer i.e. < 0.

    C. if string1 = string2 the result will be 0 i.e. $= 0$.

    D. All of the above

8. The valueOf() method returns the ....

    A. String representation of the argument

    B. int representation of the argument

    C. boolean representation of the argument

    D. character representation of the argument

9. Output of the following statement is ....

```
System.out.println("SUNDAY".substring(3));
```

    A. NDA   B. DAY   C. SUN   D. N

10. Output of the following statement is ....

```
System.out.println("WONDERFUL".substring(3,4));
```

    A. DERF   B. NDER   C. D   D. N

Assignment Questions

1. How do you create strings implicitly and explicitly?

2. Mention the purpose of the following methods along with the syntax:

(i) trim()	(v) lastIndexOf()	(ix) substring()
(ii) length()	(vi) equals()	(x) valueOf()
(iii) charAt()	(vii) compareTo()	
(iv) indexOf()	(viii) compareToIgnore()	

---

3. Differentiate between the following:

(i) `equals()` and `compareTo()`   (iv) `indexOf()` and `lastIndexOf()`

(ii) `equals()` and `==`

(iii) `startsWith()` and `endsWith()`   (v) `compareTo()` and `compareToIgnore()`

4. Write a program to input a sentence and print each word of the string along with its length in tabular form.

5. Write a program to input a sentence and arrange each word of the string in alphabetical order.

6. Write a program to input a sentence and arrange words of the string in order of their lengths from shortest to longest.

7. Write a program to input a string and print each word of the string in the reverse order.
Sample Input: Enter a string: `My name is Raman`
Sample Output: The longest word: `yM eman si namaR`

8. Write a program in Java to accept a string and display the number of uppercase, number of lowercase, number of special characters and number of digits present in the string.

9. Write a program to enter a sentence from the keyboard and count the number of times a particular word occurs in it. Display the frequency of the search word.
Sample Input:
Enter a sentence: `The quick brown fox jumps over the lazy dog.`
Enter a word to search: `the`
Sample Output:
`Search word occurs 2 times`

10. Write a program to accept a string. Convert the string to uppercase. Count and output the number of double letter sequences that exist in the string.
Sample Input: `"SHE WAS FEEDING THE LITTLE RABBIT WITH AN APPLE"`
Sample Output: `4`

11. Write a program to input twenty names in an array. Arrange these names in descending order of alphabets, using the bubble sort technique.

12. Write a program to accept the names of 10 cities in a single dimensional string array and their STD (Subscribers Trunk Dialling) codes in another single dimensional integer array. Search for a name of a city input by the user in the list. If found, display "Search Successful" and print the name of the city along with its STD code, or else display the message "Search Unsuccessful, No such city in the list".

13. Write a program to input forty words in an array. Arrange these words in descending order of alphabets, using selection sort technique. Print the sorted array.

14. Define a class named `movieMagic` with the following description:
    Instance Variables/Data Members:
    `int year` – to store the year of release of a movie
    `String title` – to store the title of the movie.
    `float rating` – to store the popularity rating of the movie.
    (minimum rating = 0.0 and maximum rating = 5.0)

    Member Methods:
    `movieMagic()` – Default constructor to initialise numeric data members to 0 and `String` data member to "".
    `void accept()` – To input and store `year`, `title` and `rating`.
    `void display()` – To display the `title` of a movie and a message based on the rating as per the table given below.

Rating	Message to be displayed
0.0 to 2.0	Flop
2.1 to 3.4	Semi-hit
3.5 to 4.5	Hit
4.6 to 5.0	Super Hit

Write a main method to create an object of the class and call the above member methods.

15. Write a program to accept name and total marks of N number of students in two single subscripts array `name[]` and `totalmarks[]`. Calculate and print:

    (i) The average of the total marks obtained by N number of students.

    [average = (sum of total marks of all the students) / N]

    (ii) Deviation of each student's total marks with the average.

    [deviation = total marks of a student - average]

16. Design a class to overload a function `check()` as follows:

    (i) `void check(String str, char ch)` – to find and print the frequency of a character in a string.
    Input: Str = "success", ch = 's'
    Output: number of s present is = 3

    (ii) `void check(String s1)` – to display only vowels from string `s1`, after converting it to lowercase.
    Input: s1= "computer"
    Output: o u e

17. Design a class to overload a function `Joystring()` as follows:

(i) void Joystring (String s, char ch1, char ch2) with one string argument and two character arguments that replaces the character argument ch1 with the character argument ch2 in the given string s and prints the new string.
Input value of s = "TECHNALAGY", ch1 = 'A', ch2 = 'O'
Output: "TECHNOLOGY"

(ii) void Joystring (String s) with one string argument that prints the position of the first space and the last space in the given string s.
Input value of s = "Cloud computing means Internet based computing"
Output: First index: 5
Last index: 36

(iii) void Joystring (String s1, String s2) with two string arguments that combines the two strings with a space between them and prints the resultant string.
Input value of s1 = "COMMON WEALTH", s2 = "GAMES"
Output: COMMON WEALTH GAMES

18. Design a class to overload a function num_calc() as follows:

(i) void num_calc (int mini, char ch) with one integer argument and one character argument, computes the square of integer argument if choice ch is 's' otherwise finds its cube.

(ii) void num_calc (int a, int b, char ch) with two integer arguments and one character argument. It computes the product of integer arguments if ch is 'p' else adds the integers.

(iii) void num_calc (String si, String s2) with two string arguments, which prints whether the strings are equal or not.

19. Design a class to overload a function compare() as follows:

(i) void compare(int, int) – to compare two integer values and print the greater of the two integers.

(ii) void compare(char, char) – to compare the numeric value of two characters with higher numeric value.

(iii) void compare(String, String) – to compare the length of the two strings and print the longer of the two.

Answers To Objective Questions

Multiple Choice Questions

1. D	3. A	5. C	7. D	9. B
2. A	4. A	6. B	8. A	10. C